CREATION SCIENTISTS ANSWER THEIR CRITICS

by Duane T. Gish, Ph.D.

Creation Scientists Answer Their Critics
Copyright © 1993

First Edition, 1993

Institute for Creation Research
P.O. Box 2667
El Cajon, CA 92021

ISBN # 0-932766-28-5
Library of Congress Catalog Card No. 92-071322

Cataloging in Publication Data
Gish, Duane T., 1921–
Creation Scientists Answer Their Critics

ii

Contents

Foreword

In recent decades there has been a notable revival of worldwide belief in the special creation of the world and its living creatures, as opposed to belief in evolution. Significantly, most of this revival can be attributed to the writing and speaking efforts, not of theologians or preachers, but of scientists.

There are now thousands of scientists who are creationists, and they come from every field of science. Many of them, like myself, once believed in evolution, but are now convinced, on the basis of abundant scientific evidence, that creationism is a far more credible model of origins than evolution.

One of the most eloquent scientific spokesmen for creation is Duane Gish, the author of this book. His scientific credentials are impeccable (Ph.D. in Biochemistry from U.C. Berkeley, many years' research experience in university laboratories and with a leading biochemical firm), and he has studied the subject of origins very thoroughly. And he is hardly alone! The Creation Research Society, of which he has been a director for 30 years, has had well over a thousand members, all with post-graduate degrees in science, since it began in 1963.

The Institute for Creation Research, which both Dr. Gish and I represent, has 9 resident faculty members and 18 adjunct faculty, 25 of whom have doctoral degrees from accredited universities. Furthermore, there are well over a hundred other creationist organizations, each with at least some scientists in their memberships. There are probably 25 other nations outside the United States with similar creationist organizations.

Thus creationism is not a fringe movement of uneducated religionists, as some have alleged. Its leadership is composed of many knowledgeable men and women of science, with excellent scientific qualifications. They have all studied the subject in at least reasonable depth and are convinced, in spite of strong peer pressure attempting to dissuade them, that creation is true and evolution is false. There may be in some cases religious and social reasons involved as well, but the fact is that they are all convinced, having studied both sides, that the *scientific* evidence strongly favors creationism.

But these creation scientists do have their critics! These critics are very vocal, often very angry and sarcastic. It is not easy for a scientist to be a creationist when the scientific and educational establishments, even including many scientists and educators who profess Christianity, regularly oppose and mock them. Their persistence in spite of this opposition speaks volumes in terms of their strong convictions about the strength of the evidence.

Consider just two of these critics, perhaps the two most articulate and influential spokesmen for evolutionism in our generation. Dr. Stephen Jay Gould of Harvard University says: "Many paleontologists, myself included, now view *Homo sapiens* as a tiny and unpredictable twig on a richly ramifying tree of life—a happy accident of the last geological moment, unlikely ever to appear again if we could regrow the tree from seed" (*Natural History*, March 1993, p. 20).

Dr. Isaac Asimov was the author of over 400 books, dealing with just about every imaginable field of science. In his last book, entitled *Asimov Laughs Again*, written shortly before his recent death, he said: "I am the president of the American Humanist Association, a thoroughgoing materialist and rationalist organization. If anyone asks me, I will admit to being an atheist. However, in the world of jokedom, God, Satan, angels, demons, Adam and Eve, and all the paraphernalia of mythology exist, and I accept them gladly. Anything for a laugh." (Cited in *The Humanist*, March/April 1993, p. 6.)

Thus to Gould, man is an accident, and to Asimov, God is a joke! (One cannot avoid wondering if Asimov is still laughing.) Both of these very eminent, widely read scientists have published bitter diatribes against creation and creation scientists.

And they are not alone. At least forty major volumes and many hundreds of articles have been written against creationism just in the past two decades, and more are coming!

Creation scientists do have their critics! It is not possible for us even to read—let alone answer—all of their books and articles.

However, their arguments do tend to center on a few major themes. It sometimes seems they are merely copying each other. Anti-creationism seems to have become a profitable mini-career, easier than doing real scientific research on origins—especially when the latter usually turns out in favor of creation!

At any rate, these major criticisms do need to be answered, and no one is better qualified to do this than Duane Gish, the author of this book. Since he joined ICR in 1971 he has participated in almost 300 formal creation/evolution debates, usually held on university campuses and opposing faculty evolutionary scientists, or—once in a while—an evolutionary philosopher or even an evolutionary theologian. And (at least in our judgment and that of most in the audiences) he always wins!

Although he is an excellent speaker, his victories are not because of his debating skills (he never took a course in debating) but because of the evidence. His opponents cannot produce scientific evidence for evolution for the simple reason that there isn't any!

I have participated in a fair number of such debates myself, and so am somewhat familiar with the arguments commonly presented by the evolutionists. Since the debates are normally framed as strictly scientific debates, the evolutionists are at a disadvantage. The best scientific evidence they can offer is a couple of questionable transitional forms, certain morphological or molecular resemblances which they misinterpret as relationships, and minor mutational changes within basic kinds.

Consequently, they will often devote much time to ridiculing the Ussher chronology or the flood or other aspects of the Genesis record. Or they will attack the credentials of creationists and their writings. They will insist that creation is strictly religion, but many will argue that one can believe in both God and evolution.

What they will *not* do is give any real *scientific* evidence for evolution! That, of course, is because they don't have any.

Most of the anti-creationist books and articles take essentially the same approach. That is, they are anti-creationist more than pro-evolutionist. Most of them repeat the same anti-creationist polemics that others have used, making the same unwarranted accusations, again and again.

Consequently, Dr. Gish has concentrated on only a few of the more influential of the anti-creationist books, showing conclusively that the criticisms are completely invalid. In the process, of course, he also shows that all the scientific evidences overwhelmingly favor creation. His arguments are easily followed, clear, and very convincing.

In this book, however, he has tried to concentrate on defending the *fact* of creation rather than the *date* of creation. These are two separate issues as far as the scientific evidence is concerned. He correctly emphasizes that, regardless of when creation took place, the evidence that it *did* take place is very powerful. The recent date of creation also can be convincingly demonstrated scientifically, but that would require another book.

Evolution, on the other hand, is defenseless! No one has ever seen real evolution take place (that is, macroevolution) in the present, or even in all human history. Since there are no true transitional forms with intermediate structures in the fossil record, there is no evidence that it ever happened in the past, any more than in the present. Furthermore, the universal laws of change in nature, especially the law of increasing entropy, seem to indicate (at least in the complete absence of evidence otherwise) that it could never take place on any significant scale at all. In fact, the more time available in the past, the more impossible evolution becomes, because the entropy principle stipulates that disintegration always tends to increase with time.

Dr. Gish has firmly documented these facts so that his book makes a strong scientific case for creation and against evolution, in addition to answering the critics of creation. The latter is the main theme of the book, of course, and I would strongly urge anyone who has been influenced by one of the anti-creationist books to read this book carefully before he decides to go along with the evolutionary world view.

Finally, I would like to comment concerning Dr. Gish himself. I have known him not only as a creationist colleague, but as a personal friend for 30 years. He is a man of high integrity, sincere compassion, consistent good humor and deep dedication to truth. He is also a man of courage, having served with distinction as an officer in the South Pacific during World War II, and he is not the least bit intimidated by the *ad hominem* arguments of his evolutionary opponents, as so many evangelicals seem to be. He is a man short in stature, but tall in knowledge, and powerful in debate. He is also a fine Christian gentleman, and in this volume, has answered with compelling effectiveness, the critics of creation.

Henry M. Morris, Ph.D., President
Institute for Creation Research

Dedication

This book is lovingly and gratefully dedicated to my wife, Lorraine (known by all as "Lolly"), the mother of my four children, faithful companion and helper, and fellow world-traveler. Without her, the labor of the past twenty years would not have been possible.

Introduction

Beginning with the publication of Charles Darwin's *Origin of Species* in 1859, a rising tide of evolutionism infiltrated the scientific and educational establishments, and even religious circles. By the turn of the century, evolution theory was being taught dogmatically in most major universities throughout the world.

In many of the textbooks used in American schools, however, a cautious approach to evolution was adopted in response to opposition to the theory in the general population. With Darwinian adulation at its height on the occasion of the Darwinian Centennial in 1959, evolutionists set about correcting what they considered a serious deficiency in education. Through the agency of the Biological Sciences Curriculum Study and a multi-million-dollar grant from the National Science Foundation, evolutionists produced three high-school biology books with evolutionary theory as their fundamental thesis, and obtained adoption of these books in the majority of high schools in the U.S.

These events served to galvanize creation scientists into action. Beginning with the publication of *The Genesis Flood*, by John Whitcomb and Henry Morris in 1961, the organization of the Creation Research Society, the Bible-Science Association, and the Institute for Creation Research, in 1963, 1964, and 1972, respectively, as well as many other creation-science organizations throughout the world, the creation scientists fought back.

In response to the highly effective lectures, seminars, and debates (almost always won by creationists, according to evolutionists), and the many books and publications produced by creation scientists, evolutionists finally awakened and reacted vigorously to this challenge to their dogmatic control of the scientific and educational establishments and domination of public thinking. As part of their campaign to mute the creation scientists, they poured forth an avalanche of journal articles and books attacking creation scientists and creation science. For the most part, these attacks have been vicious, with creation scientists being accused of all sorts of perfidy, distortion, dishonesty, and poor science. Evolution theory and evolutionists have suffered severely as a result of exposure by creation scientists, and it shows. This book is a response to these attacks. The main strategies and arguments of evolutionists are analyzed, creationist arguments are defended, and charges by evolutionists that creation scientists have used distortion, dishonesty, misquotes, quotes out of context, and poor science are refuted. Having read this book, a reader should be in a position to judge whether or not these charges are true, regardless of which position he takes on the subject of origins.

1

Creation Scientists Challenge the Dogma of Evolution

The year 1959 marked the centennial of the publication of Charles Darwin's epochal book, *The Origin of Species—Or the Preservation of Favored Races in the Struggle for Life.* During the 100 years since the publication of this book, those who opposed the theory of evolution on scientific grounds, though not silent, had become largely muted. The theory of evolution had become the dogma of the scientific and educational establishments. It became difficult, if not entirely impossible, for a professing creationist to obtain admission to a Ph.D. program in one of the natural sciences in a major university, let alone gain tenure as a professor in one of these universities. The lifeblood of a scientist is publication of his work and theories in refereed scientific journals. These journals, through editorial policies and the system of referees, came under the tight control of evolutionists. Thus, while it is easy enough for a creation scientist to publish the results of his research in a narrow technical field, or even to criticize a particular evolutionary mechanism or phylogeny, most attempts to publish an article which challenged the validity of evolutionary theory itself or to suggest that creation is a preferable or even a credible alternative to evolution simply became futile.

Having gained a considerable propaganda victory from the Scopes Trial, evolutionists became very smug, secure in both the power of their theories to explain and the power of their entrenched positions to successfully resist challenges to either. Leading evolutionists such as George Gaylord Simpson, Julian Huxley, Ernst Mayr, Theodosius Dobzhansky, and G. Ledyard Stebbins had modified Darwin's original theory into what became known as the neo-Darwinian theory, or the modern synthesis. This neo-Darwinian mechanism, embracing as its main postulate that most of evolution had proceeded slowly and gradually through a combination of micromutations and natural selection interacting with the environment, had become established orthodoxy by the mid 1950's. Mayr, in a major work published in 1966, speaking of the many symposia held to celebrate the Darwinian centennial, declared: ". . . we are almost startled at the complete unanimity in the interpretation of evolution presented by the participants. Nothing could show more clearly how internally consistent and firmly established the synthetic theory is."[1]

Furthermore, the paleontologists, whose business it is to study and interpret the fossil record, offered no challenge to the neo-Darwinian mechanism. In fact, Simpson, America's premier evolutionary paleontologist during those years, strongly maintained that the same evolutionary forces involved in the production of variations within species, if extrapolated over vast time spans, were sufficient to explain all of evolution.

Evolutionists, however, were concerned about the fact that most high school biology textbooks used in the United States devoted limited space to evolutionary theory. In January of 1959, the Biological Sciences Curriculum Study (BSCS) was organized, drawing most of its members from the American Institute of Biological Scientists. Winning a $7,000,000 grant from the National Science Foundation, the BSCS hired a group of science educators, writers, editors, illustrators, and support personnel and produced three high-school biology texts, each emphasizing one of three different aspects of the biological sciences: cell biology, molecular biology, and ecology. All emphasized evolutionary theory throughout. Thousands of high schools in the U.S. adopted one or more of these books as their basic biology texts.

With this successful assault on secondary education, with the oft-repeated assurance that no serious scientist questions the fact of evolution, and with little if any challenge to the neo-Darwinian synthesis, evolutionists were extremely confident. Never in the history of science had a notion gripped its practitioners so firmly. The dogma of evolution reigned supreme.

The voices of scientific reason were not altogether silent during these years, of course. Henry Morris, in one of his classics, *The History of Modern Creationism,*[2] has described the efforts of creationists during the past 50 years to expose the fallacies and weaknesses in evolutionary theory and to describe the admirable way in which the evidence related to origins can be correlated and explained by creation. Few of these voices were heard, however, and they were almost entirely ignored by the establishment.

Even among evolutionists, however, there were some who rejected the neo-Darwinian mechanism of evolution during these heady days. Richard Goldschmidt, a German geneticist who abandoned Nazi Germany for the University of California at Berkeley, rejected the Darwinian mechanism entirely. Noting that every one of the major types of plants and animals (that is, the families, orders, classes, and phyla) have appeared in the fossil record essentially complete at the start with no transitional forms connecting them, Goldschmidt postulated that evolution occurred in big jumps, or saltations.[3,4] He referred to this notion as the "hopeful monster" mechanism, and postulated, for example, that "the first bird hatched from a reptilian egg."[5]

In 1966, the Wistar Institute in Philadelphia hosted a symposium in which six mathematicians challenged the neo-Darwinian mechanism before a group of evolutionary biologists. One of the mathematicians, Professor Murray Eden of the Massachusetts Institute of Technology, declared on that occasion that ". . . an adequate scientific theory of evolution must await the discovery and elucidation of new natural laws—physical, physico-chemical, and biological."[6] Thus, while rejecting the neo-Darwinian mechanism, Eden and his colleagues had no alternative mechanism to suggest, forcing them into the unenviable position of admitting that evolution was devoid of any explanation.

The same could be said of Pierre Grassé, France's foremost zoologist, whose knowledge of the scientific world was encyclopedic, according to Dobzhansky.[7] Grassé rejects both mutations and natural selection as contributing factors in evolution, but he has nothing to put in their place. Grassé asserts that biology can tell us nothing about evolution, and perhaps must yield to metaphysics.[8]

Marjorie Grene, the well-known philosopher and historian of science at the University of California, Davis, also voiced her dissent. Pointing out that the Darwinians, and now the neo-Darwinians, in their attempts to explain how evolution works, dealt only with the last minutiae of development, she went on to declare:

> That the color of moths or snails or the bloom on the castor bean stem are "explained" by mutation and natural selection is very likely; but how from single-celled (and for that matter from inanimate) ancestors there came to be castor beans and moths and snails, and how from these there emerged llamas and hedgehogs and lions and apes—and

men—that is a question which neo-Darwinian theory simply leaves unasked.[9]

In spite of all of this, evolutionists hardly felt threatened as we entered the decade of the sixties. Neo-Darwinism was textbook orthodoxy. Evolution theory poured forth unchallenged on television, over radio, in the daily press, and in popular magazines, such as the *National Geographic, Reader's Digest, Life,* and newspaper weeklies. But events began to occur in the early sixties that were to change all of that.

The first significant event in the renaissance of the scientific force for creation was the publication of the book, *The Genesis Flood,* by John Whitcomb and Henry Morris in 1961.[10] This book was much more than an exposition challenging uniformitarian geology (present processes acting essentially at present rates over hundreds of millions of years are sufficient to account for all of geology), and setting forth Biblical and physical evidences for the worldwide Flood described in Chapters 6-8 of Genesis. The book was a direct assault on the entire evolutionary concept of the origin and history of the earth and of living things. At the time of its publication, Dr. Whitcomb, a theologian with a keen scientific mind, was Professor of Theology and Old Testament at Grace Theological Seminary in Winona Lake, Indiana, and Dr. Morris was Professor and Chairman of the Civil Engineering Department at Virginia Polytechnic Institute, one of the largest and most successful civil engineering departments in the U.S.

Although publication of *The Genesis Flood* may not have attracted much attention in secular circles, it did have considerable impact in Christian circles, even though its main themes, the support for the Genesis Flood and the attack on evolution theory, were rejected by most of the science faculty at such Christian colleges as Calvin College and Wheaton College. The book was widely and enthusiastically welcomed by evangelical Christians, and served as the catalyst to ener-

gize and bring together those Christian scientists, scattered throughout academia and industry, who held similar views.
One of the most significant events that followed was the founding of the Creation Research Society in 1963 with Dr. Walter Lammerts, famous horticultural scientist, as its first president.[11] Beginning with 10 members, it now has about 600 voting members, all of whom hold advanced degrees in some area of science. The Society publishes a quarterly journal, and membership is available to all scientists or laymen who subscribe to its statement of faith. During the latter part of the sixties, creation scientists became more and more active, lecturing mainly to church groups but also in some secular schools and colleges.

During these years, evolutionists chose to ignore the efforts of creation scientists, since they felt that the threat to their monopolistic control of the scientific and educational establishments was non-existent. This was soon to change. One event that caught their attention and galvanized them into action was the efforts of creationists before the Board of Education of the State of California in 1972 to institute the teaching of the scientific evidence for creation along with evolution theory in public schools. This effort met with very little success, but these activities did serve to alert evolutionists and the public in general to the burgeoning activities of creation scientists.

Two other events challenged the arrogant smugness of evolutionists and let them know a war was on. In 1970, Dr. Morris resigned his position at Virginia Polytechnic Institute to help found Christian Heritage College in San Diego, California. Included as a division of the college was a creation science research center. In the fall of 1971, the author left his position at The Upjohn Company to join Dr. Morris in this research effort; and in 1972, it was reorganized as the Institute for Creation Research with Dr. Morris as Director and the author as Associate Director. During the decade of the seventies, additional scientists were added to the staff, including

science educator Dr. Richard Bliss; biologist Dr. Kenneth
Cumming; and geologist Dr. Steven Austin (who was later on
leave for several years to get his Ph.D. at Penn State). More
recently, geological engineer Dr. John Morris (who had initially joined the team in 1972, but later went on leave for
several years to get his Ph.D. and serve on the faculty at the
University of Oklahoma), nuclear physicist Dr. Gerald Aard-
sma, physicist Dr. Larry Vardiman, and a science educator
from Australia, Ken Ham, have joined the staff of the Institute.

Soon after the founding of the Institute for Creation Research (or ICR, as it is popularly known), Dr. Morris and the
author began to challenge the evolutionary establishment directly as they presented creation science lectures on major
university campuses throughout the United States, Canada,
and many other countries. As others joined the staff, they too
carried the challenge against evolution theory to high school
and college campuses. Soon the notion was conceived of
conducting debates between creation scientists and evolution
scientists on university campuses, in city auditoriums,
schools, and churches. The creation scientists, feeling confident that the scientific evidence was solidly on their side,
readily accepted invitations to participate in these debates.
These debates usually attract audiences of from one to three
thousand, and on some occasions, have attracted as many as
five thousand. Evolutionists have freely admitted that the creationists have won most of the debates.[12]

While the Institute for Creation Research is recognized as
the leading creation science organization in the world, many
other creation science organizations now exist in the U.S. and
other countries. In his book, *The History of Modern Creationism,* Dr. Morris lists 76 national, state, and local creationist
organizations in the U.S. and 33 creationist organizations in
other countries. Creationist efforts are not limited to Christians, but include the efforts of Jewish and Moslem scientists
as well. Literally thousands of scientists throughout the world
are professing creationists, while the number of those who

accept creation but choose to keep silent for fear of loss of position or promotion cannot be estimated, although it must be considerable. There are others, not insignificant in number, who accept creation as a more credible explanation than evolution but who make no religious profession of any kind. There is also a very considerable number of scientists who, while not accepting creation as an alternative, nevertheless are severely critical of modern evolutionary theory. A goodly number of these critics have now published books recording these criticisms.[13]

Other events which drew great interest from both creationists and evolutionists from all around the world were the legal battles that erupted in the states of Arkansas and Louisiana over laws passed by the legislatures of those two states requiring balanced treatment of creation science and evolution science in the public schools. The law in Arkansas was declared unconstitutional by Federal Judge William Overton in a trial held in his Little Rock courtroom in December of 1981. The decision was not appealed. The Louisiana law was likewise declared unconstitutional by Federal Judge du Plantier of New Orleans by summary judgment without trial. On appeal to the Fifth Circuit Court of Appeals, a three-judge panel supported the lower court 3-0. The case was then appealed to the entire bank of 15 judges of the Fifth Circuit Court, and by a vote of 8-7, they sustained the decisions already reached. The case has been heard before the U.S. Supreme Court and the Court supported the lower court decisions by a 7-2 vote, with Justice Scalia and Chief Justice Rehnquist voicing powerful dissent.

More than anything, evolutionists fear an open, free, and thorough scientific challenge to evolutionary theory in the public schools. They have learned from their experiences in debates and other open exchanges that evolutionary theory comes off second best when faced with a scientific challenge from well-informed creation scientists. With their tight control of scientific journals and with the humanistic materialist philosophy that dominates the mass media, they feel secure in those areas.

The tax-supported public schools, in our pluralistic, democratic society are, however, subject to more democratic forces. A nationwide poll taken by the Associated Press—NBC News Poll in 1981 revealed that 76% of the American people want both creation and evolution taught in public schools, 10% want creation only taught, and only 8% want evolution only taught (6% had no opinion).

Evolutionists have reacted vigorously, even viciously, to these threats to their monopolistic control of science and education. They apparently are determined to use whatever means they feel are necessary to blunt and eventually to destroy the efforts of creation scientists to make known the empty rhetoric that makes up evolutionary stories and the nature of the scientific evidence that supports creation. During the past ten years or so, over 30 books have been published attacking creationists and creation science, and a blizzard of articles have appeared in scientific and quasi-scientific journals attacking creationists. In fact, today almost every issue of these journals either contains an anti-creationist article or contains an article which includes an attack against, or a reference to, creationists or creation science. One thing is certain—creationists and their scientific arguments are no longer being ignored by the evolutionary establishment!

One tactic commonly employed by evolutionists is to viciously attack the intellectual honesty and scientific integrity of creation scientists. Creation scientists are not only accused of lacking scientific objectivity, but they are accused of misquoting, quoting out of context, distorting science, and telling outright lies. For example, a professor at a college in Tennessee was quoted in a Knoxville newspaper as stating "Gish is a notorious liar." Many similar examples will be documented in this book.

References

1. Ernst Mayr, *Animal Species and Evolution,* The Belknap Press of Harvard University Press, Cambridge, 1966, p. 8.

2. Henry Morris, *The History of Modern Creationism,* Master Books Publishers, San Diego, 1984.

3. R. B. Goldschmidt, *The Material Basis of Evolution,* Yale University Press, New Haven, CT, 1940.

4. R. B. Goldschmidt, *American Scientist* 40:97 (1952).

5. R. B. Goldschmidt, Ref. 3, p. 395.

6. Murray Eden, in *Mathematical Challenges to the Neo-Darwinian Interpretation of Evolution,* P. S. Moorhead and M. M. Kaplan, Eds., Wistar Institute Press, Philadelphia, 1967, p. 109.

7. Theodore Dobzhansky, *Evolution* 29:376 (1975).

8. Pierre-Paul Grassé, *Evolution of Living Organisms* (English edition of *L'Evolution du Vivant*), Academic Press, New York, 1977.

9. Marjorie Grene, *Encounter,* November 1959, p. 54.

10. J. C. Whitcomb and H. M. Morris, *The Genesis Flood,* The Presbyterian and Reformed Pub. Co., Philadelphia, 1961.

11. Creation Research Society. Membership Secretary Dr. Glen Wolfrom, P.O. Box 28473, Kansas City, MO 64118.

12. Niles Eldredge, *The Monkey Business. A Scientist Looks at Creationism,* Washington Square Press, New York, 1982, p.17.

13. See Bibliography at back of this book.

2

Evolutionists Mount a Counterattack

Educators became alarmed by the effects on students of the lectures, seminars, and debates involving creation scientists, as evidenced by the essays and classroom questions and challenges supporting creation. Especially disturbing to evolutionists were the many appearances by creation scientists on TV and radio, the numerous books and other literature pouring forth from creation scientists, particularly from those on the staff of the Institute for Creation Research, and the equal emphasis laws passed by overwhelming majorities in the state legislatures in Arkansas and Louisiana, and similar efforts in other states. Evolutionists began to organize their forces for a counterattack. The opening salvo was a Manifesto issued by the American Humanist Association in 1977. The AHA is the leading atheist organization in the U.S. The 1977 Manifesto declared that evolution is an accepted fact of science in the view of the scientific community. It urged publishers, teachers, school boards, and other educators to defeat the efforts to teach the evidence for creation in public schools. It was signed by 102 leading humanistic evolutionary scientists and was published in *The Humanist,* the AHA publication, and was distributed to educational authorities throughout the U.S.

In 1972, the theme of the annual convention of the National Association of Biology Teachers, held in San Francisco, was "Biology and Evolution." Dr. John N. Moore, then professor in the Natural Science Division at Michigan State University, and the author succeeded in obtaining an invitation from the program committee to present a two-hour mini-symposium describing evidences for creation. This invitation was bitterly resented by the leaders of the NABT. After such luminaries as geneticist Theodosius Dobzhansky, botanist G. Ledyard Stebbins, and anthropologist Sherwood Washburn had presented lectures supporting evolution and attacking creation in preceding days, Moore and Gish presented their lectures before an audience of 1500 of these biology teachers. In an unprecedented action, Dr. William Cory, of St. Mary's College, the moderator of the symposium, saying that he had been instructed to do so, delivered a 15-minute rebuttal before allowing questions from the audience. His rebuttal was weak and boring, and was more damaging than helpful to the evolutionist cause.

Dr. Jack Carter, then the editor of *The American Biology Teacher,* the monthly publication of the NABT, an evolutionist, but a man of unusual fairness and integrity, suggested to Moore and Gish that they submit manuscripts to him so he could publish them in the *American Biology Teacher.* The papers were subsequently published.[1,2] Dr. Joan Creager, the editor who succeeded Dr. Carter, made it clear that under her editorship, no further articles about creation were to be published except those that were critical. In about 1980, Dr. Wayne Moyer, then the executive secretary of the NABT and now on the staff of Norman Lear's so-called "People for the

American Way," an ultra-liberal organization that wars against the precepts of Biblical Christianity, began circulating a newsletter specifically dedicated to fighting the efforts of creation scientists and to help and advise evolutionists in their anti-creationist cause.

It was also about this time that a quarterly journal began publication, the sole purpose of which was to defend evolution theory and to attack creation science in general, and to attempt to personally discredit creation scientists. The journal, *Creation/Evolution*,[3] was founded by and is still edited by Fred Edwords, a philosopher who was then president of the San Diego Humanist Society and is now an Administrator of the American Humanist Association. Edwords has aspired to leadership in the anti-creationist crusade and has debated the author on several occasions, as well as other creation scientists. Considerable assistance to Edwords in his work with the journal has been given by Drs. Frank Awbrey and William Thwaites, professors in the Biology Department of San Diego State University. *Creation/Evolution* has proven to be the main organ in the counterattack against creationists. This journal contains some articles that make a serious attempt to defend evolution against creationist arguments, as well as many that seek to vilify individual creation scientists by attacking their scientific objectivity and personal integrity. In fact, so many of the arguments presented in the journal are so shallow in scientific and intellectual content, and personal attacks on individual creation scientists are so frequent and intemperate, it is difficult for creationists to take the journal seriously.

Awbrey and Thwaites have carried on a personal anti-creationist crusade, engaging creation scientists in debate on a number of occasions, and teaching a creation/evolution course at San Diego State University. The author participated in this class each year for several years. It is interesting to note how this class has "evolved" during the past few years. Apparently feeling confident that they could prevail against creation scientists on an equal-time basis, Awbrey and Thwaites invited scientists from the ICR staff to participate in the class, offering them half of the 26 lectures and even permitting them to prepare the test questions for their portion of the lectures. This situation prevailed for about three years and then suddenly the ICR staff was informed that they were to be given only nine of the 26 lectures, with Awbrey and Thwaites taking the other 17. Furthermore, the ICR staff was no longer permitted to prepare test questions for their lectures.

In the 1986-1987 fall semester, the class was switched to evening hours, and of the 15 class sessions, the ICR staff was given only two of these sessions. The ICR staff is understandably suspicious that Thwaites and Awbrey felt they weren't doing too well on an equal-time basis, and were even failing when taking two-thirds of total class time, and so they finally settled on taking 13 of the 15 class sessions. The creationists do agree that this does even things out a bit!

Also in about 1980, another important effort against creation scientists was launched. Stanley Weinberg, a biology teacher and science supervisor for most of his career and active in the National Association of Biology Teachers, initiated a system of "Committees of Correspondence." The members of each local committee are dedicated to the fight against creationists, and the committees function by monitoring the activities of creationists, analyzing creationist arguments, preparing countermeasures, devising strategy, and exchanging advice and ideas. Creation scientists soon began to hear the same arguments and see some of the same slides as they debated evolutionists around the country. As of 1985, there were Committees of Correspondence in all but two states, as well as in several provinces of Canada. For a more complete history of these and other organized efforts against creation science and creation scientists, consult *The History of Modern Creationism,* by Henry Morris (cited in Chapter 1).

The first book published against creation science, *Science Textbook Controversies and the Politics of Equal Time,*[4] was authored by Dorothy Nelkin, Professor of Sociology at

Cornell University, in 1977. Dr. Nelkin had spent considerable time interviewing staff members at the Institute for Creation Research, and Dr. Morris, the author, and other staff members courteously and gladly cooperated with her fully, carefully explaining in detail the scientific evidence which had convinced them that creation was a far more credible explanation of origins than the theory of evolution. Unfortunately, her book contained numerous factual errors, and failed to give a fair appraisal of ICR and of creation science. Nelkin's book was at least moderate in tone.

It would be nearly impossible to critique every critical book written by evolutionists against creation science, or to answer in great detail each of their arguments. In this book, therefore, an effort will be made to arrange their arguments into various categories and to answer each set of arguments. Several of the books deemed to be the most important will also be answered in detail. The reader should then be in a position to decide for himself whether creation scientists have assembled a reasonably convincing case or whether their arguments are nothing more than pseudo-science rooted in religious ideas.

References

1. J. N. Moore, *The American Biology Teacher* 35(1):23-26 (1973).
2. D. T. Gish, *The American Biology Teacher,* March 1973, p. 132.
3. *Creation/Evolution,* P.O. Box 146, Amherst, New York, 14226-0146.
4. Dorothy Nelkin, *Science Textbook Controversies and the Politics of Equal Time,* The MIT Press, Cambridge, Massachusetts, 1977.

3

Creation, Evolution, Science, and Religion

One of the most frequent criticisms hurled against creation science by evolutionists, especially in the context of public education, is that it is religion, not science. We will cite only a few examples. Godfrey states flatly, "Scientific creationism is not science, it is religion."[1]

John Patterson charges that:

"Scientific creationism" is an evangelical movement of fundamentalist ministries dedicated not to the advancement of science but to the advancement of biblical inerrancy often at the expense of science.[2]

Edwords asserts that:

. . . Special Creationists aren't really fighting for fairness but rather are fighting to have their religion taught in the public schools at taxpayer expense.[3]

Wilson claims that:

After listening to creationist speakers, reading creationist writings, and talking with creationist students, we could see that creationism was nothing more than a particular version of fundamentalist Christianity having no valid scientific content.[4]

Dolphin says that:

Scientific creationism is not science. Its core is a narrow fundamentalist religious interpretation of Christianity.[5]

Waters states that:

Strict creationism, or the so-called scientific creationism, is simply the selective use of available data to support a particular theological perspective and understanding of biblical authority.[6]

Futuyma claims that:

Creationist theories rest not on evidence that can withstand the skeptical mind, but on wishful thinking and the Bible, the voice of authority which is the only source of creationist belief.[7]

And so it goes on and on.

Before we examine the scientific status of creation and evolution, let us consider the religious nature of evolution. Pierre Teilhard de Chardin, a French priest whose real faith was evolution, stated that:

(Evolution) is a general postulate to which all theories, all hypotheses, all systems must henceforward bow and which they must satisfy in order to be thinkable and true. Evolution is a light which illuminates all facts, a trajectory which all lines of thought must follow—this is what evolution is.[8]

Ayala quoted that statement in his eulogy to Dobzhansky, and stated that Dobzhansky believed that this passage from Teilhard de Chardin best expressed the place of biological evolution in human thought. Nothing can be thinkable or true unless it bows before evolution, so states Teilhard de Chardin. The Bible says that God is light. Teilhard de Chardin says evolution is a light that illuminates all facts. The passage by Teilhard de Chardin, approved so warmly by Dobzhansky, and quoted approvingly by Ayala, is religion, pure and simple.

A pamphlet from the Humanist Society explains that:

> Humanism is the belief that man shapes his own destiny. It is a constructive philosophy, a non-theistic religion, a way of life.[9]

Later, it quotes the late British biologist, atheist, and evolutionist, Sir Julian Huxley, who stated that:

> I use the word 'Humanist' to mean someone who believes that man is just as much a natural phenomenon as an animal or plant; that his body, mind and soul were not supernaturally created but are products of evolution, and that he is not under the control or guidance of any supernatural being or beings, but has to rely on himself, and his own powers.

We thus see that humanism is a non-theistic religion, with evolution as one of its fundamental dogmas. A statement very similar to Huxley's may be found in Simpson's book, *Life of the Past.*[10]

Richard Lewontin, a Marxist atheist who is a professor of biology at Harvard University, has said that:

> Yet, whatever our understanding of the social struggle that gives rise to creationism, whatever the desire to reconcile science and religion may be, there is no escape from the fundamental contradiction between evolution and creationism. They are irreconcilable world views.[11]

Yes, indeed, evolution and creation are irreconcilable world views. If, as Lewontin and his fellow evolutionists claim, creation is religion, then precisely the same must be said about evolution.

L. Harrison Matthews, British biologist and evolutionist, in his Introduction to a 1971 publication of Darwin's *Origin of Species,* stated that:

> The fact of evolution is the backbone of biology, and biology is thus in the peculiar position of being a science founded on an unproved theory—is it then a science or a faith? Belief in the theory of evolution is thus exactly parallel to belief in special creation—both are concepts

which believers know to be true but neither, up to the
present, has been capable of proof.[12]

Thus again, if creation is religion, then precisely the same
must be said about evolution. The only part of Matthew's
statement with which creationists disagree is his belief that
evolution is the backbone of biology and that biology is
founded on the theory of evolution. Biology, by its very name,
is the study of *living* organisms, while evolution is an attempt
to infer how these organisms, and organisms now extinct,
came into existence in the first place. There *is* a difference
between empirical science and history.

The powerful, underlying religious foundation of evolution was aptly expressed by Bozarth when he proclaimed that:

> Christianity has fought, still fights, and will fight science
> to the desperate end over evolution, because evolution
> destroys utterly and finally the very reason Jesus' earthly
> life was supposedly made necessary. Destroy Adam and
> Eve and the original sin, and in the rubble you will find the
> sorry remains of the son of God. If Jesus was not the
> redeemer who died for our sins, and this is what evolution
> means, then Christianity is nothing.[13]

Creation scientists hasten to point out that they have no
fight with science. In fact, it is precisely the facts of science
that convince them that creation is far more credible, scientifically, than is evolution. The battle is with the evolutionary
philosophy and faith, not science. According to Bozarth, then,
evolution is a powerful religious concept, which if correctly
understood, negates all of Christianity. Of course, Bozarth
would also agree with Julian Huxley when he stated that "In
the evolutionary pattern of thought there is no longer either
need or room for the supernatural."[14] Thus, all theistic faiths,
whether Christian, Jewish, Muslim, or any others that proclaim faith in God, are rendered obsolete by evolution, according to Huxley.

Julian Huxley made no effort to conceal the fact that he
viewed evolution as a new faith, a new religion. He, in fact,

set about to establish a new religion based on evolution. Huxley declared that:

> . . . the evolutionary vision is enabling us to discern, however incompletely, the lineaments of the new religion that we can be sure will arise to serve the needs of the coming era.[15]

In the book that Huxley co-authored with the British evolutionist Jacob Bronowski, Huxley and Bronowski stated that:

> A religion is essentially an attitude to the world as a whole. Thus evolution, for example, may prove as powerful a principle to coordinate man's beliefs and hopes as God was in the past.[16]

Marjorie Grene, as noted earlier, a well-known philosopher and historian of science (she has authored chapters in books along with prominent evolutionists), proclaimed that:

> It is as a religion of science that Darwinism chiefly held, and holds men's minds. . . . The modified but still characteristically Darwinian theory has itself become an orthodoxy, preached by its adherents with religious fervor, and doubted, they feel, only by a few muddlers imperfect in scientific faith.[17]

Colin Patterson, a senior paleontologist at the British Museum of Natural History, is an evolutionist who, while not converting to creation, has expressed serious doubts about some aspects of evolution theory which we will discuss later. Patterson has declared that:

> Just as pre-Darwinian biology was carried out by people whose faith was in the Creator and His plan, post-Darwinian biology is being carried out by people whose faith is in, almost, the deity of Darwin.[18]

Can there be any doubt, regardless of what else one may say about it, that in the minds of its leading exponents evolution is religious orthodoxy? The evolutionary fundamentalists among the ranks of its supporters demand unbending allegiance to its tenets. Those who remain within its ranks but who, for example, dare to begin a statement with the words

"If the theory of evolution is true . . ." are branded as rank heretics,[19] and of course the worst abuse is reserved for those who declare forthrightly that creation is a more credible explanation than evolution.

Now let us return to a discussion of the scientific status of creation and evolution. To do this we must define science, and what is meant by a scientific theory, and then evaluate the nature of all theories on origins, and more particularly, the theories of creation and evolution.

What is science? Loosely defined, one could say that science is what a scientist is doing when he is thinking. Of course, science, properly defined, would exclude much of the thinking done by scientists. Strictly defined, *empirical science* is our attempt to observe, understand, and explain events, processes, and properties that are repeatably observable. On the basis of such theories predictions can be made concerning related natural phenomena or future natural events. Thus, experiments can be conceived and performed to test the theory and which may possibly show that the theory is wrong, if it is wrong. This property of potential falsifiability is an important element of a true scientific theory. Empirical science and scientific theories thus are restricted to attempts to explain the *operation* of the universe and of the living things it contains. They are about the real world out there, the here and now.

Theories about origins, whether creation or evolution theories, are of necessity basically very different from empirical scientific theories. There were no human witnesses to the origin of the universe, to the origin of life, or to the origin of a single living thing. These events were unique, unrepeatable, historical events which happened in the past. No one has ever seen a worm, a fish, an ape, or a man created. Neither has anyone ever seen a fish evolve into an amphibian or an ape evolve into a man. Furthermore, one cannot go into the laboratory and test a theory on how a fish might have evolved into an amphibian or how an ape may have evolved into a man. Creation and evolution are inferences based on circumstantial evidence. They are attempts to explain events which have taken place in the past. Evolution theories do attempt to employ processes still acting today to explain how evolution may have occurred, but the time spans required to see if such ideas are correct involve tens of thousands of years, even millions of years, so no test of the theories is possible.

The ultimate question in the two conflicting theories on origins—creation and evolution—is: How did the universe and its living inhabitants come into existence? Did the universe come into existence by a process of self-transformation via naturalistic, mechanistic processes due to properties inherent in matter, or was it created by the design, purpose, and deliberate creative acts of an intelligent, omnipotent Creator? Ultimately, it is not possible to falsify either general proposition, although from each there emerges subsidiary hypotheses which are potentially capable of falsification.

First, let us consider creation. Many, and probably the majority, of creation scientists believe that it is very likely that the earth and the cosmos are quite young. A figure of ten thousand years, plus or minus a few thousand years, is often mentioned. Let us suppose that eventually, to the satisfaction of most of these scientists, it is finally established that the earth is four to five billion years old and the universe itself is 10 to 20 billion years old. Would that constitute a falsification of creation theory? Of course not. There are, in fact, right now many creationists who accept an old age for the cosmos. Creation theories would merely be realigned so that all such theories would incorporate long time intervals between the creative acts of God.

Another example that has actually already taken place is the belief relative to the fixity of species. Pre-Darwinian creationists, and in fact many creationists who did battle with Darwin and his transformist notions, held to the fixity of species. At that time, genetic data were limited and many scientists of that day had considerable confidence in man's ability to discover the limits of variability within a basic kind, which they assumed could be equated with what was defined as a species. Since then empirical evidence has accumulated to demonstrate not only that the science of taxonomy—that is, our attempts to classify organisms into categories such as species, genera, families, orders, classes, and phyla—is arbitrary and fallible, but even attempts to define a species are arbitrary and disputable. Thus, a species is often defined as a population of individuals that interbreed, producing fertile offspring, and thus experiencing a flow of genetic material between individuals of the species, and which are non-fertile with respect to other species. This is not really true at all, however. Our common household pet, the dog (*Canis familiaris*), interbreeds with wolves (*Canis lupus*), coyotes (genus *Canis*), and jackals (genus *Canis*), producing fertile offspring. Ordinarily, however, they do not interbreed and there are minor morphological differences, so they have been placed in separate species. Many similar examples of hybridization of species, even some of which are in different genera, both plant and animal, could be cited.

To modern-day creation scientists, therefore, it seems very likely, if not certain, that dogs, wolves, coyotes, and jackals have been derived from a single basic created kind through a natural, though limited, sorting out of genetic factors that were all part of the gene pool of the original created "dog" kind. As species are often defined, therefore, modern creationists no longer hold to the fixity of species, but to the fixity of created kinds. (This issue will be discussed in more detail later.) Thus, abandonment of the fixity of created species concept did not falsify the theory of special creation. These and similar events demonstrate that creation scientists do not dogmatically cling to outmoded hypotheses and that creation theory is a dynamic theory, with subsidiary hypotheses subject to test, being held tentatively by creation scientists.

Although it is easy enough to conceive of observations that might falsify, or at least cast into doubt, one or more of the subsidiary hypotheses which are derived from the general creation model, yet it seems difficult, if not impossible, to conceive of an observation or an experiment that could ultimately falsify the general concept of special creation. The details of the general concept can always be modified to accommodate new facts. We hasten to add that precisely the same can be said to be true of the general model, or theory, of evolution.

The non-falsifiability of the general theory of evolution, that is, the notion that the ultimate origin of the universe and of its living inhabitants can be ascribed solely to a mechanistic, naturalistic, evolutionary process, has been asserted by evolutionists as well as by creationists. As a matter of fact, because of this and other reasons, Sir Karl Popper, one of the world's leading philosophers of science and an evolutionist himself, has stated that:

> I have come to the conclusion that Darwinism is not a testable scientific theory but a *metaphysical research programme*—a possible framework for testable scientific theories.[20] (The emphasis is Popper's.)

Popper published a letter in *New Scientist,* the British quasi-science journal, in which he modified his position a bit.[21] On the basis of that letter, many evolutionists insist that Popper has retracted the statement quoted above. That is simply not true. In the above statement, Popper was referring to Darwinian evolutionary theory, but in his later letter his remarks referred only to the theory of natural selection. Michael Ruse, an ardent Darwinian and arch anti-creationist, in fact has said, in reference to the statement quoted above, that:

> Since making this claim, Popper himself has modified his position somewhat; but, disclaimers aside, I suspect that even now he does not really believe that Darwinism in its modern form is genuinely falsifiable.[22]

Murray Eden, certainly not a creationist, agrees that evolution is a non-falsifiable theory. He states that:

> Even in biology, I recall one occasion on which I helped develop a very ingenious and very plausible theory

regarding the countercurrent mechanism in the kidney. It was not only falsifiable, it was false. My point is that for such a theory, one could propose a crucial experiment and check as to whether or not the theory was false or not.

This cannot be done in evolution, taking it in its broad sense, and this is really all I meant when I called it tautologous in the first place. It can, indeed, explain anything. You may be ingenious or not in proposing a mechanism which looks plausible to human beings and mechanisms which are consistent with other mechanisms which you have discovered, but it is still an unfalsifiable theory.[23]

In the symposium in which Eden made those remarks there were several other evolutionists who apparently agreed with Eden's position on the non-falsifiability of evolution. Thus, Alex Fraser, then Professor of Genetics, University of California, Davis, stated on that occasion:

It would seem to me that there have been endless statements made and the only thing I have clearly agreed with through the whole day has been the statement made by Carl [sic] Popper, namely, that the real inadequacy of evolution, esthetically and scientifically, is that you can explain anything you want by changing your variables around.[24]

On that same occasion, Marcel Schützenberger, then Professor of Mathematics, University of Paris, with reference to evolutionary explanations, said:

A science consists also of a selection of questions or problems and of a general framework within which it can be decided if a question has been answered or not.

Now, we are very happy that fireflies meet each other by making light. I am sure that they have an extreme pleasure in that; but it would be interesting to know why only the fireflies do it? Is there any general reason which could be given for them inventing the idea of light? Why does this species need such a complicated mechanism for mating when anybody does otherwise?

For any specific question you can provide me with a specific answer, but I would claim that in most of the circumstances there was no general principle on which you could decide in advance which type of specific explanation you would use for it. I think this is exactly what it means to be a nonfalsifiable theory.[25]

Drs. Paul Ehrlich and L. C. Birch, biologists at Stanford University and the University of Sydney, respectively, summarized the problem in *Nature,* the journal published by the British Association for the Advancement of Science:

> Our theory of evolution has become . . . one which cannot be refuted by any possible observations. Every conceivable observation can be fitted into it. It is thus "outside of empirical science" but not necessarily false. No one can think of ways to test it. Ideas, either without basis or based on a few laboratory experiments carried out in extremely simplified systems have attained currency far beyond their validity. They have become part of an evolutionary dogma accepted by most of us as part of our training.[26]

What Ehrlich and Birch seem to be saying is that evolution theory has become so plastic that it no longer makes any difference what the data may be, there will be some way to fit the data into the theory. The theory thus is untestable and consequently non-falsifiable. And, of course, dogma is supposed to be a property of religion, not science.

Evolutionists, in their stance before the lay public and the courts, often pretend that it is only ignorant and misguided creationists who are challenging the scientific status of evolutionary theory. When one reads the scientific literature and the philosophy of science literature, however, one finds that these evolutionists, when discussing challenges to the scientific status of evolution theory, do not even mention creationists! The main challenges are coming not from creationists but from their fellow evolutionists. Thus Douglas Futuyma, in his anti-creationist book, states that:

> Two major kinds of argument about evolutionary theory occur within scientific circles. There are philosophical arguments about whether or not evolutionary theory qualifies as a scientific theory, and substantive arguments about the

details of the theory and their adequacy to explain observed
phenomena. . . . A secondary issue then arises: Is the
hypothesis of natural selection falsifiable or is it a tautology? . . . The claim that natural selection is a tautology is
periodically made in the scientific literature itself. . . .[27]

A tautology is a circular argument in which the conclusions
are merely a restatement of the premises employed in the first
place. For example, if one asks, "What survives?" The reply
is, "The fittest survive." When one then asks, "What are the
fittest?" the answer is, "Those that survive." Thus, survivors
survive. Please note that Futuyma states that the challenge to
the scientific status of evolutionary theory comes from within
"scientific circles." This is a term that evolutionists reserve
only for fellow evolutionists.

Francisco Ayala, a biologist and ardent anti-creationist,
admits that:

Two criticisms of the theory of natural selection have been
raised by philosophers of science. One criticism is that the
theory of natural selection involves circularity. The other
is that it cannot be subjected to an empirical test.[28]

Again, we need to be reminded that any theory that cannot be
subjected to empirical test cannot qualify as a scientific theory.
Ayala, of course, does not agree with those philosophers of
science who challenge the scientific status of evolutionary
theory, but he, as we shall see shortly, unwittingly revealed
the fact that evolutionary theory, because it is so constructed
that it explains everything and anything, no matter what the
data are, does not qualify as a scientific theory.

In his chapter, "Scientific Hypotheses, Natural Selection
and the Neutrality Theory of Protein Evolution," in a book
published in 1975, Ayala got off to a good start when he
correctly pointed out that:

A hypothesis or theory compatible with all possible states
of affairs in the world of experience is uninformative. . . . The
important point is that the empirical content of a hypothesis
is measured by the class of its potential falsifiers.[29]

What he is saying here is that a theory that is stated in such broad or vague terms that there is no way to show that it is wrong (if it is wrong) is a very poor theory; at the very least it is not a scientific theory. A theory, to qualify as a scientific theory, must make definite predictions, the failure of which would falsify the theory. Any theory that is thus so plastic that all possible results, no matter what they may be, can be accommodated within its general concepts, is not a scientific theory.

Now let us see what Ayala has to say on the very next page of his article. Perhaps he has a very short memory, or perhaps a considerable time span elapsed between the time he wrote the material on the first page and the material on the second page. On the next page of his chapter, Ayala states:

> Natural selection can account for the different patterns, rates, and outcomes of evolutionary processes. Adaptive radiations in some cases, as well as lack of phyletic diversifications in others, rapid and slow rates in evolutionary change, profuse and limited genetic variation in populations; these and many other alternative occurrences can all be explained by postulating the existence of appropriate environmental challenges.

In other words, it makes no difference what the data turn out to be, one can imagine an evolutionary scenario to account for the data.

Thus, the theory of natural selection can be used to explain anything and everything:

1. *Adaptive radiations* which produce numerous and widely diverse evolutionary products; or *little or no adaptive radiations,* producing practically no phyletic diversification

2. *Rapid rates* in evolutionary change or *slow rates* in evolutionary change

3. *Profuse* genetic variations, or *limited* genetic variations

4. Many other alternative occurrences by postulating the existence of appropriate environmental challenges.

In other words, the "explanatory" power of natural selection in evolutionary theory to account for what we see in the fossil record and among living creatures today is limited only by the powers of human imagination. Thus, Ayala's cherished theory of natural selection, the driving and guiding force in evolution according to Ayala and textbook orthodoxy, is compatible with all possible states of affairs in the world of experience and therefore, according to Ayala himself, is uninformative. Furthermore, the empirical content of the theory is practically non-existent because its class of potential falsifiers is empty.

No doubt it was facts similar to those above that inspired Marjorie Grene's lack of enthusiasm for the neo-Darwinian theory of evolution. In describing her objections, she stated:

> . . . but one may also ask, as some eminent biologists do, whether evolution, on a large as well as on a small scale, is essentially a matter of adaptation at all. To such biologists—such as A. M. Dalcq of Brussels, O. Schindewolf of Tubingen, or A. Vandel of Toulouse—there appear in fact to be two divergent directions in the evolutionary story. There are, indeed, all the minute specialized divergences like those of the Galapagos finches which so fascinated Darwin; it is their story that is told in the *Origin* and elaborated by the selectionists today. But these are dead ends, last minutiae of development; it is not from them that the great massive novelties of evolution could have sprung. For this, such dissenters feel, is the major evolutionary theme: great new inventions, new ideas of living, which arise with startling suddenness, proliferate in a variety of directions, yet persist with fundamental constancy—as in Darwinian terms they would have no reason in the world to do. Neither the origin and persistence of great new modes of life—photosynthesis, breathing, thinking—nor all the intricate and coordinated changes needed to support them, are explained or even made conceivable on the Darwinian view. And if one returns to read the *Origin* with these criticisms in mind, one finds, indeed, that for all the brilliance of its hypotheses, for all the splendid simplicity

of the "mechanism" by which it "explains" so many and so varied phenomena, it simply is not about the origin of species, let alone of the great orders and classes and phyla, at all. Its argument moves in a different direction altogether, in the direction of minute, specialized adaptations, which lead, unless to extinction, nowhere. And the same is true of the whole immense and infinitely ingenious mountain of work by present-day Darwinians: *c'est magnifique, mais ce n'est pas la guerre!* That the colour of moths and snails or the bloom on the castor bean stem are "explained" by mutation and natural selection is very likely; but how from single-celled (and for that matter from inanimate) ancestors there came to be castor beans and moths and snails, and how from these there emerged llamas and hedgehogs and lions and apes—and men—that is a question which neo-Darwinian theory simply leaves unasked.[30]

If modern neo-Darwinian evolutionary theory leaves unasked these vital questions, one thing is certain—it provides no answers to those questions, and therefore is not about origins at all but is simply a lot of story telling about matters irrelevant to the basic question: How could and how did the living creatures on this earth come into existence?

David Hull, in his review in *Science*, the publication of the American Association for the Advancement of Science, of the book *Dimensions of Darwinism,* edited by Marjorie Grene, states that:

The problem with explaining the structure of organisms in terms of past adaptations is that neither available evidence nor current theories of evolutionary mechanisms constrain such explanations very much. Indefinitely many alternative stories seem equally plausible.[31]

This statement by Hull is strongly reminiscent of the admission by Ehrlich and Birch and the unintended admission by Ayala.

In an earlier statement with reference to the criteria of a scientific theory, not only was falsifiability mentioned but mentioned also (and related to it) was the necessity of repeatable observation (and thus the applicability of the experimental method). But what can we say about these possibilities with reference to the general theory of evolution? This is what the late Theodosius Dobzhansky, one of the main architects of the neo-Darwinian mechanism, had to say about that:

> These evolutionary happenings are unique, unrepeatable, and irreversible. It is as impossible to turn a land vertebrate into a fish as it is to effect the reverse transformation. The applicability of the experimental method to the study of such unique historical processes is severely restricted before all else by the time intervals involved, which far exceed the lifetime of any human experimenter. And yet it is just such impossibility that is demanded by anti-evolutionists when they ask for "proofs" of evolution which they would magnanimously accept as satisfactory.[32]

Note that Dobzhansky is bitter with creation scientists because they demand the applicability of the experimental method to evolutionary theory, which he admits is an impossibility. Yet it is precisely because of the impossibility of applying the experimental method to creation that Dobzhansky and most of his evolutionist colleagues demand the exclusion of creation explanations in science and in the science classrooms! Evolutionists employ a double standard with reference to the teaching of creation science and evolution science.

"Transformed cladists" are those taxonomists who, although they may be evolutionists, do not employ evolutionary theory in their practice of classifying organisms into species, genera, etc. Their classification system is based on similarities, particularly morphological characteristics that are unique and restrictive, rather than on assumed evolutionary ancestors or history. Colin Patterson, whom we have referred to earlier in this chapter, is one of these. In an article based on a radio interview with Patterson published in *The Listener,* the publication of the British Broadcasting Corporation, the author of the article states:

So now we can see the full extent of the doubts. The transformed cladists claim that evolution is totally unnecessary for good taxonomy; at the same time they are unconvinced by the Darwinian explanation of how new species arise. To them, therefore, the history of life is still fiction rather than fact and the Darwinian penchant for explaining evolution in terms of adaptation and selection is largely empty rhetoric.[33]

Later in this article Patterson is quoted as saying:

But it seems to me that the theoretical framework has very little impact on the actual progress of the work in biological research. In a way some aspects of Darwinism and of neo-Darwinism seem to me to have held back the progress of science.

If what Patterson and his fellow transformed cladists are saying is true, then two things seem obvious. First, if indeed the Darwinian explanations are no more than empty rhetoric, then Darwinian orthodoxy, taught in schools, colleges, and universities throughout the world, is deficient in empirical content and cannot be given the dignity of a scientific theory (and may even be nothing more than fiction). Secondly, if the theoretical framework of evolutionary theory has very little impact on the progress of work in biological research and actually in some respects retards the progress in science, the oft-repeated statement that evolution theory is the great unifying concept of biology or that, as Matthews put it, "evolution is the backbone of biology," is not only without foundation but is objectively false. As we stated earlier, biology is the study of the *operation* of living organisms, while evolution is an attempt to reconstruct their histories.

In support of Patterson, one can readily cite several instances in which evolutionary theory has retarded progress in science. For decades much research in embryology had been mis-directed by the now thoroughly discredited theory of embryological recapitulation. This theory, sometimes referred to in the past as the "biogenetic law," is the notion that, for example, as the human embryo develops it recapitulates its evolutionary history by starting out as a single cell, then later resembling a fish, then a tadpole, later a reptile, then an ape, and finally a human. Research in embryology would have been more fruitful and thus would have made more rapid progress if it had been realized then, as it is now, that each embryo, plant or animal, is doing only what it must do to develop from a single, fertilized cell into an adult organism, without any influence of a supposed evolutionary ancestry.

For many years research on the true importance and function of such organs and structures as the pineal gland, the tonsils, and the appendix were neglected because, according to evolutionists, these were useless vestiges left over from our evolutionary history. The number of unnecessary and even harmful tonsillectomies and appendectomies that have been performed because of evolutionary teachings is probably in the millions.

One also wonders at the cost, in countless thousands of man-hours of research, of devising evolutionary phylogenies which not only serve no practical purpose but all of which are eventually discarded. In fact, the only sure thing that can be said about any evolutionary phylogeny or hypothetical evolutionary history is that it is certain to be discarded by future generations of evolutionists. Derek Ager, a professor of geology at the university in Swansea, Wales, and a vigorous anti-creationist, declared that:

> It must be significant that nearly all the evolutionary stories I learned as a student, from Trueman's *Ostrea/Gryphea* to Carruther's *Raphrentis delanouei,* have now been "debunked." Similarly, my own experience of more than twenty years looking for evolutionary lineages among the Mesozoic Brachiopoda has proved them equally elusive.[34]

Ager is abandoning gradualistic evolutionary theories for a jerky mode, involving, at least in part, catastrophic geological events.

Michael Ruse, who received a Ph.D. from the University of Bristol and is now a professor of history and philosophy of

biology at the University of Guelph, Ontario, is an avid
anti-creationist and totally devoted to the defense of neo-
Darwinian orthodoxy. He was the main witness on the philosophy of science for the evolutionist side in the trial held in
Judge William Overton's Federal courtroom in Little Rock,
Arkansas, in which Overton ruled that Act 590 of the Arkansas
legislature, mandating equal treatment for creation science
and evolution science, was unconstitutional. Much of Judge
Overton's reasoning in his decision concerning the nature of
science was based on Ruse's testimony. Overton's decision
has been severely criticized by Dr. Larry Laudan, professor of
the Philosophy of Science at the University of Pittsburgh when
he penned his criticism, but who is, nevertheless, an evolutionist. Laudan declared that:

> The victory in the Arkansas case was hollow, for it was
> achieved only at the expense of perpetuating and canoniz-
> ing a false stereotype of what science is and how it works.
> If it goes unchallenged by the scientific community, it will
> raise grave doubts about that community's intellectual in-
> tegrity.[35]

Not only has the decision not been challenged by most of those
in the "scientific community" (the community of evolutionists), but evolutionists have gleefully and incessantly trumpeted Overton's decision wherever the subject of creation
science is mentioned or discussed.

Philip L. Quinn, a philosopher of science, has also published a review that is critical of Overton's decision and is
especially harshly critical of Ruse's contribution to that decision. He says:

> If the expert's views are not representative of a settled
> consensus of opinion in the relevant community of schol-
> ars, then policy based on those views will lack credibility
> within that community, and the members of that commu-
> nity are likely to regard such lack of credibility as discred-
> iting the policy in question. This was the major problem in
> *McLean v. Arkansas.* Ruse's views do not represent a set-
> tled consensus of opinion among philosophers of science.

Worse still, some of them are clearly false and some are based on obviously fallacious arguments.[36]

Ruse has published a spirited defense of evolutionary theory in general and of neo-Darwinism in particular.[37] He bemoans the fact that today Darwinism is not only under attack by scientific creationists, but is under attack even among committed evolutionists and among others, many of whom are professional philosophers, who agree as to the inadequacy of Darwinism, citing serious internal conceptual flaws.[38] In his book, beginning on p. 131, Ruse has a section describing the objections to Darwinian evolutionary theory (or more particularly, neo-Darwinism) under the heading, "Darwinism as Metaphysics." As one reads this section it becomes clear that almost all of the critics are evolutionists, or at least not creationists. Extensive quotes will be taken from this section in order to document these challenges to the scientific status of evolutionary theory.

Ruse begins by stating:

The objection is as straightforward as it is popular and devastating, if well taken. *It is claimed that Darwinian evolutionary theory*—the critics usually lump together indifferently both past and present versions—*is no genuine scientific theory at all.* Despite appearances, it is just not about the empirical world; it is rather, at most, *a speculative philosophy of nature,* on a par with Plato's theory or forms of Swedenborgian theology. It is, in short, a metaphysical wolf masquerading as a scientific lamb. And, although the critics hasten to assure us that there is nothing wrong with metaphysics, it is usually not too long before words like "slight" or "inadequate" or even "dismal" start to slip into the talk. All in all, we are left with the impression that Darwinism says nothing, and even if it did say something, it would not be *that* worth listening to. "Evolution is not a fact but a theory" is a charitable epitaph.

Later Ruse says:

It seems fairly clear that what distinguishes science from nonscience is the fact that scientific claims reflect, and somehow can be checked against, empirical experience—ultimately, the data that we get through our senses. The wave theory of light is about this physical world of ours; in some very important sense, God is not part of this world. We see light; we do not see God. But, how exactly does science reflect its empirical base? One might think that it is all simply a question of finding positive empirical evidence for scientific claims—evidence that is unobtainable for other sorts of claims. However, matters are a little more complex than this, because science does not deal with particulars, at least not directly and exclusively, but with generalities and universals. One's interest is not in this planet or that planet as such. Rather, one asks what each and every planet does, just as one asks what each and every light ray does. But, this being so, simple checking and confirmation obviously cannot be enough.

Then, Ruse continues:

Given this fact, many thinkers have therefore tried the opposite tack. Perhaps what distinguishes science is not that one can ever show it true, but that one can always knock it down! As T. H. Huxley was wont to say, the scientist must be prepared always to sit down before the facts, as a little child, ever prepared to give up the most cherished of theories should the empirical data dictate otherwise. Teasingly, Huxley used to say of his friend Herbert Spencer that his idea of a tragedy was that of a beautiful theory murdered by an ugly fact. Perhaps the edge to this quip reflects Huxley's belief that Spencer would go to any lengths to prevent murder being done—even to the extent of taking his theories out of science altogether (L. Huxley, 1900).

Recently, the thinker who has stood most firmly and proudly in Huxley's tradition has been the philosopher Karl Popper (1959, 1962, 1972, 1974). Starting from the logical point that, although many positive instances cannot confirm a universal statement, one negative instance can refute it, Popper argues that the essential mark of science—the "criterion of demarcation"—is that it is *falsifiable.*

After some further remarks, Ruse continues:

Turning to science, or, more precisely, to claims that are made in the name of science, Popper and his sympathizers make short shrift of many areas of the social sciences. Freudian psychoanalytic theory is dismissed as incontrovertibly and irreparably unfalsifiable. *But then moving on to biology, coming up against Darwinism, they feel compelled to make the same judgment: Darwinian evolutionary theory is unfalsifiable.* Hence, the critical evaluation given at the beginning of this section: I have come to the conclusion that Darwinism is not a testable scientific theory but a *metaphysical research programme*—a possible framework for testable scientific theories (Popper, 1974, p. 134, his italics).

Since making this claim, Popper himself has modified his position somewhat; but, disclaimers aside, I suspect that even now he does not really believe that Darwinism in its modern form is genuinely falsifiable. If one relies heavily on natural selection and sexual selection, simultaneously downplaying drift, which of course is what the neo-Darwinian does do, then Popper feels that one has a nonfalsifiable theory. *And, certainly, many followers agree that there is something conceptually flawed with Darwinism.* (See Bethell, 1976; Cracraft, 1978; Nelson, 1978; Patterson, 1978; Platnick and Gaffney, 1978; Popper, 1978, 1980; and Wiley, 1975).

Just how precisely do the various critics make their case? Simply, it is argued that there is no way, either in practice or in principle, to put Darwinism (for ease, let us concentrate here on neo-Darwinism) to the test. For a start, testing requires prediction. One predicts something on the basis of a theory, checks to see if the prediction turns out true or false, and then rejects or retains one's theory on the basis of the results. But how can one make genuine predictions with Darwinism? Who could possibly predict what will happen to the elephant's trunk twenty-five million years down the road? Certainly not the Darwinian! And even if he could, there would be no one around to check out the prediction. Analogously, no one could step back to the Mesozoic to see the evolution of mammals and check if indeed natural selection was at work, nor could anyone spend a week or two (or century or two) in the Cretaceous to see if the dinosaurs, then going extinct, failed in the struggle for existence.

More importantly, argues the critic, even if one had a machine to go forward or back in time, it would make little difference! An essential claim of Darwinism devolves on the ubiquity of organic adaptation. The presumption is that physical characteristics have an adaptive value; they were preserved and selected because of their useful natures in the struggle for existence. But, in fact, it is easy to see that even in principle Darwinians guard themselves against counterarguments.

Take something much discussed by evolutionists: the sail on the back of the Permian reptile, *Dimetrodon*. The possibility that this may have absolutely no adaptive value is given no credence at all, as Darwinians plunge into their favorite parlour game: "find the adaptation." The sail was a defense mechanism (it scared predators), or it served for sexual display (not much chance of mistaking someone's intentions with that thing along one's backside), or, as many evolutionists (including Raup and Stanley) suppose, it worked as a heat-regulating device to keep the cold-blooded *Dimetrodon* at a more constant temperature in the fluctuating environment. The animal would move the sail around in the sunlight and wind, heating or cooling the blood in the sail, which could then be passed through to the rest of the body. In short, as this example shows, *there has to be some reason for anything and everything. One can be sure that if the Darwinian can think of no potential value in the struggle for existence, then value will be found in the struggle for reproduction.* Even the most absurd and grotesque of physical features are supposed to have irrepressible aphrodisiac qualities. Like the Freudians, Darwinians get a lot of mileage out of sex.

There must be something dreadfully wrong with Darwinism. How can it be that something, which seems at first sight to be so all-encompassing and so impressively empirical, fails so dreadfully when subjected to searching inquiry? The critics think they know the source of all the trouble. Darwinism is no genuine scientific theory because it rests on a bogus mechanism: natural selection. Far from being an empirically testable, putative cause of evolutionary change, *natural selection is no scientific claim at all: it is a vacuous tautology.* Consider that natural selection states simply that a certain proportion of organisms, by definition the "fitter," survive and reproduce, whereas others do not. But which are the "fitter"? Simply they are those that survive and reproduce! In other words, natural selection collapses into the analytically true statement that those that survive and reproduce are those that survive and reproduce. No wonder all the subareas of evolutionary thought come apart on close inspection. They put their trust in an empty statement *(Peters, 1976).* Indeed, one might feel that Popper is charitable in describing Darwinism as "metaphysical." Like Freudianism, it tells us nothing about the real world and fraudulently pretends that it does!

Only one more nail is required to make the lid to the Darwinian coffin secure. Why is it that something so bogus, so clearly inadequate when judged by the stringent criteria of genuine science, should have gone so far? Why has Darwinism been such a success for 100 years, despite the sense of unease that so many clear thinkers have felt? *It is simply because Darwinism has no rivals!* It exists on its own, filling a gap, with no personal struggle for existence to fight. Indeed, when the occasional dissenter has suggested a possible alternative, it has always been dismissed out of hand, "possibly not on very adequate evidence" (Manser, 1965).

First, we wish to note, Ruse does not accuse any of these critics of being creationists. All, or most, would be included by evolutionists as members of the "community of scientists." Next we note that Ruse immediately leaps to the defense of Darwinism. The section quoted above is followed by a section entitled "Darwinism as Genuine Science."[39] Ruse begins this section by declaring, "I believe this whole line of objection to be mistaken, absolutely and entirely." Ruse then applies what he no doubt believes to be the ultimate insult to these critics when he states, "Protestations notwithstanding, the critics' arguments look suspiciously like those of Darwin's religious opponents." Ruse no doubt intended this remark as an attempt to discredit the critics, but perhaps it only serves to lend credibility to Darwin's "religious opponents"!

Ruse's defense is much weaker and less convincing than the case laid out by the critics. His application of a double standard in evaluating the scientific status of creation and evolution soon becomes evident. If he were attacking the scientific status of creation, he would apply the severest of tests, which he did do in the Arkansas trial. In his defense of evolution, however, he immediately loosens the restrictions to be applied. He says:

> The first point I want to make is that, although the major mark of science is undoubtedly the way in which it brushes against experience, and although undoubtedly falsifiability is important here, one must be careful not to take too literal or too narrow a reading of one's criteria.

To creation scientists, what Ruse seems to be recommending and to have done is to establish proper criteria for science in general and scientific theories in particular and then to apply these criteria strictly, relative to creation. When it comes to applying these same criteria to the scientific status of evolutionary theory, however, Ruse insists that we avoid a too literal or too narrow reading of the rules. That way evolution gets in and creation is left out.

Ruse first defends Darwinism by attacking the importance of the application of the criterion of falsifiability, which he wishes to weaken, even to eliminate, when judging Darwinian evolutionary theory. He claims that if the theory is supported by many observations but appears to be falsified by only a few, then the scientific status of the theory is sustained. Thus, he says:

> If claims seem to go a little against the evidence, or (per-haps more importantly) Darwinians seem determined to fit

the facts into their own pattern, then before condemning,
one must judge the whole.

Here Ruse is forgetting, however, that one can never prove a theory to be correct, but can only prove it to be incorrect, if, indeed, it is false. Einstein is reported to have said that one may perform a thousand experiments, the results of all of which may support a theory, but finally one may perform a single experiment, the results of which falsify the theory. Ruse wishes to accept all the evidence that can be interpreted as supporting Darwinian evolutionary theory while ignoring or rationalizing all contradictory evidence.

Next, Ruse wishes to blunt the criticism of the failure of Darwinian evolutionary theory to predict the future course of evolutionary processes. Ruse, of course, freely admits that no one can predict the future course of the elephant's trunk, or the giraffe's neck, or the camel's hump, etc. But this is so, he says, because the future path of evolution is dependent on all sorts of unknown external factors. He does claim, however, that predictions can be made in what he calls "causal theory," and he refers to studies on fruit flies, or *Drosophila*. But this is not really about evolution at all, because fruit flies remain fruit flies from beginning to end. Grene's objections to the employment of such evidence for Darwinian evolution applies with full force here.

Ruse then points out that the Darwinian can make predictions about what one should find in the present and in the past (the fossil record). What Ruse fails to mention, as clearly pointed out by the critics (as earlier described), is that it really makes no difference whether the data do or do not agree with predictions, the Darwinian always has some way to "explain" it. It is strictly a "heads, I win, tails, you lose" proposition, as Ayala's description unwittingly made clear.

Later, Ruse admits that it is difficult to know which adaptations, if any, were responsible for the origin of the huge "sail" on the back of *Dimetrodon* or for the extinction of dinosaurs, stating: "Now, let me admit quite candidly that at this point in evolutionary theorizing one does get an element of speculation." He then seeks to protect evolutionary theory from this weakness by claiming that "from our evolutionary studies of the present, we have unequivocal, testable, empirical evidence about the importance of adaptation." He then proceeds to cite the Cain-Sheppard study on snails, which was open to falsification. "Had the thrushes killed more banded snails from varied backgrounds and vice versa, their hypotheses about adaptive value of shell color would have been shown false," Ruse states. That may be so, but negative results would only have falsified their hypothesis, but no doubt numerous other hypotheses could have been invented by Darwinians to replace it. Furthermore, the adaptive or non-adaptive value of the color on the shells of snails gives us absolutely no information on how snails arose in the first place. Just as Grene reminded us that neo-Darwinian theory leaves unasked, let alone unanswered, how castor beans, moths, and snails emerged from single-celled organisms, so Ruse's example of the assumed value of the color of the shell of the snail says nothing about the origin of one species of snail from another or the origin of snails from another basically different type of creature.

Ruse then has a section entitled "Is Natural Selection a Tautology?" He begins this section by stating that this claim is the strongest and most crucial objection of all, because if this is so then the whole Darwinian edifice collapses into a truism. Of course, Ruse rejects this claim most emphatically. He maintains that in at least three respects, there is an empirical, nontautological, falsifiable basis to the mechanism cherished by Darwinians. "First," he says, "there is the claim that in the organic world there is a struggle for reproduction." How Ruse could maintain that this constitutes a test for Darwinism in general or for the theory of natural selection in particular seems unfathomable, even ludicrous. That there is a struggle for reproduction was obvious to pre-Darwinian creationists, long before Darwin announced his theory, and it is obvious to all who have seen animals compete for mates and even, or perhaps especially, to humans who employ every reasonable device to attract mates. This competition is rooted in the basic drive to reproduce, which is necessary for the survival of all species.

Secondly, Ruse says, there is the central claim of Darwinians that they can apply their theory throughout the organic world, because success in the struggle is, on average, not random but a function of the distinctive characteristics possessed by organisms. Again, this is hardly more than a statement of the obvious and was in fact employed by pre-Darwinian creationists and by Darwin's creationist contemporaries to explain why variants from the norm of a species would be eliminated, thus preserving the species against change. It is also the reason that humans employ devices, such as perfume, cosmetics, hairdressers, beautiful clothes, body-building exercises, etc., in order to make themselves attractive to members of the opposite sex.

Thirdly, Ruse says that there is the claim that selection is systematic—what selection favors in one situation will be what selection favors in identical situations. That may be so, if the principle of *ceteris paribus* (all things being equal) applies.

If things do not really turn out the way the Darwinian predicts, then he can, of course, say that the *ceteris paribus* clause does not apply in this case, for obviously (he assumes) all things were not equal. The actual example that Ruse chose to support his third claim was unfortunate, for it can be shown that at least one feature of his example is erroneous. Ruse says:

> Thus, upon finding an arctic mammal with a white coat, an evolutionist confidently puts it down to an adaptive response to the snowy terrain, because this has been found to be the case for other arctic organisms.

The white coat color of the polar bear cannot be adaptive, however, since he has no predator. The white coat color thus cannot provide him any selective value, since failure to detect him against the snowy terrain cannot protect him against a non-existent predator. And by the way, the polar bear and the brown bear, placed in separate species by taxonomists, and even in separate genera by some, do interbreed and produce fertile offspring.

Ruse actually has made little, if any, attempt to answer the critics of neo-Darwinian evolution, which incorporates natural selection as its main driving force, or "creative" force. One of the main objections of the critics is that there is no criterion other than survival to test the theory of natural selection, therefore it collapses into a tautology (those that survive are the fittest, and the fittest are those that survive, so simply, it is the survivors that survive, which we knew in the first place). Tom Bethell, a writer who has a degree in philosophy from Oxford University, published an article in Harper's Magazine in 1976, entitled "Darwin's Mistake,"[40] which was given wide attention in evolutionary circles. In this article, Bethell makes a strong case for the fact that, at least in all methods used to test the theory, natural selection is tautological. Concerning the debate about the efficacy of Darwin's theory that had arisen in the 1960's and was now flourishing in the 1970's, Bethell remarks:

> It is surprising that so little word of it has leaked out, because it seems to have been one of the most important academic debates of the 1960s, and as I see it the conclusion is pretty staggering: Darwin's theory, I believe, is on the verge of collapse.

Bethell closes his article with the statement that:

> Darwin, I suggest, is in the process of being discarded, but perhaps in deference to the venerable old gentleman, resting comfortably in Westminster Abbey next to Sir Isaac Newton, it is being done as discreetly and gently as possible, with a minimum of publicity.

Bethell's study of the problem had been going on intensely for a year preceding the publication of his article and had been inspired by his reading of Norman Macbeth's *Darwin*

Retried,[41] an incisive full-bore attack on all kinds of Darwinism, in which non-creationist Macbeth attacks both the scientific status of these theories as well as their adequacy to explain the data related to origins. Macbeth's book was one of the earlier and best of the books critical of evolutionary theory of recent times. E. O. Wiley, then icthyologist (specialist on fishes) at the American Museum of Natural History and City University of New York, and now at the University of Kansas, published a favorable review of Macbeth's book in 1975.[42] Speaking of the various theories competing as explanations for evolution, none of which, Wiley says, provides a satisfactory explanation, he goes on to say:

> Most of us might opt for rejection in most circumstances. Yet, in the case of the synthetic theory, we hold it, not with a light hand as advocated by T. H. Huxley, but with an ironclad grasp, unwilling to let go, unwilling to explore alternatives.

So much for the tentative nature of evolution theory, so loudly trumpeted by evolutionists as one of the necessary characteristics of true science!

Bethell points out that some prominent Darwinians frankly admit that, in practice, the theory of natural selection is a tautology. Thus, C. H. Waddington, a British biologist and fervent neo-Darwinian, speaking at the Darwin Centennial in Chicago, frankly stated that:

> Natural selection, which was at first considered as though it were a hypothesis that was in need of experiment or observational confirmation turns out, on closer inspection, to be a tautology, a statement of an inevitable although previously unrecognized relation. It states that the fittest individuals in a population (defined as those which leave most offspring) will leave most offspring.[43]

Macbeth found this statement "staggering," but it hardly raised an eyebrow in evolutionary circles.

Today many biologists accept the definition of natural selection as nothing more than differential reproduction. This redefinition was performed by the British geneticist and statistician, R. A. Fisher, in a widely acclaimed book, *The Genetical Theory of Natural Selection*.[44] Fisher applied mathematical formulae to his theories and from this emerged what has come to be known as population genetics. This development was happily welcomed by evolutionary biologists, because it seemed to provide a more sure scientific undergirding for their theory. But that can hardly be the case if the following statement by Waddington about this matter is a true approximation:

> The theory of neo-Darwinism is a theory of the evolution of the population in respect to leaving offspring and not in respect to anything else. . . . Everybody has it in the back of his mind that the animals that leave the largest number of offspring are going to be those best adapted also for eating peculiar vegetation, or something of this sort, but this is not explicit in the theory. . . . There you do come to what is, in effect, a vacuous statement: Natural selection is that some things leave more offspring than others; and, you ask, which leave more offspring than others; and it is those that leave more offspring, and there is nothing more to it than that. The whole real guts of evolution—which is how do you come to have horses and tigers and things—is outside the mathematical theory.[45]

Here we find another confirmation of the severe limitations to Darwinian theory that affirm once more, as creation scientists have always maintained and as Marjorie Grene has so aptly stated, that Darwinian theory doesn't even attempt to explain the really significant events in origins.

According to Dobzhansky, the evolutionary process is "blind, mechanical, automatic, impersonal." Sir Gavin de Beer, the British biologist and evolutionist, stated that evolution was "wasteful, blind, and blundering." When it comes to selling evolution, however, and extolling the processes involved, evolutionists wax eloquent. Dobzhansky likened natural selection to "a human activity such as performing or composing music." de Beer described it as a "master of ceremonies." Simpson compared natural selection to a poet and a builder. Ernst Mayr, formerly a professor of zoology at Harvard, likened selection to a sculptor. Sir Julian Huxley compared natural selection to William Shakespeare.[46] To say that these evolutionists had a fondness for Darwinism bordering on obsession would hardly be an overstatement.

Ronald H. Brady, a professor of philosophy at Ramapo College, has written one of the most thorough and objective critiques of the problem. His paper, entitled "Natural Selection and the Criteria by Which a Theory is Judged," was published in *Systematic Zoology* in 1979.[47] Brady explains that, as formulated by Darwin, the theory of natural selection is not a tautology, but whenever any attempt is made to test the theory, the procedure degenerates into a tautology, because the only empirical test that can be applied is survival. Brady thus states that:

> Natural selection is free of tautology in any formulation that recognizes the causal interaction between the organism and its environment, but most recent critics have already understood this and are actually arguing that the theory is not falsifiable in its operational form. Under examination, the operational forms of the concepts of adaptation and fitness turn out to be too indeterminate to be seriously tested, for they are protected by ad hoc additions drawn from an indeterminate realm.[48]

Stephen Jay Gould, a professor at Harvard University teaching geology, biology, and the history of science, is a prolific writer and one of the chief spokesmen for evolutionary theory in the U.S. and, of course, a tireless anti-creationist. Much more will be said about Gould later. Gould took offense at Bethell's claim that the theory of natural selection was a tautology and hastened to challenge Bethell's attack on this cornerstone of Darwinism, although Gould is not really a good Darwinian himself, as we will see later. Gould maintained that there was a criterion for judging fitness independent of

survival: the evidence of good engineering design. Gould thus
states:

> Now the key point: certain morphological, physiological,
> and behavioral traits should be superior *a priori* as designs
> for living in these environments. These traits confer fitness
> by an engineer's criterion of good design, not by the em-
> pirical fact of their survival and spread.[49]

But how can one know whether any particular trait confers
fitness, and is thus presumably the product of good engineering design, without using survival as a measure of fitness?
How else can we test the hypothesis that a trait fulfills the
criterion of good engineering design? A number of Gould's
fellow evolutionists gave him credit for providing an answer
to Bethell's arguments, but Gould actually did not escape the
trap that so badly weakens the claim for the testability of the
theory of natural selection and of neo-Darwinian evolution, of
which natural selection is the key element. In this contest
between Bethell and Gould, Brady awards the prize to Bethell.[50]

Many evolutionists today are beginning to de-emphasize
the importance of natural selection in evolution and some wish
to discard its role almost completely. Steven M. Stanley, a
professor at John Hopkins University, made a frontal attack
on the neo-Darwinian selection theory in an article published
in the *Proceedings of the National Academy of Science* in
1975.[51] Stanley maintained that:

> Gradual evolutionary change by natural selection operates
> so slowly within established species that it cannot account
> for the major features of evolution.[52]

Stanley is so impressed by the apparent sudden appearance
(on a geological time scale) in great diversity of various types
of animals that he maintains that the neo-Darwinian model of
gradualistic change by natural selection cannot account for
such rapid origins. He believes that evolution has occurred by
abrupt, random production of new species, a notion originally
propounded by Stephen Gould and Niles Eldredge, and now

growing increasingly popular in evolutionary circles. Stanley, and others who hold this view (of which we will say more later), offer no explanation as to how a species may abruptly, at random, produce new species. Assuming evolution to be a fact, and maintaining that the fossil record clearly contradicts the neo-Darwinian theory of gradual change through small mutations and natural selection, Stanley simply assumes that evolution must have occurred rapidly by "random speciation events." He asserts that:

> If most evolutionary changes occur during speciation events and if speciation events are largely random, natural selection, long viewed as the process guiding evolutionary change, cannot play a significant role in determining the overall course of evolution.[53]

He even goes so far as to say that "The reductionist view that evolution can ultimately be understood in terms of genetics and molecular biology is clearly in error."[54] But if evolution cannot be understood in terms of genetics and biology, then the mechanism of evolution will always remain an intractable mystery.

Pierre-Paul Grassé, the famous French zoologist mentioned earlier in this chapter, would not only agree with the foregoing statement by Stanley but would also go much further in rejecting the neo-Darwinian mechanism of micromutations acted upon by natural selection. He states flatly that "No matter how numerous they may be, mutations do not produce any kind of evolution."[55] Later, he says:

> Mutations, in time, occur incoherently. They are not complementary to one another, nor are they cumulative in successive generations toward a given direction. They modify what preexists, but they do so in disorder. . . .[56]

Furthermore, as far as natural selection is concerned, Grassé maintains that it has nothing to do with evolution. He says:

> The role assigned to natural selection in establishing adaptation, while speciously probable, is based on not one single sure datum. . . . To assert that population dynamics gives a

picture of evolution in action is an unfounded opinion, or rather a postulate, that relies on not a single proved fact showing that transformations in the two kingdoms have been essentially linked to changes in the balance of genes in a population.[57]

Grassé provides devastating evidence, in several passages in his book, against the notion that chance can account for evolution. Speaking to the vital part that chance is assigned in all Darwinian schemes, Grassé says:

> Directed by all-powerful selection, chance becomes a sort of providence, which, under the cover of atheism, is not named but which is secretly worshipped.[58]

Grassé, an evolutionist, refuses to be forced to make a choice between randomness and the supernatural but believes that there must be some unknown inner natural laws that direct evolutionary processes, a notion that is vigorously denied by most evolutionists, and by creationists, of course.

What is really significant about this evaluation of the status of evolutionary theory by this agnostic evolutionist is that most of what he is saying is almost precisely what has long been asserted by creation scientists. As noted earlier in this chapter, Grassé despairs of ever discovering how evolution has occurred. In the final sentence in his book, Grassé states resignedly, "Perhaps in this area biology can go no further: the rest is metaphysics." Grassé's evaluation provides strong undergirding for Macbeth's flat-out statement, "Darwinism is not science."[59]

Michael Ruse, a philosopher and unabashed propagandist for neo-Darwinian evolution, brushes aside all doubt as to the "fact" of evolution and any question concerning the sufficiency of neo-Darwinian formulations to explain how evolution has occurred. Pierre-P. Grassé, the most distinguished of all French zoologists, whose knowledge of the living world is encyclopedic, vigorously disagrees. Of these two, concerning the efficacy of mutations and natural selection, creation scientists are very pleased to have Grassé on their side.

Gould and Eldredge are among others who are leaning away from the primacy of natural selection as the creative force in evolution. Gould, for example, says:

> Many evolutionists now doubt exclusive control by selection upon genetic change within local populations. Moreever, even if local populations alter as the synthesis maintains, we now doubt that the same style of change controls events at the two major higher levels: speciation and patterns of macroevolution.[60]

Roger Lewin, in his review[61] of a paper by E. O. Wiley and Daniel Brooks[62] which was a direct challenge to neo-Darwinian theories, states:

> Natural selection, a central figure of neo-Darwinism, is allowed for in Brooks and Wiley's theory, but only as a minor influence. "It can affect survivorship," says Brooks. "It can weed out some of the complexity and so slow down the information decay that results in speciation. It may have a stabilizing effect, but it does not promote speciation. It is not a creative force as many people have suggested."
>
> Competition, another important feature of neo-Darwinism, is again relegated to a minor role in Brooks and Wiley's theory. "We haven't thrown out natural selection and competition," explains Brooks. "They are real, but are not important in explaining the hierarchy that is surely central to understanding evolution."

Thus the doctrine of natural selection, the crowning jewel of all forms of Darwinism, is being discarded or seriously weakened by a growing number of evolutionists, both as to its status as a scientific theory and as to its ability to account for most of evolution.

Furthermore, their arguments for doing so sound startlingly similar to arguments of creation scientists from Darwin's time down to the present. Creation scientists, understandably, are beginning to smell victory.

This discussion on the scientific and religious nature of creation and evolution, while extensive, could be continued almost endlessly, as many more experts on each side could profitably be cited, but time and space impose limits. From our discussion, it can be seen that both creation and evolution contain an important dimension of metaphysics. They are thus, as Popper has stated, metaphysical research programs. Strictly defined, neither creation nor evolution is a scientific theory. This does not mean that they do not have scientific character or that they cannot be discussed in scientific terms and their credibility evaluated on the basis of scientific evidence. This is just as true of creation as it is of evolution. In fact, in the more than 300 debates that have been conducted throughout the U.S. and in other countries during the past 20 years, creationists have carefully avoided all references to religious concepts and literature and have based their arguments strictly on scientific evidence, such as the fossil record, the laws of thermodynamics, the complexity of living organisms and probability relationships, etc. The fact that evolutionists themselves admit that creationists have won most of the debates does seem to be saying something important.

Important facets of this scientific evidence will be discussed in detail throughout this book. The credibility of creation and evolution as explanations for origins can be discussed and compared on the basis of that scientific evidence. One very important element of that evidence, for example, is the fossil record. There is absolutely no doubt that the fossil record provides a basis for choosing between creation and evolution. Certainly the fossil record, expected on the basis of creation, should be most significantly different from that expected on the basis of evolution. Thus Glenister and Witzke, in their chapter in an anti-creationist book, state:

> The fossil record affords an opportunity to choose between evolutionary and creationist models for the origin of the earth and its life forms.[63]

Futuyma, in his anti-creationist book, declares that:

> Creation and evolution, between them, exhaust the possible explanations for the origin of living things. Organisms either appeared on the earth fully developed or they did

not. If they did not, they must have developed from preexisting species by some process of modification. If they did
appear in a fully developed state, they must indeed have
been created by some omnipotent intelligence.[64]

It is precisely the argument of creation scientists that the fossil
record provides decisive evidence that all basic types of plants
and animals have appeared fully formed on this planet.

Kenneth Hsu, in a recent paper published in the *Journal
of Sedimentary Petrology,*[65] decries the neglect of the fossil
record by Darwinists. He declares, "The record of history is
stored in archives, and sedimentary rocks constitute the most
important data-storage of the history of life." A bit earlier, he
had complained that Darwin all but ignored the fossil record,
complaining about the imperfections of the geologic record.
"He and his followers wrote the history of life on the basis of
what they thought the history should be."

Later in his paper, Hsu, a committed evolutionist, states:

> We all have heard of *The Origin of Species,* although few
> of us have had time to read it; I did not secure a copy until
> two years ago. A casual perusal of the classic made me
> understand the rage of Paul Feyerabend (1975). He consid-
> ers science an ideology. Feyerabend wrote, "All ideologies
> must be seen in perspective. One must read them like fairy
> tales which have lots of interesting things to say, but which
> contain wicked lies." I do not want to follow his lead to
> lend "three cheers to the fundamentalists in California who
> succeeded in having a dogmatic formulation of the theory
> of evolution removed from the textbooks and an account
> of Genesis included" (p. 163). Nevertheless I agree with
> him that Darwinism contains 'wicked lies'; it is not a
> 'natural law' formulated on the basis of factual evidence,
> but a dogma, reflecting the dominating social philosophy
> of the last century.

It could be said with equal force that modern evolutionary
theory, in whatever guise it is found, is the dominating social
philosophy of the 20th century, a dogmatic ideology.

We can easily see that regardless of whether or not creation and evolution are metaphysical concepts, whether or not creation and evolution fulfill the criteria of a scientific theory, or whether or not natural selection is a tautology, the fossil record *does* afford an opportunity to choose between the creation and evolution models. If what we are seeking to establish is the truth concerning origins, then evolutionists should stop bleating about the supposed religious nature of creation and produce the fossils that document the suggested transition of a single-celled organism into the plants and animals on this earth that now exist and have existed in the past.

Evolutionists have made the charge that creation theory is solely a religious concept, and have made this charge along with the claim that evolutionary theory is pure, unadulterated science, the centerpiece in their political campaign to keep the scientific evidence for creation out of science textbooks and out of biology classes. This is sheer hypocrisy and is designed to avoid a scientific challenge by creation scientists to their precious theory of evolution. Enough slips through the cracks, from time to time, however, to reveal the true nature of the relationships of theories on origins. Richard D. Alexander, a professor of zoology at the University of Michigan, in his chapter in an anti-creationist book, says, "Evolution is an explanatory theory about history."[66] In his note of praise for Ernst Mayr on the occasion of the award of the Balzan prize to Mayr, Gould stated:

> The Nobel prizes focus on quantitive nonhistorical, deductively oriented fields with their methodology of perturbation by experiment and establishment of repeatable chains of relatively simple cause and effect. An entire set of disciplines, different though equal in scope and status, but often subjected to ridicule because they do not follow this pathway of "hard" science is thereby ignored: the historical sciences, treating immensely complex and nonrepeatable events (and therefore eschewing prediction while seeking explanation for what has happened) and using the methods of observation and comparison.

Evolutionary biology is a quintessential historical discipline.[67]

There you have it. Evolution is an explanatory theory about history, "a quintessential historical discipline," included within a set of disciplines often subject to ridicule because they do not follow the pathway of "hard science"—eschewing prediction while seeking to explain what has already happened. Is not the same true of creation? Do not creation scientists seek to explain what has already happened? Is not creation an explanatory theory about history, often subject to ridicule because it does not follow the pathway of "hard" science? Indeed, just as L. Harrison Matthews stated, creation and evolution are exactly parallel.

"Wait!" the evolutionist cries. "Creation requires a creator, and the creator by definition must be external to and independent of the natural universe, and thus by nature, supernatural. Science deals only with natural phenomena, excluding supernatural intervention. Evolution theory bases its premises on natural laws and natural processes still operating in the universe today. Therefore, evolutionary theory is admissible in biology textbooks and classrooms, but creation theory must be excluded."

Creationists agree totally with evolutionists that the supernatural must be excluded from the empirical sciences, the "hard sciences." Creation scientists perform their scientific experiments in exactly the same way evolutionists perform their experiments. Creation scientists assume that what they see happening today happened yesterday and will happen in the future. This is the only way a scientist can operate. No creation scientist undertakes an experiment with the expectation that God must perform a miracle for the experiment to succeed. Science is about the real world out there; a world that functions according to natural laws and processes.

Theories on how the universe came into existence in the first place are, however, outside of the limits of empirical science. To say that we can positively exclude the possibility that the universe and its living inhabitants were supernaturally created is absurd. If that possibility exists, then no one, if he approaches the question objectively, should be unwilling to consider the evidence for such a possibility and to permit that evidence to be examined by students in a science classroom when the subject of origins is being discussed.

References

1. L. R. Godfrey, in *Scientists Confront Creationism,* L. R. Godfrey, Ed., W. W. Norton & Company, New York, 1983, p. xiii.

2. J. W. Patterson, *ibid.,* p. 146.

3. Frederick Edwords, *ibid.,* p. 314.

4. D. B. Wilson, in *Did the Devil Make Darwin Do It?,* D. B. Wilson, Ed., The Iowa State University Press, Ames, 1983, p. viii.

5. W. D. Dolphin, *ibid.,* p. 35.

6. B. P. Waters, *ibid.,* p. 154.

7. D. J. Futuyma, *Science on Trial,* Pantheon Books, New York, 1983, p. 219.

8. P. T. de Chardin, as quoted by F. J. Ayala, *Journal of Heredity* 68:3-10 (1977).

9. Anonymous, "What Is Humanism?" a pamphlet distributed by the Humanist Community of San Jose, California, 95106.

10. G. G. Simpson, *Life of the Past,* Yale University Press, New Haven, 1953.

11. R. C. Lewontin, in Ref. 1, p. xxvi.

12. L. H. Matthews, Introduction to *The Origin of Species,* C. Darwin, reprinted by J. M. Dent and Sons, Ltd., London, 1971, p. xi.

13. G. R. Bozarth, *American Atheist,* September 1978, p. 30.

14. Julian Huxley, as quoted in an Associated Press dispatch, November 27, 1959, commenting on Huxley's keynote speech at the Darwinian Centennial Convention at the University of Chicago.

15. Julian Huxley, in *Issues in Evolution,* Vol. 3 of *Evolution After Darwin,* Sol Tax, Ed., University of Chicago Press, Chicago, 1960, p. 260.

16. Julian Huxley and Jacob Bronowski, *Growth of Ideas,* Prentice-Hall, Inc., Englewood Cliffs, N.J., 1968, p. 99.

17. Marjorie Grene, *Encounter,* November 1959, p. 49.

18. Colin Patterson, *The Listener* 106:390-392 (October 8, 1981). *The Listener* is a publication of the British Broadcasting Corporation.

19. Anonymous, *Nature* 289:735 (1981).

20. Karl Popper, in *The Philosophy of Karl Popper,* P. A. Schilpp, Ed., Open Court, La Salle, Illinois, 1974, p. 134.

21. Karl Popper, Letter to the Editor, *New Scientist* 87:611 (1980).

22. Michael Ruse, *Darwinism Defended,* Addison-Wesley Pub. Co., London, 1982, p. 133.

23. Murray Eden, in *Mathematical Challenges to the Neo-Darwinian Interpretation of Evolution.* P. S. Moorhead and M. M. Kaplan, Eds., Wistar Institute Press, Philadelphia, 1967, p. 71.

24. Alex Fraser, *ibid.,* p. 67.

25. M. P. Schützenberger, *ibid.,* p. 70.

26. Paul Ehrlich and L. C. Birch, *Nature* 214:352 (1967).

27. D. J. Futuyma, Ref. 7, p. 171.

28. F. J. Ayala, in *The Role of Natural Selection in Human Evolution,* F. M. Salzano, Ed., North-Holland Pub. Co., 1975, p. 19.

29. F. J. Ayala, *ibid.,* p. 19.

30. Marjorie Grene, Ref. 17, p. 54.

31. David Hull, *Science* 223:1923 (1984).

32. Theodore Dobzhansky, *American Scientist* 45:388 (1957).

33. Colin Patterson, Ref. 18, p. 390.

34. D. V. Ager, *Proceedings of the Geological Association* 87:132 (1976).

35. Larry Laudan, in *Creationism, Science and the Law: The Arkansas Case,* M. C. La Follette, Ed., The MIT Press, Cambridge, Massachusetts, 1983, p. 166.

36. P. L. Quinn, "The Philosopher of Science as Expert Witness," in *Science and Reality,* J. T. Cushing, C. F. Delancy, and G. M. Gutting, Eds., University of Notre Dame Press, Notre Dame, Indiana, 1984, p. 51.

37. Michael Ruse, Ref. 22. This material is quoted by permission of the author and of the publisher, Addison-Wesley Publication Company, London, and the author.

38. Michael Ruse, *ibid.,* p. xv.

39. Michael Ruse, *ibid.,* p. 135.

40. Tom Bethell, *Harper's Magazine* 252:70-75 (February 1976).

41. Norman Macbeth, *Darwin Retried,* Gambit, Inc., Boston, 1971.

42. E. O. Wiley, *Systematic Zoology* 24(2):270 (1975).

43. C. H. Waddington, in *The Evolution of Life,* Vol. 1 of *Evolution After Darwin,* Sol Tax, Ed., University of Chicago Press, Chicago, 1960, p. 385.

44. R. A. Fisher, *The Genetical Theory of Natural Selection,* Clarendon Press, Oxford, 1930.

45. C. H. Waddington, Ref. 23, p. 14.

46. Tom Bethell, Ref. 40, p. 75.

47. Ronald H. Brady, *Systematilc Zoology* 28:600-621 (1979).

48. Ronald H. Brady, *ibid.,* p. 600.

49. S. J. Gould, *Natural History* 85:24-30 (1976).

50. Ronald H. Brady, Ref. 47, pp. 605, 606.

51. Steven Stanley, *Proceedings of the National Academy of Science* 72:640-660 (1975).

52. Steven Stanley, *ibid.,* p. 646.

53. Steven Stanley, *ibid.,* p. 648.

54. Steven Stanley, *ibid.,* p. 650.

55. P.-P. Grassé, *Evolution of Living Organisms,* Academic Press, New York, 1977, p. 88.

56. P.-P. Grassé, *ibid.,* pp. 97, 98.

57. P.-P. Grassé, *ibid.,* p. 170.

58. P.-P. Grassé, *ibid.,* p. 107.

59. Norman Macbeth, *American Biology Teacher,* November 1976, p. 496.

60. S. J. Gould, *Paleobiology* 6(1):121 (Winter 1980).

61. Roger Lewin, *Science* 217:1239 (1982) (Review of Ref. 62).

62. D. R. Brooks and E. O. Wiley, *Evolution as Entropy,* The University of Chicago Press, Chicago, 1986.

63. B. F. Glenister and B. J. Witzke, in Ref. 4, p. 58.

64. D. J. Futuyma, Ref. 7, p. 197.

65. Kenneth Hsu, *Journal of Sedimentary Petrology* 56(5):729-730
     (1986).
66. R. D. Alexander, in *Evolution versus Creationism: The Public
     School Controversy,* J. P. Zetterberg, Ed., Oryx Press, Phoenix,
     1983, p. 91.
67. S. J. Gould, *Science* 223:255 (1984).

4

Scientific Integrity

Intense rivalries, generating great personal animosity, such as that between O. C. Marsh and E. D. Cope in the late 19th century, and sharp controversies in science, even within the evolutionary camp, such as that created by Richard Goldschmidt's "hopeful monster" attack on neo-Darwinism, which earned for Goldschmidt ridicule and the role of an outcast, have punctuated the history of science from time to time. The attacks by evolutionists against creation science and creation scientists, however, have been especially vicious and slanderous. Creation scientists have been accused of distorting science, quoting out of context, misquoting, and outright lying. These vicious, ad hominem attacks on creation scientists are actually counterproductive. Many whom they seek to convince by such attacks sense that these tactics reveal the fact that evolutionists, in doing so, are acknowledging that their scientific case is weak and that their attacks on the personal integrity of the creation scientists constitute a smoke screen behind which they seek to conceal the fallacies and weaknesses in evolution theory.

Only a few examples of these attacks will be cited. Stephen Jay Gould says, concerning what he termed "militant fundamentalists who label themselves with the oxymoron 'scientific creationists' . . . ," that "I'm used to their rhetoric, their dishonest mis- and half-quotations, their constant repetition of 'useful' arguments that even they must recognize as nonsense. . . ."[1] Richard C. Lewontin states:

> The recent massive attack by fundamentalist Christians on the teaching of evolution in the schools has left scientists indignant and somewhat bewildered. Creationist arguments have seemed to them a compound of ignorance and malevolence, and, indeed, there has been both confusion and dishonesty in the creationist attack.[2]

Alice B. Kehoe draws on a characterization of American patriotism by Robert Hewett to illustrate her view of creation scientists. She says:

> . . . the American patriot becomes "a perfectly clean and basically passive hero, committed to lawful obedience, carrying out his highest form of faithfulness by violating cleanliness, law, and passivity" (for example, the marshall gunning down the Bad Guy on Main Street at high noon) (Jewett 1973, p. 153). Jewett's ironic insight well describes the scientific creationist.[3]

In other words, according to Kehoe, the creation scientists are willing to stoop to most any device, dishonest, unlawful, or otherwise, to further what they consider their high calling.

John W. Patterson, who makes no secret of either his atheism or his hatred of creationists, has attempted to refute the creationists' arguments based on the Second Law of Thermodynamics (much more will be said about this later). While acknowledging the effectiveness of the creationists' arguments on "unwitting audiences," Patterson explains:

> Because the second law of thermodynamics is nonintuitive and because few people have studied it in depth, it is ideally suited to the apologists' favorite techniques of obscurantism.

Moreoever, the second law does provide a criterion for determining if certain processes are impossible in nature. Hence, by misinterpreting the second law, whether by ignorance or deliberate deception, or both, the creationists are able to convince unwitting audiences that evolution is impossible.[4]

David B. Wilson, in his Introduction to a 1983 anti-creationist book which he edited, with reference to creationists' arguments against evolution, states:

Underlying these areas of disagreement is the view of scientists that creationists frequently distort scientific theories, purposely misleading their audiences.[5]

It may be noted here that a very common ploy of anti-creationists is to refer to evolutionists as "scientists," while creation scientists are referred to merely as "creationists." This is designed to convey the notion that all scientists are evolutionists, while creationists are non-scientists.

Futuyma, in his anti-creationist book, charges that:

To analyze creationist literature is to scale a fortress of facts and quotations taken from the evolutionary literature, distorted and quoted out of context, haphazardly glued into a defense around their faith.[6]

Later on in the same book, Futuyma says:

Like the purveyors of cigarettes, laetrile, nuclear superiority, and instant spiritual enlightenment, scientific creationism teaches by its tactics more than by its words: truth is not the object of brave and honest search. Truth is whatever you can convince people it is. But to accede to these standards in education is to teach dishonesty and cowardice.[7]

Throughout his book, Futuyma makes similar charges, either explicitly or implicitly, often confusing or distorting the details himself, as I will document later.

In his anger at the catastrophist interpretation of geology involving the postulate of a worldwide flood, Eldredge goes far beyond merely challenging the geological wisdom of such an interpretation, when he vituperates that:

Creationists are the liars, freely slinging mud at all who
cross their peculiarly myopic view of the natural world.[8]

Henry Morris is one of the chief theoreticians among creationists who have offered the catastrophic view of geology versus
the uniformitarian view of evolutionary geology. In all of his
many writings on the subject, of which *The Genesis Flood*[9]
(which he coauthored with John Whitcomb) is the chief, and
in the writings of many other creationist geologists, such as
Steven Austin, Harold Coffin, and Clifford Burdick, I have
yet to see anything that could be characterized as mud slinging
at their theoretical opponents, but calling those scientists who
disagree with your interpretation of geological data "liars" is
certainly mud slinging at its worst!

As the reader may have noted, one of the frequent charges
made against creation scientists is that they quote evolutionists
out of context. Whether the scientist is a creationist or an
evolutionist, research in the field and in the laboratory frequently turns up evidence that is contradictory to predictions
based on evolution theory. Sometimes this evidence finds its
way into the scientific literature, although evolutionists, in
their fear of creation scientists, are becoming more and more
cautious about what they publish, as will be documented later.
Creation scientists quite reasonably believe that when facts or
ideas are placed in the scientific literature, that information,
whether published by evolutionists or creationists, belongs to
everybody. In fact, creation scientists feel that facts published
by evolutionists are especially valuable, because it cannot be
charged by evolutionists that these data were produced by
individuals biased against evolution. Evolutionists, on the
other hand, somehow feel that it is unfair and even unscrupu-
lous for creationists to utilize facts published by evolutionists
that are damaging to evolutionary theory, or that support creation. Furthermore, often unable to refute the logic of the
arguments of creation scientists based on facts derived from
publications of evolutionists, evolutionists attempt to discredit

the arguments by claiming that the creation scientists have quoted out of context.

Two examples from Philip Kitcher's anti-creationist book will help to illustrate this point. In Kitcher's attempt to discredit my refutation of the fossil record of horses as an example of evolutionary transitional forms, Kitcher charges:

> At this point a new tactic emerges. Instead of offering a detailed argument, Gish simply appeals to authority. His sources are various. The maverick evolutionary theorist Richard Goldschmidt is quoted out of context.[10]

Here Kitcher does not offer one shred of evidence to support that charge—he does not because he cannot. In fact, he neither quotes the statement by Goldschmidt, nor does he give a reference to Goldschmidt's publication from which it was taken. In other words, he provides no opportunity for the reader to verify his charge.

The statement by Goldschmidt that I quoted, found in my book, *Evolution: The Fossils Say No!*,[11] reads as follows:

> Moreover, within the slowly evolving series, like the famous horse series, the decisive steps are abrupt without transition.

What is the context of this statement? It was taken from Goldschmidt's publication, "A Geneticist Looks at Evolution,"[12] in which he was attacking the neo-Darwinian mechanism of evolution involving slow and gradual evolution via micromutations and natural selection. This attack was based mainly on the evidence provided by the fossil record, the evidence so powerfully employed by creation scientists, namely that the gaps between the major categories, phyla, classes, orders, and families, are systematic and almost always large, demonstrating beyond doubt that each basic type of plant and animal has appeared on this earth fully formed from the start. Creation scientists point out that this is powerful positive evidence for creation. Richard Goldschmidt would entertain no such thought, but rather proposed what he called the "hopeful monster" mechanism for evolution. Goldschmidt suggested that the major categories arose instantaneously by major saltations, or systemic mutations. In his major work, *The Material Basis of Evolution,* Goldschmidt states:

> I need only to quote Schindewolfe (1936), the most progressive investigator known to me. He shows by examples from fossil material that the major evolutionary advances must have taken place in single large steps. . . . He shows that the many missing links in the paleontological record are sought for in vain because they have never existed: "The first bird hatched from a reptilian egg."[13]

Now having established that Goldschmidt, based on his "hopeful monster" mechanism, would not even expect to find transitional forms for the horses or any other major types, let us establish the immediate context of the Goldschmidt quote concerning horses that I used. Concerning the fossil record, Goldschmidt says:

> . . . the facts of greatest general importance are the following. When a new phylum, class, or order appears, there follows a quick, explosive (in terms of geological time) diversification so that practically all orders or families known appear suddenly and without any apparent transitions. . . . Moreover, within the slowly evolving series, like the famous horse series, the decisive steps are abrupt, without transition. . . .[12]

Goldschmidt is saying that, just as is the case with phyla, classes, orders, and families, where these various categories appear suddenly without any apparent transitions, so it is also true with the horse series, where the decisive steps are abrupt, without transitions. Thus, I quoted the statement by Goldschmidt on horses perfectly in context. I doubt very seriously whether Kitcher even bothered to read Goldschmidt's publication. In any case, his charge that I quoted Goldschmidt out of context is obviously patently false.

I might point out further, that when creation scientists quote evolutionary authorities effectively, they are accused of "appealing to authority." But then, what better source for our facts than what even evolutionists consider to be authoritative?

We would certainly not help our credibility by spewing out *ex cathedra* statements or telling "Just So" stories, as is so common in evolutionary literature.

On the same page (p. 115) that Kitcher makes his charge concerning my use of the statement by Goldschmidt, Kitcher says (concerning horses):

> Paleontologists do not question the relationships, and the overall line of evolution is uncontroversial. But, as in many other sciences, when the general form of the answer to a question is known, there is frequently considerable disagreement about the specifics. So, for example, Gish is able to quote David Raup: "By this I mean that some of the classic cases of Darwinian change in the fossil record, such as the evolution of the horse in North America, have had to be discarded or modified as the result of more detailed information—what appeared to be a nice simple progression when relatively few data were available, now appears to be much more complex and much less gradualistic" (Raup 1979, quoted in Gish 1979, 103). Torn out of context, Raup's remark may make it appear that paleontologists have given up the idea that the organisms in the horse sequence are related to one another. However, this is not the issue. No paleontologist doubts that there is a process of "descent with modification" that embraces all the animals preserved in the horse sequence. What *is* at issue is *how* they are related.

Let me first state, categorically, that there was no intention at all on my part to use the statement by Raup to convey the notion that evolutionists have given up on the idea that the various horses in the "horse sequence" are related to one another. Of course evolutionists believe that. Evolutionists believe that all organisms, from amoeba to man, are related to one another. What *is* in question is the nature of the evidence related to that assumption. But, more to the point, was the statement by Raup "torn out of context"?

The title of Raup's article is "Conflicts Between Darwin and Paleontology." Now, it is certainly true that in this article,

Raup, a thorough-going evolutionist, is not intending to throw doubt on the theory of evolution or to give any deliberate help to creationists. He is asking the question, in the present-day knowledge of the fossil record, whether or not the data of paleontology support the Darwinian mechanism for evolution, namely, slow and gradual change through time due to minor variations acted on by natural selection. At the same time, however, what Raup has to say about the fossil record considerably weakens any claim that the fossil record, in general, and the fossil record of horses, in particular, support evolution; and this was, of course, my reason for emphasizing the importance of Raup's statement.

In order for the reader to judge for himself whether or not I used Raup's statement in proper context, I will quote much more extensively from his article. Raup states that:

> Darwin's theory of natural selection has always been closely linked to evidence from fossils, and probably most people assume that fossils provide a very important part of the general argument that is made in favor of Darwinian interpretations of the history of life. Unfortunately, this is not strictly true. . . . The evidence we find in the geologic record is not nearly as compatible with Darwinian natural selection as we would like it to be. Darwin was completely aware of this. He was embarrassed by the fossil record, because it didn't look the way he predicted it would, and, as a result, he devoted a long section of his *Origin of Species* to an attempt to explain and rationalize the differences. . . . Darwin's general solution to the incompatibility of fossil evidence and his theory was to say that the fossil record is a very incomplete one. . . . Well, we are now about 120 years after Darwin, and the knowledge of the fossil record has been greatly expanded. We now have a quarter of a million fossil species, but the situation hasn't changed much. The record of evolution is still surprisingly jerky, and, ironically, we have even fewer examples of evolutionary transition than we had in Darwin's time. By this I mean that some of the classic cases of Darwinian change in the fossil record, such as the evolution of the horse, in North

America, have had to be discarded or modified as a result of more detailed information—what appeared to be a nice simple progression when relatively few data were available now appears to be much more complex and much less gradualistic. So Darwin's problem has not been alleviated. . . .[14]

Darwin's mechanism of evolution requires that the fossil record produce vast numbers of intermediate or transitional forms. It did not in Darwin's time, and it does not now, and that is why Raup states that the fossil record was an embarrassment to Darwin and why he speaks of the "incompatibility of the fossil evidence and his (Darwin's) theory." Raup then goes on to explain that some of "the classic cases of Darwinian change" have had to be discarded or modified, and he includes, specifically, the alleged evolution of horses. One can make no more nor less of Raup's statement, but it does lend considerable encouragement, intended or not, to the creationist interpretation of the fossil record. Some evolutionists (much less frequently than in the past) cite the horse "series" as evidence that supports evolution. Raup, however, includes the phylogeny of the horses among his examples that either had to be discarded or modified and deemed much less gradualistic.

In order to further clarify what evolutionists are saying today about the fossil record of horses, I quote from a newspaper article, "Ideas on Evolution Going Through a Revolution Among Scientists," written by Boyce Rensberger, then a senior editor of *Science 80,* published in November of 1980.[15] Rensberger says:

Exactly how evolution happened is now a matter of great controversy among biologists. Although the debate has been under way for several years, it reached a crescendo last month, as some 150 scientists, specializing in evolutionary studies, met for four days in Chicago's Field Museum of Natural History to thrash out a variety of new hypotheses that are challenging older ideas.

Eldredge reminded the meeting of what many fossil hunters have recognized, as they trace the history of a species through successive layers of ancient sediments. Species simply appear at a given point in geologic time, persist largely unchanged for a few million years, and then disappear. There are very few examples—some say none— of one species shading gradually into another.

The popularly told example of horse evolution, suggesting a gradual sequence of changes from four-toed, fox-sized creatures, living nearly 50 million years ago, to today's much larger one-toed, has long been known to be wrong. Instead of gradual change, fossils of each intermediate species appear fully distinct, persist unchanged, and then become extinct. Transitional forms are unknown.

The context in which I used the quote from Raup's paper, and in which I have used the quote immediately above, is in a discussion of the absence of transitional forms in the fossil record in general, and with respect to the fossil record of horses, in particular. Thus, my use of the quotation from Raup's publication was not "torn out of context" as charged by Kitcher. Finally, let us be reminded that facts are facts, regardless of the context in which they are recorded. There are no transitional forms between distinct types of horses, and that remains true whether one is discussing competing theories on the mechanism of evolution or the competing theories of creation versus evolution.

Laurie R. Godfrey states that:

Duane Gish (1978) prepared the major creationist account of the fossil record for public-school use. The book is provocatively called *Evolution? The Fossils Say No!* Its treatment of angiosperm origins is typical of its treatment of other paleontological data—misleading, incomplete, full of half-truths and outright falsehoods. Gish disposes of angiosperm evolution in a single paragraph, by citing a remark made by botanist E. J. H. Corner in 1961 that despairs of the (then valid) lack of known primitive angiosperms. Gish fails to mention the major books on

angiosperm paleobiology that should have been available
to him in 1978: Beck's *Origin and Early Evolution of
Angiosperms* (1976) or Hughes's *Paleobiology of Angiosperm Origins* (1976). Anyone serious about surveying the
fossil evidence of angiosperm evolution could hardly have
missed them.[16]

Neither Gould nor Lewontin offers any documentation
whatsoever of their charges, mentioned earlier in this chapter,
concerning quotes out of context. In fact, Gould frequently
makes similar statements without a shred of actual documentation from creationist literature. This makes it difficult, therefore, for creationists to defend themselves against such
shotgun attacks. It is a simple matter, however, to expose the
totally false nature of Godfrey's charges, and to establish just
who is telling the truth in this matter. Apparently Godfrey has
failed to carefully read either of the texts she cites, nor, apparently, has she read my book, for nowhere in my book do I
discuss angiosperm origins. In fact, the word cannot be found
anywhere in that book.

The statement from Corner that I cited (found on p. 154
of my book) reads as follows:

> Much evidence can be adduced in favour of the theory of
> evolution—from biology, biogeography and paleontology,
> but I still think that, to the unprejudiced, the fossil record
> of plants is in favour of special creation.[17]

First, in order to avoid misunderstanding concerning what
Corner (and others cited in that particular chapter of my book)
believes about evolution, I stated on p. 150, with reference to
the absence of transitional forms between the higher categories, "We now propose to document this statement by citing
published statements of evolutionists." In other words, I was
careful to point out that Corner and others cited were not
creationists. Furthermore, I included the portion of Corner's
statement, "Much evidence can be adduced in favour of the
theory of evolution . . ." so as to not delete any portion of his

statement, the deletion of which would weaken his evolutionary position.

My purpose in citing this statement by Corner was to place on record the scientific facts concerning the fossil record of plants as they relate to creation versus evolution. It is especially significant that Corner, in spite of the fact that he is an evolutionist, acknowledged that the fossil record of plants supports creation.

Note that Corner's statement makes no reference to angiosperms whatsoever, but to the fossil record of plants, in general. If he had intended for his remarks to apply only to angiosperms, he would have used the terms "angiosperms" or "flowering plants," rather than the broad term "plants." Furthermore, the context shows clearly that he is not discussing the origin of angiosperms, in particular, but the origin of plants, in general. The title of his chapter is simply "Evolution." I will quote extensively from the page preceding the one from which the quote in question was taken and including most of the page on which the quote is found, so that the reader will be able to discern for himself the context of the quote.

Beginning on page 96 of Corner's chapter, we read:

> The early advocates of evolution were taxonomists, and many were concerned with the very building of the great hierarchy of classification on which we still rely. It is so immense that the modern student takes it for granted, and it is this indifference which makes me suspect that the significance of evolution is underestimated. Classification has related species into genera, genera into tribes, tribes into families, and so on, and the implication is that these genera have evolved from an ancestral genus, the tribes from an ancestral tribe, and so on. It is commonly assumed that the evolution of species, producing novelties in structure and function, has been the same as that which produced the higher taxa, the characters of which are conserved and not mutated. Indeed, it is a fashion to wave aside the higher taxa as figments convenient for nomenclature. This is a misunderstanding, because the characters of these taxa are

as real as the specific characters; they make up the more fundamental construction, of which the specific are the embellishments. Equally with the specific, they must have a protoplasmic basis, but, whether this is nuclear or cytoplasmic, genetics has been unable to investigate, since the higher taxa do not hybridize.

Considering how many of these characters depend ultimately upon the cell wall in plants, and realizing how little is known of the inheritance of the cell wall, except that it forms from the cytoplasm, I often think that the permanent characters of supra-specific taxa are maintained by cytoplasmic structure, modifiable, no doubt, by nuclear influences. We have, in fact, no evidence of how the potentialities of these higher taxa are inherited, and, what is more, in botany, we commonly have no idea of their selective value, if any; this, indeed, was the creed of Willis (1949) throughout his long life. Thus, the taxonomic characters of Myrtaceae have no evident selective value over those of Rosaceae; *Pyrus* is no better off than *Prunus,* or *Rubus* than *Rosa,* and a primitive family like Ranunculaceae thrives, along with Compositae and Papilionaceae. These are a few examples only, but every large genus and high taxon affords such, and they increase to tens of thousands. The theory of evolution is not merely the theory of the origin of species, but the only explanation of the fact that organisms can be classified into this hierarchy of natural affinity. Much evidence can be adduced in favour of the theory of evolution—from biology, biogeography, and palaeontology, but I still think that, to the unprejudiced, the fossil record of plants is in favour of special creation. If, however, another explanation could be found for this hierarchy of classification, it would be the knell of the theory of evolution. Can you imagine how an orchid, a duckweed, and a palm have come from the same ancestry, and have we any evidence for this assumption? The evolutionist must be prepared with an answer, but I think that most would break down before an inquisition.

Textbooks hoodwink. A series of more and more complicated plants is introduced—the alga, the fungus, the bryophyte, and so on, and examples are added eclectically in support of one or another theory—and that is held to be a presentation of evolution. If the world of plants consisted only of these few textbook types of standard botany, the idea of evolution might never have dawned, and the backgrounds of these textbooks are the temperate countries which, at best, are poor places to study world vegetation. The point, of course, is that there are thousands and thousands of living plants, predominantly tropical, which have never entered general botany, yet they are the bricks with which the taxonomist has built his temple of evolution, and where else have we to worship?

It is evident that Corner's essay is directed at the problem of the evolution of plants, in general. Algae, fungi, and bryophytes are not flowering plants, while other examples Corner cites *are* flowering plants. I thus quoted Corner perfectly in context, contrary to Godfrey's allegation.

But what about angiosperms? The flowering plants do make up a very important part of the fossil record of plants, and their origin has been a baffling mystery to evolutionists from the time of Darwin to the present day. Darwin called the origin of the flowering plants "an abominable mystery."[18]

Let us take a look at the books cited by Godfrey. First, the book by Hughes.[19] The fossils of about 43 families of flowering plants appear in rocks of the so-called Cretaceous Period. The sudden appearance of this great variety of flowering plants in Cretaceous rocks has forced evolutionists to believe that flowering plants must have evolved many millions of years before the Cretaceous, well down into what is called the Jurassic Period, or earlier. These rocks have been intensely searched for ancestors of flowering plants, with total lack of success.

In order to obtain a clearly objective evaluation of the conclusions drawn by Hughes concerning the origin of flowering plants, I will quote what an evolutionist has to say. W. G. Chaloner, in his review of Hughes' book published in *Nature*, states:

Two important facts emerge from his thorough and well-illustrated analysis. First, there is no acceptable evidence of angiosperms before the early Cretaceous. Second, all those characteristic attributes of angiosperms which have a sporting chance of surviving in a fossil (wood with vessels, dicot-type leaves, multiaperturate tectate pollen and seeds enclosed in a fruit) appear within the timespan of one geological stage, during or close to the Aptian (late early Cretaceous).

The author offers us no snap answer to the mystery of angiosperm origins. But he has faith that the fossil record, properly documented, will eventually yield an answer.[20]

Godfrey clearly implied that if I had read Hughes' book, I would have been able to see that the origin of angiosperms no longer poses a mystery to evolutionists. It is obvious, however, that Godfrey has not read the book carefully and thoroughly, or she would know, as Chaloner points out, that Hughes has no answer to "the mystery of angiosperm origins," but only faith that the fossil record will eventually provide an answer. Godfrey actually had no need of reading more than a page or so of Hughes' "Introduction and Proposition" (pp. 1-3) to discover the above facts. Here we find that Hughes states:

The evolutionary origin of the now dominant land-plant group, the angiosperms, has puzzled scientists since the middle of the nineteenth century. . . .

As evolutionary studies in fossil animals became relatively well documented, three interdependent 'escape' hypotheses were developed to explain, in the plant kingdom, the continuing failure to deal with the angiosperm 'mystery'. These were: (a) general incompleteness of the plant fossil record, in addition to the admitted lack of fossils of the flowers themselves; (b) slowness of evolution in land plants, calling for a long developmental history to produce such a complication as angiospermy; and (c) cryptic evolution of early angiosperms in upland areas, from which few, if any fossils could have been preserved. Although all these hypotheses were depressingly negative, palaeobotanical search continued, and still does. With few exceptions of detail, however, the failure to find a satisfactory explanation has persisted, and many botanists have concluded that the problem is not capable of solution, by use of fossil evidence; geologists have displayed little interest in the matter, apparently owing to a general lack of coherence of philosophical treatment of palaeobiological information (pp. 1-2).

Thus, Hughes admits that with a few exceptions of detail, the failure to find a satisfactory explanation of the origin of angiosperms has persisted, and even that many botanists have concluded that the problem is not capable of solution, by use of fossil evidence. Hughes advocates a fresh new approach to the problem, and as Chaloner has stated, Hughes *does* have faith that the fossil record, properly documented, will eventually provide an answer. I must admit that I am a bit shy of such evolutionary faith.

In the book, *Origin and Early Evolution of Angiosperms,*[21] edited by Beck, Beck does state, in the Preface, that although the problem of the origin of the angiosperms is a long way from solution, progress in recent years has been substantial. A bit later, however, in his chapter, "Origin and Early Evolution of Angiosperms: A Perspective," Beck states (p. 1):

In a speech in 1960 to the British Association on the origin of angiosperms, Tom Harris set the stage by the following rather pessimistic statement: "I ask you to look back, not on a proud record of the success of famous men, but on an unbroken record of failure." Indeed, the mystery of the origin and early evolution of the angiosperms is as pervasive and as fascinating today as it was when Darwin emphasized the problem in 1879. Progress has been made, however, and some of the most significant accomplishments have come since 1960. Still, we have no definitive answers, because we are forced to base our conclusions largely on circumstantial evidence, and they must usually, of necessity, be highly speculative and interpretative.

Thus, Beck must admit that there are still no definitive answers, so that the mystery of the origin of flowering plants is as pervasive today as it was in Darwin's time. As Beck states, evolutionists are forced to base their conclusions largely on circumstantial evidence, and these conclusions must, of necessity, be highly speculative and interpretative.

Beck believes that one possible reason for the failure to solve the mystery of angiosperm origins is the notion, up until this time, that angiosperms originated much earlier than the Cretaceous. He thus states (p. 2) that:

> It seems possible, therefore, that we may not have to look beyond the Cretaceous to find very primitive angiosperms. Indeed, past failure to look for them in the Cretaceous may well be a primary reason that the origin of angiosperms is still a mystery.

Later on (p. 5), Beck states:

> One thing is clear: we shall not be able to determine the ancestral affinities of the angiosperms or even to recognize the significance of certain angiospermlike fossils until we have a series of fructifications connecting the primitive angiosperms with their nonangiospermous precursors. The absence of any known series of such intermediates imposes severe restrictions on morphologists interested in the ancestral source of angiosperms, and leads to speculation and interpretation of homologies and relationships on the basis of the most meager circumstantial evidence.

Thus, evolutionists, because of the total absence of the necessary fossil intermediates, are left with nothing but speculations and interpretations based on the most meager of circumstantial evidence. If one reads through this book edited by Beck, one can read page after page of speculations and interpretations by various workers in this field, but speculations are no substitute for definitive evidence.

Godfrey first implied that I had quoted Corner out of context, and secondly, of treatment of paleontological data that is misleading, incomplete, full of half-truths and outright falsehoods. It is seen, however, that it is her accusations that are false and misleading. Her culpability is compounded by the fact that her intent was not to challenge a competing interpretation of the data, but to slanderously impugn the integrity of a fellow scientist. Furthermore, resort to such tactics is an admission that her case cannot stand on its own merits.

Kenneth Miller is a professor of biology at Brown University. He has assumed the role of one of the chief evolutionist debaters. He has debated Henry Morris, me, and perhaps other creation scientists on a number of occasions. He has adopted the tactic of what I am told is called "spread debating." That is, the tactic of speaking very rapidly and producing so much material that it is impossible for his creationist opponent to answer all of his arguments. This is designed, of course, to leave the audience with the impression that his opponent simply had no answers to these arguments. Another favorite tactic of Miller's is to create ridiculous caricatures of several of the creation scientists' theories and then to poke fun at them. Miller does have a unique ability to reel off, in rapid succession, one argument after another, and this no doubt impresses many in the audience, regardless of whether or not they grasp much of what he is talking about.

The book, *Evolution Versus Creationism: The Public Education Controversy,*[22] edited by J. Peter Zetterberg, was published following a conference entitled "Evolution and Public Education," held at the University of Minnesota, December 5, 1981. The material in the book is a revised version of a resource manual compiled for the conference. Of the approximately 470 pages of text, only about 60 pages were devoted to material from creation scientists. Included in the evolutionist material was an article by Miller (pp. 249-262) which he had originally published in the Winter 1982 issue of the evolutionist organ, *Creation/Evolution.* The article bears the title "Answers to the Standard Creationist Arguments." This is a poor choice of a title, for his book does not provide answers to the standard arguments of creation scientists, but his article is an attempted refutation of the arguments I advanced in a nationally televised debate I had with Russell Doolittle, a professor of biochemistry at the University of California at San Diego. The debate was sponsored by the Old Time Gospel Hour, moderated by Jerry Falwell, and was held before approximately 5,000 people at Liberty University. In his description, Miller gets off to a rather poor start when he states that the debate was held in the spring of 1982. Actually, the debate took place on October 13, 1981. The debate went rather poorly for the evolutionist side. The article describing the debate that appeared the next day on the front page of the *Washington Post*, was headlined, "Science Loses One to Creationism," with sub-headlines, "How Am I Going to Face My Wife?" enclosed in quotes. The author of the article, Philip Hilts, had heard Doolittle make this anguished remark after the debate. *Science,* in its report of the debate,[23] termed it a rout.

Miller thus felt compelled to provide what he believed to be effective counter arguments to the presentation I made in the debate. After complimenting Doolittle for "an excellent case for the exclusion of creationism from science classrooms," Miller says:

> Dr. Gish in a stunning presentation, made an effective summary of the standard debate arguments. Because his performance was so widely viewed, the points he made have become the creationist arguments most familiar to millions of television viewers. We will see them crop up again and again in school board controversies, legislative battles, and court cases. It would be practical, therefore, that answers to these standard arguments be made available. The purpose of this article is to provide them.

In a critique later in this book, we will return to a discussion of Miller's attempt to provide answers, but in the context of this chapter I wish to discuss Miller's charge in this article that I not only quoted E. J. H. Corner out of context (a charge we have just refuted), but that I also misquoted him. Miller (p. 258) charges:

> In a classic out-of-context quote, he voiced the words of Dr. Corner, a Cambridge botanist, who wrote, "Much evidence can be adduced in favor of evolution, but I still think

that to the unprejudiced the fossil record of plants is in favor of creation." However, what Dr. Corner actually said was that ". . . the fossil record of *higher* plants is in favor of *special* creation" (emphasis added). What did Corner mean by that? He meant that the major form of higher plants (the angiosperms or flowering plants) appeared on earth about 135 million years ago, and we have no good fossil evidence as to what forms they evolved from. Corner meant to emphasize, in his statement, just that lack of ancestral evidence, and pointed out that the higher plants appear so suddenly, one could almost believe that they had been *specially* created—just as if a creator had said, "Let there be angiosperms," and so they appeared.

In the debate, each debater was limited to just 18 minutes for his initial arguments. After I had completed the first draft of these arguments, I discovered that considerably more than 18 minutes would be required to deliver them. I had to repeatedly delete and abridge these prepared statements, in order to deliver my initial arguments within the allotted time span. I thus abridged, somewhat, the direct quotation of Corner's statement, being careful, however, to leave in "Much evidence can be adduced in favor of evolution," so as to leave Corner's position clear. The omission of the word "special" from Corner's original term "special creation" actually weakens the statement from the creationist perspective, since the simpler term "creation" is taken to mean various things, even theistic evolution, while the term "special creation" is restricted (as Miller actually concedes in his statement) to the concept of creation I was supporting.

The important point is that Miller accuses me of leaving out the word "higher," deliberately misquoting Corner for the purpose of making him appear to be saying something that he did not say, thus using a dishonest and invalid argument. Now, I believe everyone will agree, that in order to charge someone of deliberately leaving out a word in a quotation, the accuser, either 1) must have accurate copies before him of both the original statement and the quotation used by the accused, or

2) failing this, the accuser is guilty of inexcusable carelessness for not possessing accurate information before making such serious charges, or 3) the accuser himself is guilty of deliberate falsehood.

One thing is certain—the word "higher" does not appear in Corner's statement. I will repeat the statement here as I have quoted it repeatedly in my books and elsewhere, and as it appears in Corner's publication:

> Much evidence can be adduced in favor of the theory of evolution—from biology, biogeography, and paleontology, but I still think that to the unprejudiced, the fossil record of plants is in favor of special creation.

In his accusation against me, Miller attaches great significance to the adjective "higher." How then would he *dare* make the specific accusation that I had left out that important word, unless he had a copy of Corner's statement right before his eyes? And if he had the statement right in front of him, how could he possibly not be aware of the fact that the word "higher" does not appear in Corner's statement? Miller's charge, obviously false and slanderous, was due either to an inexcusable failure to possess the necessary documentary evidence, or he knew it was false when he made it, which is much worse.

Miller was involved, indirectly, in another case in which false and misleading information was used against me. On February 18, 1985, I debated Philip Kitcher at the University of Minnesota. As is usual in debates, one of the main positive arguments I used to support creation was the abrupt appearance, fully formed, of each major category, or basic type, of plant and animal. Kitcher argued that evolutionists *do* possess some examples of transitional forms. To support his case, he displayed a slide showing alleged reconstructions of a series of mammal-like reptiles, supposedly bridging the gap between reptiles and mammals. In an especially dramatic moment in the debate, Kitcher strode across the stage with the challenge, "Gish, if there are any gaps there, please point them out!"

Never having seen that particular illustration or the article in which it is found, I was at a loss to do so. I did state that there were obvious gaps, because every mammal, living or fossil, has three bones in the ear and a single bone in the jaw, while every reptile, living or fossil, has a single bone in the ear and multiple bones in the jaw, and there are no intermediates. I further challenged Kitcher to explain how the intermediates managed to hear and chew, while they were dragging two bones from the jaw up into the ear. Kitcher, nevertheless, scored powerfully with his illustration there for everyone to see.

After being tipped off that there was some skullduggery involved in the use of the illustration, I wrote to Kitcher for the documentation used for that particular slide. He graciously supplied the information, saying that he actually had obtained the slide from Kenneth Miller.[24] I obtained a copy of the publication,[25] and found the illustration on page 430. The text that accompanied the illustration revealed the fact that 1) two of the "intermediates" in the series were totally hypothetical, 2) hypothetical structures had been added to some of the "intermediates," 3) the "intermediates" were not arranged in a true time sequence, and 4) the "intermediates" were not drawn to scale. If a creationist had used an illustration which incorporated any of these doctorings of the facts, even a single one, and evolutionists came into possession of that evidence, the creationist would be thoroughly roasted for distorting science and for deliberate falsehood.

Of course I could not point out any gaps! The gaps had been filled, either with totally hypothetical reconstructions, or with "intermediates" manufactured by adding hypothetical structures. Furthermore, since the "intermediates" were not arranged in a true time sequence, they could not be true intermediates, even if they actually existed as represented. Furthermore, by not drawing them true to scale, they were made to appear more similar to one another than is actually true. I do not know whether Kitcher was aware of these facts when he used the slide. I personally doubt it. I did, in later correspondence, challenge Kitcher with the question, why, if the case for evolution is good, he had to use such manufactured data. There can be no doubt, however, that Miller, the supplier of the slide, was aware of these facts. The audience at the University of Minnesota was hoodwinked by the use of false and misleading data, but the credibility of evolutionary protagonists has suffered seriously, as a result.

During a debate I had with Miller at Tampa, Florida, on March 20, 1982, Miller wished to support his contention that something akin to Goldschmidt's "hopeful monster" mechanism can and does occur. He used two examples: four-winged flies and Ancon sheep. He maintained that each of these examples lend support to Goldschmidt's suggestion that sudden large evolutionary changes, caused by macromutations, can give rise to abrupt, large evolutionary advances. As a professional biologist, Miller would possess knowledge of the true nature of the changes involved, and would know, or should know, that the changes involved are pathological and would bring about the extinction of these creatures in a natural environment, rather than an advance through natural selection. The suggestion, by Miller, that the four-winged fly and the Ancon sheep represent evolutionary advances was simply a deceptive ploy.

In the fruit fly, *Drosophila melangaster,* the wings develop on the second thoracic segment, and the halteres, organs necessary for balance and control of flight, develop on the third thoracic segment. A mutation causes a bizarre transposition, such that the second thoracic segment, bearing wings, doubles, but the third thoracic segment, which normally bears the halteres, does not develop at all. Thus, the poor fly, although now possessing two sets of wings, cannot fly because it has lost its halteres, essential for balance. It could not survive, of course, in a natural environment, and would simply die. Stephen Jay Gould, in his article on four-winged flies and similar mutants, says:

We must avoid, I believe, the tempting but painfully naive
idea that they represent the long-sought "hopeful monsters"
that might validate extreme saltationist views of major
evolutionary transitions in single steps. . . .[26]

I was aware of these facts, and so explained them to the
audience. Miller's example of the Ancon sheep caught me off
guard, however, as I was not aware, at that time, concerning
the true nature of these deformed creatures.

Ancon sheep are also the product of a pathological condition, called achondroplasia. In his presentation, Miller
pointed out that these sheep have been bred by sheep breeders
because they are short-legged and thus cannot jump fences—
an advantage for those who raise sheep. What he did *not* say
was that their condition is caused by a mutation which results
in the failure of the cartilage between the joints to develop.
There is thus little or no cartilage between the joints of their
legs, causing them to be short. This abnormal condition would,
of course, result in their rapid extinction in a natural environment and could never be considered an evolutionary advance.
Miller did not explain this to the audience, of course, and much
to my chagrin, neither was I able to do so, since I was not
aware of these facts at that time. As was the case with Kitcher
and his string of "intermediates" between reptile and mammal,
the audience was hoodwinked.

Chicanery also came into play during a debate I had with
Dr. Russell Doolittle on the origin of life at Iowa State University, Ames, Iowa, on October 22, 1980. Doolittle is Professor of Biochemistry at the University of California at San
Diego, and is well known in evolutionary circles for his work
on protein homologies. One of my major thrusts in the debate
was the mathematical impossibility of random chemical as-
sembling of amino acids in the precise, or nearly precise, order
required for biological activity of the several hundred proteins
necessary to get life started. During the rebuttal period, Doolittle set about to refute my probability arguments. He first asked
the audience to consider the "impossibility" of all those 2,000

people being in that auditorium at that particular time, and yet, there they were. I easily rebuffed that ludicrous argument by pointing out that there was absolutely no difficulty for accounting for that fact, since not one of them had gotten there by chance!

In his final rebuttal, Doolittle used a trick for which, unfortunately, at that time, I did not have an answer. Taking the first row of spectators, he asked them, one by one, to name their birthdays. By the time he had gone through about 20-25 in the first row, two of their birthdays had fallen on the same day. Doolittle then exulted that, in spite of the extremely low probability of such an occurrence, he had found two people in the front row whose birthdays fell on the same day. Therefore, he declared, probability arguments are worthless, and Gish's arguments based on them are discredited. What Doolittle knew (obviously) and what I, and those in the audience did not know at the time, was the high probability of such an occurrence. If one is not familiar with probability calculations, one might suppose that with 30 people, there would be a probability of only 30/365 of two people having their birthdays on the same day. Actually, of 30 people, the probability is better than two to one that two people will have their birthdays on the same day, and if the number is 35, the odds are three to one!

The probability is calculated by adding $0 + 1/365 + 2/365 + 3/365 + 4/365 + 5/365 + \ldots n-1/365$ (where n = total number of people queried) (see the Time-Life publication, *Mathematics,* p. 142). Doolittle thus had played a game with the audience that he knew he was almost certain to win, while pretending that the odds were greatly against him. Once more, an audience had been hoodwinked. Of course, I must bear a major share of the blame, for it is my responsibility in a debate to be prepared to counter such fallacious arguments and to expose such trickery.

The November 1972 issue of the Biological Sciences Curriculum Study (BSCS) newsletter contained an article (anonymous, apparently by the editor) entitled "Will the Real John Moore Please Stand Up?" (p. 16). In the article, the author claimed creationists had deliberately confused their Dr. John N. Moore, a creationist and professor of Natural Science at Michigan State University, with Dr. John A. Moore, an evolutionist and Professor of Biology at the University of California, Riverside. The author claimed that creationists were dishonestly attempting to place John A. Moore in their camp, in order to appropriate, for their cause, the prestige of a University of California professor, and particularly the prestige held by John A. Moore.

I wrote a letter to the editor of the newsletter in which I stated that, first of all, we creationists were perfectly happy with our John N. Moore and didn't need their John A. Moore. Secondly, I asked the editor to either document his charge that creationists had deliberately confused John N. Moore with John A. Moore or retract the charge. Thirdly, I stated that I had done some research of my own, and that I could find only two instances where John N. Moore had been confused with John A. Moore. One case was in a publication by evolutionist geologist Preston Cloud, of the University of California, Santa Barbara,[27] and the other was in a publication by, of all people, John A. Moore![28] I told the editor that I thought his readers might find this a bit amusing. The editor, however, did not find it amusing, nor did he wish to acknowledge just who had been guilty of confusing John N. Moore with John A. Moore. He thus did not publish my letter, nor did he publish a retraction of his false and slanderous charge.

On March 4-6, 1977, I attended a symposium on human origins at the University of California, Davis. The symposium was jointly conducted by the Foundation for Research into the Origins of Man, and the University Extension, University of California, Davis. The faculty included Richard Leakey (son of Louis and Mary Leakey) who has gained much fame in the past decade and a half as a fossil hunter in Africa; Donald Johanson, the discoverer of "Lucy"; Alan Walker, now of

Johns Hopkins University, who has worked with Richard Leakey; David Pilbeam, then of Yale University; Garniss Curtis, of the University of California, Berkeley; Owen Lovejoy, of Kent State University; and Glynn Isaac, of the University of California, Berkeley.

Curtis is a radiochronologist who has dated a number of samples for anthropologists. He presented a lecture at the symposium on the technique of radiometric dating. He and other radiochronologists, using radiometric dating, had obtained dates for certain events that are quite divergent from the dates suggested for these events by those who employ the "protein clock" hypothesis developed by A. C. Wilson, Vincent Sarich, and others at the University of California, Berkeley. Before development of the "protein clock" hypothesis, it had been suggested, for example, that the divergence of man and the apes from their common ancestor had occurred sometime between 20 and 30 million years ago. Wilson and Sarich, however, on the basis of their "protein clock," have suggested that this divergence had occurred no more than four or five million years ago.

This divergence of opinion, between the radiochronologists and the "protein clock" people, naturally had created tension between those holding strong views on each side. Curtis therefore wished to put down the "protein clock" hypothesis and the dates that might be obtained using this technique. He mentioned that, according to comparisons based on the structures of certain serum albumins, humans were nearly as similar to bullfrogs as they were to apes. Using the "protein clock" idea, then, one could assume that man had split off from the amphibians about the same time he had split off from the apes—clearly a ludicrous suggestion, according to evolutionists.

Dr. Gary Parker, then a member of the Institute for Creation Research staff, had suggested another unacceptable conclusion based on comparison of the structures of proteins. I had heard him describe this situation in a lecture.

Subsequently, he published the account. After describing the problems evolutionists have with the hemoglobins, Parker says:

> The same seems to be true for a fascinating protein called lysozyme. . . . By comparing lysozyme and lactalbumin, Dickerson was hoping to "pin down with great precision," where human beings branched off the mammal line. The results are surprising. In this test, it turned out that humans are more closely related to the *chicken* than to any living mammal tested! Every evolutionist knows that can't be true, but how can he get around the objective evidence? In his concluding diagram, Dickerson slips in a wiggly line for rapid evolution, and that brings the whole thing back in line again with his evolutionary assumptions. But notice that his protein data, the facts that he observed, did not help him at all with his evolutionary idea.[29]

On the basis of what I had heard from Garniss Curtis and Gary Parker, on two occasions I stated that, following the reasoning of evolutionists based on the similarity of certain protein molecules, one would assume that man is as closely related to bullfrogs and chickens as he is to apes. One occasion was during a debate with John W. Patterson on a radio station in Ames, Iowa, and the other was during the videotaping of a program for Public Broadcasting Television. Evolutionists have vigorously contested that statement and have challenged me to provide documentation.

Robert Schadewald, a free-lance writer and a virulent anti-creationist, wrote to Garniss Curtis to check out my story after I had informed him concerning the source of my information on serum albumins. Curtis, in his reply, reported that he had indeed told the story the way I had revealed it. Now Curtis claimed, however, that he had told this story with tongue in cheek, more or less as a joke.[30] It was perfectly clear to me at the time Curtis gave his talk that there was a joke involved, all right, but it was equally clear that Curtis intended for the joke to be on the "protein clock" people, and not in the nature of the data he presented. Thus, if the data were faulty on which I had based my remarks about the serum albumins of man, apes, and bullfrogs, the responsibility for the faulty data (if indeed it is faulty) is due to false information provided in a public address by an evolutionist.

The documentation for the claim concerning the relationship of the lysozymes of humans, mammals, and chickens is available in the scientific literature. Dickerson and Geis, in their book, *The Structure and Action of Proteins,* provide this documentation.[31] According to Dickerson and Geis, and other evolutionists, lactalbumin, a protein found in milk, and lysozyme, an enzyme found in most plant and animal cells and which catalyzes the digestion of bacterial cell walls, are descended from a common ancestral protein. It is believed that the genes for lysozyme and lactalbumin resulted from a gene duplication about the time of the divergence of the amphibians and reptiles.

If one compares the differences in amino acid sequences of mammalian lactalbumins (including humans) and human and chicken lysozymes, the results pose a surprising puzzle for evolutionists. It is found that human lysozyme is more similar to chicken lysozyme than it is to lactalbumin. As Dickerson and Geis point out, on the basis of the usual evolutionary assumption that amino acid differences can be used to date times of divergence, one would arrive at the conclusion shown in Figure 1.

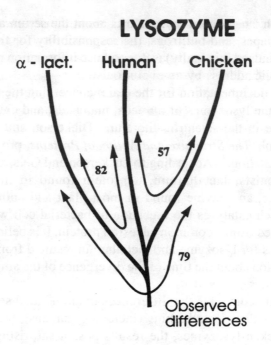

Figure 1

Thus, if one approaches these results in all innocence, using the commonly accepted assumptions of evolutionists concerning the meaning of amino acid sequence differences in proteins, humans are more closely related to chickens than they are to the mammals, including the apes. Of course, to evolutionists, this conclusion is completely unacceptable, even ludicrous. What makes this conclusion outrageously ridiculous is the fact that, based on these data, humans would be more closely related to chickens than they are to themselves! What this really demonstrates is that amino acid sequence similarities or differences do not reveal the degree of relatedness in an evolutionary sense. Evolutionists attempt to explain away the contradictions these data pose for evolutionary theory by making the ad hoc assumption that for some unknown reason, amino acid substitutions occurred much more rapidly in the various mammalian lactalbumins than in the mammalian lysozymes. In this case, then, the "protein clock" notion is deceptive, because the clock is running at different rates in these two different cases. Therefore, such a clock can never be trusted. In any case, evolutionists should spend more time straightening up their own house, instead of hurling accusations against creation scientists.

Another charge hurled against me is that I continued to repeat an error in my description of the remarkable defense mechanism of the bombardier beetle, even after I had become aware of the error.[32,33] I described this complex mechanism in my book on dinosaurs for children, *Dinosaurs: Those Terrible Lizards*,[34] and used it first publicly in a debate that Dr. Henry Morris and I had with Professors Frank Awbrey and William Thwaites at San Diego State University on April 26, 1977.

The bombardier beetle has a remarkable defense mechanism and, after describing this incredible mechanism, I challenged Awbrey and Thwaites to explain how an ordinary beetle, through a series of random, accidental mutations, acted upon by natural selection, could gradually change into a bombardier beetle. Neither at that time nor since have Awbrey and Thwaites been able to explain how this could have taken place. Awbrey and Thwaites subsequently, however, did utilize the common evolutionist ploy of ignoring the challenge and grasping for a flaw, even minor, in the creationist's argument.

When a bombardier beetle (*Brachinus*) is threatened by a predator or an offensive invader of any kind, at the appropriate point of approach the bombardier beetle swings his tail end around in just the right direction (he never misses) and hot, noxious gases, heated to 212°F (the boiling point of water), are explosively released from twin combustion tubes right into the face of his enemy. This is, of course, sufficient to discourage any further notion of an attack on the bombardier beetle. Research has revealed the fact that this beetle has a double set of apparatus. In twin storage chambers, he stores an aqueous solution of two chemicals—10% hydroquinone (a reducing agent used in photographic developing fluids) and 23% hydrogen peroxide (a powerful oxidizing agent). Remarkably, these chemical agents do not react, the solution remaining as crystal clear as pure water. Apparently the bombardier beetle adds an inhibitor which prevents the chemicals from reacting. If these chemicals are mixed in the laboratory, the solution soon becomes discolored, as the hydrogen peroxide oxidizes the hydroquinones to quinones (in the bombardier beetle a mixture of hydroquinone and methylhydroquinone is used).

When the bombardier beetle is ready to fire his defensive spray, he squirts a charge of the chemical solution into each of the combustion tubes. There an enzyme, catalase, catalyzes the extremely rapid decomposition of hydrogen peroxide into oxygen and water, and another enzyme, peroxidase, catalyzes the oxidation of the hydroquinones to quinones—noxious, irritating chemicals. The chemical reaction generates sufficient heat to raise the temperature of the mixture to 212°F, and the excess oxygen produced provides the high pressure, and valves in the ends of the combusion tubes are opened at the appropriate time.[35-37]

My original source of information (and the only source available to me early on) was a little pamphlet, "Darwin and the Beetles," published in the early sixties by Dr. Robert E. Kofahl, then president of Highland College and now science consultant to the Creation Science Research Center, San Diego. In his reading of the article by Schildknecht and Holoubek, Kofahl apparently mistranslated the German word for "unstable" to read "explosive." Kofahl in his pamphlet thus reported that a mixture of 10% hydroquinones and 23% hydrogen peroxide was explosive. Following Kofahl, as I told the story of the bombardier beetle in lectures, in the debate at San Diego State University, and in the book, *Dinosaurs: Those Terrible Lizards,* I said that ordinarily a mixture of these chemicals at those concentrations was explosive. Awbrey and Thwaites, anxious to find a way out of the dilemma posed by the bombardier beetle, diligently searched for any possible slip in my story. As soon as they discovered that the mixture was *not* explosive, they made no attempt whatever to explain how the bombardier beetle could have evolved, but trumpeted loudly, everywhere, this minor slip in the story. Other evolutionists eagerly grabbed onto the story, and it found its way even into *Nature,* the prestigious British science journal.[33]

As soon as I learned of this little hitch in the story of the bombardier beetle, I modified the story I related in my lectures. I had to wait until the publisher was ready to publish a revised edition of *Dinosaurs: Those Terrible Lizards,* however, to correct the story there. In the meantime, the first edition was continuing to be sold. That apparently was the source of the charge that I had continued to tell the original story even after the problem had been called to my attention.

Dr. Kofahl, in an article entitled "The Bombardier Beetle Shoots Back," which he published in the evolutionist journal *Creation/Evolution,*[38] in response to the critical article by Weber,[32] accepted the responsibility for the slip in the story. He further argued powerfully that Weber's attempt to explain the evolution of the bombardier beetle from an ordinary beetle was exceedingly weak and seriously flawed. In spite of this explanation, published in 1981 in the major anti-creationist journal, evolutionists have continued to bring up the story, implying that I have persisted in using a flawed case, even after having been made aware of the problem. As recently as my debate with Grover Krantz at Washington State University on March 3, 1987, an evolutionist professor from the University of Idaho brought up this subject during the question/answer period. It is long past time that this old tired story should be laid to rest.

Even if the mixture of hydroquinones and hydrogen peroxide is not explosive, a mixture of these two chemicals in the presence of the two enzymes in a confined space *is* explosive. The beetle, on his way to becoming a bombardier beetle, would have to be smart enough to carefully store the chemicals in a storage chamber apart from the enzymes but in the presence of an inhibitor to prevent them from reacting prematurely with one another. He also would have to be smart enough to know which enzymes he needs to catalyze the chemical reactions involved, and he would have to be smart enough to secrete them into the combustion chamber. The combustion chamber itself must be very special, able to resist the corrosive effect of the hot, irritating chemicals and strong enough to contain the high pressure without rupturing. The combustion chamber must also be equipped with a highly efficient valve, and the appropriate muscles must exist to manipulate the combustion tube and point it in the right direction. Of course, all of this incredibly complex apparatus would be totally useless without a precisely designed and perfectly functional communication system to squirt the charge of chemicals into the combustion tube, secrete the enzymes into the combustion tube, activate the valve at the appropriate moment, and send the correct signals to all of the muscles involved, in order to point the combustion tube in the right direction. Evolutionists would have us believe that all of the hundreds, and most likely thousands, of genes required to direct the construction and operation of all of this arose through a series of copying errors. Furthermore, these complex genetic changes had to occur in just the right order, so that at every stage of development the beetle was not only able to survive but also was actually superior to the preceding stage. Creation scientists reject this notion as more than scientifically untenable; it is simply preposterous, a fairy tale! But once again, evolutionists have resorted to an *ad hominem* attack on a creation scientist in order to obscure their failure to explain fatal flaws in evolutionary theory.

The book, *Holy Terror,* by Flo Conway and Jim Siegelman,[39] has as its subtitle, "The Fundamentalist War on America's Freedoms in Religion, Politics and Our Private Lives." Throughout their book it is next to impossible to find a single good thing they have to say about anyone they would characterize as a fundamentalist Christian. For example, after the report of their visit to Rev. Jerry Falwell's Thomas Road Baptist Church, in Lynchburg, Virginia, they describe their visit around the city of Lynchburg (p. 78). From the description of their inquiries in the city, one is left with the impression that there was no one in the city who didn't either hate or fear Rev. Falwell. According to Conway and Siegelman, no one had a good word to say about Jerry Falwell. Do all the 20,000 members of his church come from outside the city of Lynchburg? Since people like Conway and Siegelman view all creationists as radical, far-out fundamentalists, their attitudes toward creationists are perfectly predictable.

Thus, Conway and Siegelman has this to say (p. 122):

> Although their arguments have been judged to be not a scientific discipline but a branch of Christian apologetics, the "big lie" proliferates, fueled by zealotry, intellectual chicanery and a broadening economic base. And few realize the extent to which the continuing scam is an integral part of the larger picture of Holy Terror in America. In fact, as we found, to a large extent, creationism is a wholly owned and operated subsidiary of the fundamentalist right political network.

On the flap of the book, with reference to the "Holy Terror" they claim is assaulting America, it is stated, ". . . Conway and Siegelman traveled 10,000 miles cross country and back, interviewing people on all sides of the issue. . . ." Their investigation of scientific creationists, however, involved a single interview with a single creation scientist, Dr. Richard B. Bliss, Director of Curriculum Development for the Institute for Creation Research. This interview is described on pp. 122-128 of their book. Based on some of their remarks, one would be inclined to doubt their objectivity. For example, they describe the ICR library as a "small library overflowing with creationist texts." At that time the ICR library was indeed small, but it certainly wasn't overflowing with creationist texts. In fact, evolutionist texts in the ICR library vastly outnumber creationist texts, and this has always been true. The ratio is certainly as high as 50 to 1.

The report of their interview with Bliss involved a great deal of fencing, or, as they put it (p. 124), a "cat-and-mouse game." They tried hard to draw Bliss into making what they would consider embarrassing or damaging admissions, but Bliss eloquently defended his two-model approach for teaching origins in science education in public schools. Drawing on his 23 years as a science educator, director of science education in the Racine, Wisconsin, school district (one of the largest in the state), and the one who pioneered the two-model approach in the Racine district, Bliss defended that approach, based on good science, good education, and academic and religious freedoms. This apparently was not what Conway and Siegelman wished to hear. After reporting Bliss's statement (p. 128) that,

> If we establish a two-model approach and the inquiry that goes along with it, it's going to spill over into the social sciences and history.

Conway and Siegelman state:

> The prospect of a spillover was even more frightening. Bliss's vision exposed the creationists' role in the long-range plan of Holy Terror. . . . Was that the goal: to expunge all critical thinking and non-fundamentalist philosophy from the culture?

During the entire interview, Bliss was urging the value of unfettered inquiry in science education. On p. 123, Conway and Siegelman give Bliss the credit for being, more than anyone else, the man behind the two-model approach, which he pioneered in the Racine school district. Yet after all of this, and Bliss's pleading against programming young minds to accept a single view of origins, but rather to train them, via the scientific method and critical thinking, to evaluate each model of origins and to decide for themselves which seems more credible, more reasonable, now Conway and Siegelman accuse Bliss of the goal of expunging all critical thinking and non-fundamentalist philosophy from our culture! It seems clear that it is Conway and Siegelman who wish to expunge all critical thinking from public education and to institutionalize evolution and secular humanism as dogma in public schools, rather than to employ the two-model approach advocated by Bliss and other creation scientists.

In all of the thousands of lectures and debates involving creation scientists, and in the many hundreds of articles and books published by creation scientists, it is possible, of course, that a few errors, a few misquotes, and some misunderstanding of evolutionist literature may have crept in. Creation scientists are, after all, fallible, and prone to mistakes in the same manner as are evolutionists. If such errors do occur, it is legitimate, of course, for evolutionists to point these out and to ask that they be corrected. Even evolutionists have misunderstood their fellow evolutionists. Thus, Sewall Wright, in a paper published in 1980,[40] related the fact that such prominent evolutionists as Julian Huxley, R. A. Fisher, and Ernst Mayr had seriously misunderstood some of his theories.

It is unfair, unethical, and demeaning to science as a profession for evolutionists to incessantly charge creation scientists with quoting out of context, misquoting, distorting science, and telling outright falsehoods. These tactics are simply an admission of weakness on the part of evolutionists and of their inability to refute scientific challenges to their sagging theory. If the facts are on their side, they should simply state the facts, and the facts would speak for themselves.

References

1. S. J. Gould, *Discover,* January 1978, p. 64.

2. R. C. Lewontin, in *Scientists Confront Creationism,* L. R. Godfrey, Ed., W. W. Norton & Co., New York, 1983, p. xxiii.

3. A. B. Kehoe, *ibid.,* p. 11.

4. J. W. Patterson, *ibid.,* p. 114.

5. D. B. Wilson, in *Did the Devil Make Darwin Do It?,* D. B. Wilson, Ed., Iowa University Press, Ames, 1983, p. xi.

6. D. J. Futuyma, *Science on Trial,* Pantheon Books, New York, 1983, p. 178.

7. D. J. Futyma, *ibid.,* p. 220.

8. Niles Eldredge, *The Monkey Business. A Scientist Looks at Creationism,* Washington Square Press, New York, 1982, p. 112.

9. J. C. Whitcomb and H. M. Morris, *The Genesis Flood,* Presbyterian and Reformed Pub. Co., Philadelphia, 1961.

10. Philip Kitcher, *Abusing Science,* The MIT Press, Cambridge, Massachusetts, 1982, p. 115.

11. D. T. Gish, *Evolution: The Fossils Say No!,* Creation-Life Pub., San Diego, 1979, p. 101.

12. R. B. Goldschmidt, *American Scientist* 40:97 (1952).

13. R. B. Goldschmidt, *The Material Basis of Evolution,* Yale University Press, New Haven, 1940, p. 395.

14. D. M. Raup, *Field Museum of Natural History Bulletin* 50:22 (1979).

15. Boyce Rensberger, *Houston Chronicle,* Section 4. p. 15, November 5, 1980.

16. L. R. Godrey, Ref. 2, p. 202.

17. E. J. H. Corner, "Evolution," in *Contemporary Botanical Thought,* A. M. MacLeod and L. S. Cobley, Eds., Quadrangle Books, Chicago, 1961, p. 97.

18. Charles Darwin, *Origin of Species,* 1859.

19. N. F. Hughes, *Paleobiology of Angiosperm Origins: Problems of Mesozoic Seed-Plant Evolution,* Cambridge University Press, Cambridge, Eng., 1976.

20. W. G. Chaloner, *Nature* 260:402 (1976).

21. C. B. Beck, in *Origin and Early Evolution of Angiosperms,* C. B. Beck, Ed., Columbia University Press, New York, 1976.

22. *Evolution Versus Creationism: The Public Education Controversy,* J. P. Zetterberg, Ed., Oryx University Press, Phoenix, 1983.

23. Roger Lewin, *Science* 214:638 (1981).

24. Personal Communication to D. T. Gish from Philip Kitcher.

25. E. F. Allin, *Journal of Morphology* 147:403-438 (1975).

26. S. J. Gould, *Natural History* 89:6-15 (October 1980).

27. Preston Cloud, *The Humanist,* Jan./Feb. 1977, p. 7.

28. J. A. Moore, *Daedalus* 103:173-189, Summer 1974. In the bibliography John A. Moore lists the editors of the Creation Research Society high school biology text as John A. Moore and Harold Slusher. John N. Moore was co-editor with Slusher.

29. H. M. Morris and Gary Parker, *What Is Creation Science?* Master Book Pub., San Diego, 1982, pp. 24, 25.

30. Personal Communication to D. T. Gish from Robert Schadewald.

31. R. E. Dickerson and I. Geis, *The Structure and Action of Proteins*, W. A. Benjamin, Inc., Menlo Park, California, 1969, pp. 77, 78.

32. C. G. Weber, *Creation/Evolution* 2(1):4 (1980).

33. T. H. Jukes, *Nature* 308:398 (1984); *Trends in Biochemical Sciences* 6(7):1 (1981).

34. D. T. Gish, *Dinosaurs: Those Terrible Lizards,* Master Books, El Cajon, California, 1977, pp. 50-55.

35. H. Schildknecht and K. Holoubek, *Angewandte Chemie* 73(1):1 (1961).

36. T. Eisner and D. J. Aneshansky, *Science* 215:J83 (1982).

37. J. A. Miller, *Science News* 115:330 (1979).

38. R. E. Kofahl, *Creation/Evolution* 2(3):12 (1981).

39. Flo Conway and Jim Siegelman, *Holy Terror,* Doubleday and Co., Garden City, NY, 1982.

40. Sewall Wright, *Evolution* 34:825 (1980).

5

Attack and Counterattack:
The Fossil Record

Discussions concerning the fossil record have, appropriately, occupied a preeminent place in the creation/evolution controversy. The fossil record provides the only direct evidence concerning the history of life on this planet. It is true, of course, that there were no human witnesses to the origin of a single one of these fossil organisms, and thus scientific conclusions concerning the origin of these organisms are, at best, inferences based on circumstantial evidence.

There are many billions times billions of invertebrate fossils, many billions of fossil fish, untold millions of fossil amphibians, reptiles, and mammals locked in fossil-bearing strata. Fossils of some creatures, man for example, are, on the other hand, quite rare. In the natural history museums of the world are to be found more than 250,000 different fossil species, represented by tens of millions of catalogued fossils.

These fossils have been taken from every one of the so-called geological periods. Thus, the fossil record is almost immeasurably rich. An appeal to the "poverty of the fossil record" is no longer legitimate.

If, as evolutionists believe, several millions of species have gradually evolved during hundreds of millions of years, a vast number of intermediate stages would have arisen, and the number of intermediate or transitional forms that would have lived and died during that enormous stretch of time would have been many billions times billions, and most likely, times billions again. If evolution is true, then at least many tens of thousands of the quarter of a million fossil species in our museums should consist of unquestionable transitional forms. This would be true even if one invokes the so-called "punctuated equilibria" mode of evolution. There would be absolutely no challenge to the fact of evolution, no Institute for Creation Research, no Creation Research Society, no scientific creationists. If, on the other hand, creation *is* true, the picture presented by the fossil record would be very different from that expected on the basis of evolution. On the basis of creation, one would expect the abrupt appearance, fully formed, of each of the basic types of plants and animals, or created kinds, with no intermediate or transitional forms to suggest their gradual origin from a common ancestor. The gaps between the higher categories—the phyla, classes, orders, and families, would be systematic and almost always large.

The fossil record comes down heavily on the creationist side. As a matter of fact, there is simply no contest! Creation wins hands down! This was apparent to Darwin, and he admitted that the fossil record was one of the strongest arguments against his theory. Paleontologists have searched intensely for the anticipated transitional forms, but today, about 130 years after Darwin, the "missing links" are still missing. These facts have been documented by creation scientists[1-3] and by non-creationist anti-Darwinists.[4-8]

Present-day evolutionists respond to this dilemma in a variety of ways. Some downplay the importance of the fossil record relative to the creation/evolution question. Thus British zoologist Mark Ridley declares:

> ... the gradual change of fossil species has *never* been part of the evidence for evolution. In the chapters on the fossil record in the *Origin of Species,* Darwin showed that the record was useless for testing between evolution and special creation because it has great gaps in it. The same argument still applies. . . . In any case, no real evolutionist, whether gradualist or punctuationist, uses the fossil record as evidence in favor of the theory of evolution as opposed to special creation.[9]

This is truly an incredible statement. First, Ridley echoes Darwin's appeal to the poverty of the fossil record. Present-day geologists recognize the fact that our museums are so loaded down with fossils, that this attempt to circumvent the difficulties the fossil record poses for evolution theory is no longer valid.[10-12] T. N. George states, for example:

> There is no need to apologize any longer for the poverty of the fossil record. In some ways it has become almost unmanageably rich, and discovery is outpacing integration.[12]

Here in the U.S., with a nation of 260 million people, national polls seek responses from about 2,000 people in order to get a fairly accurate view on issues. Surely, even if the total number of species that have ever lived totalled 25 million, an excessive estimate, 250,000 would represent a one percent sampling. A one percent sampling of the U.S. adult population would exceed 1.5 million!

What evidence does Ridley suggest as support for evolution? He states:

> So just what is the evidence that species have evolved? There have traditionally been three kinds of evidence, and it is these, not the 'fossil evidence,' that critics should be thinking about. The three arguments are from the observed

evolution of species, from biogeography, and from the hierarchical structure of taxonomy.

All of these arguments are emphasized, to some degree, by most evolutionists, as we will see. We will leave a detailed refutation of each of these arguments until later. Suffice it to say at this point that all of the evidence within those three categories can readily be interpreted within a creationist framework, and if, on the other hand, that is the strongest evidence that can be cited as support for evolution, then the case for evolution is, indeed, appallingly weak.

As we have mentioned in an earlier chapter, Pierre-Paul Grassé refutes, directly, Ridley's assertion concerning the relative unimportance of the fossil record. Grassé states:

> Naturalists must remember that the process of evolution is revealed only through fossil forms. A knowledge of paleontology is, therefore, a prerequisite. Only paleontology can provide them with the evidence of evolution and reveal its course or mechanisms. Neither the examination of present beings, nor imagination, nor theories, can serve as a substitute for paleontological documents. If they ignore them, biologists—the philosophers of nature—indulge in numerous commentaries and can only come up with hypotheses.[13]

Grassé thus makes clear that it is the fossil record, and only the fossil record, that could potentially produce any real evidence for evolution. Sir Gavin de Beer, British biologist and evolutionist, has said, "The last word on the credibility and course of evolution lies with the paleontologists. . . ."[14] As recorded in an earlier chapter, Glenister and Witzke have said that:

> The fossil record affords an opportunity to choose between evolutionary and creationist models for the origin of the earth and its life forms.[15]

Similar statements by other evolutionists could be cited. According to Ridley, however, any evolutionist who attempts to defend evolution versus creation on the basis of the fossil record is not a real evolutionist at all!

There are two huge gaps in the fossil record that are so immense and indisputable that any further discussion of the fossil record becomes superfluous. These are the gap between microscopic, single-celled organisms and the complex, multicellular invertebrates, and the vast gap between these invertebrates and fish. There are now many reports in the scientific literature claiming the discovery of fossil bacteria and algae in rocks supposedly as old as 3.8 billion years. Paleontologists generally consider that the validity of these claims is beyond dispute. In rocks of the so-called Cambrian Period, which evolutionists believe began to form about 600 million years ago, and which supposedly formed during about 80 million years, are found the fossils of a vast array of very complicated invertebrates—sponges, snails, clams, brachiopods, jellyfish, trilobites, worms, sea urchins, sea cucumbers, sea lilies, etc. Unnumbered billions of these fossils are known to exist. Supposedly, these complex invertebrates had evolved from a single-celled organism.

The rocks that generally underlie the Cambrian rocks are simply called Precambrian rocks. Some are thousands of feet thick, and many are undisturbed—perfectly suitable for the preservation of fossils. If it is possible to find fossils of microscopic, single-celled, soft-bodied bacteria and algae, it should certainly be possible to find fossils of the transitional forms between those organisms and the complex invertebrates. Many billions times billions of the intermediates would have lived and died during the vast stretch of time required for the evolution of such a diversity of complex organisms. The world's museums should be bursting at the seams with enormous collections of the fossils of transitional forms. As a matter of fact, not a single such fossil has ever been found! Right from the start, jellyfish have been jellyfish, trilobites have been trilobites, sponges have been sponges, and snails have been snails. Furthermore, not a single fossil has been found linking, say, clams and snails, sponges and jellyfish, or trilobites and crabs, yet all of the Cambrian animals supposedly have been derived from common ancestors.

For a time, evolutionists believed that the Ediacaran Fauna, originally discovered in Australia but now known to be worldwide in distribution, contained creatures that, even though already very complex in nature, might be ancestral to many of the Cambrian animals. Some of the Ediacaran creatures were placed in the same categories as the Cambrian jellyfish, worms, and corals. According to Adolph Seilacher, a German paleontologist, the Ediacaran creatures are, however, basically different from all of the Cambrian animals, and so could not possibly have been ancestral to them. It is believed that all of the Ediacaran creatures became extinct without leaving any evolutionary offspring.[16] Thus, the Cambrian "explosion," as it is commonly called, remains an unsolved mystery for evolutionists.

It is extremely interesting to observe how evolutionists deal with this tremendous contradiction to evolutionary theory. The attempt by Niles Eldredge, an invertebrate paleontologist at the American Museum of Natural History, to explain away this problem is not only interesting but even amusing. In his anti-creationist book, [17] following his discussion of the Ediacaran Fauna (now invalidated by the later revelations of Seilacher), Eldredge says:

> Then there was something of an explosion. Beginning about six hundred million years ago, and continuing for about ten to fifteen million years, the earliest known representatives of the major kinds of animals still populating today's seas made a rather abrupt appearance. This rather protracted "event" shows up graphically in the rock record: all over the world, at roughly the same time, thick sequences of rocks, barren of any easily detected fossils, are overlain by sediments containing a gorgeous array of shelly invertebrates; trilobites (extinct relatives of crabs and insects), brachiopods, mollusks. All of the typical forms of hard-shelled animals we see in the modern oceans

appeared, albeit in primitive, prototypical form, in the seas of six hundred million years ago.

Creationists have made much of this sudden development of a rich and varied fossil record where, just before, there was none. . .

Indeed, the sudden appearance of a varied, well-preserved array of fossils, which geologists have used to mark the beginnings of the Cambrian Period (the oldest division of the Paleozoic Era) does pose a fascinating intellectual challenge.[18]

Eldredge offers several possible solutions to the problem. One suggestion is that the level of atmospheric oxygen rose to a critical point, so that the oxygen level in the ocean became sufficient to support a large variety of animal life.[19] He admits, however, that red beds, or rocks containing a high content of ferric oxide (the highest oxidation state of iron) are found at least as far back as two billion years, indicating the presence of a relatively high percentage of oxygen in the atmosphere. If, on the evolutionary time scale, oxygen was abundant by two billion years ago, and the Cambrian explosion did not occur until 600 million years ago (a difference of 1.4 billion years), it seems obvious that the sudden appearance of all these complex invertebrates had nothing to do with the oxygen content of the atmosphere.

Eldredge's main argument is that evolution does not necessarily proceed slowly and gradually, but that some episodes in evolution may, geologically speaking, proceed very rapidly.[19] Thus, just before the advent of the Cambrian, for some reason or other, there was an evolutionary burst—a great variety of complex multi-cellular organisms, many with hard parts, suddenly evolved. This evolution occurred so rapidly (perhaps in a mere fifteen to twenty million years, more or less) there just wasn't enough time for the intermediate creatures to leave a detectable fossil record.

This notion of explosive evolution is really not a new idea at all, as it has been employed in the past to explain the absence of transitional forms.[20] This notion will not stand up under scrutiny, however. First, what is the *only* evidence for these postulated rapid bursts of evolution? *The absence of transitional forms!* Thus, evolutionists, like Eldredge, Simpson, and others, are attempting to snatch away from creation scientists what these scientists consider to be one of the best evidences for creation, that is, the absence of transitional forms, and use it as support for an evolutionary scenario!

What is predicted on the basis of evolution—namely, the *presence* of transitional forms—is not forthcoming, so rather than admitting that the evidence falsifies their theory, the new scenario predicts just the opposite—the *absence* of transitional forms. Furthermore, the science of genetics is solidly against the notion of rapid bursts of evolution. As a matter of fact, evolutionists argue that the reason we have never witnessed any really significant evolutionary changes in all of human observation is because evolution moves so slowly. Indeed, the genetic apparatus of a lizard, for example, is totally devoted to producing another lizard; and the idea that there could be processes that somehow overcome this genetic bulwark against change and convert a lizard into a different creature without leaving fossilized intermediates is wishful thinking and contrary to science. Even more incredible is the idea that this could have happened to a whole host of complex creatures. Finally, while fifteen to twenty million years may seem brief to evolutionists, it *is* a very, very long time—plenty of time to leave a rich fossil record.

Later in the book by Eldredge quoted above, Eldredge suggests the most incredible notion of all to explain away the vast Cambrian explosion. He states:

> We don't see much evidence of intermediates in the Early Cambrian because the intermediates had to have been soft-bodied, and thus extremely unlikely to become fossilized.[21]

It is difficult to believe that Eldredge or any other scientist could have made such a statement. Whatever they were, the evolutionary predecessors of the Cambrian animals had to be complex. A single-celled organism could not possibly have suddenly evolved into a great variety of complex invertebrates without passing through a long series of intermediates of increasing complexity. Surely, if paleontologists are able to find numerous fossils of microscopic, single-celled, soft-bodied bacteria and algae, as Eldredge does not doubt they have, then they could easily find fossils of all the stages intermediate between these microscopic organisms and the complex invertebrates of the Cambrian. Furthermore, in addition to the many reported findings of fossil bacteria and algae, there must be many hundreds of finds of soft-bodied, multicellular creatures, such as worms and jellyfish, in the scientific literature. The creatures of the Ediacaran Fauna, which have been reported from five continents, are soft-bodied.

Even more incredible is Eldredge's suggestion that all of the intermediates leading up to the creatures that abruptly appear fully-formed in Cambrian rocks were soft-bodied. As Eldredge describes above, the Cambrian animals include a gorgeous array of shelly invertebrates—creatures with hard parts. If, as Eldredge says, *all* of the intermediates were soft-bodied, that means that a great variety of creatures with hard parts suddenly arose directly from soft-bodied creatures. That is simply impossible. The anatomy, the physiology, the very way of life of an invertebrate with hard parts is intimately intertwined with and dependent on those hard parts. Thus the anatomies of soft-bodied animals are very different from the soft anatomies of animals with hard parts. If invertebrates with hard parts evolved from soft-bodied creatures, that change had to be gradual, and there would have been many intermediate stages, permitting a gradual acquisition of hard parts and changes in the way of life of these creatures. This gradual acquisition of hard parts by these many creatures should be abundantly documented in the fossil record. Fossils of thousands of these intermediate stages should grace museum displays. None have been found.

Evolutionists believe that the vast array of invertebrates represented in the Cambrian rocks evolved from common ancestors, but of course there is not a single fossil of an intermediate to document this notion. Billions times billions of these creatures would have lived and died, but none can be found in paleontological collections. Vast unbridged gaps separate such creatures as jellyfish, sponges, worms, sea urchins, sea cucumbers, trilobites, brachiopods, sea lilies, and others.

This leaves evolutionists with what Simpson calls the major mystery of the history of life. In a review[22] of a recent book on the origin of the major invertebrate groups,[23] Runnegar states that:

> As might be expected, the paleontologists have concentrated on the fossil record and have therefore provided a wealth of information on the early history of a great variety of invertebrate groups, but little insight into their origins.

Eldredge admits that "The Cambrian evolutionary explosion is still shrouded in mystery."[24] But creation scientists say, what greater evidence for creation could the rocks give, than this abrupt appearance of a great variety of complex creatures without a trace of ancestors? Thus we see, right from the beginning, on the basis of an evolutionary scenario, the evidence is directly contradictory to predictions based on evolution but is remarkably in accord with predictions based on creation.

The late George Gaylord Simpson, one of the world's leading paleontologists during his lifetime, struggled with the problem but could provide no solution, terming the absence of ancestors for the Cambrian animals the "major mystery of the history of life."[20]

The remainder of the history of life reveals a remarkable absence of the many transitional forms demanded by the theory of evolution. There is, in fact, a systematic deficiency of transitional forms between the higher categories, just as predicted by the creation model.

Laurie Godfrey, a professor of anthropology at the University of Massachusetts and one of the leading anti-creationists, in her chapter, "Creationism and Gaps in the Fossil Record," in the anti-creationist book she edited, all but ignores the largest gap of all—that between single-celled organisms and the complex Cambrian invertebrates. All she has to say about the subject is, "We *have* found sources in Pre-Cambrian rocks for the famous Cambrian explosion of multicellular life forms."[25] Note that she claims only to have found *sources* for the Cambrian explosion, rather than the actual Precambrian ancestors. One of the publications she cited in support of that statement was a paper by Valentine. In another book she edited, published two years later, she included a chapter by Valentine entitled "The Evolution of Complex Animals." Valentine devotes considerable space to the problem of the origin of the complex Cambrian invertebrates. He candidly states that:

> The fossil record is of little use in providing direct evidence of the pathways of descent of the phyla or of invertebrate classes. Each phylum with a fossil record had already evolved its characteristic body plan when it first appeared, so far as we can tell from the fossil remains, and no phylum is connected to any other via intermediate fossil types. Indeed, none of the invertebrate classes can be connected with another class by series of intermediates.[26]

Valentine estimates that about 300 major body plans and sub-plans made their appearance during that time, including at least 50 phyla.

In a later discussion (p. 268) of his chapter, Valentine describes the close correlation between the soft anatomy of a brachiopod and its shell. He says:

> Thus we cannot imagine a long period of existence of brachiopods lacking mineralized skeletons; when the first brachiopod skeletons appear in the fossil record we are witnessing the origination of the brachiopod ground plan, or as near to it as the spotty fossil record permits us to approach.

Valentine's only way out is that proposed by some other evolutionists. He states that most likely the time available for the development of the brachiopod ground plan was only a few million years. In the first place, that is plenty of time to leave fossils, equal to the entire span of the Pliocene and Pleistocene Epochs combined on the evolutionary time scale. Furthermore, as Valentine points out, this would assign less time to the origin of a new basic life plan than the average life span of a single species. The possibility that evolution, totally dependent on random, accidental genetic mistakes, could so very rapidly produce a single, drastically new fundamental life pattern, coordinated nearly perfectly at every stage of its development, let alone the vast array of 50 phyla with a total of 300 new body plans that appear in the Cambrian fully formed at their first appearance, is simply an outrageous suggestion.

We thus see that Valentine provides absolutely no help towards resolving this great dilemma for evolutionary theory. In fact, he makes crystal clear that paleontologists have failed to find evolutionary ancestors for a single one of the complex Cambrian invertebrates, and that, in fact, this is true not only of every one of the phyla but also of the classes as well. Godfrey's use of Valentine in her 1983 book to gloss over this monumental problem was sheer bluff, knowing that very few of her readers would ever check to see what Valentine actually had to say on the subject.

Kitcher, in his anti-creationist book,[27] devotes 15 pages (pp. 106-120) in an attempt to refute creationists' arguments based on the fossil record, particularly the material found in the 1979 edition of my book, *Evolution? The Fossils Say No!*[28] In this section of his book, Kitcher discusses in detail the creationists' critique of the alleged transitions between fish and amphibians, reptiles and mammals, and reptiles and birds. He does not, however, say one single word about the intractable mystery that the Cambrian "explosion" poses for evolutionary theory. In fact, the word "Cambrian" is not to be found anywhere in his book. Perhaps it is at least to his credit that he simply ignored the problem, rather than attempting to bluff through it, as did Godfrey. Nevertheless, what Kitcher does not say in his book about the fossil record speaks much louder than what he does say.

Futuyma, in his anti-creationist book, devotes a single short paragraph to the problem. He writes:

> Animal fossils do not appear in profusion, however, until the beginning of the Cambrian period, 580 to 600 million years ago, and within the next 50 million years or so all the animal phyla that have fossilizable skeletons appear in the geological record. At first glance, it seems as if all the major groups of animals arose in a very short time, but this is clearly an illusion; 700-million-year-old Precambrian rocks have a rather diverse fauna, and the very fine-grained Cambrian shales of British Columbia show that there was an enormous diversity of animals that lacked skeletons. Very possibly this 'rapid' diversification of animals in the Cambrian was due to the rapid evolution of hard parts by groups that had evolved long ago.[29]

His reference to a 700-million-year-old Precambrian fauna is to the Ediacaran Fauna discussed earlier in this chapter. We note that Futuyma mentions not a single word about the possible existence of transitional forms for the Cambrian invertebrates. His only suggestion is that there were soft-bodied creatures which could have given rise to the Cambrian animals with hard parts. This suggestion has already been critiqued in the earlier discussion of the same suggestion by Eldredge, and cannot be taken seriously. Furthermore, it is immaterial whether all of the Cambrian animals appeared simultaneously or sequentially. Each appeared fully formed from its first appearance, and not one of these creatures is supposed by evolutionists to be ancestral to one of the others.

In the essentially anti-creationist book *Evolution Versus Creationism: The Public Education Controversy* (22 chapters are by anti-creationists and four are by creationists), only two of the anti-creationists even mention the Cambrian explosion of complex invertebrates. One of these, Fred Edwords, a philosopher, uses essentially the same argument employed by Futuyma, again ignoring the fact that not a single ancestor has ever been discovered for the complex invertebrates.[30] Preston Cloud, a Professor Emeritus of Biogeology and Environmental Studies at the University of California, Santa Barbara, also makes brief mention of the problem. He says:

> In the creationist scientist-joke cartoon-strip, "Have you been brainwashed?" D. T. Gish states that *billions of highly complex animals—trilobites, brachiopods, corals, worms, jellyfish, etc.—just suddenly appear in the geological record at the base of the Cambrian.* He can be forgiven for this misstatement, because part of it could be derived from careless reading of source materials, including my own writings. But it is not true. Since 1954, a variety of primitive microorganisms have been found to occur through a long sequence of rocks dating back to more than two billion years ago. We now also have evidence that a limited variety of multicellular animal life began about 680 million years ago, perhaps 80 million years before shell fossils of the Cambrian, and that higher forms appeared sequentially up to, through, and beyond the Cambrian.[31]

One of Cloud's main interests and research efforts has been the search for Precambrian ancestors. As a biogeologist, and one who has searched intensely for the ever elusive ancestors of the complex Cambrian invertebrates, he, of all people, has no excuse for such unmitigated evasion and obfuscation as found in that statement. First of all, why does he quote from my little pamphlet, "Have You Been Brainwashed?" rather than from my more authoritative book, *Evolution? The Fossils Say No!*, a thoroughly referenced book, including a reference to a publication by Cloud in support of the statement he seeks to refute? That the book was available to Cloud at the time is obvious, since he included a reference to it in this publication (p. 141), erroneously giving its publication date, however, as 1937. Furthermore, he resorts to ridicule in calling the pamphlet a "creationist scientist-joke cartoon-strip." The pamphlet is serious in tone throughout, and is illustrated conservatively, definitely not in cartoon style.

My reading of Cloud's publications was careful and thorough, not careless, as Cloud alleges. In *Evolution? The Fossils Say No!*, I stated:

> As recently as 1973, Preston Cloud, an evolutionary geolo-gist, expressed his conviction that there are as yet no re-cords of unequivocal Metazoa (multicellular forms of life) in undoubted Precambrian rocks.[32]

This is practically a direct quote from Cloud's paper. He is the one who has been most skeptical of reports of the discoveries of Precambrian fossils, both microscopic and macroscopic, and has exposed the erroneous nature of some of those reports. At the time of the statement quoted, he did believe that some reports of the discovery of Precambrian microorganisms were valid. Furthermore, Cloud knows that mention of Precambrian microorganisms is completely irrelevant to the mystery of the origin of the Cambrian invertebrates, but he mentions them, as is frequently done by evolutionists, in the expectation that many unsuspecting lay readers will be misled into believing that these mircoorganisms could have been direct ancestors of the Cambrian animals.

The "limited variety of multicellular animal life [that] began about 680 million years ago" that Cloud mentions is, of course, a reference to the Ediacaran Fauna, which we have discussed earlier. As Cloud knew at the time, these creatures were already highly complex at their first appearance and so would in no case provide transitional forms between single-celled microorganisms and complex invertebrates, and as later research showed, they certainly were not ancestral to the Cambrian invertebrates. Furthermore, he mentioned that it had not yet been established whether the Ediacaran Fauna was Precambrian or Cambrian. Finally, as we have stated earlier, it makes no difference whether the Cambrian invertebrates did actually all appear at the same time or whether they appeared sequentially in evolutionary reconstructions, for wherever or whenever they appeared, they were complete at the very first, and no transitional forms have ever been found. This is not only contradictory to evolutionary theory, it is also absolutely incompatible with the theory.

Glenister and Witzke, in their chapter in the anti-creationist book edited by D. B. Wilson, have a section entitled, "Precambrian fossils."[33] In that section, they state:

> Megascopic animals first appeared in the late Proterozoic Vendian (Ediacaran) period beginning about 650 million years ago, and groups of shelly fossils appeared successively in the Cambrian about 560 million years ago. Diversification of organisms from the Vendian through the Middle Ordovician was rapid, presumably because of the crossing of one or more biologic or ecologic thresholds as well as expansion into underutilized environments.

It will be noted that they smoothly glide over the monstrous gap between microscopic organisms and the Cambrian invertebrates. From reading this, unsuspecting readers would believe that there is no problem whatsoever here. By the way, when evolutionists wish to cover up a gap in the fossil record, they claim that evolution was "rapid."

The gap between single-celled, microscopic organisms and the complex invertebrates is both immense and unchallengeable. Furthermore, the search has been so thorough, intense, and of such long duration, that if the fossils exist, they would have been found by now. A great variety of highly diverse, complex invertebrates appears explosively in the fossil record. Each is fully formed at its first appearance. The time span involved supposedly stretched through hundreds of millions of years. The number of transitional forms that would have lived and died during the vast time span required for the evolution of the complex invertebrates would have been many billions times billions. If evolution is true, museums should have an immense storehouse of the fossil transitional forms. *Yet, not one has ever been found!* One of the absolute requirements of evolutionary theory is continuity—there can be no break in the sequence of living things from the origin of life up to the appearance of man. The history of life in the evolutionary view must be a continuum, yet right here at the start we have one of the most immense breaks in the history of life that one could imagine. **This break establishes beyond doubt that evolution has not occurred.** This evidence is powerful, positive, irrefutable evidence of the fact of creation. Further discussion of the fossil record is actually unnecessary. Why beat a dead horse?

The remainder of the fossil record only serves to reinforce the fact of creation as established by the abrupt appearance, without ancestors, of the complex invertebrates. In fact, there is another immense gap in the fossil record that documents, beyond a shadow of a doubt, that evolution has not taken place. This is the gap between the invertebrates and the vertebrates—a gap that is also beyond dispute. According to evolutionists, the first vertebrates were the fishes. The evolution of an invertebrate into a fish would have required a revolution in structure. Either a simple, soft-bodied creature, such as a worm or a jellyfish, or a creature with soft inner parts and either a hard shell or an exoskeleton would have evolved into a fish with hard inner parts, or skeleton, and soft outer parts. This evolution supposedly required many tens of millions of years. Again, many billions times billions of the transitional forms would have lived and died. Hundreds of thousands of fossils of these transitional forms should rest on museum shelves. **Yet not one has ever been found!**

The transition from invertebrate to vertebrate supposedly passed through a simple chordate stage. The fossil record, however, fails to provide any evidence for this. Thus Ommaney states:

> How this earliest chordate stock evolved, what stages of development it went through to eventually give rise to truly fish-like creatures, we do not know. Between the Cambrian, when it probably originated, and the Ordovician, when the first fossils of animals with really fish-like characteristics

appeared, there is a gap of perhaps 100 million years which we will probably never be able to fill.[34]

Errol White, an ichthyologist (specialist on fishes), in his presidential address to the Linnaean Society of London on lungfishes, said:

> But whatever idea authorities may have on the subject, the lungfishes, like every other major group of fishes I know, have their origins firmly based in *nothing*. . . .[35]

In his discussions concerning theories on the origin of bony fishes, Gerald Todd of U.C.L.A. states:

> All three subdivisions of the bony fishes appear in the fossil record at approximately the same time. They are already widely divergent morphologically and they are heavily armored. How did they originate? What allowed them to diverge so widely? How did they come to have heavy armor? And why is there no trace of earlier intermediate forms?[36]

Why, indeed, is there no trace of transitional forms leading up to the three widely divergent major subdivisions of bony fishes? Why, in fact, does every major type of fish, as White states, appear from nowhere?

Again, this discontinuity in the fossil record, a gap both immense in scope and beyond dispute, destroys the pseudo-scientific notion of evolution. I thoroughly searched a number of the most prominent anti-creationist books and could find no mention whatsoever concerning the origin of fishes. This was true of the earlier book edited by Godfrey,[25] her later book,[26] the book edited by Zetterberg,[30] the book by Kitcher,[27] and the book edited by D. B. Wilson.[15] Futuyma (Ref. 29, p. 74) and Eldredge (Ref. 17, p. 49) each briefly mention fishes, but neither mentions a single word about the huge gap between fishes and invertebrates nor attempts to give any explanation whatsoever as to why each major group of fishes appears fully formed at the start. These anti-creationists have enshrouded this profound discontinuity in the history of life in an enormous fog of silence. They not only make no attempt to offer

"Just-so" stories how this may have occurred, they completely ignore it. It is too embarrassing to evolutionary theory even to discuss in their anti-creation polemics.

Evolutionists have employed clever tactics in their debates with creationists, both on platforms before live audiences and in their anti-creationist publications. In public debates, they rarely respond to the creationists' challenges concerning the immense gaps between microorganisms and complex inverte-brates and between complex invertebrates and fishes, and, as mentioned above, in their publications, they either simply ignore these problems or offer stories which even they must realize lack credibility. Rather, they spend much time discuss-ing a few disputable claims concerning the existence of al-leged transitional forms. These claims most often center around *Archaeopteryx,* a bird which, many evolutionists main-tain, gives some indications of being intermediate between reptiles and birds; the so-called "mammal-like reptiles," sup-posedly showing a transition between reptiles and mammals; a few alleged intermediates between ape and man, such as *Australopithecus* and *Homo erectus;* and much less often, fossil horses.

Although the "evolution" of horses used to be one of the evolutionists' favorite examples, it is now being mentioned less and less frequently. It is rarely brought up by evolutionists in public debate, and almost fails to appear at all in the more prominent anti-creationist books. No mention of the origin of horses appears in the books by Eldredge and Kitcher, or in the books edited by Zetterberg, D. B. Wilson, or Godfrey. Fu-tuyma, on the other hand, has an extensive discussion in his book (Ref. 30, pp. 85-94). It contains numerous errors and faulty conclusions. For example, Futuyma claims that the condylarth, *Phenacodus* was a "close relative of *Hyracoth-erium*" (usually designated by evolutionists as the first horse), and that "the differences between *Phenacodus* and *Hyracoth-erium* are equivalent to those that can often be seen within species." George Gaylord Simpson, however, has stated that nowhere in the world is there any trace of a fossil that "would close the considerable gap between *Hyracotherium* and its supposed ancestral order Condylarthra."[37] Surely this "considerable gap" is greater than the differences that can often be seen within species.

Futuyma then describes a more or less smooth transition of the horses, all the way from *Hyracotherium* to the modern horse, even though he later says (p. 90) that:

> The history of horses, then, is very complex, and not at all the steady progress from *Hyracotherium* to the modern horse that is taught in introductory biology books.

Bearing in mind that when an evolutionist uses such terms as "sudden," "abrupt," or "rapid," with reference to evolutionary transitions, he is usually inferring that no transitional forms have been found, it is interesting to read the story of horse "evolution" as told by Birdsell. He says:

> The evolution of the foot mechanisms proceeded by rapid and abrupt changes rather than gradual ones. The transition from the form of foot shown by miniature *Eohippus* [*Hyracotherium*] to larger consistently three-toed *Miohippus* was so abrupt that it even left no record in the deposits . . . their foot structure changed very rapidly to a three-toed sprung foot in which the pad disappeared and the two side toes became essentially functionless. Finally, in the Pliocene the line leading to the modern one-toed grazer went through a rapid loss of the two side toes on each foot.[38]

He then goes on to say that this evolution was not gradual, but that it had proceeded by rapid jumps. One gets a very different impression about the course of things from reading this description as compared to reading Futuyma's story.

In Futuyma's Figure 17 (p. 91) we have illustrated for us what Futuyma describes as the "Evolution of the front foot in members of the horse family." He indicates here that there is an evolutionary line leading from the five-toed condylarth *Phenacodus* through *Eohippus* [*Hyracotherium*] to *Miohippus* to *Parahippus* to *Pliohippus,* and, finally, to the modern horse *Equus.* He also states, "In South America, the 'pseudo-horses,'

Diadiophorus and *Thoatherium,* underwent a parallel evolutionary change," and Figure 17 includes lines leading from *Phenacodus* to the three-toed *Diadiaphorus* to the one-toed *Thoatherium.* This is, however, totally erroneous, even if one accepts the theory of evolution. As I describe in the section on horses in *Evolution: The Challenge of the Fossil Record*[1] (p. 83), fossils of *Diadiaphorus* and *Thoatherium* appear simultaneously in Miocene rocks, not successively from three-toed to one-toed. *Diadiaphorus* has reduced side toes, while a third form, *Macrauchenia,* is a fully three-toed form. *Macrauchenia,* however, is the *last form to appear, according to the evolutionary time scale, occurring in Pliocene rocks.* The Pliocene is supposed to be the geological epoch that follows the Miocene epoch. In fact, it is believed that the one-toed *Thoatherium* became extinct before the three-toed *Macrauchenia* made its appearance. In other words, the sequence in South America was opposite to that in North America, going from a one-toed "horse" to a three-toed "horse," rather than from a three-toed horse to a one-toed horse as supposedly happened in North America. The illustration used by Futuyma (his Figure 17) indicates, however, that both sequences included a change from a three-toed horse to a one-toed horse. Apparently it would be a bit embarrassing for an evolutionist to explain why evolution converted a three-toed horse to a one-toed horse in North America, while converting a one-toed horse into a three-toed horse in South America.

In Chapter 3 the comments of Raup, Goldschmidt, and Rensberger concerning the fossil record of horses was discussed. Goldschmidt and Rensberger especially emphasized in their articles the absence of transitional forms. Finally, it must be realized that neither the sequence suggested by Futuyma nor by anyone else could constitute a phylogeny, or family tree, for the horses. These fossil horses have been discovered in various parts of the world, some widely scattered, and, even assuming the geological sequence accepted by evolutionists, these horses did not appear in the particular

sequence in which they have been arranged. It is hardly legitimate to suggest that horse B is intermediate between horses
A and C, if horse B is found only in North America, while
horses A and C are found only in Europe, or if horses B and
C were contemporary. The so-called family tree of horses has
been constructed from non-equivalent parts. That different
kinds of "horses" existed in the past that are now extinct is a
fact for all to see, but the notion that these creatures had
evolved from a common ancestor is fictional—part of the
evolutionary myth.

In most of the anti-creationist books will be found extensive sections on *Archaeopteryx,* the mammal-like reptiles, and
human origins. In the discussion above, on horses, we have
already allowed ourselves to fall into the trap of engaging
evolutionists in a debate concerning alleged transitional
forms—an exercise totally unnecessary, and part of their
smokescreen designed to cover up the complete failure to find
ancestors for the invertebrates and the vertebrates (fishes).
Therefore, rather than devoting space here to a point-by-point
refutation of the claims by evolutionists concerning these
alleged transitional forms, the reader is referred to the discussions found in the creationist books[1-3] and the non-creationist
anti-Darwinist books[4-8] referred to early in this chapter.

It might be noted here that every recent investigation of
important structures in *Archaeopteryx* has shown them to be
bird-like rather than reptile-like. Furthermore, a very recent
find of fossil birds in Texas has greatly strengthened the case
for the creationist side. Sankar Chatterjee and colleagues at
Texas Tech University have discovered the fossil remains of
two crow-sized birds near Post, Texas.[39,40] These fossils were
recovered from the Dockum Formation, allegedly 225 million
years old. Therefore, these fossil birds are supposedly 75
million years older than *Archaeopteryx.* Evolutionists would,
of course, expect that fossil birds 75 million years older than
Archaeopteryx would be considerably more reptile-like than
Archaeopteryx. Just the reverse is true, however! The fossil

bird discovered by Chatterjee (named *Protoavis,* for "ancestral bird") had, for example, a keel-like breastbone, a skull entirely like that of modern birds, and hollow bones, in addition to all of the other bird-like features possessed by *Archaeopteryx*. A date of 225 million years for this newly discovered fossil bird would place it right at the time the dinosaurs supposedly first appeared, destroying a popular notion that birds had evolved from dinosaurs. In any case, rather than getting a fossil of a creature just emerging from its supposed reptilian ancestor, evolutionists got a bird even more bird-like, if anything, than *Archaeopteryx,* supposedly 75 million years younger. So much for the ancestral status of *Archaeopteryx*!

Another very recent find that has produced results opposite to that which should be expected on the basis of evolution theory is the discovery of a fossil of *Homo habilis*. This fossil was discovered in the Olduvai Gorge in Tanzania by Donald Johanson and colleagues.[41,42] Fossils of this creature had first been described by Leakey, Tobias, and Napier.[43] Although this creature was very similar to *Australopithecus,* Leakey and his colleagues had maintained that it was sufficiently "advanced" to place it in the genus *Homo*. Today, most anthropologists reject this notion and maintain that *H. habilis* was a variety of *Australopithecus,* albeit perhaps somewhat more "advanced." Johanson's *H. habilis* (designated OH62, for Olduvai Hominid 62) is dated at 1.8 million years, thus supposedly nearly two million years younger than his *Australopithecus afarensis* ("Lucy"), dated at 3.8 million years. If OH62 is really a more advanced creature than the australopithecines and two million years younger than "Lucy" and her fellow creatures (*A. afarensis*), then OH62 should exhibit a considerable advance in man-like characteristics, as compared to "Lucy."

The OH62 creature is believed to be an adult female, barely more than three feet tall. For the first time, enough of the arm was recovered to make it possible to estimate accurately the length of the arms of these creatures. It was discovered that the arms were long and powerful, extending practically to the knees, as in apes. Furthermore, there were essentially no differences in the postcranial skeletons of "Lucy" and the OH62 *H. habilis* fossil. All of these creatures, *H. habilis* and the australopithecines, had long curved fingers and long curved toes. Now, what does a creature use long, powerful arms and long curved fingers and toes for? Only for swinging through trees, of course, surely not for walking around on the ground in the bipedal human manner! These findings certainly reinforce the conclusions of Lord Zuckerman and Charles Oxnard (both evolutionists) that the australopithecines (and *H. habilis*) *did not walk upright in the human manner, and were not intermediate between ape and man*.[44]

Just as it was the case with Chatterjee's fossil bird, so it is with OH62—evolutionists' expectations have been frustrated, and support for the contentions of creation scientists is strengthened. In spite of the supposed two million years between "Lucy" and the OH62 *Homo habilis,* there has been no change, no advance towards the human condition in the postcranial skeleton. In fact, just the opposite effect is seen, as the arms turn out to be long and powerful, or ape-like, rather than man-like. "Lucy," her fellow australopithecines, and *Homo habilis* are slipping down out of the family tree of man and will eventually be put back up into ordinary trees, along with the rest of the apes.

The track record of evolutionists, in their search for man's fossil ancestry, has been a dreary record of failures and fraud, with their bogus Piltdown Man, their pig's tooth (Nebraska Man), their orangutan (*Ramapithecus*), and their Neanderthal Man (now upgraded to full human status, *Homo sapiens*), even though it required almost a hundred years to debunk some of these. It may require another hundred years to discover sufficient material to place "Lucy" and other australopithecines in this same dismal category, but recent developments have certainly moved us in that direction. The record of evolutionists, in general, has not been significantly different. Thus, avowed evolutionist Derek Ager, British geologist and vigorous anti-creationist, states:

> It must be significant that nearly all the evolutionary stories I learned as a student, from Trueman's *Ostrea/Gryphea* to Carruther's *Raphrentis delanouei*, have now been debunked. Similarly, my own experience of more than twenty years' looking for evolutionary lineages among Mesozoic Brachiopods, has proved them equally elusive.[45]

The fossil record is powerful, positive evidence for creation, and every new discovery strengthens the case for creation and exposes additional difficulties for evolutionary theory. Evolutionary theory is, of course, dead, as long as the two huge gaps between single-celled organisms and the complex invertebrates and between complex invertebrates and fishes continue to exist. The total failure to reduce these gaps, let alone close them, in spite of an intense search by thousands of paleontologists during more than 125 years, establishes beyond doubt that the required transitional forms will never be found. The fact that the gaps between all higher taxa, such as families, orders, classes, and phyla, are systematic and almost always large, is simply additional confirmatory evidence for creation.

In closing this chapter, it might be interesting to examine how evolutionists contradict one another, and even themselves, as they attempt to escape the quagmire the fossil record presents to evolutionists. Stephen Jay Gould, in the anti-creationist article he published in 1981, states that:

> Transitional forms are generally lacking at the species level, but are abundant between large groups.[46]

This is precisely opposite to the assessment of George Gaylord Simpson, who states:

> Gaps among known species are sporadic and often small. Gaps among known orders, classes and phyla are systematic and almost always large.[47]

Two statements could hardly be more contradictory than these statements by Gould and Simpson.

Which one is nearer the truth? Gould himself provides the answer. In an article he co-authored with Niles Eldredge and published in 1977, Gould and Eldredge state:

> At the higher level of evolutionary transition between basic morphological designs, gradualism has always been in trouble, though it remains the 'official' position of most Western evolutionists. Smooth intermediates between Baupläne are almost impossible to construct, even in thought experiments: there is certainly no evidence for them in the fossil record (curious mosaics like *Archaeopteryx* do not count).[48]

They thus state that it is at the *higher* level that gradualism has *always* been in trouble. Bauplan (Baupläne is the plural) is the German word meaning basic building plan, or basic morphological design, as used by Gould and Eldredge. The last vestige of doubt concerning what they meant by "higher level" or "basic morphological design" is the example they cite—*Archaeopteryx*. Many evolutionists have claimed that *Archaeopteryx* is an intermediate form between reptiles and birds. Reptiles are classified within the class Reptilia, and birds are classified within the class Aves. The class is the highest level of classification next to phyla, the phylum being the highest level of classification. The higher levels refer to families, orders, classes, and phyla. Lower levels are species and genera. Here, Gould states that it is at the *higher level* that gradualism has always been in trouble—*not* at the *lower level* of species.

Note, further, that Gould and Eldredge admit that at this higher level one can't even imagine what a series of smooth intermediates would look like. Why not? If evolution has produced millions of species, including many thousands of different basic morphological designs, via intermediates, whereby sea urchins changed into fish, fins changed into legs, scales changed into feathers, forelimbs changed into wings, legs changed into flippers, ape-like skulls changed into human skulls, etc., why can't evolutionists imagine what the intermediates may have looked like? Perhaps Gould and Eldredge have tried. They may have attempted, for example, to imagine what viable, functional intermediates between a land animal and a whale may have looked like. Evolutionists have suggested that some hairy, four-legged mammal, perhaps something that may have resembled a pig, a cow, or a buffalo (or perhaps a carnivore of some kind) ventured into the water in search of food or sanctuary. Over eons of time, it is imagined, the tail changed into flukes, the hind legs gradually disappeared, the front legs changed into flippers, the nostrils gradually migrated to the top of the head, and the skin was replaced by a heavy coat of blubber, just to name a few of the changes required. It may be that Gould and Eldredge tried to imagine what the intermediates looked like, in going from a land animal to a whale, and discovered that such an attempt was impossible.

Gould and Eldredge further seem to specifically exclude *Archaeopteryx* as an intermediate form. It is a "strange mosaic," they say, "that doesn't count." Yet *Archaeopteryx* is most frequently cited, by evolutionists, as an example of a transitional form! It is to be noted that Gould made no mention of *Archaeopteryx* when he cited examples of alleged transitional forms in two recent publications in *Discover*.[46,49] The examples he cited were the mammal-like reptiles and alleged ape-to-man intermediates.

In any case, Gould's statement that transitional forms are lacking at the species level but are abundant between large groups (families, orders, classes, and phyla) is clearly contradicted, not only by Simpson but also by the statement he had published four years earlier. Gould apparently finds it necessary to make contradictory claims when he is seeking support for his punctuated equilibria model of evolution, as he and Eldredge were doing in their 1977 paper in *Paleobiology*,[48] in contrast to those times when he is attempting to support evolution versus creation, as he was doing in the 1981 article in *Discover*.[46] Finally, it seems clear that it is between the higher taxa, the families, orders, classes, and phyla, that transitional forms are systematically absent.

Another case, in which Gould seems to reverse himself, is in his discussion of Richard Goldschmidt's "hopeful monster" mechanism of evolution. In earlier chapters, I have discussed Goldschmidt's "hopeful monster" mechanism, whereby Goldschmidt contended that all big steps in evolution—that is, those giving rise to phyla, classes, orders, and families, and in most cases even those giving rise to genera and species—occurred all at once by means of saltations. These saltations, he believed, were caused by macromutations that drastically altered an organism's basic morphological design, or Bauplan, so that essentially an entirely new creature suddenly came into existence. In 1977, in the pages of *Natural History*, Gould published an article entitled, "The Return of Hopeful Monsters."[50] In this article, after recalling the "official rebuke and derision" poured out on Goldschmidt by his fellow evolutionists because of his "hopeful monster" mechanism, Gould says:

> I do, however, predict that during the next decade Goldschmidt will be largely vindicated in the world of evolutionary biology.

The reasons he gives include his assessment of the fossil record. For example, Gould says:

> The fossil record with its abrupt transitions offers no support for gradual change. . . . All paleontologists know that the fossil record contains precious little in the way of intermediate forms; transitions between major groups are characteristically abrupt.

Here again, Gould is stating that it is between major groups that the transitional forms are characteristically missing. This was exactly what Goldschmidt had maintained, for, as it may be recalled from an earlier chapter, it was he who said that:

> When a new phylum, class, or order appears, there follows a quick, explosive (in terms of geological time) diversification,

so that practically all orders or families known appear suddenly and without any apparent transitions.[51]

Gould also mentions another argument against gradual change and in support of Goldschmidt's notions. Gould says:

> Even though we have no direct evidence for smooth transitions, can we invent a reasonable sequence of intermediate forms, that is, viable, functioning organisms, between ancestors and descendants? Of what possible use are the imperfect incipient stages of useful structures? What good is half a jaw or half a wing?[52]

Indeed, what good is half a jaw or half a wing? There is nothing particularly astounding about that question, since creationists have been asking that question ever since Darwin. What is astounding, is that it is now such a virulent, anticreationist as Gould who is asking the question! Creationists have used such questions as this to point out the impossibility of evolution and the necessity of creation. The idea of creation, however, was as unacceptable to Goldschmidt as it is now to Gould, so Goldschmidt and Gould, since it is impossible to imagine that half a jaw or half a wing could have any function at all, must suggest that evolution proceeded directly from no jaw to a jaw, and no wings to wings.

Nowhere in his article does Gould qualify his acceptance of Goldschmidt's theory, or disavow any portion of it. If one reads Gould's paper in all innocence, one comes away with the impression that Gould heartily supports Goldschmidt's theory. Thus, after thoroughly discussing Goldschmidt's ideas and Gould's support for them in my book, *Evolution: The Fossils Say No!,* I state:

> According to Goldschmidt, and now apparently according to Gould, a reptile laid an egg from which the first bird, feathers and all, was produced. How, one may ask, were entirely new and novel structures, such as feathers, produced all at once by small variations in rates of development of entirely different structures? A feather is an amazingly complex structure, with many elements marvelously designed to function together in such a way that the

feather performs its task in an optimal fashion. Its very existence speaks of deliberate design. To believe that a feather, or an eye, or a kidney, let alone a new plant or animal, could be produced from an animal that possessed none of these by small variations in rates of development, is absolutely incredible.[53]

I went on to say apparently, according to Gould, that is what evolutionists must believe. I then quoted one of Gould's final statements, in which he said:

> Indeed, if we do not invoke discontinuous change by small alteration in rates of development, I do not see how most major evolutionary transitions can be accomplished at all. Few systems are more resistant to basic change than the strongly differentiated, highly specified, complex adults of "higher" animals groups. How could we ever convert a rhinoceros or a mosquito into something fundamentally different? Yet transitions between major groups must have occurred in the history of life.

My exposure of Gould's endorsement of Goldschmidt's ideas was apparently a bit embarrassing to Gould, so Gould vented his fury by accusing me (as well as Luther Sunderland, who also had referred to Gould's acceptance of the "hopeful monster" notions of Goldschmidt) of distorting Goldschmidt's theory by creating a caricature of his theory. Gould says:

> Goldschmidt argued, in a famous book published in 1940, that new groups can arise all at once through major mutations. He referred to these suddenly transformed creatures as "hopeful monsters." (I am attracted to some aspects of the non-caricatured version, but Goldschmidt's theory still has nothing to do with punctuated equilibrium) . . . Duane Gish writes "According to Goldschmidt, and now apparently according to Gould, a reptile laid an egg from which the first bird, feathers and all, was produced." Any evolutionist who believed such nonsense would rightly be laughed off the intellectual stage. . . .[54]

I wrote to the editor of *Discover* and asked him for permission to publish an article in *Discover,* presenting a critique of Gould's article. He refused, but did say he would publish a one-page Letter to the Editor. (Almost all science journals and quasi-science journals refuse to publish articles by scientists which question the "fact" of evolution, or which suggest the credibility of creation, then these same evolutionists turn around and criticize creation scientists for not publishing their articles in standard journals!) In my letter to the Editor, along with other comments, I wrote:

> Finally, Gould assails Sunderland and me for linking him to a hopeful monster mechanism whereby a reptile laid an egg and a bird was hatched. He says an evolutionist who believed such nonsense would rightly be laughed off the intellectual stage. Let's see, then, what Goldschmidt really did say. In *The Material Basis of Evolution*, Goldschmidt says, "I need only quote Schindewolfe (1936), the most progressive investigator known to me. He shows by examples from fossil material that the major evolutionary advances must have taken place in single large steps. . . . He shows that the many missing links in the paleontological record are sought for in vain because they have never existed: 'The first bird hatched from a reptilian egg.'" By Gould's own testimony, then, Goldschmidt, Gould's hero of the next decade, should be laughed off the intellectual stage.[55]

Gould felt constrained to reply, via his own Letter to the Editor.[56] In this letter, Gould accused me of displaying:

> . . . that charming mixture of selective misquotation and plain old-fashioned ignorance for which he, as intellectual leader of the creationist movement, is so widely and justly acclaimed.

Let me hasten to say, regardless of what attributes this virulent anti-creationist wishes to hang on me, I am not the "intellectual leader of the creationist movement." The creationist movement has many outstanding scientists in its leadership, both here in the United States and in many countries around the world.

Gould goes on to say:

In his most egregious misinterpretation, Gish continues what must be a willful caricature of Goldschmidt's "hopeful monster" concept. He has consistently interpreted Goldschmidt's idea—that new groups of organisms arise perfectly and fully formed in a single grand evolutionary burp—as a blind flailing born of despair. Gish writes that Goldschmidt termed his mechanism the "hopeful monster" mechanism and proposed, for instance, that at one time "a reptile laid an egg from which the first bird, feathers and all, was produced." I called Gish on this caricature by stating that any evolutionist believing such nonsense would be "laughed off the intellectual stage." Gish retorts by selectively quoting Goldschmidt's metaphor (well known to me since I wrote the introduction for the Yale University Press's reissue of Goldschmidt's work). Let us examine what Gish leaves out:

> Goldschmidt's hypothesis (which I accept only in part, by the way) was an interesting attempt to explain how small genetic changes might produce large effects on adult morphology by altering rates of development early in embryology with cascading effects thereafter. Goldschmidt never held, as Gish claims, that a fundamentally new type of organism could appear at once in perfected form, but only that certain key features might arise abruptly as a result of these small embryonic shifts with accumulating consequences through growth. He repeatedly argued that many subsequent adaptations must be built around this key feature to produce a new basic form. He used the reptilian egg metaphor to make the point that the transitional creature (basically still a reptile with a new key feature characteristic of birds) would, in our taxonomic schemes, be called the first bird.

Gould thus, in accusing me of "selective misquotation" and "egregious misinterpretation," and by labelling Goldschmidt's statement that "the first bird hatched from a reptilian egg" as nothing more than a metaphor, is rapidly backpedalling from his 1977 endorsement of Goldschmidt's "hopeful monster" mechanism. My quotation from

Goldschmidt's book was selective, of course—all quotations are selective—but it certainly was not a misquotation. I quoted Goldschmidt in a precisely correct fashion. But is my description of Goldschmidt's theory either a misinterpretation or nothing more than a caricature? Did not Goldschmidt say that when a new phylum, class, or order appears, there follows a quick, explosive (in geological time) diversification, so that practically all orders or families known appear suddenly and *without any apparent transitions*? Did Goldschmidt not say that the major evolutionary advances must have taken place in *single large steps*? Did he not say that the many missing links in the paleontological record are sought for in vain because *they have never existed*? Did he not really say *that the first bird hatched from a reptilian egg*? Did not Goldschmidt, himself, term his theory the "hopeful monster" theory? If Goldschmidt didn't really mean what I said he did, then what *did* he mean?

An absolutely clear answer to that question comes from Gould's fellow evolutionists. The fervent anti-creationist Futuyma, speaking of Goldschmidt, says:

> He pushed his conclusion to extremes, and theorized that each major taxonomic group had arisen as a macro-mutation, a 'hopeful monster,' that in one jump had passed from worm to crustacean, or reptile to bird.[57]

No mention here of a "metaphor"! Eldredge, a close collaborator with Gould in their punctuated equilibria theorizing, states:

> Schindewolfe interpreted the gaps in the fossil record as evidence of the sudden appearance of new groups of animals and plants. Not a creationist, Schindewolfe believed all forms of life to be interrelated, but felt that the fossil record implied a *saltational* mode—literally, sudden jumps from one basic type (called a *Bauplan,* or fundamental architectural design—conceptually if tangentially related to creationists' 'basic kinds').[58]

The views of Goldschmidt and Schindewolfe on evolution were essentially identical, sharing precisely the same views concerning the saltational, or "hopeful monster" mechanism.

Steven Stanley, who shares the punctuated equilibria view of evolution with Gould and Eldredge, writes:

> Goldschmidt's most controversial construct was the "hopeful monster," the single animal supposed to constitute a new genus or family at birth. Otto Schindewolf, a German paleontologist, was driven to similar views by the anti-gradualistic evidence of the fossil record. As I have already noted, Schindewolfe envisioned the first bird hatching fully formed from a reptile egg![59]

John R. G. Turner, professor of genetics at Leeds University, states:

> The biggest mistake that any punctuationist could make would be to assume, as Goldschmidt did, that this "hopeful monster," if that is what one wants to call it, would be perfect to the point of undergoing no further modification. Goldschmidt did his better ideas a disservice by attaching them so firmly to this perverse view.[60]

Gould insisted that:

> Goldschmidt never held, as Gish claims, that a fundamentally new type of organism could appear at once in perfected form. . . .

Gould's fellow evolutionist, Turner, stated that Goldschmidt assumed that his "hopeful monster" would be *perfect* to the point of undergoing no further modification. Stanley, another fellow evolutionist, says that Schindewolfe, who shared similar views with Goldschmidt, envisioned the first bird hatching *fully formed* from a reptile egg. Eldredge writes that Schindewolfe believed the fossil record implied sudden jumps from one basic type, and equated this with the creationists' basic kinds (conceptually, if tangentially!). Futuyma says that Goldschmidt believed each major taxonomic group had arisen as a macromutation, a "hopeful monster," that had in *one step* passed from worm to crustacean, from reptile to bird.

Now, who has failed to tell the truth in this matter? Who is guilty of misinterpretation? Who has created a caricature of Goldschmidt's "hopeful monster" theory of evolution? Who has displayed "old-fashioned ignorance"? Unless Turner, Eldredge, Futuyma, and Stanley have likewise created a caricature of Goldschmidt's views due to their misinterpretation of his theory, then Gould is the guilty one—he is guilty of all the accusations he hurled at me. In the closing paragraph of Gould's letter,[56] he states:

> I repeat: any scientist accepting Gish's ridiculous caricature of Goldschmidt would rightly be laughed off the intellectual stage. They could then join Mr. Gish in the pits.

If the interpretations of Gish, Turner, Futuyma, Stanley, and Eldredge are correct, Mr. Gould should retrieve Gish from the pits!

In June 1979, an interesting article on the radical, largely Marxist, politico-scientist group, called Science for the People (SftP) appeared in *Bioscience*.[61] Gould, a Marxist, is one of the more prominent members of the group (along with microbiologist Jonathan Beckwith, biologist Richard Levins, and geneticist Richard Lewontin, all Marxists, and professors at Harvard University, as is Gould). According to the article, the opponents of SftP see it "as a danger to the freedom of inquiry and objectivity for which academic science prides itself." Referring to E. O. Wilson, a Harvard professor who, although a humanistic evolutionist, finds his views on sociobiology bitterly opposed by Marxists, the author says:

> When the issues are brought close to home, the rhetoric against SftP gets heated. Wilson, for example, has accused his colleague Stephen Gould, an outspoken critic of sociobiology, of "destroying the whole countryside to kill a few guerillas. . . . He's willing to denigrate his own field of evolutionary biology in order to downgrade the enemy, human sociobiology, which is a small but important branch of evolutionary biology. When Darwin conflicts with Marx, Darwin goes."

Wilson here is accusing Gould of what many scientists consider sacrilegious: to sacrifice Darwin, a symbol of scientific knowledge, at the altar of Marx, who symbolizes pure politics.

If, as Wilson claims, Gould is willing to destroy the whole countryside "to kill a few guerillas," to denigrate even his own cherished field of evolutionary biology, and to sacrifice his precious Darwin at the altar of Marx, woe be unto scientific creationists, for they would be especially bitterly despised by Gould and his fellow Marxists.

The God of creation was anathema to Marx, Engels, and Lenin. Furthermore, if Science for the People is seen "as a danger to the freedom of inquiry and objectivity" by ordinary evolutionary scientists, surely creation scientists should not expect Gould and his fellow Marxists, who now occupy so many key professorships and leading positions in scientific and academic establishments, to display the slightest degree of freedom of inquiry and scientific objectivity towards creationists.

References

1. D. T. Gish, *Evolution: Challenge of the Fossil Record,* Creation-Life Publishers, El Cajon, California, 92022, 1985.

2. J. K. Anderson and H. G. Coffin, *Fossils in Focus,* Zondervan Publishing House, Grand Rapids, Michigan, 1977.

3. Wilbert Rusch, *The Argument: Creation versus Evolution,* Creation Research Society Books, 5093 Williamsport Drive, Norcross, GA.

4. Michael Denton, *Evolution: A Theory in Crisis,* Burnett Books, London, 1985 (available from Woodbine House, 5615 Fishers Lane, Rockville, MD 20852).

5. W. R. Fix, *The Bone Peddlers - Selling Evolution,* Macmillan Pub. Co., New York, 1984.

6. Francis Hitching, *The Neck of the Giraffe,* Ticknor and Fields, New Haven, CT, 1982.

7. Jeremy Rifkin, *Algeny,* The Viking Press, New York, 1983.

8. Fred Hoyle and Chandra Wickramasinghe, *Evolution from Space,* J. M. Dent and Sons, London, 1981.

9. Mark Ridley, *New Scientist* 90:830 (1981).

10. N. E. Newell, *Proceedings of the American Philosophical Society,* April 1959, p. 267.

11. D. M. Raup, *Field Museum Natural History Bulletin* 50:22 (1979).

12. T. N. George, *Science Progress* 48:1 (1960).

13. P.-P. Grassé, *Evolution of Living Organisms,* Academic Press, New York, 1977, p. 4.

14. Gavin de Beer, *Science* 143:1311 (1964).

15. B. F. Glenister and B. J. Witzke, in *Did the Devil Make Darwin Do It?*, D. B. Wilson, Ed., Iowa State University Press, Ames, 1983, p. 58.

16. S. J. Gould, *Natural History* 93:14 (1984).

17. Niles Eldredge, *The Monkey Business,* Washington Square Press, New York, 1982.

18. Niles Eldredge, *ibid.,* p. 44.

19. Niles Eldredge, *ibid.,* p. 47.

20. G. G. Simpson, *The Meaning of Evolution,* Yale University Press, New Haven, 1949, p. 18.

21. Niles Eldredge, Ref. 17, p. 130.

22. B. Runnegar, *J. Paleont.,* 55:1138 (1981).

23. M. R. House, Ed., *The Origin of Major Invertebrate Groups,* Systematics Assoc. Special Vol. 12, Academic Press, New York, 1979.

24. N. Eldredge, Ref. 17, p. 46.

25. L. R. Godfrey in *Scientists Confront Creationism,* L. R. Godfrey, Ed., W. W. Norton & Co., New York, 1983, p. 198.

26. J. W. Valentine, "The Evolution of Complex Animals," in *What Darwin Began,* L. R. Godfrey, Ed., Allyn and Bacon, Inc., Boston, 1985, p. 263.

27. Philip Kitcher, *Abusing Science,* The MIT Press, Cambridge, Massasachusetts, 1982.

28. D. T. Gish, *Evolution? The Fossils Say No!* Creation-Life Pub., San Diego, California, 1979.

29. D. J. Futuyma, *Science on Trial,* Pantheon Books, New York, 1983, p. 72.

30. Fred Edwords, in *Evolution versus Creationism: The Public Education Controversy,* J. P. Zetterberg, Ed., Oryx Press, Phoenix, 1983, pp. 361-385.

31. Preston Cloud, in Ref. 30, p. 145.

32. D. T. Gish, *Evolution? The Fossils Say No!,* Public School Edition, Creation-Life Pub., San Diego, 1978, p. 63.

33. B. F. Glenister and B. J. Witzke, Ref. 15, p. 80.

34. F. D. Ommaney, *The Fishes,* Life Nature Library, Time-Life, Inc., New York, 1964, p. 60.

35. Errol White, *Proceedings of the Linnaean Society,* London 177:8 (1966).

36. G. T. Todd, *American Zoologist* 20(4):757 (1980).

37. G. G. Simpson, *Tempo and Mode in Evolution,* Columbia University Press, New York, 1944, p. 105.

38. J. B. Birdsell, *Human Evolution,* Rand McNally College Pub. Co., 1975, p. 169.

39. S. Weisburd, *Science News,* August 16, 1986, p. 103.

40. T. Beardsley, *Nature* 322:677 (1986).

41. Roger Lewin, *Science* 236:1061 (1987).

42. Donald Johanson (and nine co-authors), *Nature* 327:205 (1987).

43. L. S. B. Leakey, P. V. Tobias, and J. R. Napier, *Nature* 202:7 (1964).

44. See D. T. Gish, Ref. 1, pp. 144-180, for a discussion of *Australopithecus* and *Homo habilis.*

45. D. V. Ager, *Proceedings of the Geological Association* 87:132 (1976).

46. S. J. Gould, *Discover,* May 1981, p. 37.

47. G. G. Simpson, in *Evolution of Life,* Sol Tax, Ed., University of Chicago Press, Chicago, 1960, p. 149.

48. S. J. Gould and Niles Eldredge, *Paleobiology* 3:147 (1977).

49. S. J. Gould, *Discover,* January 1987, p. 64.

50. S. J. Gould, *Natural History* 86:22 (1977).

51. R. B. Goldschmidt, *American Scientist* 40:97 (1952).

52. S. J. Gould, Ref. 50.

53. D. T. Gish, Ref. 32, pp. 161, 162; Ref. 28, p. 174.

54. S. J. Gould, Ref. 46.

55. D. T. Gish, *Discover,* July 1981, p. 6.

56. S. J. Gould, *Discover,* October 1981, p. 10.

57. D. J. Futuyma, Ref. 29, p. 65.

58. Niles Eldredge, Ref. 17, p. 66.

59. S. M. Stanley, *The New Evolutionary Timetable,* Basic Books, Inc., New York, 1981, p. 135.

60. J. R. G. Turner, in *Dimensions of Darwinism,* Marjorie Grene, Ed., Cambridge University Press, Cambridge, Eng., 1983, p. 158.

61. R. M. Henig, *Bioscience* 29(6):341 (1979).

6

Attack and Counterattack: The Science of Thermodynamics

The science of thermodynamics is critical to the question of origins and has thus been one of the main battlegrounds where the intellectual war between creation scientists and evolutionists has been waged. Creation scientists maintain that the science of thermodynamics, more particularly, the Second Law of Thermodynamics (henceforth referred to as the Second Law) is the Achilles heel of all naturalistic, mechanistic evolutionary theories on origins. Although there are no absolute proofs in science, the proper understanding of the science of thermodynamics and the theory of evolution from the origin of the universe through the origin of life to the origin of man comes as close as is possible to providing proof that the theory of evolution is scientifically untenable. All evolutionists believe otherwise, of course—they have no choice. They accept as an article of faith that evolution is true. As evolutionist Robert Shapiro has said, relative to the origin of life, evolutionists believe that some principle exists that moved matter across the gap between the non-living and the living. "The existence of the principle," Shapiro says, "is taken for granted in the philosophy of dialectical materialism . . . it is accepted as an article of faith."[1] Evolutionists would not dare to question the validity of the Second Law—one of the most well-established natural laws in science. Thus they reason: Evolution is a fact; the Second Law is a fact; obviously there is no contradiction between the Second Law and evolution.

The First Law of Thermodynamics is the law of the conservation of energy (or mass/energy, since energy and mass are equivalent). This law states that the total quantity of energy in the universe is a constant. Energy may be transformed from one form into another and energy may be transformed into matter and matter into energy, but the total quantity remains constant—energy can be neither created nor destroyed. The Second Law has to do with the quality or usability of that energy—its availability to do work. The law is of such general application that it can be defined, or its applicability described, in several ways. This natural law first came to be recognized during a study of the energy consumed and the work produced by heat engines. It was noted that, without exception, as energy is utilized to perform work, some of the energy becomes unavailable to perform further work. In other words, energy can never be 100 percent converted into work. This application is referred to as classical thermodynamics. It was later discovered that the Second Law could be applied to problems relative to the energy required to construct and maintain complex systems. This is generally referred to as statistical thermodynamics and is related to the tendency of all organized complex systems to become more random, more disorderly. It is easy to see why this is so. The construction and maintenance of complex systems (by systems is meant anything from molecules to machines to galaxies) requires the expenditure of energy, and as this energy is consumed to perform work, some of the energy becomes unavailable to perform further work—thus the system tends to run down and deteriorate. Finally, it has been discovered that the Second Law also applies to the transmission and storage of information—there is always a tendency for information to become lost or garbled. Again, this is easy to understand, for the transmission and the maintenance of information requires the expenditure of energy—work must be performed. This application is called informational thermodynamics.

In our discussion here, we will be most concerned with statistical and informational thermodynamics because the origin of the universe, the origin of life, and the evolution of a single-celled organism into man would have required an enormous increase in complexity, organization, and information content, and, certainly, biological evolution would require the transmission and storage of information and a net increase in information content.

Let us consider, first of all, what is postulated to have taken place during the evolutionary process from the cosmic egg to the human brain. According to one of the current notions on the origin of the universe, the so-called Big Bang theory, some billions of years ago all of the energy and matter in the universe was crammed together in a huge cosmic egg. The size, temperature, and density of this primeval cosmic egg varies according to who is telling the story, but its temperature and density were enormous, while its radius has been estimated to be from no more than that of an electron up to some fraction of a light-year.[2] The cosmic egg was so hot that no elements could exist—the egg consisted of subatomic particles and radiation.

Nobody knows where the cosmic egg came from or how it got there—it is simply assumed it was there (someone suggested perhaps the Cosmic Chicken laid the cosmic egg). No one knows how long it sat there, but, as the story goes, the cosmic egg exploded (nobody knows why), and as the expanding primeval fireball expanded, it cooled sufficiently that hydrogen gas and helium gas (minor in amount relative to hydrogen) could form. These gases expanded out into the vast stretches of the nascent universe until a very low temperature and a very low pressure were reached. At that time only hydrogen (the lightest element in the universe with an atomic weight of about one) and helium (with an atomic weight of about four, the next lightest element) existed. There were no carbon, oxygen, sulfur, nitrogen, copper, lead, iron, uranium, or any other elements except hydrogen and helium. All that existed consisted of hydrogen, helium, and residual radiation—in fact, it might be said, hydrogen gas was the universe.

From these highly dispersed hydrogen and helium gases at a very low temperature (100° Kelvin or less, or about -173° centigrade), somehow, evolutionists believe, stars and galaxies created themselves, our solar system created itself, life created itself, and from that first primordial form of life all other forms of life evolved, including man, with his three-pound human brain containing about 12 billion brain cells with about 120 trillion connections. Thus, so the story says, we have gone from hydrogen gas to people. It was George Mulfinger who reminded us that if this is true, then we could say that hydrogen is an odorless, tasteless, invisible gas which, if given enough time, becomes people!

A number of problems with this scenario immediately are apparent. The initial cosmic egg was in a homogeneous state of mass/energy in thermal equilibrium which somehow converted itself into a heterogeneous state of mass/energy not at thermal equilibrium, a very unlikely event.[3] As Gregory and Thompson have stated:

> Can the path from homogeneity to the rich assortment of present day structures be traced? . . . The more conventional model assumes that individual galaxies arose out of nearly homogeneous primordial soup. The main trouble with this model is explaining how the universe proceeded from its

smooth state to the state in which matter was gathered into galaxies.[4]

An article entitled "Why Is the Cosmos Lumpy?" was published by Ben Patrusky in the Mysteries Section of *Science 81*. In that article, Patrusky says:

> Few cosmologists today would dispute the view that our expanding universe began with a bang—a big, hot bang—about 18 billion years ago. Paradoxically, no cosmologist could now tell you how the Big Bang—the explosion of a superhot, superdense atom—ultimately gave rise to galaxies, stars, and other cosmic lumps.
>
> As one sky scientist, IBM's Philip E. Seiden put it: "The standard Big Bang model does not give rise to lumpiness. That model assumes the universe started out as a globally smooth, homogeneous expanding gas. If you apply the laws of physics to this model, you get a universe that is uniform, a cosmic vastness of evenly distributed atoms with no organization of any kind." No galaxies, no stars, no planets, no nothing. Needless to say, the night sky, dazzling in its lumps, clumps, and clusters, says otherwise.[5]

Sir Fred Hoyle, famous British astronomer, has lost all patience with the Big Bang theory. Speaking of this idea, Hoyle says:

> But the interesting quark transformations are almost immediately over and done with, to be followed by a little rather simple nuclear physics, to be followed by what? By a dull-as-ditchwater expansion which degrades itself adiabatically until it is incapable of doing anything at all. The notion that galaxies form, to be followed by an active astronomical history, is an illusion. Nothing forms, the thing is as dead as a door-nail.[6]

Another problem that is immediately apparent is the origin of the cosmic egg. Why should it have been there at all? The First Law tells us that the total quantity of energy in the universe is a constant. If one holds to the belief that these natural laws are all there is and all there ever has been, then it must be accepted that the cosmic egg could not have come into being from nothing. If even a single atom cannot come into being from nothing, surely the matter and energy equivalent to that presently existing in the universe could not have come into being from nothing. Where did all this mass/energy come from? How long did it sit there before it exploded? What caused it to explode? But why worry about these little problems while playing games? And all of this is just a game. George Abell tells us, "We are playing games—cosmology is the best sport of all, because it is the ultimate game."[7] There is a multitude of other problems with the Big Bang theory and with its erstwhile variant, the Inflationary Universe theory, not the least of which are the contradictions between these theories and the Second Law.

In order to see clearly the contradictions to evolutionary theory imposed by the science of thermodynamics, the nature of the supposed evolutionary process needs to be emphasized. Gamov put it this way:

> We may also assume in the distant past our universe was considerably less differentiated and complex than it is now and that the state of matter at that time could be accurately described by the classical concept of "primordial chaos" . . . the problem of scientific cosmogony can be formulated as an attempt to reconstruct the evolutionary process which led from simplicity of the early days of creation to the present immense complexity of the universe around us.[8]

Similarly, Victor Weisskopf informs us:

> This evolutionary history of the world, from the "big bang" to the present universe, is a series of gradual steps from the simple to the complicated, from the unordered to the organized, from the formless gas of elementary particles to the morphic atoms and molecules, and further to the still more structured liquids and solids, and finally to the sophisticated living organisms.[9]

Julian Huxley, one of the chief architects of the neo-Darwinian mechanism of evolution, tells us:

> Evolution in the extended sense can be defined as a directional and essentially irreversible process occurring in

time, which in its course gives rise to an increase of variety and an increasingly high level of organization in its products. Our present knowledge indeed forces us to the view that the whole of reality is evolution—a single process of self transformation.[10]

Thus, it is seen that evolutionary theory requires an enormous increase in complexity, organization, and information (the amount of information required to describe or define a homogeneous universe of hydrogen and helium gases is vastly less than that required to describe a universe containing 100 billion galaxies, each containing 100 billion stars, a complex solar system, including millions of incredibly complex living organisms here on planet earth, or that required to describe even a single bacterium).

As Huxley describes, evolution is a process of self transformation—no outside agency of any kind was required or involved. God, by definition, is excluded from the process. Notice further, as all evolutionists believe, the process was directional, giving rise to an increase in variety and an increasingly high level of organization in its products. Chaos generated the cosmos, disorder was transformed into order, the complex arose from the simple. Notice further that everything is included—the whole of reality—stars, galaxies, the solar system, the beginnings of life, all plants, animals, and man, including our consciousness, our ability to remember the past, cope with the present, and plan for the future—even our faith in God—is nothing more than the product of an evolutionary process. The process is totally naturalistic and mechanistic, due solely to properties inherent in matter.

If all of this has really happened, then there must exist a universal, natural tendency of matter to transform itself from disorder to order, from simple to complex. This tendency must be all pervasive, all unfailing, if hydrogen gas has transformed itself into people via a multitude of other elements which must possess this same property. This led Hoyle to assert:

If there were some deep principle that drove organic systems toward living systems, the operation of the principle
should easily be demonstrable in a test tube in half a
morning.[11]

On the basis of creation, predictions concerning the inherent tendency of matter would be just the opposite of that
predicted on the basis of evolutionary theory. If an omniscient,
omnipotent Creator (the least we could say is that He was
certainly adequate for the job) created the universe and all it
contains, the universe would have started out in a state of
perfection. Thus, matter would have no natural tendency to
promote itself to higher and higher levels of order and complexity. If, however, something has happened since creation
to change the original created state (and obviously it has), the
only effect possible would be to cause matter to change in
such a way that it would now have an intrinsic tendency to
become less ordered and less complex. Thus, on the basis of
evolutionary theory, the prediction is for matter to possess an
all-pervasive tendency to increase in order and complexity.
On the basis of creation, on the other hand, it would be
predicted that matter would have a universal tendency to
degenerate, to decay, to become more random, less complex.

Now let us go out into the real world and take a look—let's
see what's really going on out there. After all, science is
nothing more than common experience. From common experience, or by the most sophisticated efforts scientists can arrange, it is apparent, first of all, that matter does not have an
inherent tendency or intrinsic ability to transform itself from
disorder to order, from simple to complex. No scientist has
ever detected such a property of matter—it is not known in
science. No natural law that describes such a tendency of
matter exists. There is, however, a natural law which describes just the opposite tendency—the Second Law of Thermodynamics. R. B. Lindsay, a physicist at Brown University,
tells us:

There is a general natural tendency of all observed systems to go from order to disorder, reflecting dissipation of energy available for future transformation—the law of increasing entropy.[12]

Harold Blum, a biologist and professor at the State University of New York, Albany, has authored a book titled *Time's Arrow and Evolution,*[13] comments from which will be discussed later. While believing, as an evolutionist, that the direction of evolution has been upward, he acknowledges that Time's Arrow—the Second Law—always points downward. Thus he says:

All real processes go with an increase of entropy. The entropy also measures the randomness, or lack of orderliness of the system; the greater the randomness, the greater the entropy.[14]

A thermodynamicist would define entropy as a function of several variables in a form that can be used to calculate the quantity of this property called entropy. Thus, in one formulation:

$$G = H\text{-}TS$$

where G is the Gibbs free energy, H is enthalpy, T is the temperature in degrees Kelvin, and S is the entropy. A layman could examine several such formulas without understanding the importance of this property called entropy relative to the question of origins, or have a feel for what entropy really is. Its importance is readily apparent, however, when the statements of Lindsay and Blum are examined. From these statements, we can see that in statistical thermodynamic terms, entropy is a measure of the disorderliness or randomness of a system—the greater the randomness, the greater the entropy. As things run down, deteriorate, and decay, their entropy increases. As a system becomes more highly organized and complex, its entropy decreases. Blum states that in all real processes (irreversible processes, those processes that occur spontaneously and naturally without any outside help), the entropy, or randomness always increases. There are no exceptions—this is a natural law—the Second Law of Thermodynamics.

Isaac Asimov, as has been previously indicated, is an avid anti-creationist and is thus convinced that there can be no contradiction between the Second Law and evolution. He has described the present situation of the universe in terms of the Second Law in a way that can easily be understood by the layman. He says,

Another way of stating the second law then is: "The universe is constantly getting more disorderly." Viewed that way we can see the second law all about us. We have to work hard to straighten a room, but left to itself, it becomes a mess again very quickly and very easily. Even if we never enter it, it becomes dusty and musty. How difficult to maintain houses, and machinery, and our own bodies in perfect working order; how easy to let them deteriorate. In fact, all we have to do is nothing, and everything deteriorates, collapses, breaks down, wears out—all by itself—and that is what the second law is all about.[15]

If that is what the Second Law is all about, it does indeed appear that evolutionary theory is in trouble. Everything in the universe, at every level, has a tendency to run down, to deteriorate, to decay—there are no exceptions (it is even being suggested today by some physicists that protons decay). If, however, some billions of years ago, all that existed in the universe were highly dispersed and homogeneous hydrogen and helium gases, and one of the laws that governed these elements—the Second Law—is a universal law of deterioration—an all pervasive, never-failing law that causes matter to inevitably become more random, less complex—how could these simple gases have transformed themselves into higher and higher levels of organization—into stars, galaxies, and eventually into people?

The Second Law always applies, without exception, to isolated systems. An isolated system is a system which exchanges neither energy nor matter with its surroundings—it is truly isolated. Evolutionists believe the universe is an isolated system—nobody on the outside did any work on the system; no energy or matter entered the system from the outside. The Second Law tells us that an isolated system can never increase in order, complexity, organization, or information content. An isolated system, according to the Second Law, will inevitably, with time, become more random, more disorderly, less complex, less organized. Contrary to the Second Law, evolutionists believe that the universe began with the chaos of the big bang, soon generating a homogeneous mixture of hydrogen and helium gases, and this sytem then transformed itself from the simplicity of hydrogen and helium gases into the incredibly complex universe we have today, including the human brain with its 120 trillion connections, the most complex arrangement of matter in the universe. This is a clear violation of the Second Law. Creation scientists reject this notion as unscientific and irrational, and point out that since the universe could not have created itself naturally, it had to be created supernaturally. It thus cannot be an isolated system. There must exist a Creator, external to and independent of the natural universe, who was responsible for the introduction of the organization, complexity, and information content of the universe.

The importance of accounting for the origin of information cannot be overemphasized. Evolutionists believe that order and complexity come out of chaos, that nonsense generates sense, that information has spontaneously arisen *within* systems with no help from the outside. Our human observations and experiences tell us, however, that this never happens. The ink and paper, the typewriter, the type-setting machine, the printing press—none of these—were responsible for the information content within this book. All of the information within this book was introduced from the outside. The ink (or carbon) and paper, the typewriter, the type-setting machine, the printing press were all necessary for the *transmission* of the information, but not for the *generation* of that information.

As noted earlier, information is not generated spontaneously. Rather, there is a universal, natural tendency for information to be lost or garbled as it is transmitted (witness the typographical errors in this book). Professor A. E. Wilder-Smith, a creation scientist holding three earned doctorates from European universities, has emphasized this vital point in all of his writings.[16]

Evolutionists, realizing the extremely damaging effect that the evidence against evolution based on the Second Law has had on their precious theory, have counterattacked vigorously, and in some instances, viciously, against creation scientists and their arguments based on the Second Law. They portray creation scientists as confused, ignorant, incompetent, and at the worst, downright dishonest in their use of Second-Law arguments against evolution. As will be seen, however, creation scientists are not confused, ignorant, incompetent, or dishonest in their treatment of these data. On the other hand, in most instances, arguments advanced by evolutionists have been extremely simplistic, irrelevant, and totally unconvincing. In the most important details, evolutionists have skirted the real issues, and have often attempted to avoid the evidence advanced by creation scientists through vicious personal attacks, which demonstrate that they realize their arguments are weak or non-existent.

Almost without exception, evolutionists advance the "open-system" argument against the contradiction the Second Law generates versus evolutionary theory. With reference to the Second Law arguments of creation scientists, evolutionist Warren Dolphin asserts:

> What they completely overlook, of course, is that in biological systems order can be created from disorder at the expense of energy input from an external source, the sun. Their arguments are spurious at best and are based on a misleading simplistic approach to a complex, quantitative scientific concept. In brief, they have created a clever word game by introducing thermodynamics into their arguments.[17]

Chris McGowan says:

We must emphasize that the laws of thermodynamics apply *only to closed systems,* and are concerned with the behavior of molecules.

What you may well ask, has all this got to do with the appearance of new organisms on the earth? Absolutely nothing! The origin of life, and the evolution of progressively more complex organisms, took place on the earth's surface, and this cannot possibly be described as operating in a closed system. Energy is free to flow in and out of the system, and the laws of thermodynamics are therefore absolutely irrelevant.[18]

Asimov says:

To lift the argument a notch above the kindergarten level, the second law of thermodynamics applies to a "closed system"—that is, to a system that does not gain energy from without, or lose energy to the outside. The only truly closed system we know of is the universe as a whole. . . . Evolution can proceed and build up the complex from the simple, thus moving uphill, without violating the second law, as long as another interlocking part of the system—the sun, which delivers energy to the earth continually—moves downhill (as it does) at a much faster rate than evolution moves uphill.[19]

Alice Kehoe declares that:

Most evolutionists simply dismiss the Second Law of Thermodynamics as irrelevant to the central questions of their field because it deals with closed systems and does not preclude local build-ups of more highly organized energy in open systems. . . .[20]

And so it goes, on and on. Evolutionists believe that just throwing out the terms "open systems" and "closed systems" demolishes the arguments against evolution by creation scientists. They even attempt to propagate the nonsense that creation scientists do not take into account the matter of open and closed systems and are even completely ignorant of the matter of considering differences between open and closed systems. This is what Warren Dolphin was arguing when, as noted above, he began his statement on the Second Law with "What they [creation scientists] completely overlook. . . ."

First, it must be pointed out that the Second Law *does* apply to *all* systems, open or closed. Every system, whether open or closed, *tends* to deteriorate, to become less orderly, more random—all open systems eventually reach a state of maximum disorder, or entropy. Living organisms are exceedingly complex, they are all open systems free to take in energy—but they all die and decay. Evolutionists maintain that for evolutionary processes to succeed, to proceed from disorder to order, from simple to complex; from molecules to man, all that is needed is for the system to be an open system and the existence of an adequate flow of energy into the system from the outside. Creation scientists maintain that these *are necessary* conditions but *not sufficient* conditions for the evolutionary process to avoid the consequences of the Second Law. Furthermore, when the literature of evolutionists who consider, in depth, the relationship of evolution and the Second Law is carefully searched, it is discovered that *they agree with creation scientists that more is required than simply having an open system and a flow-through of energy.* This is true, as will be seen, in the case of John Patterson, a virilent anti-creationist who accuses creation scientists of gross errors, incompetence, and dishonesty in their case against evolution based on the Second Law. Ultimately, the disagreement rests on whether the additional conditions required are available to the evolutionary process anywhere in the earth-sun system.

Before we proceed further, it must be emphasized that the discussion of open and closed systems and what else, if anything, is required for evolution to proceed other than an open system and a flow-through of energy, is completely irrelevant concerning the origin of the universe. Creation scientists and evolutionists all agree that, as far as natural processes are concerned, the universe is an isolated system—no energy is flowing into the natural universe from the outside now, and certainly evolutionists believe the universe has always been an isolated system during its entire history, from the beginning of its origin to the present day. Therefore, there is absolutely no doubt that the Second Law applies to the origin of the universe. There is no doubt that the Second Law applies to all isolated systems, without exception. There is no doubt that the Second Law tells us that such a system goes in one direction, and one direction only—down. All such systems constantly become less orderly, more random, less complex. They *never* become more complex, more organized. This is ultimate proof that the universe could not have created itself. If evolutionists really believe in the laws of science, they would abandon their religious faith in evolution. They persist in believing that the universe began in the chaos of the big bang and transformed itself from the simplicity of hydrogen gas to higher and higher levels of organization until the present highly complex universe was produced—a clear violation of the Second Law.

Some evolutionists frankly admit the failure of science to solve the fundamental problem of the origin of the universe. Evolutionist Hugo Franzen, in his chapter, "Thermodynamics: The Red Herring," says:

> The scientist does not consider it a failing that science does not at all explain the origin of the universe or completely explain the origin of life. . . . While there is a problem at some point of reconciling the apparent degradation of useful energy (that is, increase in entropy) with the constant energy content of the universe if the process is followed backward in time, it requires a leap of faith to conclude that this problem is solved only by accepting a supernatural event.
>
> The alternative to this leap of faith is to recognize that our present ability to reason meaningfully about the origin or end of the universe is not adequate to the job.[21]

Isaac Asimov, on the other hand, chooses to meet head on the problem that an evolutionary origin of the universe encounters with the Second Law. In a debate between Asimov and me in the pages of *Science Digest,* he asserts that, according to the

Big Bang theory, the universe at the beginning, in the form of
the cosmic egg, was in a state of high order, although it had
no organization. The cosmic egg then exploded and the universe has been running down ever since, fully in accord with
the Second Law.[22] In order to evaluate this notion, it is necessary first to review the events which supposedly occurred
according to this scenario. After the fireball cooled sufficiently
for elements to form, hydrogen and helium began to form.
After some time, matter was decoupled from radiation, and
these gases expanded as previously described until they were
distributed homogeneously at a very low temperature and at
almost a perfect vacuum. Then somehow portions of these
highly dispersed gases collapsed by gravitational forces to
form one hundred billion galaxies, each containing about one
hundred billion stars. Later, our solar system evolved and life
arose on this planet and evolved into all living things on the
earth—plants, animals, and man.

It is true that matter in a highly dense homogeneous form
at an enormous temperature, as in the hypothetical cosmic egg,
would have a low entropy relative to highly dispersed, homogeneous gases at a very low temperature, as visualized for the
hydrogen and helium gases after the expansion. Thus, if all
that ever happened in this scenario was the big bang, followed
by a never-ending expansion of the gases that formed, there
would be no problem with the Second Law (nor would there
be humans to worry about it). The gases would continue to
expand forever—a dull-as-ditchwater expansion in which
nothing forms—the thing would be as dead as a doornail, as
Fred Hoyle put it. It is also remembered that Philip Seiden
asserted that if you apply the laws of physics to such a globally
smooth, homogeneous expanding gas, you can't get the universe we have today.

Asimov claims that the universe has been running down in
accord with the Second Law ever since the big bang. Would
Asimov have us believe that the conversion of globally smooth
homogeneous gases into stars and galaxies is a "running

down" process? Does he believe that hydrogen, in the form of a hundred billion galaxies, each containing a hundred billion stars—highly condensed, complex forms of matter at a very high temperature—is a less complex, less organized, more random arrangement of matter than a homogenous highly dispersed cloud of gas? Does he really believe that his brain is a run-down product of hydrogen gas? That notion is absurd on the face of it. The present universe in all of its complexity is obviously not the run-down product of a homogeneous cloud of gas. The formation of even a single star from a cloud of gas requires a *decrease* in entropy, which is forbidden by the Second Law. That is, any process which involves a decrease in entropy will not occur spontaneously. Work must be performed on any system which undergoes a decrease in entropy. An enormous decrease in entropy would thus be required to form one hundred billion times one hundred billion stars. A *decrease* in entropy reflects an *increase* in complexity, structure, and organization, just the opposite of that required for the origin of the universe according to Asimov's scenario. Now, in its present state, the universe *is* running down—the entropy of the universe is increasing—but the conditions of the *present* universe must not be confused for those conditions that must have existed during the *origin* of the universe.

As Asimov has stated, the present universe is constantly getting more disorderly. The entropy of the universe is steadily increasing as the supply of energy available to do work constantly decreases. As heat and radiation from the sun and other stars pass out into interstellar space, they become unavailable to do further work. This energy does not become nonexistent—it is still there—but it cannot be used to do work. According to present estimates, billions of tons of fuel in the sun are being consumed every second. Every star in the universe is burning up its fuel. It is obvious that if there is no God, or if God would choose not to intervene, the day will inevitably come when every star in the universe will have exhausted its fuel. At that moment the lights will go out—the universe will be dead. It will still be here, but it will be a dead universe. All activity, all life will cease. The temperature throughout the universe will be uniform—thus no further exchange of energy will be possible—the universe will have reached a state of maximum entropy. *If the natural laws and natural processes now governing the universe are leading inexorably to its death and destruction, and if, as evolutionists believe, these natural laws and processes are all there is and all there ever has been, how could these very same natural laws and processes create the universe in the first place? Could the natural laws and processes now destroying the universe also be responsible for its creation?* What sort of tortured logic would one have to use to reach such an impossible conclusion? Evolutionary scenarios for the origin of the universe are scientifically untenable, and such scenarios survive simply because the authors and supporters of these scenarios refuse to believe any explanation that does not involve a totally mechanistic, naturalistic, non-theistic explanation.

In their attempts to circumvent the Second Law, evolutionists have at times offered truly juvenile arguments. One argument often encountered is that if what creation scientists claim is true about evolution and the Second Law, then, using the same kind of reasoning, it would be impossible for a fertilized egg to develop into the adult animal. Speaking of the laws of thermodynamics, Futuyma says:

> Creationists take these laws of physics to mean that organized living systems could not have evolved from less organized matter, and that complex organisms could not evolve from simpler ones: "For the evolution of a more advanced organism, however, energy must somehow be gained, order must be increased, and information added. The Second Law says this will not happen in any natural process unless external factors enter to make it happen."
>
> But order arises from disorder all around us. A human body arises from the relative formlessness of a fertilized egg; disordered water molecules form ordered ice crystals in our refrigerators.[23]

(In his quote of a creation scientist, Futuyma is quoting Henry Morris's *Scientific Creationism*, 1st Ed., p. 40).

Of course, no creation scientist believes that the conversion of a fertilized egg into an adult creature in any way violates the Second Law. The conversion of a fertilized egg into an adult has nothing whatsoever to do with evolution. A fertilized egg contains all of the information in its genetic apparatus to produce the adult creature—no new information is added during the developmental process. Furthermore, it is fully equipped with the metabolic machinery required for life. All that is required is a steady supply of nutrients and energy. On the other hand, the *origin* of life, the *origin* of each basic type of creature which produces a fertilized egg, and the *origin* of its reproductive process has everything to do with evolution. It is incredible, by the way, to note that Futuyma, a biologist, refers to what he calls the "relative formlessness of a fertilized egg." A biologist simply cannot be that ignorant concerning the true nature of a fertilized egg. A fertilized egg is so complex that if scientists could study it forever, there would probably still be much about it that they would not understand. "Relative formlessness," indeed, is a ridiculous term to use in describing a fertilized egg—it is just the opposite. Use of this term by Futuyma appears to be deliberately misleading.

John Patterson, mentioned earlier, uses a similar type argument. He says:

> Growing organisms are but additional examples of localized entropy reductions. One cannot insist that the second law of thermodynamics contradicts evolution without simultaneously maintaining that growth—development, "morphogenesis"—is similarly impossible.[24]

This statement is simply absurd. *Growth and development* of a plant or an animal has absolutely nothing to do with evolution. The *origin* of a plant or animal, or the conversion of a plant or animal into a basically different kind of creature, certainly is what evolution supposedly is all about. To imply

that using the same reasoning that creationists use concerning
the origin of the universe, the origin of life, or the evolution
of a single-celled organism into a human, relative to the Second Law, would also mean that growth and development of
living organisms could not take place, is juvenile in the extreme. It is evident from this remark and similar statements of
his that Patterson either doesn't understand what evolution
involves or he doesn't understand thermodynamics; he certainly doesn't understand the relationship between the two.

The statement quoted above from Futuyma also includes
another simplistic and totally false argument against creation
scientists and their case against evolution based on the Second
Law. He says: ". . . disordered water molecules form ordered
ice crystals in our refrigerators." This reference to crystallization as a refutation of the argument against evolution based
on the Second Law is one frequently encountered by creation
scientists. A variation on that argument, which also involves
crystallization of water, is the argument based on snowflakes
used by Patterson. He says:

> Localized entropy reduction is an extremely common phe-
> nomenon in living and nonliving systems alike. Indeed, it
> occurs each time a snowflake forms. . . . *Moreover, each
> one forms completely spontaneously and completely natu-
> rally from a completely disorganized ensemble of airborne
> vapor molecules! . . . Surely the creationists do not mean
> to argue since the entropy principle is a universal law,
> snowflake formation is impossible!* To be sure, scientists
> do not completely understand the genesis of snowflakes or
> the evolutionary process, but a declaration that either is
> "impossible" does not follow from the second law of ther-
> modynamics.[25]

No, of course creation scientists do not argue that since
the entropy principle (the Second Law) is a universal law,
snowflake formation is impossible. What Patterson is saying,
however, is that since the Second Law does not prevent snowflake formation, similarly it does not prevent evolution. Futuyma, Patterson, and others who use similar arguments based

on crystallization obviously do not understand the difference between crystallization and evolution. In crystallization, the material crystallizing goes to a *lower* energy level, to a *more probable* state. In fact, a crystal exhibits no activity whatsoever. It is at equilibrium. On the other hand, every step in the origin of life would require movement to a *higher* energy level, to *a less probable* state. A crystal is highly ordered, but it has very little complexity—it has a totally repetitive structure. Knowledgeable evolutionists, unlike Futuyma, Patterson, and others who cite crystallization in their Second Law arguments, know that crystallization gives no information on how the origin of life could take place in spite of the Second Law. For example, Peter T. Mora says:

> The second law of classical thermodynamics postulates an overall increase in entropy. Of course, certain local areas where entropy is decreasing are common, as in crystallization. In crystallization, the full process is determined by the valency, the molecular structure of the components, whether atoms, molecules, or polymers. Crystallization occurs because it leads to the lowest energy state and to the most stable arrangements of atoms or molecules under the given conditions. Crystallization leads to simple, very uniform repeating structures, which are inert. These structures do not function, and are not designed by function.[26]

Jeffrey Wicken also is aware of the differences between crystals—ordered systems—and systems that are part of a living organism—organized system. He points out that:

> "Organized" systems are to be carefully distinguished from "ordered" systems. Neither kind of system is "random," but whereas ordered systems are generated according to simple algorithms and therefore lack complexity, organized systems must be assembled element by element according to an external "wiring diagram" with a high information content.[27]

Evolutionist Wicken is admitting here exactly what Wilder-Smith and other creation scientists have long argued: Information (even a high information content) must be introduced from the outside to construct or originate complex, organized systems, in contrast to that required to form mere ordered systems, such as crystals, where a simple algorithm based on internal forces yield repetitive structures.

As will be seen later, Ilya Prigogine, the Belgian scientist who won the Nobel Prize in physics for his work in thermodynamics, is the man Patterson believes will lead evolutionists out of the trap that thermodynamics has laid for evolutionary theory. Patterson should read all that Prigogine has to say about thermodynamics and evolution. If he did, he would learn that crystallization in no way contradicts the arguments of creation scientists based on the Second Law. Prigogine (with co-authors Nicolis and Babloyants) says:

> The point is that in a non-isolated system there exists a possibility for formation of ordered, low-entropy structures at sufficiently low temperatures. This ordering principle is responsible for the appearance of ordered structures such as crystals as well as for the phenomena of phase transitions.
>
> Unfortunately this principle cannot explain the formation of biological structures. The probability that at ordinary temperatures a macroscopic number of molecules is assembled to give rise to the highly ordered structures and to the coordinated functions characterizing living organisms is vanishingly small.[28]

Patterson boasts that he is an expert in thermodynamics, having a doctorate in metallurgical engineering and having taught thermodynamics at Iowa State University for many years. It is strange, then, that he would advance the sophomoric notion that crystallization destroys the argument against evolution based on the Second Law. We have just witnessed the statements by Prigogine and his co-workers, and of others, that there is no relevancy between the two. Furthermore, if he had read the book on the origin of life co-authored by Charles Thaxton, Walter Bradley, and Roger Olsen, he would know why this is true based on a technical thermodynamic treatment of the subject. Thaxton, Bradley, and Olsen point out that:

As ice forms, energy (80 calories/gm) is liberated to the surroundings. The change in the entropy of the system as the amorphous water becomes crystalline ice is -0.293 entropy units (eu)/degree Kelvin (K). The entropy change is negative because the thermal and configuration entropy (or disorder) of water is greater than that of ice, which is a highly ordered crystal. Thus, the thermodynamic conditions under which water will transform to ice are seen from equation 7-9 to be:

$$-0.293 - \left(\frac{-80}{T} \right) > 0 \qquad (7\text{-}10a)$$

or

$$T \leq 273K \qquad (7\text{-}10b)$$

For condition of T <273 K energy is removed from water to produce ice, and the aggregate disordering of the surroundings is greater than the ordering of the water into ice crystals. This gives a net increase in the entropy of the universe, as predicted by the second law of thermodynamics.

It has often been argued by analogy to water crystallizing to ice that simple monomers may polymerize into complex molecules such as protein and DNA. The analogy is clearly inappropriate, however. The $\Delta E + P \Delta V$ term (equation 7-9) in the polymerization of important organic molecules is generally positive (5 to 8 kcal/mole), indicating the reaction can never spontaneously occur at or near equilibrium. By contrast the $\Delta E + P \Delta V$ term in water changing to ice is a negative, -1.44 kcal/mole, indicating the phase change is spontaneous as long as T <273 K, as previously noted. The atomic bonding forces draw water molecules into an orderly crystalline array when the thermal agitation (or entropy driving force, $T\Delta S$) is made sufficiently small by lowering the temperature. Organic monomers such as amino acids resist combining at all at any temperature, however, much less in some orderly arrangement.[29]

Now Patterson, the "expert" in thermodynamics, if he reads this book or the book by Thaxton, Bradley, and Olsen, will know why, based on the science of thermodynamics, the crystallization of water is totally irrelevant to the thermodynamics of evolution. It is seen here that the thermodynamics of the process permits water to spontaneously crystallize when the temperature is lowered to 273 K (0° Centigrade, 32° Fahrenheit). At that low temperature, the bonding energy between the water molecules is sufficient to overcome the thermal agitation energy, and crystallization occurs. With the organic monomers involved in the formation of proteins (amino acids), DNA and RNA (nucleotides), and carbohydrates (sugars), just the opposite is true—the attraction between molecules is never great enough to form more than a vanishingly small quantity of polymer, no matter what the temperature may be.

Evolution supposedly is a spontaneous process. According to evolutionary theory, hydrogen spontaneously condensed from a highly dispersed state at a very low temperature to form stars, highly concentrated gaseous structures with internal temperatures of millions of degrees. Galaxies—billions of stars each—spontaneously created themselves. Through the action of energy from the sun bathing simple gases on the earth—hydrogen, methane, ammonia, nitrogen, carbon dioxide, water vapor—these gases spontaneously formed more complex molecules—amino acids, nucleotides, sugars, etc. These molecules spontaneously combined to form proteins, DNA, RNA, and complex carbohydrates, requiring only an external source of energy. Then, somehow, these molecules spontaneously separated from the mixed-up mess constituting the hypothetical primordial "soup" to form complex metabolic cycles, which later spontaneously arranged themselves in a highly coordinated fashion to produce life. No planning was involved. The process had no purpose or goal. No directing force existed to orchestrate the process. No intelligence was required. No engineers were involved. No instructions on how to proceed were available—no information was fed into the system from the outside. Everything that happened can be ascribed to properties inherent in matter. The universe created itself. Life created itself. The microbe-to-man evolutionary process resulted from the unplanned, spontaneous generation of all the information required to specify every living organism on the earth (and all extinct organisms), including man with his three-pound human brain with 12 billion brain cells and 120 trillion connections. All of this occurred, evolutionists tell us, by a simple flow-through of energy acting on matter due to properties inherent in this matter, starting with hydrogen gas. Evolutionists thus maintain that all that is required for evolution to proceed is an open system with an adequate flow-through of energy from the outside. The earth-sun system is an open system—energy flows freely from the sun to the earth's surface, and the energy from the sun is more than adequate to fuel the evolutionary process. Thus, we are told, there is no contradiction between evolution and the Second Law. As described earlier, the universe is an isolated system which could not experience a flow-through of energy, so doubtlessly, the Second Law does apply to its origin.

As earlier stated, creation scientists point out that an open system and an adequate outside source of energy are necessary *but not sufficient* conditions for the complexity, structure, and organization of a system to increase. In fact, the flow of uncontrolled, raw energy into a system is *destructive,* not constructive. Life on the earth is possible only because it is protected by the ozone layer, a shield about 20-35 kilometers (12-21 miles) above the surface of the earth. Ozone is triatomic oxygen (O_3) and is produced from molecular oxygen (O_2) by radiant energy from the sun. If there were no oxygen in our atmosphere there could be no ozone. Evolutionists must, of absolute necessity, postulate that there was no oxygen in the atmosphere before and during the origin of life. This is so because oxygen would destroy all organic molecules, such as ammonia, methane, amino acids, nucleotides, sugars, etc., by oxidation. If there were no oxygen, then, of course, there could be no ozone. All of the energy from the sun, including the highly energetic, short-wave, deadly destructive ultraviolet light would flow unimpeded to the surface of the earth. Far from being a means of producing low entropy substances on the earth, this radiation would destroy any organized systems that might exist. Of course, there would be no organized systems on the earth because they could not exist, let alone originate, in the presence of this destructive energy.

All of us are familiar with the destructive effects of ultraviolet (UV) light. A very effective and rapid means of killing bacteria or inactivating viruses is to irradiate them with UV light. Scientists have a dreadful fear of the slightest decrease in the ozone layer surrounding the earth. They know that a decrease in the ozone layer would result in an increase in the amount of UV light reaching the earth, resulting in an increase in the mutation rate. If a substantial amount of the ozone were removed, life, from microbes to man, would no longer be possible. Even the relatively simple molecular substance of ammonia, NH_3, would be rapidly decomposed into nitrogen and hydrogen by ultraviolet light.[30] If even a simple substance such as ammonia would be rapidly destroyed by the radiant energy from the sun bathing the primordial earth, how could more complex substances that are more unstable and thus more easily destroyed, survive, let alone be produced? How could living organisms, the most complex, most unstable arrangements of matter on the earth, survive, let alone evolve in the presence of this deadly radiation? Proteins, DNA, and RNA can be synthesized by organic chemists using very carefully controlled conditions and employing specially devised chemical reagents as energy donors. No organic chemist would be foolish enough, however, to try such syntheses using UV light as his energy donor. He would know the only result would be the destruction of his starting materials.

In order for low entropy complex organized systems to be produced, at least four conditions must be satisfied:

1. The system must be an open system;

2. An adequate outside supply of energy must be available;

3. An energy conversion system must exist to convert the raw, uncontrolled energy coming in from the outside to a controlled form that can be utilized in a constructive way by the system undergoing change;

4. There must be a control system capable of regulating the activities of the system undergoing change, such that the changes are progressive and integrative rather than meaningless and destructive.

Although most evolutionists declare simplistically that all that is required for progressive evolutionary changes to take place is an open system and a flow-through of energy, some agree with creationists that more is required. Charles J. Smith writes:

> The thermodynamicist immediately clarifies the latter question by pointing out that the Second Law classically refers to isolated systems which exchange neither energy nor matter with the environment; biological systems are open, and exchange both energy and matter. The explanation, however, is not completely satisfying, because it still leaves open the problem of how or why the ordering process has arisen (an apparent lowering of the entropy), and a number of scientists have wrestled with this issue. Bertalanffy (1968) called the relation between irreversible thermodynamics and information theory one of the most fundamental unsolved problems in biology.[31]

George Gaylord Simpson and W. S. Beck, both evolutionists, have clearly seen the problem. They say:

> We have repeatedly emphasized the fundamental problems posed for the biologist by the fact of life's complex organization. We have seen that organization requires work for its maintenance and that the universal quest for food is in part to provide the energy needed for this work. But the

simple expenditure of energy is not sufficient to develop
and maintain order. A bull in a china shop performs work
but he neither creates nor maintains organization. The work
needed is particular work; it must follow specifications; it
requires information on how to proceed.[32]

In this passage, Simpson and Beck are speaking as scientists, and what they are saying is good science. When they
forget science and speculate as evolutionists, however, they
must suggest exactly what they have denied in the above
statement. They believe that life arose on this planet by some
mechanistic evolutionary process by the simple expenditure
of energy from the sun. That brutal energy is nothing more
than a bull in a china shop—it would perform work, but it
could neither create nor maintain organization. There were no
specifications to follow, no information on how to proceed.
The results would be destructive—the same sort of results
brought about by a bull wandering through a china shop.

Angrist and Hepler have accurately outlined the true situation. They state:

> Life, the temporary reversal of a universal trend toward
> maximum disorder, was brought about by the production
> of information mechanisms. In order for such mechanisms
> to first arise it was necessary to have matter capable of
> forming itself into a self-reproducing structure that could
> extract energy from the environment for its first self-
> assembly. Directions for the reproduction of plans, for the
> extraction of energy and chemicals from the environment,
> for the growth of sequence and the mechanism for trans-
> lating instructions into growth all had to be simultaneously
> present at that moment. This combination of events has
> seemed an incredibly unlikely happenstance and often di-
> vine intervention is prescribed as the only way it could have
> come about.[33]

As mentioned earlier in this chapter, Harold Blum has
wrestled with the problem of the origin of life and thermodynamics. When I obtained his book, *Time's Arrow and Evolution*,[13] I eagerly read the book, searching for Blum's solution

to the problem rendered by the fact that Time's Arrow, thermodynamics, always points downward but (in the evolutionist's view) evolution has proceeded upward. When I had finished the book, I realized that Blum had no solution whatsoever. In the first place, he just simplistically denies that there is a problem, giving the same answer so often heard from the evolutionist camp—an appeal to open systems. He says:

> Since any increase in order within the biosphere must be very small compared to the increase of entropy in the sun-earth system there is no reason to think that evolution controverts the second law of thermodynamics, even though it may appear to do so if viewed as a thing apart.[34]

A careful reading of Blum's book reveals, however, that the answer is not that simplistic and that the problem is serious and remains unsolved. He writes:

> Since the reproduction of proteins could not have gone on without a means of energy mobilization, it might almost be necessary to assume that these two processes had their origin at the same time, unless indeed the latter actually antedated the former. . . . the problem of energy supply for the first organism seems fundamental.[35]

In living organisms today, the energy for their multitude of activities is provided by energy-rich organic compounds derived (in plants) from photosynthesis, and indirectly from photosynthesis for animals, since they either eat plants or eat animals which do eat plants. Blum thus says:

> There would seem to be no way of replenishing the supply of such compounds except by capturing energy of sunlight by means of some photosynthetic process.[36]

Later, Blum writes:

> However we regard the problem, we must admit that photosynthesis of some kind, perhaps very different from any we know today, arose very early in the course of organic evolution, *if indeed it was not involved from the beginning* [emphasis added].[37]

Here Blum pinpoints the problem and brings himself almost to the point of admitting the necessity of the existence of an energy conversion mechanism right from the start. As an evolutionist, he can't quite bring himself to admit, without reservation, that the energy conversion or mobilization system had to be there at the beginning, because he knows such an admission would be fatal to evolutionary theory. In saying that an energy mobilization system must have arisen "very early in the course of organic evolution, if indeed it was not involved from the beginning," he can say it, and at the same time make it possible for him to deny that he really said it. After his in-depth study of the problem, it appears that Blum actually realizes that an energy conversion system had to be there right from the beginning for any dynamically active biological system to exist, and he half admits it. Creation scientists point out that there is absolutely no doubt that such a mechanism had to exist from the very beginning—no biological system is capable of harnessing energy of any kind without such a mechanism, whether it be radiant energy from the sun, heat energy, or energy derivable from organic compounds.

John W. Patterson, mentioned earlier, is one who pours out vituperation of all kinds against creation scientists, accusing them of being not only ignorant and incompetent but also downright dishonest in their treatment of evolution and the Second Law. He has recommended that creation scientists be dismissed from university positions, that research grants be denied creation scientists, and that, if possible, earned Ph.D.'s should be taken away from creation scientists. His charges of blatant dishonesty and incompetence on the part of creation scientists have been published in anti-creationist books,[24,38] in the *Proceedings of the Iowa Academy of Science,*[39] and in *The American Atheist.*[40] For our critique of Patterson's attempt to reconcile evolution with the Second Law, his chapter, "Thermodynamics and Evolution," in *Scientists Confront Creationism,*[41] will be used.

Patterson begins by accusing creation scientists of using "completely fallacious and deceptive" arguments against evolution based on the Second Law. He states that the Second Law does indeed describe an overall tendency in nature toward decay, but, he says, a great many processes in nature are coupled to predominant downhill fluxes, and are coupled in such a way that they are actually driven in the backward or uphill direction. Creation scientists have no quarrel with the facts contained in the preceding sentence. They certainly do believe that there must exist a coupling mechanism linking thermodynamically unfavored uphill processes to thermodynamically favored downhill processes in order for the uphill processes involved in the origin and maintenance of complex organizations to occur. He then describes the formation of snowflakes, and, as described earlier in this chapter, he implies that this process weighs against the creation scientists' arguments based on the Second Law. Snowflake formation is, of course, only a special case of the crystallization of water and is irrelevant to the question of evolution.

Patterson begins to get into the meat of the situation when he says:

> Growing organisms are but additional examples of localized entropy reductions. . . . Of course, the living organism must draw its energy from its surroundings, and, of course, to maintain a highly ordered internal condition, it must rid itself of all the entropy it produces while alive. That is how the second law affects living organisms [p. 105].

Later, Patterson states:

> It is clear that the second law of thermodynamics does not contradict the formation of snowflakes, the synthesis of chemicals over a Bunsen burner, the growth and development of living organisms, or the "uphill" evolution of life in the bioshpere. However, this still doesn't explain how uphill processes occur [p. 106].

First, note how Patterson slides from an obviously true statement about snowflakes, chemical synthesis, and growth

and development of living organisms, to the totally presumptuous statement about the uphill evolution of life. This is the
old trick of coupling obviously true statements to what you
want your listeners to believe, the latter of which is nothing
more than an unproved assumption. At least Patterson admits
that he must explain how the required uphill process can occur.
Patterson then goes on to explain:

> As suggested above, an uphill or backward process can
> spontaneously occur in nature by being somehow coupled
> to a more dominant downhill process. By virtue of cou-
> pling, the downhill process can actually drive the other
> process "backward" or in the so-called uphill direction
> [p. 106].

Patterson chooses, as his example, the self-operating ram
pump developed in Britain in the late 1700's. An hydraulic
ram pump is so constructed that the energy derived from a
relatively large amount of water moving downhill will pump
a relatively small amount of water up a net lift of as much as
90 feet into a storage tank, where it can be used as needed.
He chides Henry Morris for Morris's failure to mention the
ram pump in his chapter on thermodynamics entitled, "Can
Water Run Uphill," in a 1975 book.[42] Later, he writes:

> The energy requirements of living systems are derived from
> the foodstuffs that flow "downward" through the food-
> chains. Were one to neglect the downhill stream of water
> in a ram or the downhill flow of food energy in living
> systems, the attendant uphill processes would appear to
> violate thermodynamic laws. Taking a broader view, how-
> ever, reveals that the "violations" are only superficial
> [p. 108].

What Patterson has proven here with his ram pump concerning evolution—the origin of life, for example—and how
it is related to thermodynamics is—absolutely nothing. Of
course Morris doesn't mention the ram pump in his discussion
of evolution and thermodynamics—it is simply irrelevant. It
is Patterson who warrants chiding, not Morris. First of all, and
this apparently completely escapes Patterson, the ram pump

is a device constructed by engineers—intelligent human beings. It was not produced spontaneously by an evolutionary process! Furthermore, the pumping up of the water and the uphill processes in living organisms require, even as Patterson admits, a *coupling* to downhill processes, just as creation scientists have repeatedly pointed out. A mechanism must exist to utilize the flow-through of energy in a manner that can be productively used by the system—in case of the ram pump it is the pump itself, and in the case of living organisms it is photosynthesis and a vast multitude of other metabolic systems tightly coordinated in time and space. In his discussion here, Patterson is not giving us any explanation of how these complex devices arose in the first place, and that is what evolution theory is supposed to explain.

Another indication that Patterson doesn't understand evolution and the relationship between evolution and the Second Law is his astounding claim that the ram pump provides an analog for natural selection. He says (pp. 107,108):

> The reason, in my view, is that the ram is spectacularly inconvenient to his [Henry Morris's] argument, and, in fact, it provides a nice analog for "explaining" how natural selection works. In evolution the vast majority of mutations can be regarded as degenerative, and that same vast majority disappears. Natural selection saves the slight majority that represent an improvement. Similarly, in the ram pump, most of the water flows downhill through the pump and disappears. The flap valve in a ram pump diverts only a tiny amount to the elevated tank. In the ram, the elevation energy is derived from the downward-flowing stream. Natural selection depends upon the energy that keeps organisms alive as mutation and reproduction work their wiles.

In the ram pump, the only thing happening is that a small amount of water is being lifted by the energy of much water flowing downhill. The water does not undergo any changes, or "mutations," whatsoever, and it does not undergo reproduction. The "analogy" is no analogy at all. The two systems, one a physical system, the other a living system, are as different as apples and bolts.

Patterson cites another spurious example—the flow of a current of electricity from a battery. He describes how a current flows from a battery due to chemical reactions in the battery, stating that if these reactions are left to themselves, they proceed in one way only because of the energy and entropy changes that result. Then he says:

> Nevertheless, virtually all these unidirectional, internal processes can be made to go "backward" merely by properly coupling the battery to another one with larger terminal voltage [p. 108].

Exactly! But what has this to do with the *origin* of the batteries or the *origin* of the universe or the *origin* of life? The batteries are complex devices created by man, and the stronger battery had to be heavily charged. The batteries did not create themselves, and the stronger battery did not spontaneously charge itself. If Patterson were able to explain how ram pumps and batteries could spontaneously create themselves and spontaneously coordinate themselves into the systems they are serving, then perhaps he would have a start on explaining the spontaneous evolutionary origin of life.

Patterson finally gets to the basic part of the whole discussion of evolution and the Second Law, and in doing so, *he admits precisely what creation scientists have insisted from the beginning:* that the central problem is the **origin** of the required organization by a spontaneous evolutionary process that is energized by nothing more than raw, uncontrolled energy. On p. 110, Patterson begins a section entitled, "Self-organization." He starts out by saying:

> Closely related to the apparent "paradox" of ongoing uphill processes in nonliving systems is the apparent "paradox" of spontaneous self-organization in nature. It is one thing for an internally organized, open system to foster uphill processes by tapping downhill ones, *but how did the required internal organization come about in the first place? Indeed the so-called dissipative structures that produce*

> *uphill processes are highly organized (low entropy) mo-*
> *lecular ensembles, especially when compared to the dis-*
> *persed arrays from which they assembled. Hence, the*
> *question of how they could originate by natural processes*
> *has proved a challenging one* [emphasis added].

Right on, John! Right on! Patterson has finally admitted what the real problem is all about, precisely the problem creation scientists have pointed out from the very start. Patterson takes his readers through a fairyland of snowflakes, growing organisms, ram pumps, and supercharged batteries, but he finally comes back into the real world to discuss real problems. Patterson, of course, would not admit for a minute that there is any problem here with thermodynamics; the paradox is only illusory, he says, and has only to do with how self-organization occurs, not whether it does. This *ex cathedra* statement by Patterson is sufficient, he apparently believes, to simply cause the problem to vanish. There is no problem because Patterson says there is no problem.

How spontaneous self-organization occurs, if it does occur, is indeed the problem, and the Second Law does erect an insuperable barrier to a spontaneous origin of the complex organization required to get life started.

Patterson pours contempt on creation scientists for their interpretation of the evidence related to evolution and the Second Law; yet, step by step, he concedes point after point: For an organism to draw energy from its surroundings it must possess and maintain a highly complex internal organization; uphill processes involving a decrease of entropy must be *coupled* to downhill processes which result in an increase of entropy; and the *origin* of the required internal organization must be explained. In other words, simply to say that all that is required to create complex organizations is an open system and an adequate energy supply is a totally inadequate explanation—it really explains nothing.

Patterson likes to believe that Ilya Prigogine and his colleagues have explained how spontaneous self-organization could take place in spite of the Second Law. At least, Patterson believes, they are on the right track. Patterson states (pp. 110, 111):

> Current thinking holds that self-organization can be understood in terms of theories advanced by Prigogine and his colleagues . . . who have devised some very plausible explanations based upon statistical physics and new instability principles. The new instability principles apply to systems in highly nonuniform states, what Prigogine calls "far-from-equilibrium" states, but do not apply to the uniform states treated in classical thermodynamics. . . . It has been found that the imposition of naturally occurring temperature gradients, pressure gradients, or composition gradients can force a system into highly nonuniform configurations that eventually become unstable relative to (and hence transform into) highly organized configurations. . . . Prigogine calls these highly organized configurations *dissipative structures* and a fairly wide variety have been described in theoretical analyses. Moreover a good many have also been produced in laboratory experiments carried out in inorganic and organic media. The overwhelming majority of biochemists and molecular evolutionists who have looked into this matter realize Prigogine's dissipative structures provide a very viable, perfectly natural mechanism for self-organization, perhaps even for the genesis of life from nonliving matter (abiogenesis). These structures can be induced merely by imposing strong temperature, pressure, or composition gradients.

Patterson, a metallurgical engineer, certainly could not be expected to be competent in biochemistry and molecular biology. Thus, when Prigogine moves out of his theoretical world (he hasn't spent any time in the laboratory in years) into the real world of biochemistry and molecular biology with his speculations, Patterson is in no position to evaluate the validity of Prigogine's notions. Prigogine's theoretical ideas are buttressed with a large amount of complicated mathematics which few biochemists and molecular biologists can understand, but it all does look deliciously scientific. Since

Prigogine's speculations lend comfort to his fellow evolutionists among the biochemists and molecular biologists, they are only too eager to bow to the authority of this Nobel Prize winner.

Actually, although he believes that he is on the right track, Prigogine does not claim he has solved the problem of the origin of life or the origin of complex biological organizations. In a book he co-authored in 1977, the year he won the Nobel Prize, Prigogine says:

> There seems to be no doubt that dissipative structures play an essential role in the function of living systems as we see them today. What was the role of dissipative structures in evolution? It is very tempting to speculate that prebiotic evolution corresponds essentially to a succession of instabilities leading to an increasing level of complexity.[43]

What is the answer that Nicolis and Prigogine give to their question, "What was the role of dissipative structures in evolution?"—It is very *tempting* to *speculate*! No doubt it was tempting for Nicolis and Prigogine to speculate about such matters, but since when have tempting speculations become scientific solutions to an extremely vexing and complex problem? Patterson has no solution for the origin of complex biological systems, let alone for the origin of life, except to suggest the speculative ideas of Prigogine in a field where Patterson has no expertise whatsoever.

Patterson speaks of the many examples of these "highly organized configurations," which serve as examples of Prigogine's dissipative structures that Prigogine touts speculatively as models for self-organization. One of the most compelling examples offered by Prigogine is the so-called Benard's principle. As a vessel of water is heated, heat energy begins to flow through the water by convection. Suddenly, as the water reaches a critical point where the system has reached a point said to be far from equilibrium, hexagonal cells form in the water as heat energy flows upward through the water. The hexagonal cells form what

Patterson has called "highly organized configurations," and supposedly serve as a model for self-organization that may have led to the origin of life. Actually, this model is light years short of models that might give some hint of what could possibly move in that direction. The Benard principle is exhibited by liquid water, hardly the type of self-organization that might lead to proteins, DNA, and a living cell. The phenomenon is extremely temporary—once the heat is removed, the hexagonal cells immediately disappear. Prigogine visualizes the possibility that the Second Law might be circumvented by a series of such fluctuations, eventually leading to a living cell. What he and most of his fellow evolutionists forget is the fact that if a fluctuation of a system far from equilibrium did just happen to move to a more highly organized state, the probability is overwhelming that the next fluctuation would move to a lower state of organization, wiping out all organization that had been gained. After all, an explosion is an example of a fluctuation of a system far from equilibrium. Other similar examples one might cite are volcanoes, landslides, earthquakes, lightning, and other such natural calamities.

As mentioned earlier, when Prigogine moves his speculations off of paper, where they are embellished with a world of mathematics, and places them in the real world of biochemistry, then it is possible for a biochemist to evaluate Prigogine's speculations. It is apparent to this author, a biochemist, that when Prigogine attempts to construct a model using polynucleotide polymers, simulating primordial DNA to demonstrate fluctuations, his assumptions are totally devoid of any foundation and his model would lead nowhere. Detailed critiques of Prigogine's notions are included as Appendix I to this book. These critiques were composed by Dr. Henry Morris and this author and were originally published in the ICR *Impact* series.[44]

We would be accused by evolutionists of prejudice, of course, whose criticisms should be ignored. Whether these criticisms are valid, however, should be judged by readers solely on their merits. Critiques are available, moreover, from those who are not creationists, thus those who could not be accused of evaluating Prigogine's speculations with preconceived ideas. One of these critics is Peter Engels, who published a review[45] of the book, *Order Out of Chaos*[46] by Prigogine and Isabelle Stengers in *The Sciences*. Excerpts from Engels' review follow:

> Prigogine is a Belgian citizen in his mid-sixties who teaches at the Universite Libre in Brussels, and, for part of the year, at the University of Texas at Austin. In 1977, he received the Nobel Prize in chemistry for using thermodynamics, in the words of the committee, "to bridge the gap that exists between the biological and the social scientific fields of inquiry." . . . enter Prigogine and Stengers, *dei ex machina*, with their plan for resolving the paradox of the second law. Theirs is, at the least, an earnest and noble attempt. Whether they ultimately succeed or merely add their names to the roster of scientists who have tried, they tackle this most formidable of challenges in a truly novel and exciting way. . . . The most compelling example of this process that the authors offer is the Benard instability. . . . The book's examples of self-organization range from carefully conducted laboratory experiments to wild, untested (and perhaps untestable speculations). . . . "We are tempted to go so far as to say," they conclude, "that once the conditions for self-organization are satisfied, life becomes as predictable as the Benard instability or a falling stone." . . . The obvious question is: What are the conditions for self-organization? But, disappointingly, the authors fail to identify the physical mechanisms underlying most of their examples of self-organization, leading one to wonder if the fluctuations really exist.
>
> How can there be system-wide decreases in entropy on the scale of life itself, in seeming contradiction of the second law? . . . Unfortunately, whatever they achieve in this regard remains obscure. Just as they approach the

issues of greatest moment, their writing, awkward and dis-
jointed to begin with, takes a turn for the worse.

According to Engels' reading of the citation awarding
Prigogine the Nobel Prize, Prigogine was not awarded the
Nobel Prize for solving the "paradox" of the Second Law and
the origin of life, but for using thermodynamics "to bridge the
gap that exists between the biological and the social scientific
fields of inquiry." A common mistaken notion, often voiced
by evolutionists, is that he received the Nobel Prize for using
thermodynamics to explain how organized systems leading to
the origin of life could arise out of chaos by fluctuations. As
mentioned earlier, Prigogine made no such claim in his 1977
book, saying only, in this respect, "it is tempting to speculate."
Patterson claims that there is no problem whatsoever between
evolution and the Second Law. Such an approach is obviously
all bluff. This problem is often referred to as "the paradox of
the Second Law." Engels quite apparently recognizes this as
a critically important question, "this most formidable of challenges," as he puts it, and he credits Prigogine and Stengers
for, at the least, making an earnest and noble attempt at solving
the problem. Certainly they must be given credit for recognizing that there is a formidable problem, which is much more
than can be said for Patterson.

A Harvard scientist, Dr. John Ross, states:

> . . . there are no known violations of the second law of
> thermodynamics. Ordinarily the second law is stated for
> isolated systems, but the second law applies equally well
> to open systems. . . . there is somehow associated with the
> field of far-from equilibrium phenomena the notion that the
> second law of thermodynamics fails for such systems. It is
> important to make sure that this error does not perpetrate
> itself.[47]

One of the most formidable problems to overcome, relative to a mechanistic, evolutionary origin of life, is to explain
how the vast reduction in entropy required for the production
of the precise sequences necessary for biologically active

protein, DNA, and RNA molecules could be accomplished in spite of the Second Law, which tells us that the tendency is always towards randomness. This reduction in entropy, related to biologically active sequences, is called configurational entropy. Concerning Prigogine and his speculations, Thaxton, Bradley, and Olsen say:

> But such analogies have scant relevance to the origin-of-life question. A major reason is that they fail to distinguish between order and complexity. The highly ordered movement of energy through a system as in convection or vortices suffers from the same shortcoming as the analogies to the static, periodic order of crystals. Regularity or order cannot serve to store the large amount of information required by living systems. A highly irregular, but specified, structure is required rather than an ordered structure. This is a serious flaw in the analogy offered. There is no apparent connection between the kind of spontaneous ordering that occurs from energy flow through such systems and the work required to build aperiodic information-intensive macromolecules like DNA and protein. Prigogine et al suggest that the energy flow through the system decreases the system entropy, leading potentially to the highly organized structure of DNA and protein. Yet they offer no suggestion as to how the decrease in thermal entropy from energy flow through the system could be coupled to do the configurational entropy work required. . . . Nicolis and Prigogine offer their trimolecular model as an example of a chemical system with the required nonlinearity to produce self ordering. They are able to demonstrate mathematically that within a system that was initially homogeneous, one may subsequently have a periodic, spatial variation of concentration. To achieve this low degree of ordering, however, they must require boundary conditions that could only be met at cell walls, i.e. at membranes, relative reaction rates that are atypical of those observed in condensation reactions, a rapid removal of reaction products, and a trimolecular reaction (the highly unlikely simultaneous collision of three atoms). Furthermore the trimolecular model requires chemical reactions that are essentially irreversible.

But condensation reactions for polypeptides or polynucleotides are highly reversible unless all water is removed from the system.

They speculate that the low degree of spatial ordering achieved in the simple trimolecular model could potentially be orders of magnitude greater for the more complex reactions one might observe leading up to a fully replicating cell. The list of boundary constraints, relative reaction rates, etc., would, however, also be orders of magnitude larger. As a matter of fact, one is left with so constraining the system at the boundaries that ordering is inevitable from the structuring of the environment by the chemist. The fortuitous satisfaction of all of these boundary constraints simultaneously would be a miracle in its own right. . . . No, the models of Prigogine et al, based on nonequilibrium thermodynamics, do not at present offer an explanation as to how the configurational entropy work is accomplished under prebiotic conditions. The problem of how to couple energy flow through the system to do the required configurational entropy work remains.[48]

We have seen that Patterson, the self-proclaimed expert on thermodynamics, has charged creation scientists with ignorance, incompetence, and even blatant dishonesty, in their treatment of evolution and the Second Law. Where is the incompetence, ignorance, and dishonesty in the treatment of this subject by Thaxton, Bradley, and Olsen? Where is the incompetence and dishonesty in non-creationist Engels' evaluation? In some non-democratic countries, certain people have become non-persons, as their names were completely blotted out, with absolutely no mention of their names permitted in any official publications—newspapers, magazines, history books, etc. Similarly, Patterson declares that the Second Law poses no problem for the origin of the complex organized structures required for the origin of life and their further organization into the coordinated system required for a living cell. If Patterson had his way, this would be declared a non-problem, and all mention of it would be banished from the scientific literature and textbooks, and creation scientists, who persist in describing the problem, would be banished from universities, government laboratories, and any other position under government control, and exiled to a scientific Siberia of some kind after their Ph.D.s had been stripped from them.

Many knowledgeable scientists reject Patterson's sophomoric approach and at least acknowledge the problem. Thaxton, Bradley, and Olsen obviously reject Patterson's simplistic approach. They summarize the problem as follows:

> Throughout Chapters 7-9 we have analyzed the problems of complexity and the origin of life from a thermodynamic point of view. Our reason for doing this is the common notion in the scientific literature today on the origin of life that an open system with energy and mass flow is *a priori* a sufficient explanation for the complexity of life. We have examined the validity of such an open and constrained system. We found it to be a reasonable explanation for doing the chemical and thermal entropy work, but clearly inadequate to account for the configurational entropy work of coding (not to mention the sorting and selecting work). We have noted the need for some sort of coupling mechanism. Without it, there is no way to convert the negative entropy associated with energy flow into negative entropy associated with configurational entropy and the corresponding information. Is it reasonable to believe such a "hidden" coupling mechanism will be found in the future that can play this crucial role of a template, metabolic motor, etc., directing the flow of energy in such a way as to create new information?[49]

Thaxton, Bradley, and Olsen devote three chapters of their book to discussing the problem of evolution and the Second Law, which Patterson dismisses in one sentence. Now, who are the real scientists? Who are the experts in thermodynamics? Who has honestly faced the problem? Patterson has villified creation scientists, slandering them in all of his publications as incompetents and liars. Slander, however, is no substitute for science. It needs to be said, again, that when one uses a vicious *ad hominem* attack against an opponent in an intellectual discussion, it is an indication that he knows his case is weak, and his opponent, on the other hand, has compelling evidence to support his own case.

The science of thermodynamics is indeed the Achilles Heel that destroys evolutionary theory. It was stated that four conditions must be satisfied for complex organizations to arise within a system or for relatively simple systems to increase in complexity. In the hypothetical evolutionary origin of the universe *none* of these conditions are satisfied—the universe is not an open system (in the evolutionists' view), there is no flow-through of energy from the outside, there are no energy conversion systems, and there is no coding or control system to direct the system to produce low entropy highly organized systems, such as stars, galaxies, and solar systems. The hypothetical primordial earth would satisfy two of the requirements: it would have been an open system, and more than an adequate supply of energy would have been available from the sun. The other necessary conditions would not exist, however. There would have been no photosynthesis or any other energy mobilization system to harness the highly destructive raw energy of the sun and convert it into chemical energy that could be used to construct the monomers (amino acids, etc.) and the polymers (proteins, DNA, RNA) necessary for life, nor would there be a coding and control system necessary to construct the organized systems with specified complexity, which are a vital part of a living cell. Evolutionists must postulate that order spontaneously arose from chaos, that nonsense spontaneously generates sense, that simple, disordered systems spontaneously gave rise to an incredibly complex living cell. This is nothing more than a twentieth century myth that man has invented to explain his origin without God. As with all myths, it is intellectually bankrupt and devoid of any real scientific support.

One of the charges that Patterson has made against creation scientists is that their organizations are dominated by engineers, perhaps competent in their narrow engineering specialties, but obviously scientifically ignorant and incompetent otherwise. Patterson's allegations are unfounded on both counts. The Creation Research Society, the largest membership society of creation scientists, has 600 voting members who hold postgraduate degrees in the sciences. Engineers make up a relatively small proportion of members of the Creation Research Society. Biologists make up the largest category of membership. At present, the Executive Board of 18 members has only two engineers. Of the nine scientists on the staff of the Institute for Creation Research, Dr. Henry Morris, its president, has a doctorate in engineering with a specialty in hydraulics, and Dr. John Morris, administrative vice-president, has a doctorate in geological engineering. Serving on the Technical Advisory Board are several engineers, which would be expected, since many of Dr. Morris's friends in the sciences are engineers.

Who are these incompetents that Patterson finds among engineers? Patterson himself provides a list.[50] These, of course, include Dr. Henry Morris, Ph.D. from the University of Minnesota, who served for 13 years as chairman of the Civil Engineering Department of Virginia Polytechnic Institute and State University, one of the largest civil engineering departments in the U.S., with 28 professors; Dr. David R. Boylan, Ph.D. in chemical engineering, who served for 18 years as Dean of Engineering at Iowa State University, until voluntarily relinquishing his position as dean very recently (he was, of course, Patterson's superior); Dr. Edward Blick, professor of aerospace, mechanical, and nuclear engineering, and formerly associate dean of engineering at the University of Oklahoma; Dr. Harold R. Henry, Ph.D. in fluid mechanics, professor and chairman of civil and mining engineering at the University of Alabama; Dr. Malcolm Cutchins, Ph.D. in engineering mechanics, professor of aerospace engineering at Auburn University; Dr. William Bauer, Ph.D. in hydraulics, president of his own engineering consulting firm; Dr. John

Morris, Ph.D. in geological engineering, assistant professor in geological engineering at the University of Oklahoma before joining the ICR staff; and Dr. Walter T. Brown, Ph.D. in mechanical engineering, formerly Colonel and Professor of Engineering, Air Force Academy, now retired. This is quite an impressive list, several of whom held or hold positions as deans or chairmen of engineering departments, and practically all holding professorships at major universities. It is further obvious that the university training of all of them would have included courses in thermodynamics, and the positions held by several of them would require special expertise in thermo-dynamics. It is amazing how several of these "incompetents" have managed to receive prestigious appointments as deans or chairmen of engineering departments, while Patterson, their intellectual superior, has failed to obtain such an appointment. Perhaps "incompetency" reaches on up to those university authorities responsible for making such appointments.

Patterson has especially singled out his own Dean of Engineering, Dr. David R. Boylan, in his charges of incompe-tency, especially in thermodynamics. In this respect, he is a bit careless. In a cartoon appearing in his article, "Thermody-namics and Evolution," which appeared in *The American Atheist,*[40] is found a balloon, and riding in the basket beneath the balloon are three people. Attached to the basket is a streamer with the names "Morris," "Williams," and "Boy-land." Patterson apparently has difficulty with spelling the name of his own dean!

Patterson's charges of incompetency and of gross errors in thermodynamics against Dr. Boylan have appeared in his articles in *The American Atheist,*[40] *Proceedings of the Iowa Academy of Sciences* and in *Evolution Versus Creationism.* Prior to these publications, Patterson wrote to me accusing Dr. Boylan of making gross errors in his article, "Process Con-straints in Living Systems," which appeared in the *Creation Research Society Quarterly* in 1978.[51] In his May letter, Patterson accused Boylan of making two blatant errors and attached a sheet detailing what he termed Major Error I and Major Error II.[52] In an earlier letter to me, dated April 17, Patterson said:

> I think you should be ashamed of yourself for letting Dr. Boylan commit his "Process Constraints . . ." paper to print in the December, 1978 *C.R.S.Q.* The mistakes in it are so gross as to make a laughingstock of him, of the Editorial Board of the *Quarterly,* and of all *C.R.S.Q.* readers who have read the paper and failed to even comment on its colossal blunders. They are so bad, only a Creationist such as yourself could have missed them.

I mailed a copy of the sheet detailing the "major errors" to Boylan for his comments, and, I also mailed a copy to Dr. Emmett Williams, Ph.D. in materials engineering from Clemson University, one of the Executive Board members of the *Creation Research Society,* and employed by Lockheed-Georgia Company, Norcross, Georgia, asking for his evaluations of Patterson's charges. Copies of the paper by Boylan, the "Major Errors" alleged by Patterson, and the detailed responses by Boylan and Williams, plus follow-up memos by Patterson and Boylan, will be found in Appendix II in the back of this book.

After receiving a copy of the "Major Errors I and II," Boylan responded with a detailed answer in a letter dated July 9, 1980 (see Appendix II). In that letter, as will be noted, Boylan states:

> First, let me comment on Patterson's criticisms of my paper. I am surprised that there are only two alleged "errors," after he characterized it as "so bad." His citations are, in fact, not errors at all. They show either a misunderstanding of my paper or a lack of understanding about the subject.

What follows is a detailed explanation showing why Patterson's alleged errors are not errors, and pointing out that Boylan's treatment of thermodynamics is scientifically correct. After completing his explanation, Boylan says:

If these citations of Patterson's are the "Major Errors," the paper in no way is ". . . so gross as to make a laughingstock of him (Boylan), of the Editorial Board of the *Quarterly,* or of all the *C.R.S.Q.* readers who have read the paper and failed even to comment on its "colossal blunders." Patterson himself has failed to find even one "colossal" blunder! His critique shows the extent to which he will go to discredit the views of those with whom he disagrees.

In a letter to me dated August 22, 1988, Boylan writes:

My memo to him (Patterson) of July 16, 1980 should have stopped any further criticism. As you know it didn't, and he continued to press the false charge of "gross errors." I now believe he really didn't understand my paper, and he was trying any tactic to prove me incompetent. Although I didn't say so in this memo, it was intended to show him he didn't understand the First Law, let alone the Second Law. His first criticism was that my Equation 3 was "nonsense." Since it is the most common expression of the First Law, he should have been embarrassed. Of course, he wasn't, and to save face he started the diatribe of letters that followed.

There is one fact that destroys all his arguments. He criticizes my development on the grounds that I didn't recognize the constraints of irreversibility. As many have pointed out, organic reactions are generally considered reversible for the most part. In fact, it is hard not to have them reversible. Patterson didn't recognize this and kept on pursuing the irreversible argument.

Also included here are his papers published in *The American Atheist.* The one on "Thermodynamics and Evolution" is the "crowning blow" to his incompetence. He states that ". . . the (hydraulic) ram . . . provides a nice analog for 'explaining' how natural selection works. . . ." Nothing could be further from the truth. If he believes that natural selection is analogous to a hydraulic ram, he simply doesn't understand either.

In a letter to me dated July 9, 1980 (see Appendix II for a copy of the complete letter), Dr. Emmett Williams defends

Boylan's derivations against Patterson's allegations. A copy of Dr. Williams' letter was mailed to Patterson on August 13, 1980. Dr. Williams writes: "I read Boylan's paper over a year ago and thought it was excellent. I saw no problems with it then and I see none now."

As noted earlier, on July 16, 1980, Boylan sent a memo to Patterson (see Appendix II) in which he clarified for Patterson what Patterson alleged were the two major errors in Boylan's paper, that is, errors in Boylan's Equation 3 and Equation 10. Patterson responded with a memo dated July 18, 1980 (see Appendix II). As will be noted, Patterson conceded Boylan's major points, although he says that he still has reservations concerning Boylan's second law (entropy derivation), holding that Boylan's attempt to embrace both the typical process and the corresponding reversible process with one derivation or one expression is "out of order."

This point is thoroughly discussed, clarified, and defended in the second page of Boylan's letter to me of July 9. There is no error here, let alone a "major error." Also, Boylan responded to Patterson's memo with one dated July 21 (see Appendix II) in which he offered further clarification. On August 20, Patterson sent another memo to Boylan (see Appendix II), expressing great interest in Williams' reference to a steady-state, steady-flow (SSSF) system. I do not know whether or not Boylan replied. A final letter on the subject from Williams, dated September 11, 1980, is found in Appendix II. As Williams points out, Patterson by this time had moved away from his original allegations and was discussing new problems he claimed existed in Boylan's paper. The allegations appeared in his paper published in the *Proceedings of the Iowa Academy of Sciences*[39] and in the anti-creationist book, *Evolution Versus Creationism*,[38] pp. 155-157. This book was published in 1983, and Patterson's chapter was a reprint of the paper he had published in June 1982, in the *Proceedings of the Iowa Academy of Sciences*. Patterson says:

The most error-ridden thermodynamic analysis I have seen in print is the one by creationist D. R. Boylan which appears in the December 1978 issue of *Creation Research Society Quarterly*.

To begin with, Boylan virtually equates two of the most distinguishable introductory level concepts in engineering thermodynamics, namely *systems* and *processes*. In effect, he directs his reader to "consider life processes as systems." This is like a would-be mechanic directing us to consider gas combustion (a process) as being like a tire or an engine, which are mechanical systems.

After teaching beginners the profound difference between a process and a system, the next most important issues are (a) how to define or describe the system (e.g. closed, open, isolated, etc.) to which one's analysis is to apply; (b) how to specify the system's boundaries; and (c) how to specify the nature of the processes taking place within or over these boundaries (e.g. are they reversible, irreversible, steady state, etc.). If these specifications are not done properly, the results of one's analysis can come out garbled or self-contradictory. Boylan's paper exemplifies such confusion because he fails to specify properly the system to which his analysis applies and the nature of the "life processes" of which he speaks. Only after I submitted a harsh criticism of the paper to the *Creation Research Society Quarterly (CRSQ)*—which led to a heated correspondence with editorial board members Gish and Williams—were the system process specifications made clear. Williams proved to the satisfaction of both Gish and Boylan that the first and second law analysis and the derivation of the entropy change by Boylan are for an open system subjected to a special kind of steady state condition: the so-called *steady state steady flow* (SSSF) condition. But this was also a blunder, since by definition of steady state there can be no change in the entropy inventory (nor of any other extensive property) for steady state systems. All these properties including entropy must remain steady or fixed in value. Hence, Boylan's central result—i.e. his erroneous formula for the entropy change—should have come out to be identically zero (!) and not the non-vanishing sum whose limiting cases he discusses at great length.

In other words, Boylan's analysis implies a profound and unmistakable self-contradiction. And yet it is clear from the subsequent correspondence that neither Boylan, Williams, nor Gish realized this. In fact, at last contact, Gish inferred from Williams's analysis that "there are no errors at all" in Boylan's paper and actually suggested that I apologize for the criticisms I had submitted which I have not done. Also, as of this date (Spring 1982) no letters questioning Boylan's analysis have appeared in the CRSQ.

Several conclusions can be drawn from all of this. First, one must conclude that Boylan, a Ph.D. and Professor in Chemical Engineering, has committed to print worse errors than those for which beginning thermodynamic students are penalized, if not failed in their homework and examinations. Secondly, Williams, and especially Gish, are at least as devoid of thermodynamic understanding and knowledge as is Boylan. Thirdly, the same can be said for all engineers in the CRSQ readership who read but did not question Boylan's analysis. If there were any who did submit criticisms, I have a feeling the public will be the last to know.

Thus Boylan's paper is best viewed as a poor attempt to make a scientific case for creationism. The paper is self-contradictory, and hopelessly garbled when viewed from the perspective of science.

Notice how Patterson has shifted his charges. Nowhere do we find "Major Error I" and "Major Error II." He now charges that Boylan equated system with process, that Boylan failed to specify properly the system to which his analysis applies and the nature of the "life processes" of which he speaks, and then charges Boylan with a third blunder—that "the first and second law analysis and the derivation of the entropy change by Boylan are for an open system subjected to a special kind of steady-state condition: the so-called *steady-state steady-flow* (SSSF) condition." Because of this, Patterson declares,

"Boylan's analysis implies a profound and unmistakable self-contradiction." Please note: Nowhere in all of his previous correspondence did Patterson mention this "profound and unmistakable self-contradiction." He was not aware that Boylan's paper contained such a "profound and unmistakable" contradiction. His concern was with "Major Error I" and "Major Error II." I do not recall whether or not I sent a copy of Williams' letter to Boylan, thus, whether he approved Williams' statement concerning the SSSF condition. Whether or not Boylan's first and second law analysis and the derivation of the entropy change by Boylan are for an open system subjected to a steady-state steady-flow system, and whether or not this is a colossal blunder, one thing is certain: Patterson was not aware of it, in spite of his intense searching of Boylan's paper for alleged errors. It was not until Williams pointed this out that Patterson became aware of it. But note—he condemns Williams, Gish, and all engineers in the CRSQ readership who read Boylan's paper and did not find errors in that paper, but yet he himself "missed" what he claims is a profound and unmistakable blunder!

Recently the controversy was reopened by the reprinting in *The Christian Connection*[53] of the article that Patterson had published in the *Proceedings of the Iowa Academy of Sciences.*[39] I sent a copy of this article to Dr. Boylan and asked for his comments. The following are excerpts from a letter dated December 26, 1989, that I received from Dr. Boylan in response:

> As to my interaction with Patterson, I can only add a few thoughts. At the beginning, I thought that he might have found some mistakes. I told him that anyone could make a mistake and that I would be willing to address any errors he might have found. He declined to point out any errors, saying it was a 'professional' matter, and instead tried to vilify me in the media. The "The Major Error I and Major Error II" never materialized. He called my Equation 3 (in the CRS article) "nonsense" until I pointed out that it was the generally accepted expression of the First Law for open

systems and referred him to Van Wylen and Sonntag's "Fundamentals of Classical Thermodynamics".

As you point out, Patterson kept changing his mind on just what were the errors. He tried to make a point of my use of "systems" and "processes" by some strange analogy of ". . gas combustion (a process) being like a tire or an engine . .". He apparently hasn't worked any thermodynamic problems related to gas combustion. In thermodynamic analysis one is at liberty to choose the "system", as Van Wylen puts it (p.17), as "a quantity of matter of fixed mass and identity upon which attention is focused for study . ." And, on page 220, Van Wylen states ". . the principle of the increase of entropy can be considered as a quantitative general statement of the second law from the macroscopic point of view, AND APPLIES TO COMBUSTION OF FUEL in our automobile engines, the cooling of our coffee, and the processes that take place in our body . ." Note these examples. They are all 'processes'. Obviously, he [Patterson] either doesn't understand the terms himself, or he is just making up criticisms to justify his own personal vendetta of creationists.

The article in the Proceedings of the Iowa Academy of Science, which I had not seen until reprinted by the Spirit of the Lord Charitable Fund, is by far the most telling "blunder" that Patterson has made. In his article "An Engineer Looks at the Creationist Movement" he states ". . by definition of steady state there can be no change in the entropy inventory (nor of any other extensive property) for steady state systems . . All these properties including entropy must remain steady or fixed in value . ." He references Van Wylen, page 235. Unfortunately, he is not well read in the book he references. On page 127 of that book, the authors state under the heading Steady-State, Steady Flow Process, ". . consider a centrifugal air compressor that operates with constant mass rate of flow into and out of the compressor, constant properties AT EACH POINT across the inlet and exit ducts, a constant rate of heat transfer to the surroundings, and constant power input. At each point in the compressor the properties are constant with time, even though the properties of a given elemental mass of air VARY AS IT FLOWS THROUGH THE COMPRESSOR." What Patterson didn't read in his reference on page 235 were the words ". . at any point within the control volume . .". Even so, only the first term of the second law control volume equation equals zero. On the very next page, 236, the authors give the resulting equation which has a change in entropy term for the mass crossing the control volume boundary. Again, the claimed "blunder" is his own, not mine.

As I told Patterson, I am willing to correct any error which might have been made. The letters to the editor of most scientific journals show that errors do creep in the best of manuscripts. Most of these letters are gracious attempts to help the scientific community. This is not the case with Patterson. His purpose, unfortunately, is to discredit anyone who holds the creationist position.

A careful and thorough reading of Boylan's paper and all of the correspondence that resulted from Patterson's allegations of major errors in the paper will show that, if there are any errors in the paper, they are minor and of little consequence relative to the thesis that Boylan established.

Patterson's objective in all of this is to discredit his Dean of Engineering, a creation scientist who published a paper pointing out contradictions between evolutionary theory and thermodynamics. By this diversion, Patterson deliberately attempts to conceal the fact that he cannot, point by point, refute Boylan's arguments on evolution and the Second Law. This is a common practice among evolutionists—remember that evolutionists made no attempt to answer my challenge to explain how an ordinary beetle could have evolved into a bombardier by any mode of evolution. They sought only for any possible slip-up, no matter how minor, so they could rave about that without feeling obligated to answer the challenge—for which they knew they had no answer.

Patterson's charges that David Boylan is grossly incompetent in thermodynamics is ridiculous, on the face of it.

Boylan's Ph.D. is in chemical engineering, and during all the years he held the position of Dean of Engineering at Iowa State University, he also served as a professor of chemical engineering. Thermodynamics is especially important in chemical engineering, even as Patterson himself has admitted. How could the administration at Iowa State University, especially in engineering, be so inept as to appoint a faculty member, incompetent in one of his most important disciplines, to the position of professor of chemical engineering and then later elevate him to the prestigious position of Dean of Engineering? No—the only motive behind Patterson's campaign of vicious charges against Dean Boylan is the fact that Dr. Boylan is a creation scientist—an unforgivable sin in Patterson's eyes.

In many cases, evolutionists have simply brushed aside the challenges of creation scientists to evolution based on thermodynamics, by resorting to tactics similar to those employed by Patterson—charging creation scientists with incompetence, and suggesting absurd examples of apparent circumventions of the Second Law by evolution, such as tornadoes, crystallization, ram pumps, batteries, and fertilized eggs developing into adult animals, and employing the old closed-system, open-system argument. The most vitally important questions, however, they have failed to answer—how the universe, an isolated system, could transform itself from chaos and simplicity into order and complexity, when the Second Law tells us this is impossible; how the natural laws and processes now destroying the universe could also create it; and how the incredibly complex internal organization of a living cell could create itself in spite of all the work that had to be done to create the enormous amount of information required to specify that organization. It is strange that evolutionists believe that random, blind, chance natural processes have managed to create this universe and man, with his incredible brain, in spite of the Second Law, but man, an open system with a steady flow-through of energy, equipped with the most complex machinery in the universe and endowed with that incredible brain, cannot devise a way to circumvent the Second Law—*and live forever!*

References

1. Robert Shapiro, *Origins - A Skeptic's Guide to the Creation of Life on Earth,* Bantam Books, New York, 1986, pp. 207,211.

2. E. L. Williams, "The Initial State of the Universe - A Thermodynamic Approach," in *Design and Origins in Astronomy,* George Mulfinger, Ed., Creation Research Society Monograph Series: No. 2, Creation Research Society Books, P.O. Box 28473, Kansas City, MO 64118.

3. E. L. Williams, *ibid.,* p. 33.

4. S. A. Gregory and L. A. Thompson, *Scientific American* 246(3):113 (1982).

5. Ben Patrusky, *Science 81,* June 1981, p. 96.

6. Fred Hoyle, *New Scientist* 92:524 (1981).

7. G. O. Abell, in *What Darwin Began,* L. R. Godfrey, Ed., Allyn and Bacon, Boston, 1985, p. 240.

8. G. Gamov, *The Creation of the Universe,* Viking Press, New York, 1955, p. 20.

9. V. F. Weisskopf, *American Scientist* 65:409 (1977).

10. Julian Huxley, "Evolution and Genetics" in *What Is Science?,* J. R. Newman, Ed., Simon and Schuster, New York, 1955, p. 278.

11. F. Hoyle, as quoted by Robert Shapiro, Ref. 1, p. 208.

12. R. B. Lindsay, *American Scientist* 56:100 (1968).

13. H. F. Blum, *Time's Arrow and Evolution,* Princeton University Press, Princeton, 3rd Ed., 1968.

14. H. F. Blum, *American Scientist* 43:595 (1955).

15. Isaac Asimov, *Smithsonian Institution Journal,* June 1970, p. 6.

16. See for example A. E. Wilder-Smith, *The Scientific Alternative to Neo-Darwinian Evolutionary Theory: Information Sources and Structures,* TWFT Publishers, Costa Mesa, CA 1987.

17. Warren D. Dolphin, in *Did the Devil Make Darwin Do It?*, D. B. Wilson, Ed., The Iowa State University Press, Ames, IA, 1983, p. 31.

18. Chris McGowan, *In the Beginning . . .*, Macmillan of Canada, Toronto, 1983, pp. 10,11.

19. Isaac Asimov, in *Science and Creationism*, Ashley Montagu, Ed., Oxford University Press, Oxford, 1984, pp. 187,188.

20. Alice B. Kehoe, in Ref. 7, p. 179.

21. H. F. Franzen, in Ref. 17, pp. 127,128,129.

22. Isaac Asimov, in "The Genesis War," *Science Digest,* October 1981, p. 82.

23. D. J. Futuyma, *Science on Trial,* Pantheon Books, New York, 1983, p. 183.

24. J. W. Patterson, in *Scientists Confront Creationism*, L. R. Godfrey, Ed., W. W. Norton & Company, New York, 1983, p. 105.

25. J. W. Patterson, *ibid.,* pp. 104,105.

26. P. T. Mora, *Nature* 199:216 (1963).

27. J. S. Wicken, *Journal of Theoretical Biology* 77:349 (1979).

28. Ilya Prigogine, Gregoire Nicolis and Agnes Babloyants, *Physics Today* 25(11):23 (1972).

29. C. B. Thaxton, W. L. Bradley, and R. L. Olsen, *The Mystery of Life's Origin: Reassessing Current Theories,* Philosophical Library, New York, 1984, pp. 119-120. This is the finest critique of origin-of-life theories by creation scientists. Thaxton has a Ph.D. in chemistry, Bradley holds a Ph.D. in materials science, and Olsen has a Ph.D. in geochemistry. This book may be obtained from the Foundation for Thought and Ethics, P.O. Box 830721, Richardson, TX 75083-0721.

30. P. H. Abelson, *Proceedings of the National Academy of Science* 55:1365-1372 (1966).

31. C. J. Smith, *Biosystems* 1:259 (1975).

32. G. G. Simpson and W. S. Beck, *Life: An Introduction to Biology,* Harcourt, Brace, and World, New York, 1965, p. 466.

33. S. W. Angrist and L. G. Hepler, *Order and Chaos,* Basic Books, New York, 1967, pp. 203-204.

34. H. F. Blum, Ref. 13, pp. 200-201.

35. H. F. Blum, *ibid.,* p. 160.

36. H. F. Blum, *ibid.,* p. 165.

37. H. F. Blum, *ibid.*, p. 166.
38. J. W. Patterson, in *Evolution Versus Creationism: The Public Education Controversy,* J. P. Zetterberg, Ed., Oryx Press, 1983, pp. 150-161.
39. J. W. Patterson, *Proceedings of Iowa Academy of Sciences* 89(2):55-58 (1982)
40. J. W. Patterson, *The American Atheist* 25:39-46 (1983).
41. J. W. Patterson, Ref. 24, pp. 99-116.
42. H. M. Morris, *Troubled Waters of Evolution,* Creation-Life Publishers, San Diego, 1975, pp. 111-142.
43. Gregoire Nicolis and Ilya Prigogine, *Self-Organization in Nonequilibrium Systems: From Dissipative Structures to Order Through Fluctuations,* John Wiley & Sons, New York, 1977, p. 12.
44. *Institute for Creation Research Impact Series,* No. 57, March 1978 (H. M. Morris) and No. 58, April 1978 (D. T. Gish), El Cajon, CA.
45. Peter Engels, *The Sciences* 24(5):50-55 (Sept./Oct. 1984).
46. Ilya Prigogine and Isabelle Stengers, *Order Out of Chaos,* Bantam Books, Inc., New York, 1984.
47. John Ross, *Chemical and Engineering News,* July 27, 1980, p. 40.
48. C. B. Thaxton, W. L. Bradley, and R. L. Olsen, Ref. 29, pp. 151-154.
49. C. B. Thaxton, W. L. Bradley, and R. L. Olsen, *ibid.,* p. 165.
50. J. W. Patterson, Ref. 38, p. 153.
51. D. R. Boylan, *Creation Research Society Quarterly,* 15(3):133-138 (1978).
52. J. W. Patterson, personal communication to D. T. Gish, May 27, 1980.
53. J. D. Kallmyer, Special Edition of *The Christian Connection,* December 1989, P.O. Box 546, Owing Mills, MD, 21117 (the article by Patterson was reprinted as part of this paper by Kallmyer).

7

Kitcher Abuses Science

Philip Kitcher was Associate Professor of Philosophy at the University of Vermont when his book, *Abusing Science - The Case Against Creationism*[1] was published in 1982. (He is now at the University of California, San Diego). It is a virulent attack on creation science and creation scientists by this philosopher and is one of the most widely read books of this kind. This chapter is a critique of this book. Beginning on the first page of his book, Kitcher employs the favorite tactic of evolutionists—laying down a smoke screen of religion in order to obscure the science of creation science. On p. 1, Kitcher asserts:

> In recent years, a political alliance has been forged between the self-appointed champions of virtue and religion—the Moral Majority—and a group of believers in the literal truth of the Bible. The extreme fundamentalists, who call themselves Scientific Creationists, have founded the Institute for Creation Research.

In the next few pages, he repeatedly links scientific creationists with the Moral Majority, as if any such link would in itself be sufficient to discredit the scientific credibility of scientists who support creation. The Institute for Creation Research was founded long before the founding of the Moral Majority, and there never has been a link between the two, although members of each may share the views of the other. As mentioned earlier in this book, there are many scientists who are neither Christians nor who believe in a literal reading of Genesis, but who nevertheless reject evolutionary theory in favor of some form of creation. Furthermore, as far as the scientific case for and against creation or evolution is concerned, it is immaterial what creationists or evolutionists believe about the Bible. The only relevant matter is what scientific evidence creationists can present to support creation and what scientific evidence evolutionists can present to support evolution. After all, one can be right for the wrong reason or be wrong for the right reason.

Kitcher's own dogmatism and almost religious devotion to evolution pervades his book. He leaves no doubt that to him evolution is fact, not theory (although the mechanism may be in doubt). He says (p. 150) that "there is an ongoing debate about the *mechanism* of evolution. That debate does not touch the *fact* of evolution." His dismissal of creation is as sharp as his embrace of evolutionary dogma is unrestrained. Thus Kitcher asserts, "Creationism does not merit scientific discussion" (p. 171), although his book is largely devoted to a scientific discussion of creation.

But why not have a full and free discussion of the scientific merits of creation and evolution in the public school classroom? Why not expose students to all the evidence on both sides of this controversial question? Why not let the students decide for themselves which explanation of origins is more credible? Kitcher correctly states that:

> Students would be indoctrinated if they were offered a
> single view as authoritative when rival views were equally
> well confirmed by the available evidence [p. 176].

He then goes on to assert, "Nothing like indoctrination occurs when the best-supported account of the origin and development of life is presented for what it is." First of all, it may be pointed out that numerous times in the past, theories in science that were considered to be best supported by the evidence were proven wrong and were discarded. Some of the greatest disasters in science have occurred when theories were allowed to freeze into dogma and shielded against challenge. Secondly, it may be asked, who has decided that evolutionary theory is the best-supported account of the origin and development of life? Why, evolutionists, of course! It is they who consider themselves to be the intellectual elite, the sole possessors of truth who must protect ignorant and scientifically illiterate students from error. It is this clique of favored individuals who must see to it that students are properly indoctrinated in "true science" (evolutionary theory). Fortunately, for the sake of good science and academic freedom, more and more scientists today are breaking free from the intellectual shackles that Darwinism has imposed on their thinking and are willing to consider creation, or at least to entertain anti-evolution ideas.

The beauty, the strength of evolutionary theory, according to Kitcher, is that it employs problem-solving strategies via a particular style of historical narratives. Thus he states:

> The heart of Darwinian evolutionary theory is a family of
> problem-solving strategies related by their common em-
> ployment of a particular style of historical narrative. A
> Darwinian history is a piece of reasoning. . . . Suppose we
> want to know why a contemporary species manifests a
> particular trait. We can answer that question by supplying
> a Darwinian history that describes the emergence of that
> trait [p. 50].

It is truly incredible that Kitcher, obviously intelligent and holding a Ph.D. in philosophy, cannot distinguish between history and "a piece of reasoning," or between true history and an historical narrative contrived to support a particular notion about the past. Of course it is perfectly legitimate for Kitcher, or anyone, to adopt a philosophy about the past, but to equate such a view with reality or to pretend that this view is real history is both arrogant and misleading.

Kitcher attributes great importance to what he believes to be the problem-solving strategies inherent in Darwinian evolution. He believes that since evolutionists can construct historical narratives about supposed evolutionary processes, they have employed problem-solving strategies. Now, one can certainly employ problem-solving strategies in designing programs to, say, avoid famine in a particular country in the next year or so, or in designing a spacecraft to make a soft landing on Mercury. But how can one employ problem-solving strategies to reconstruct the evolution of, say, a sea urchin into a fish, which is obviously operationally impossible in either the present or in the past? How can one employ problem-solving strategies for unobservable, one-time events which occurred in the past? If, on the other hand, Kitcher has a problem-solving strategy of, for example, evolving a fish into an amphibian, he should design and conduct the experiment. The suggestion is, of course, absurd.

And what about historical narratives? Certainly evolutionary literature is full of historical narratives, most of which have now been discredited and discarded. As noted in an earlier chapter, Derek Ager, arch anti-creationist, admitted that most of the evolutionary stories he had learned as a student have now been debunked,[2] and Colin Patterson, senior paleontologist at the British Museum, has reminded us that all we have of the evolutionary phylogenetic trees are the tips of the branches. All else is story-telling of one kind or another, and that so-called evolutionary historical narratives are nothing more than empty rhetoric.[3] Kitcher, as is true of most evolutionists, has deluded himself into believing that true science, at least as far as evolutionary theory is concerned, can be replaced by story telling.

Kitcher illustrates the supposed power of Darwinian "problem-solving" strategies and story-telling by "explaining" why tenrecs, a group of insectivorous mammals, are found on Madagascar, an island off the east coast of Africa (pp. 51-52). He says:

> A straightforward evolutionary story makes sense of what we observe. In the late Mesozoic or early Cenozoic, small, primitive, insectivorous mammals rafted across the Mozambique Channel and colonized Madagascar. Later the channel widened and Madagascar became inaccessible to the more advanced mammals that evolved on the mainland. Hence the early colonists developed without competition from advanced mainland forms and without pressure from many of the normal predators who make life difficult for small mammals. The tenrecs have been relatively protected. In the absence of rigorous competition, they have preserved their simple body plan, and they have exploited unoccupied niches, which are filled elsewhere by more advanced creatures. Tenrecs have gone up the trees and burrowed in the ground because those are good ways to make a living and because they have had nobody but one another to contend with.

There you have it! A perfectly reasonable story, Kitcher believes, to explain the presence of tenrecs on Madagascar, and demonstrating the power of Darwinian problem-solving strategies and story telling to provide the true history of the colonization of Madagascar by tenrecs. First of all, every word of Kitcher's story could be true (which it isn't), without providing one shred of evidence for evolution. Kitcher's story, for example, doesn't even pretend to explain where tenrecs came from in the first place, and isn't that what evolutionary theory was invented for in the first place? Even Kitcher supposes these creatures were tenrecs when they rafted on his ark to Madagascar. Isn't it possible, even probable that the burrowing, the tree-climbing, and the other varieties of tenrecs existed before they rafted to Madagascar?

Not only does Kitcher's story fail to explain anything significantly related to evolutionary theory, but important details are obviously incorrect. He suggests that tenrecs rafted over to Madagascar in the late Mesozoic (about 75 million years ago on the evolutionary time scale) or early Cenozoic (65-70 million years ago). He apparently is unaware of the fact that the earliest fossil record of tenrecs on Madagascar is found in the Pleistocene,[4] or about three million years ago on his time scale. This is 60 million years too late to fit Kitcher's story. According to reconstructions by those geologists who hold to the reality of continental drift, Madagascar was essentially in its present position by the Pleistocene, so the Mozambique channel was as wide then as it is now. Furthermore, in contradiction to Kitcher's story, there are and were other mammals on Madagascar, and they were there as early as the tenrecs, because their fossils are found in Pleistocene deposits of Madagascar. Furthermore, they are not "primitive" mammals, but they are found in the most "advanced" mammalian order, the Primates. These creatures are, of course, the lemurs. According to Kitcher, the tenrecs rafted across to Madagascar and colonized the island before the more advanced mammals had evolved. Even assuming the standard evolutionary scenario, this story is clearly contradicted by the evidence. If tenrecs did raft over to Madagascar from Africa and some clambered up the trees, they would have been staring right into the face of the lemurs.

Kitcher says, "In the absence of rigorous competition, they have preserved their simple body plan." Regardless of whether or not the tenrecs faced rigorous competition on Madagascar, Kitcher is faced with the problem of explaining why similar creatures, such as the otter shrew, Potamogale, of West Africa, and the Cape golden mole of South Africa, did manage to survive in spite of vigorous competition. In fact, representatives of the tenrec, otter shrew, and golden mole types are known from the Miocene of East Africa. No fossil ancestors are known.[5] No wonder Kitcher made no attempt to employ his Darwinian problem-solving strategy to explain the origin of tenrecs!

Another difficulty intrudes to muddy up Kitcher's story. According to A. Franklin Shull, then professor of zoology at the University of Michigan:

> The fauna of Madagascar is most similar, not to its continental neighbor, Africa, but to that of Asia, the gap being bridged over by the Seychelles Islands, whose animals are similar to those of Madagascar.[6]

The Seychelles Islands are 700 miles from Madagascar, and Asia is another 1,500 miles from the Seychelles, while Madagascar is no more than 300 miles from Africa. Yet, according to Shull, the fauna of Madagascar is more Asian than African. If the tenrecs rafted over from Africa, why did most of the animals found on Madagascar reach there from Asia rather than Africa? Is it not very likely that at the time tenrecs migrated to Madagascar, prevailing currents favored migration from Asia to Madagascar rather than from Africa to Madagascar, regardless of the distances involved? The route of migration of tenrecs thus could have been opposite to that suggested by Kitcher.

In any case, we can see that Kitcher's story is directly contradicted by several important facts. So much for the power of Darwinian problem-solving strategies to invent historical narratives!

But, of course, Kitcher could easily invent another story to explain the presence of tenrecs in Madagascar. Evolutionary theory has become so plastic that it can explain anything and everything, no matter what the data may be. In this respect, it is interesting to note the story recounted by evolutionist John Fentress, of the University of Rochester. Of two species of the British vole, when a predator appears overhead, one species seeks to escape detection by remaining perfectly still, while the other species seeks to escape by dashing for the nearest cover. This behavior was explained to a group of zoologists, and the zoologists were asked to explain why the differences in behavior had evolved in these two species. All came up with what they considered to be excellent solutions (based no doubt on Darwinian problem-solving strategies!). The only problem with the solutions was that the professor had switched the two species! The one that remained motionless, the professor had told the zoologists, was the one that scampered for cover, and the one that ran for cover, the professor had said, was the one that remained motionless![7]

Perhaps it was fellow evolutionists like Kitcher that Richard Lewontin had in mind when he accused Darwinists of telling "Just So" stories when they try to explain how natural selection explains evolutionary novelties.[8] In any case, Kitcher's historical narratives are nothng more than "Just So" stories and without any real scientific merit, although he devotes many pages of his book to extolling the powers of Darwinian problem-solving strategies and deriving what he calls evolutionary scenarios.

Kitcher supports, beautifully, the creation scientists' claim that evolutionary theory has been constructed so that it can explain anything and everything, no matter what the data might be. For example, beginning on p. 68 of his book, Kitcher seeks to explain how evolution could be compatible with discontinuities between organisms. He begins by stating that there are a number of answers a neo-Darwinian may offer. First, in some cases, intermediate forms may simply not be produced. He says:

> An ancestral population may split into two parts that can then diverge from one another by natural selection. After millions of years of evolution, the two descendent populations are morphologically very different, and there are no intermediates. In other cases, intermediates may arise, but lose out in competition with the extreme forms. Neither of these explanations is exactly an unrelated straw frantically clutched by Darwinians to save their favorite theory.

Thus, according to Kitcher, we can have millions of years of evolution giving rise to two descendant populations which

are morphologically very different, yet there are no intermediates! Kitcher, of course, makes no attempt to explain how
this could be. But then he goes on to say that perhaps there
were intermediates. Thus, perhaps there were no intermediates, but then again, perhaps there were. These suppositions
leave Kitcher certain to be right—either there were no intermediates or there were intermediates. Furthermore, if there
were intermediates, why is there a discontinuity between the
two species? How could there have been representatives of
the two species, both in the present and in the fossil record of
the past, but no record of any intermediates?

Kitcher admits (p. 70), "Notoriously, *The Origin of Species* is rather inexplicit about the origin of species." As other
evolutionists have similarly stated, one thing Darwin did not
cover in his book was the origin of species. Kitcher hastens
to claim, however, that this has been accomplished by later
evolutionists. He then proceeds to supply an example, hypothetical, of course. This hypothetical example involves two
related species of birds, one with a beak three centimeters long
and the other with a beak six centimeters long. Kitcher asks,
"What type of Darwinian history should we construct to describe the evolutionary process?" What kind of "history," we
may ask, is a story that is contrived for the sole purpose of
supporting what the story teller believes could have happened
according to his evolutionary notions? Evolutionary texts are
the only books in which such a bizarre notion of history is
employed.

Kitcher goes on to say that:

The general scenario is easily illustrated by our hypothetical example. Our ornithologist may propose that the
short-beaked form represents the ancestral type. (I should
emphasize, however, that the claim that both species had a
recent common ancestor does not imply that either contemporary population represents the ancestral species. It is
quite possible that the original species should* have been

───────────────

*It is possible that Kitcher meant to say "could" rather than "should."

modified in two different ways.) The long-beaked form arose from a small, isolated subgroup of the ancestral population that found itself in an environment without a handy supply of worms. In this environment, birds with longer beaks were more efficient predators. Thus, there was continuous selection in favor of those birds in the population that had the longest beaks. Our ornithologist suggests that the history of the new species consists of a sequence of populations through which average-beak length consistently increased.

Again, Kitcher, in his hypothetical reconstruction, or Darwinian historical narrative, leaves various options. Perhaps the short-beaked species was the ancestral species, but then, perhaps it was not. Perhaps the ancestral species was neither the short-beaked nor the long-beaked variety, but some unknown type that was modified to give rise to both the short-beaked and long-beaked varieties. All of this is no more than idle speculation, since there is no way to know which explanation is correct and there is no way to falsify any of the alternatives. Kitcher's hypotheses fail all the tests required of a scientific hypothesis.

Nevertheless, after discussing a few other matters in this chapter and making several claims for Darwinian evolutionary theory—some dubious and others clearly erroneous—Kitcher ends the chapter with a grandiose claim. He says (p. 81) that:

> It is also remarkable for its fecundity. Indeed, evolutionary theory has spawned so many healthy new sciences that its actual reproductive success is truly spectacular.

Kitcher does not, however, describe for us what even one of these "many healthy new sciences" might be. Obviously, it couldn't be biology, chemistry, physics, geology, or mathematics, since these sciences pre-date Darwin. It certainly couldn't be genetics, because Mendel's work was published shortly after *The Origin of Species,* and evolutionists, including Darwin, ignored Mendel's work for nearly half a century, even though they were aware of it (Kitcher states on p. 9 that Mendel had sent Darwin a copy of his paper). Darwinism

didn't give rise to the science of embryology, but actually
misled embryologists through the now thoroughly discredited
theory of embryological recapitulation. The Darwinian notion
of vestigial organs held back for many years the true discovery
of the function of the tonsils, the appendix, and many glands,
such as the thymus gland and the pineal gland. All really
significant discoveries that have been made in science since
Darwin would have been made even if evolutionary theory
had never been conceived, and many would have been made
sooner. Evolutionary theory has been a drag on real science.

In his discussion of evolution and the Second Law of
Thermodynamics, Kitcher adopts the usual dodge of evolutionists who attempt to deal with the problem—the matter of
open versus closed systems. Kitcher says (p. 91) that:

> Creationists like to present the second law either by omit-
> ting any mention of its restriction to closed systems or by
> choosing a statement that does not make this restriction
> clear.

He then quotes statements by Henry Morris, Randy Wysong,
and H. Hiebert, and says:

> In all these cases, Creationists fail to acknowledge that the
> second law states only that the entropy of *closed* systems
> increases.

As was made clear in an earlier chapter, creation scientists are
fully aware of all the restrictions that apply to the Second Law
of Thermodynamics and all of the considerations that apply
to energy transmission, storage, and utilization in any hypothetical evolutionary process. This is made clear, even by
Kitcher, for he devotes about half a dozen pages to attempting
to refute creation scientists' arguments which do take into
account the matter of open and closed systems. As a matter of
fact, Morris devotes an entire chapter to a discussion of thermodynamics, including open and closed systems, in the book
quoted by Kitcher.[9] It is Kitcher who applies simplistic arguments based solely on claims related to open systems.

Kitcher states (p. 94) that:

> Creationists now ask why some open subsystems show decreasing entropy and others (cars in junkyards) do not. That is an entirely different question, and one that has an obvious answer. The simple answer is that the open systems that do not evolve have a different physiochemical makeup from those that do evolve.

Later, he states (p. 95) that:

> Nobody alleged that having an open system is *sufficient* for decreased entropy. . . . Evolutionary theory contends that decreased entropy is *possible* in an open system, not that it must happen in *any* open system.

Of course, creationists realize that evolutionists do not believe that entropy decreases in *all* open systems, and that evolutionists believe that there must have existed some physiochemical makeup that caused highly destructive raw energy, such as ultraviolet energy from the sun, to convert simple gases into the incredibly complex machinery of a living cell. Creationists have challenged evolutionists, however, to describe the physiochemical makeup that reversed the universal natural *tendency* of all systems to go from order to disorder, especially under the impact of the tremendously destructive power of raw energy, such as ultraviolet light.

Kitcher makes no attempt whatsoever to describe what process, what machinery existed that could have converted expanding hydrogen gas into highly condensed stars, galaxies, and solar systems, or what could have transformed simple gases into proteins, DNA, and RNA, and subsequently into the intricate, highly coordinated systems found in living cells. His "explanation" of how evolution circumvented the Second Law is no explanation at all, but consists solely of a statement of his faith that it must have happened. Creationists base their case on empirically established facts, on abundantly confirmed principles of science, while evolutionists resort to "Just So" stories which contradict natural laws and processes. Kitcher miserably flunks his attempt, if that is what it can be called, to refute creationist arguments based on the science of thermodynamics.

One of the major arguments against the mechanistic, naturalistic evolutionary origin of the incredibly complex and precisely arranged systems found in living organisms is based on the mathematical improbability of the random processes involved in chemistry and physics producing such systems, even in the supposed five billion years of earth history. In a section of his book entitled "The Randomness Ploy" (p. 85), Kitcher attempts to refute these arguments. His "explanation," however, explains nothing. He devotes most of his time to discussing what he calls "apparent randomness," "irreducible randomness," and "chaotic processes," accusing the creationists of not understanding the differences. He never explains how natural processes, whether apparently random, irreducibly random, or just plain chaotic, could produce a living organism, or create a human brain with 12 billion brain cells and 120 trillion connections from a single-celled organism.

Kitcher argues that what evolutionists believe:

> is perfectly consistent with supposing that the DNA formed when a system of less complicated molecules (about whose relative abundances we are ignorant) underwent chemical combination according to the general laws that govern chemical reactions.

To suppose, however, that the general laws that govern chemical reactions were operative during the formation of DNA on the hypothetical primitive earth *is* the *problem, not* the *solution* to the problem. The general laws that govern chemical reactions would arrange the nucleotides of a DNA molecule in a nonsense fashion, so that any and all combinations would arise. Thus, the probability that a particular arrangement of nucleotides would result that specified a biologically active protein would be infinitesimally small. Certainly the general laws of chemistry and physics were operating during the construction of this sentence, but those general laws had no more to do with arranging the letters of the alphabet in the precise order required to construct this sentence than the general laws of chemistry had to do with constructing the DNA found in living organisms. Here, in his attempt to refute the case for creation based on probability considerations, Kitcher once again comes up with an argument devoid of any intellectual content.

The same deficiency in Kitcher's ability to recognize the real problems involved is evident from his attempt to deal with probability arguments as found on p. 103. He states:

> Frequently, there are ways of under-describing the starting conditions of an actual occurrence so as to make it look extremely improbable. Imagine that you are dealt a hand of thirteen cards, one after the other, from a standard deck of fifty-two cards. In Morrisian style, we might ask for the probability that you would have been dealt those cards in exactly that order. The answer is about 1 in 4×10^{21}. Of course, that makes the event look very improbable. But it happened.
>
> Cases like these should mystify us only if we overlook the obvious fact that the probability of any event can be very low relative to a *particular description of its initial conditions* even though those initial conditions actually determine that the event will occur. When you are told only that you would receive thirteen cards from a standard deck, being dealt that particular sequence of cards seems very improbable. However, the sequence is completely determined by the conditions prior to the deal—specifically, by the way in which the cards are arranged in the pile.

Precisely correct! But that *is* the *problem, not* the *solution.* Of course each of the four players is certain to receive 13 cards. But *which* 13 cards? The order of the cards in the deck has been arranged by a random process—the shuffling of the cards. It is impossible to predict, before the cards are dealt, which 13 cards a particular player will receive. He is absolutely certain to receive 13 cards of some kind, but the chances of his receiving any particular set of 13 cards is 1 in 4×10^{21}. If the cards could be dealt once every second, it would require

about 10,000 times 20 billion years before a player would have
an even probability of receiving a pre-ordained set of 13 cards.
That would require a long card game indeed! Now suppose
that this had to happen one million times to the same player!

If a monkey was supplied with a typewriter and paper and
was allowed to tap the keys of the typewriter as many times
as there are letters in this sentence, it is certain that that many
letters would appear on the page. There would only be one
chance in 26^{176}, however, that the monkey would have typed
the preceding sentence without any spelling errors. The number 26^{176} is so huge it exceeds the number of particles in
trillions times trillions times trillions times trillions times tril-
lions times trillions times trillions of universes! An evolutionary origin of life, however, would be enormously less likely
than that. People like Kitcher live in a dream world where
evolution is God—nothing is impossible with evolution. The
incredible improbability, or actually the impossibility, of evolution by strictly naturalistic mechanistic processes has been
documented by numerous creationists, anti-evolutionists, neutral investigators, and frustrated evolutionists.[10]

In a section (pp. 106-120) entitled "Fear of Fossils,"
Kitcher attempts to defend the theory of evolution against the
charge of creation scientists that the fossil record directly
contradicts predictions based on evolutionary theory and offers remarkable support for creation. Stating that although
other creationists make this claim, Kitcher indicates that he
would address his remarks primarily to the presentation of it
found in my book, *Evolution? The Fossils Say No!*, referring
to the 1979 edition of that book.[11] As do most evolutionists,
Kitcher begins by attempting to claim that the paucity and
the bias of the fossil record gives a distorted view of reality
that is exploited by creationists. Here he is immediately in
trouble, as more and more geologists in modern times are
abandoning the old Darwinian claim that the poverty of the
fossil record accounts for the fact that so few (if any) transitional forms are found. With fossils of over 250,000 different

species, represented by tens of millions of fossils from every supposed geological period of earth history resting on museum shelves, any claims concerning the purported poverty of the fossil record simply betrays the desperate situation in which evolutionists find themselves.

Part of the problem of evolutionists, Kitcher claims, rests on the bias of the fossil record. He says:

> The fossil record is not only partial. It is biased. Some organisms—such as marine invertebrates—are much more likely to be preserved as fossils than others.

This statement, however, actually runs counter to Kitcher's attempts to get around the difficulties posed by the fossil record, for it is the fossil record of *invertebrates,* which Kitcher admits has the best record, that provides the most powerful testimony against evolution. As detailed in an earlier chapter, even though many millions of fossil invertebrates are found in museum collections and billions are potentially available, all major invertebrate types—sponges, jellyfish, trilobites, sea urchins, sea cucumbers, sea lilies, clams, snails, etc.—appear fully formed right from the first, with no evolutionary ancestors preceding any of these forms, and no connecting forms between any of them. Thus, just where Kitcher claims we should have the best chance of finding transitional forms, none are found.

Kitcher argues that there are some examples of transitional forms, citing what he claims to be transitions between fish and amphibia, reptiles and mammals, and reptiles and birds. Since these suggested intermediates have been dealt with in an earlier chapter, and extensively in *Evolution: The Challenge of the Fossil Record,*[12] as well as in books by other creationists and skeptics, they will not be discussed further here. In spite of Kitcher's attempt to explain it away, the fossil record offers some of the most powerful positive evidence for creation.

It is in this section (p. 115) that Kitcher accuses me of quoting both Richard Goldschmidt and David Raup out of context, but this accusation has been thoroughly refuted in an earlier chapter. In his very next chapter (Chapter 5), Kitcher distorts the belief of the nineteenth century geologist, Adam Sedgewick. Kitcher says, "In 1831, in his presidential address to the Geological Society, Adam Sedgewick publicly announced that his own variant of Creationism had been refuted" (p. 125). Kitcher then proceeds to quote a portion of that address. It is clear from reading this portion, however, that it is not *creation* that Sedgewick is disavowing, but his previously held position concerning *catastrophism*, which he now believed to be incorrect.

Kitcher makes a feeble attempt to refute the evidence for creation based on purpose and design, in a section entitled, "To each according to his need" (pp. 135-143). Kitcher claims that recent discoveries of biochemical similarities among organisms represent "a striking new success for evolutionary theory" (p. 136). This claim is powerfully refuted by molecular biologist Michael Denton[13] and by an alternative interpretation of these data suggested by evolutionists Schwabe and Warr.[14] In attacking the evidence for creation based on design, Kitcher says (p. 137):

> If one wants to believe in Creationism, the picture can easily lull critical faculties. Yet, if we think about it, it is bizarre! Surely we should not imagine the Creator contemplating a wingless bat, recognizing that it would be defective, and so equipping it with the wings it needs. Rather, if we take the idea of a single creative event seriously, we must view it as the origination of an entire system of kinds of organisms, *whose needs, themselves, arise in large measure from the character of the system.*

It is Kitcher's beliefs about how creationists think that is bizarre. Of course creation scientists do not believe that the Creator was half-way through designing a bat when, oops, He suddenly realized that bats needed wings. Of course creation scientists believe that the Creator created each kind of plant and animal, knowing from the start what the morphological, biochemical, and physiological needs would be. If one wants to believe in evolutionism, the picture can easily lull critical faculties. Kitcher says, "Invocation of the word 'design,' or the passing reference to the satisfaction of 'need' explains nothing." The creation scientist might immediately remind Kitcher, first of all, that invocation of the words "natural selection," or a passing reference to the satisfaction of "need," when used in evolutionary theory, certainly explains nothing. Furthermore, an engineer could convincingly invoke "design" and "need" to explain the existence of each of the millions of parts in a spacecraft. Equally well, the design and purpose of every feature of the structure and function of a living cell, which is almost infinitely more complex than a spacecraft, is obvious. Why is the evidence for the creation of a living cell by an intelligent creator less compelling than the evidence for the creation of a spacecraft by intelligent engineers?

Kitcher invokes two examples that are oft repeated by evolutionists as evidence against design by an intelligent creator. The first, the panda's thumb, was made popular by Gould.[15] The claim is that some structures are clumsy and inefficient, one of which is the panda's thumb. Kitcher says, "Although they belong to the order Carnivora, giant pandas subsist on a diet of bamboo. In adapting to this diet, they needed a means to grasp the shoots. Like other carnivores, they lack an opposable thumb. Instead, a bone in the wrist has become extended to serve as part of a device for grasping. It does not work well. Any competent engineer who wanted to design a giant panda could have done better. But it works well enough" (p. 139). The problem with this story is that evolutionists have not bothered to tell the giant panda that his thumb (it really isn't a thumb) is clumsy and inefficient, and so he uses it extremely efficiently to strip the leaves off of bamboo (it wasn't designed as a grasping tool but as a tool for stripping leaves). Even Kitcher admits that "it works well enough." In fact, it works well enough that an evolutionist would be forced to admit that it has served the giant panda during his entire existence (which evolutionists believe has stretched through millions of years). Thus, the "clumsy and inefficient" giant panda's "thumb" is neither a thumb nor inefficient. It is presumptuous for evolutionists to demand that God modify the true thumb of the giant panda, which serves other important needs, for the purpose of stripping leaves, rather than add an extension to the radial sesamoid bone of the wrist, and it is arrogant of them to claim that they could have done a better job. Certainly they know that there is no way to put them to the test, for there is no way for them to redesign the panda's thumb and then check to see if their design is more efficient than the real panda's thumb.

Another example cited by Kitcher is the practice of coprophagy by rabbits. Rabbits excrete two types of fecal pellets, one type of which is brown, the other green. Rabbits reingest the green pellets. The reason for this is that the green pellets contain a considerable amount of nutritious, undigested food which thus serves as a valuable food source. Kitcher and other evolutionists claim that this is repulsive. Kitcher and his fellow evolutionists have failed, however, to ask the rabbits what they think about it. Certainly such behavior appears repulsive to humans, but obviously not to rabbits, and in this case, it is only the rabbit's opinion that counts.

There is much else in this book that we could profitably explore in order to plumb the depths of Kitcher's plea against creationists, but perhaps enough has been said to expose the nature of Kitcher's biased views. What impressed me most, after going through Kitcher's book the second time, was the lack of substance in his arguments. His supposed employment of problem-solving strategies to generate Darwinian historical narratives is nothing but empty rhetoric. He resorts, again and again, to special pleading. He rests safe in his delusion that all objections to Darwinism, even when coming from competent biologists and other scientists, is muddled thinking or fanatic fundamentalism. It is Kitcher who is guilty of abusing science, not the creation scientists.

References

1. Philip Kitcher, *Abusing Science - The Case Against Creationism,* The MIT Press, Cambridge, MA, 1982.

2. Derek Ager, *Proc. Geol. Assoc.* 87:132 (1976).

3. Brian Leith, *The Listener* 106:390 (8 October 1981).

4. A. S. Romer, *Vertebrate Paleontology,* 3rd Edition, University of Chicago Press, Chicago, 1966, p. 381.

5. A. S. Romer, *ibid.,* p. 211.

6. A. F. Shull, *Evolution,* McGraw Hill Book Co., New York, 1951, p. 70 (as quoted by J. C. Whitcomb and H. M. Morris, *The Genesis Flood,* Presbyterian and Reformed Publishing Co., Philadelphia, 1961, p. 85).

7. J. C. Fentress, in the Discussion section of the chapter, "The Problems of Vicarious Selection," George Wald, in *Mathematical Challenges to the Neo-Darwinian Mechanism of Evolution,* P. S. Moorhead and M. M. Kaplan, Eds., Wistar Institute Press, Philadelphia, 1967, p. 71.

8. Sharon Begley, *Newsweek,* April 8, 1985, p. 80.

9. H. Morris, *The Troubled Waters of Evolution,* Creation-Life Publishers, San Diego, 1974.

10. For example, see *Darwin Was Wrong - A Study in Probabilities,* I. L. Cohen, New Research Publications, Greenvale, NY, 1984; *Origins - A Skeptic's Guide to the Creation of Life on the Earth,* R. Shapiro, Bantam Books, New York, 1986; *Evolution - Possible or Impossible?,* J. E. Coppedge, Zondervan Publishing Co., Grand Rapids, MI, 1973; *Evolution: A Theory in Crisis,* M. Denton, Burnett Books, London, 1985; *The Mystery of Life's Origin,* C. B. Thaxton, W. L. Bradley, and R. L. Olsen, Philosophical Library, New York, 1984.

11. D. T. Gish, *Evolution? The Fossils Say No!,* Creation-Life Publishers, San Diego, 1979.

12. D. T. Gish, *Evolution: The Challenge of the Fossil Record,* Master Books, El Cajon, CA, 1985.

13. M. Denton, *Evolution: A Theory in Crisis*, Burnett Books, London, 1985.

14. C. Schwabe and G. Warr, *Prespectives in Biology and Medicine* 27(3):465 (Spring 1984).

15. S. J. Gould, *The Panda's Thumb,* Norton, New York, 1980.

8

Eldredge and His Monkey Business

As has been indicated earlier, Niles Eldredge, a curator at the American Museum of Natural History and an invertebrate paleontologist, is one of the chief architects of the punctuated equilibrium notion about evolution. This is the idea that evolution has not proceeded by a slow, gradual process involving innumerable micromuations, but that after long periods of stasis, or no change, each species arose very rapidly (in a few thousands of years) from preexisting species by some as yet unknown mechanism. He has been a very active anti-creationist and is the author of the book, *The Monkey Business. A Scientist Looks At Creationism.*[1] This chapter is a critique of that book.

In the preface to his book, Eldredge begins by quoting the King James translation of Genesis, Chapter 1. He describes a scientific creationist as one who respects these words as literal truth but seeks to prove the Genesis account using scientific evidence, while disproving evolution. He then describes a theistic evolutionist as one who reads Genesis metaphorically and believes that God used natural laws to create the universe and living organisms, viewing the six days of creation as six eons. Lastly, Eldredge says, we have the scientist who may have any conceivable personal opinion about Genesis but who must consider the origin of all things natural solely in natural terms. In the next paragraph, Eldredge makes rather clear that he belongs to the latter category of scientists. He states:

> It seems to me that the beauty and relevance of Genesis 1 are neither threatened nor enhanced by modern science. Why can't we just let it be and get on with the job of understanding ourselves and our world in our respective time-honored ways?

Creation scientists maintain that modern science does enhance Genesis 1 by providing powerful positive supporting physical evidence for creation. They are careful to separate evolution theory and philosophy from what should be called modern science, and they reject the notion that humanistic evolutionary thinking is a time-honored way of understanding ourselves and our world.

Eldredge, in Chapter 1, states that:

> Creationists today—at least the majority of their spokesmen—are highly educated, intelligent people (p. 17).

He thus contradicts Stephen Gould's favorite characterization of creationists as "yahoos." Concerning the debates, which he states have taken place all over the United States, Eldredge says, "The creationists nearly always win" (p. 17). He admits that creationists don't argue religion, have always done their homework, and nearly always seem better informed than their opponents, whom, he says, "are reduced too often to a bewildered state of incoherence."

The creationists, by Eldredge's admission, don't argue religion, sticking strictly to a discussion of the relevant scientific evidence. Then why, if, as Eldredge believes, evolutionists have all the scientific evidence on their side and creationists have nothing but pseudoscience to support their case, don't evolutionists blow the creationists and their arguments right out of the lecture hall? Why do creationists "almost always win?" Creationists win debates because of their canny stage appearance, and not through clarity of logic or force of evidence, Eldredge says (p. 18). Incredible! How devilishly clever of creationists. How shameful of evolutionists to allow creationists to win these very important debates and reduce them to a "bewildered state of incoherence," all because of the "canny stage appearance" of their creationist opponents (whatever Eldredge means by that). Eldredge's claim is ridiculous on the face of it. Creationists win the creation/evolution debates for one reason only—they have the truth on their side. Eldredge also admits, "Creationists have been very successful of late in converting student followers" (p. 21). Obviously, this can't be done by a canny stage appearance. This is done, Eldredge says, by the ploy of claiming that evolution and creationism are comparable belief systems. Actually, that is irrelevant to students. They are interested in where the truth lies. They are being converted because they are intelligent and realize where the truth is.

In his initial chapter, Eldredge pours out all kinds of vituperation against creation science. It is, he says, anti-intellectualism; a part of the general surge of neopopulism associated with political conservatism; arguments adduced by creationists to salvage a literal Genesis which are outmoded, false, and (in some cases) downright dishonest distortions; a blatantly religiously inspired political activity; and an attempt to dilute science curriculum with the equivalence of medical quackery. "There," Eldredge asserts, "the gloves are off." Indeed! And creation scientists accept the challenge!

In his second chapter, in a section entitled "Facts and Theories: Is the Earth Really Round?", Eldredge discusses the nature of facts, hypotheses, and theories, but he really does not understand what these terms mean, for he says, "Evolution is a fact as much as the idea that the earth is shaped like a ball" (p. 31). Now many present-day, repeatable observations, earth-bound or from satellites in space, have confirmed that the earth is shaped like a ball. Doubters, if any, can make their own observations and tests concerning this fact. No rational scientist denies this fact. No one, however, has ever seen a fish evolve into an amphibian or an ape evolve into a man. These notions are nothing more than speculation, notions that are contradicted by much scientific evidence and rejected by many thousands of intelligent and well-informed scientists. Eldredge's belief in the "fact of evolution" betrays his religious faith in evolution.

One of the most important criteria of a scientific theory is the ability, on the basis of the theory, to predict the results of experimental tests, or what may occur in nature in the future. No evolutionist will, however, venture to predict what evolutionary changes may occur in the future. Eldredge thus feels compelled to rescue evolutionary theory from this dilemma. He states (p. 33):

> All this fancy rhetoric beclouds the simple meaning of 'predictivity' in science. As we have seen, predictivity means that if an idea is true, there should be certain consequences. We should be able to go to nature to see if these expected (predicted) consequences seem to be there.

What Eldredge is saying is that in science, at least in origins, predictivity about the future course of events is not a necessary requirement—predictivity about what has taken place in the past or may exist in the present is sufficient. A bit later, Eldredge says:

> If the basic idea is correct that all organisms past and present are interrelated by a process of ancestry and descent we call evolution, what should we expect to find in the real world as a consequence? These observable consequences are the predictions we should be making—not guesses about the future.

Before we discuss examples which, according to Eldredge, support predictions based on evolution theory, let us consider other important consequences of what Eldredge has just said. His statement that predictivity means that if an idea is true, there should be certain consequences and we should be able to go to nature to see if these expected (predicted) consequences seem to be there, is just as applicable to creation as it is to evolution. Thus Eldredge has opened the door just as wide to the entry of creation as true science as he has for evolution. It is fully justifiable, therefore, to restate Eldredge's proposal to read:

> If the basic idea is correct that all organisms past and present were created by the deliberate, planned creative acts of an intelligent Creator, what should we expect to find in the real world as a consequence? These observable consequences are the predictions we should be making—not guesses about the future.

As has been described in earlier chapters, what we find in the record of the past (the fossil record) and in the present (thermodynamics, complexity of living organisms versus the laws of probability), the consequences Eldredge is talking about, speak powerfully in favor of creation.

Here Eldredge briefly refers to the fossil record, claiming that there is a three-billion-year history that supports the idea of evolution. As we have seen, however, the fossil record is actually incompatible with the theory of evolution. Eldredge claims, however, that:

> We can sharpen our predictions to the point where a fossil record isn't even necessary to test the fundamental notion that all forms of life have descended from a common ancestor. What should modern life look like if the basic idea of evolution is correct? What predictions would we make? (p. 34).

Eldredge supplies his answer. He says (p. 36):

> ... the very idea of evolution implies that each species will tend to have some features unique to itself, but each species must share some similarities in structure or behavior with

some other species. Furthermore, each group of similar species will share further features with other groups of species (the two-monk analogy again), and this common group *must* share features with still other groups. This pattern of sharing similarities with an ever-widening array of biological forms *must* continue until all of life is linked up by sharing at least one similarity in common. *This* is evolution's grand prediction: that the patterns of similarities in the organic world are arranged like a complex set of nested Chinese boxes.

Eldredge then proceeds to point out that this pattern is precisely what is found in nature. Individuals can be grouped together to form a species because they share many similarities and are interfertile. Groups of species can be placed in a genus because they share certain similarities; similar genera can be grouped into families; similar families into orders, etc. Thus, Eldredge claims, the prediction based on evolution theory has been abundantly confirmed. Furthermore, he says, one would not predict this on the basis of creation—the Creator could have fashioned species in any way imaginable.

The history of biology, however, flatly contradicts Eldredge's story. The fact that living organisms can be arranged into a hierarchy consisting of nested groups was known long before the time of Darwin, long before his theory of evolution had been spawned. The modern system of taxonomy, which groups organisms into species, genera, families, orders, classes, and phyla, was devised by Carolus Linnaeus, whose work preceded the publication of Darwin's *Origin of Species* by 100 years. How can one say that this was a *prediction* of evolutionary theory, when it was commonly known 100 years *before* Darwinism burst upon the scene?

Furthermore, the fact that creatures can be grouped into a set of nested groups is based more on differences and discontinuities than it is on similarities. The record of life, both in the present world and in the world of the past (as revealed by fossils), is a record of sharp discontinuities, not the gradual blending of one species into another, of genera gradually

arising from earlier, similar genera, etc., as would be predicted
on the basis of evolution. The very fact that taxonomy, the
system of classification, is possible, is because of the very
significant gaps between basically different types of organisms. Just as mentioned earlier in this book, Simpson admitted
that the gaps between the higher categories, orders, classes, and phyla are systematic and almost always large, while
Eldredge, Gould, and others who hold to the notion of punctuated equilibrium maintain that there are rarely, if ever, any
transitional forms at the species level. Furthermore, among the
millions of species of living organisms today, no one can point
to a single transitional form, or a nascent organ or organism,
emerging from some preexisting form.

Evolutionists like Eldredge thus point to evidence which
they believe supports their theory, but ignore evidence that is
even more telling against the theory of evolution. We see, then,
that evolution's grand prediction according to Eldredge was
no prediction at all; and, furthermore, what should be evolution's grandest prediction, that, as Darwin claimed, the record
of life would reveal the blending of one form of life into
another form of life with no discontinuities, fails miserably.
The actual record of life, showing that each basic type of plant
and animal life is separate and distinct from all other basic
types, does conform remarkably well with what would be
expected on the basis of creation. One wonders how intelligent
people can be so blinded by their preconceived notions and
religious beliefs to accept evolution theory in spite of a multitude of its failures.

In his third chapter, Eldredge devotes the few pages of
this chapter to a rather brief discussion of the fossil record.
His main thesis is that the general sequence of life, preserved
over a span of 3.5 billion years, conforms well with expectations based on evolutionary predictions. He points out that the
earliest fossils—those of blue-green algae and bacteria, which
are remarkably similar to present-day organisms—are found
in rocks allegedly 3.5 billion years old. He states that in rocks

of about 1.3 billion years of age are found fossils of single-celled eucaryotes; that is, single-celled organisms with a nucleus—algae, amoebas, and foraminiferans. Eldredge then is forced, by the record, to begin a discussion of the very complex invertebrates from the Ediacaran Fauna, found in Australia, Newfoundland, England, Siberia, and South Africa. Eldredge expresses the then prevailing belief that these fossils included those of coelenterates, resembling modern jellyfish and sea pens, others are wormlike, some are echinoderms, and others are of previously unknown forms. He then devotes the next four pages (and p. 130) to discussing the "Cambrian explosion," the sudden appearance of a great variety of complex invertebrates, both soft-bodied and hard-shelled—sponges, jellyfish, trilobites, sea urchins, sea cucumbers, sea lilies, worms, clams, snails, brachiopods, and others. In Chapter 5, a detailed discussion of Eldredge's struggle with this "fascinating intellectual challenge," as he calls it, was included, so it will not be reexamined here. Suffice it to say that in spite of all the squirming and squealing that Eldredge goes through trying to explain away this monstrous incompatibility with the theory of evolution, he must admit (p. 46), "The Cambrian evolutionary explosion is still shrouded in mystery."

What does Eldredge have to say about the origin of fish? Fish are supposed to have been the first vertebrates, thus the ancestors of all other vertebrates—amphibians, reptiles, birds, and mammals—man being the last mammal to evolve. The evolution of fish thus would be the most epochal of all evolutionary events and should be treated in great detail. Their origin should provide a fascinating evolutionary story. Many volumes on the subject should occupy library shelves. The evolution of an invertebrate into a fish would have required a revolution in structure and supposedly spanned 100 million years. Innumerable intermediate stages would have existed during that vast stretch of time. Billions times billions of the transitional forms would have lived and died. Millions of fossils of these intermediates should be resting on museum shelves, but, as documented in Chapter 5, *not one single fossil of such an intermediate has ever been found*! Right where evolutionary changes should be the most obvious and well-documented is precisely where no such evidence is forthcoming. **So, what does Eldredge have to say about the origin of fish? Absolutely nothing!**

On p. 49, Eldredge says:

> Being vertebrates ourselves, it is with the fish, amphibians, reptiles, and mammals that we are most interested. Here the fossil record has, in a sense, been deceiving, because the vertebrates conform to Darwin's expectations far better than any other group: 'fishes' of various sorts predate the earliest vertebrates to clamber out on land—'amphibians,' which were still obliged to return to the water to reproduce (as frogs and salamanders do today).

This is all that Eldredge has to say about the origin of fishes—that is, nothing.

Eldredge points out what he thinks is important evidence in the fossil record that supports evolution—the succession of simpler forms to the more complex—procaryote single-celled organisms (blue green algae and bacteria) to single-celled eucaryotes (all organisms with a nucleus, including single-celled organisms) to complex, multicellular organisms (Ediacaran and Cambrian invertebrates) to fishes and other vertebrates. He either ignores or attempts to minimize, however, the really significant characteristics of this record—the immense, indisputable gaps between the single-celled organisms and the complex invertebrates and between these complex invertebrates and fishes. These huge, unbridged gaps are far more than "fascinating intellectual challenges"—they are fatal to evolutionary theory. Neither invertebrates nor fishes (allegedly the first vertebrates) have ancestors, and all other vertebrates, including man, are the supposed lineal descendants of, first, some invertebrate, and subsequently, of some fish. They have no ancestors, thus we have no ancestors, and evolution has been effectively falsified, whether evolutionists admit this truth or not. As pointed out in Chapter 5, this renders pointless any further discussion of the fossil record.

On p. 80, Eldredge states:

> . . . creation-science isn't science at all, nor have creation scientists managed to come up with even a single intellectually compelling, scientifically testable statement about the natural world.

One of the statements about the natural world that creationists have made is that both in the fossil record and among living organisms the discontinuities between basically different types of living organisms, both plants and animals, would be systematic and almost always large. During the approximate 130 years since Darwin's *Origins of Species,* that statement has been tested, literally, many thousands of times, as paleontologists have searched intensely for the "missing links," but today the "missing links" are still missing. Thus the statement by creationists above, an intellectually compelling scientifically testable statement, has been confirmed. Furthermore, this statement by creationists did contain a very important element of predictivity, since it was first made in Darwin's time, long before it was known what the intense search of the past 130 years might produce.

Eldredge devotes his fourth chapter to a discussion on the mechanism of evolution, discussing the succession of ideas on this subject—Lamarckism, Darwinism, neo-Darwinism, the "hopeful monster" notion of Schindewolfe, Goldschmidt, and others, and his own concept of "punctuated equilibrium." He makes the interesting admission (p. 52) that:

> Superficially, it looks as if we know less now about how evolution works than we did, say, even ten years ago. This is because, as recently as a decade ago, there was something approaching unanimity in the evolutionary ranks. Today, though chaos is too strong a word, there is definitely dissent in the ranks.

Incredible! Ever since Darwin, hordes of scientists (zoologists, botanists, paleontologists, geneticists, embryologists, anatomists, physiologists, biochemists, and geologists) have devoted untold thousands of man-hours to testing Darwinian, neo-Darwinian, and other theories about possible evolutionary mechanisms, and yet they are really no closer to the truth today than Darwin was in 1859. Something must be rotten with the entire concept of evolution.

Eldredge makes another interesting statement (p. 55). Speaking of Darwin's struggle to win over scientists and laymen to his views, Eldredge says:

> And his arguments were so successful that his 1859 *On the Origin of Species* persuaded most biologists and geologists, and a substantial segment of the nonscientific public, that evolution must have occurred. Darwin reviewed all the telltale signs in nature suggesting evolution must have happened. But he convinced the world of the reality of evolution mainly by propounding a simple, believable theory on how evolution occurs.

In other words, it was not evidence from the fossil record (which even Darwin admitted was the most serious objection to his theory); it was not evidence based on comparative anatomy, so-called "vestigial" organs, or embryology; it was not evidence based on biogeography; it was not evidence based upon breeding experiments; it was the fact that Darwin persuaded the world that he had conceived a simple, believable mechanism for evolution. Today, the evidence for evolution based on comparative anatomy (homology), "vestigial" organs, and embryology is recognized as either essentially non-existent or contradictory to evolution; the fossil record is actually incompatible with evolution; artificial selection (breeding experiments) is either irrelevant or contradictory to evolution theory; biogeography and other related evidences can be equally well interpreted on the basis of either evolution or creation; the mechanism Darwin proposed has been discarded by practically every modern biologist, and the neo-Darwinian mechanism devised to replace it has been dubbed "effectively dead" by Stephen Jay Gould.[2] Thus, the one thing that Darwin supplied that won the majority to a faith in evolution, a supposedly convincing mechanism, is now being discarded, and there is absolutely no consensus concerning a replacement. Yet, Eldredge and other evolutionists dogmatically declare, "Evolution is a fact!" A rapidly increasing number of both scientists and laymen are beginning to ask, "But how do they know it's a fact?" The power of propaganda is incessant repetition, and evolutionists seek to convince everyone that they know it is a fact by incessantly repeating, "Evolution is a fact."

Concerning evolutionary biology, Eldredge says (p. 82): "It makes predictions about what we should find in nature, and it is self-correcting. It never claims to have the final truth." Now, compare that to his statement found on p. 31: "Evolution is a fact as much as the idea that the earth is shaped like a ball." This latter statement is stated in terms of final truth just about as much as could be. Evolutionists like Eldredge pretend they are objective, dispassionate scientists, seeking only to know the truth, and allowing the facts to lead them compellingly to the correct conclusion. Actually, scientists are just as biased in their views as are ordinary citizens, and evolutionists, in particular, are guilty of dogmatism and are guided by powerful, preconceived ideas. Eldredge and evolutionists of similar thinking consider themselves to be numbered among the intellectual elite, sole possessors of the truth, whose duty it is to protect innocent students and the lay public from error and to indoctrinate them in evolutionary truths.

Eldredge asserts (p. 83) that a relatively small number of creation scientists have produced the vast bulk of the articles that have appeared in the *Creation Research Society Quarterly*. "None of them," Eldredge claims, "has contributed a single article to any reputable scientific journal." This is patently false, because most of these scientists, including this author, have published articles in a variety of leading scientific journals. Eldredge apparently meant that creation scientists have not published articles in reputable scientific journals that frankly support creation and/or express doubts about the ultimate truth of evolution. This is very near the truth, for regardless of denials by Eldredge and other evolutionists, the editors and referees of those journals reject, out of hand, regardless of merit, any article supporting creation.

Eldredge states that:

> . . . anyone familiar with the scientific literature of the past twenty years knows full well that all manner of new, heretical—and sometimes rather bizarre—ideas have been mooted in the pages of many journals. . . . Indeed, heresy is cherished in some quarters—if it is compelling heresy.

Now let us see what Hannes Alfven, a Nobel Prize winning physicist, has to say about that. In his paper "Memoirs of a Dissident Scientist" Alfven states, "With the referee system which rules U.S. science today, this means that my papers rarely are accepted by the leading U.S. journals."[3] Alfven does not challenge evolution theory. He differs with the Establishment in the interpretation of anomalous redshifts and what this means to theories on the origin and expansion of the universe. If this Nobel Prize winner, who does not even challenge evolution theory, cannot get his papers published in reputable scientific journals, how would it be possible for an *ordinary* scientist to get an article published in one of those journals, an article that *does* challenge evolution theory? All pretense aside, evolutionists are absolutely determined that these journals bar access to creation scientists.

Eldredge quotes (p. 116) a long passage from my book, *Evolution: The Fossils Say No!*,[4] in which I define what is meant by a "basic kind." Eldredge's comments following his quotation of the passage makes one wonder if Eldredge has a good grip of the English language. In that quote, I say:

> It is obvious, for example, that among invertebrates the protozoa, sponges, jellyfish, worms, snails, trilobites, lobsters, and bees are all different kinds. Among the vertebrates, the

fishes, amphibians, reptiles, birds, and mammals are obviously different basic kinds.

Among the reptiles, the turtles, crocodiles, dinosaurs, pterosaurs (flying reptiles), and ichthyosaurs (aquatic reptiles) would be placed in different kinds. Each one of these major groups of reptiles could be further subdivided into the basic kinds within each.

Within the mammalian class, duck-billed platypuses, opossums, bats, hedgehogs, rats, rabbits, dogs, cats, lemurs, monkeys, apes, and men are easily assignable to different basic kinds. Among the apes, the gibbons, orangutans, chimpanzees, and gorillas would each be included in a different basic kind.

It is clear from this passage, when, in saying, "Among the vertebrates, the fishes, amphibians, reptiles, birds, and mammals are obviously different basic kinds," I did not mean that all fishes were the same basic kind, or that reptiles were all one basic kind, etc., for in the very next sentence, I state, "Among the reptiles, the turtles, the crocodiles, dinosaurs, pterosaurs (flying reptiles), and ichthyosaurs (aquatic reptiles) would be placed in different kinds." I go on further to make clear that I did not mean all turtles were a single created kind, or that all dinosaurs were a single created kind, etc., by stating, "Each one of these major groups of reptiles could be further subdivided into the basic kinds within each." I then go on to employ a similar illustration using mammals, making clear, for example, that all apes certainly are different kinds from all other mammals, and that among the apes themselves, the gibbons, orangutans, chimpanzees, and gorillas are each a separate basic kind.

It seems to me that I had so clearly and adequately described what I meant by a basic kind that any high school student with average intelligence, let alone a curator of the American Museum of Natural History, could easily understand what was meant. Eldredge seemed quite confused,

however. Immediately following Eldredge's quote, which included the above material, he says:

> Gish, of course, cannot possibly mean what he literally says
> in this passage. He says that 'variation' occurs within basic
> kinds but not between them—and proceeds to define such
> groups as 'reptiles' and 'mammals' as 'basic kinds.' By his
> very words, then, bats, whales, mankind, and the rest of the
> mammals he cites could have arisen within the basic mam-
> malian 'kind.' But he then defines these subgroups of mam-
> mals as *themselves* constituting 'basic kinds'—which
> means they cannot have shared a common ancestor by
> creationist tenets. Bats beget bats, whales beget whales,
> and so forth, but Gish implies there is no common ancestral
> connection between these basic sub-units of mammals.
> This, of course, is inconsistent, at best, and at worst, sense-
> less. One cannot but agree that creationists, indeed, have
> trouble with the notion of 'basic kinds.'

It seems transparently clear I in no way implied that all
mammals constitute a single basic kind, or that all reptiles
constitute a single basic kind, or that all birds constitute a
single basic kind. What I was saying, is that we know, unhesitatingly, that any reptile is a different basic kind than any
mammal, that we would unhesitatingly know that any mammal is a different basic kind than any bird, just as a taxonomist
immediately assigns a reptile to the Class Reptilia and immediately assigns a bird to the Class Aves. I also make transparently clear we would unhesitatingly know that an ichthyosaur
is a different basic kind than a turtle, although both are included in the Class Reptilia. That doesn't mean, of course, that
all ichthyosaurs constitute a single basic type, or that all turtles
constitute a single basic type. We could illustrate this as shown
in Figures 1 and 2. The Order Primates is subdivided into two
suborders, and each suborder is further subdivided into six
families (Figure 1). The Family Pongidae is divided into three
genera, one of which, *Pan*, is further subdivided into two
species (Figure 2). The basic type, or created kind, may, in
some cases, be at the species level, as is the case with mankind,

Homo sapiens; or at the genus level, as perhaps in the case of *Pan*, or even perhaps at the family level, as, for example, the "dog" kind, or Canidae. The fact, of course, that several small circles are included within a larger circle does not mean that all creatures within the larger circle necessarily constitute a single basic type, or created kind, any more than all creatures the taxonomist places in a genus constitute a single species.

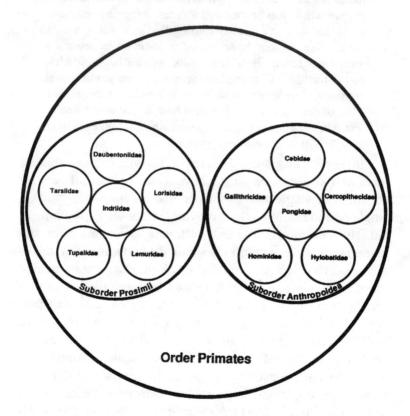

Figure 1.   *Classification of the Order Primates*

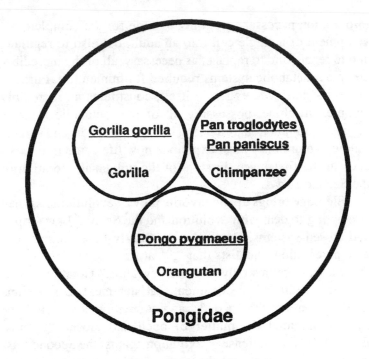

Figure 2.   *Classification of the Family Pongidae*

Eldredge reveals his ignorance, as do most evolutionists, concerning the problem that the science of thermodynamics poses for evolutionists. Since this subject has been discussed in considerable detail in an earlier chapter, what Eldredge has to say about it (pp. 88-91) will be only briefly critiqued. He cites the example of the development of a fertilized human egg cell into an adult human as "an apparent exception to the Second Law." This is silly, of course. First, if there were exceptions to the Second Law of Thermodynamics, it obviously would not be a law but a mere generalization. Secondly, of course, a human egg is an open system which receives a constant supply of energy and food from an external source, but it is even much more. It contains all of the genetic information necessary, not only to code for the complete development of a single cell into an adult, but also to regulate, and to repair, and to replace, as necessary, all of the incredibly complex metabolic systems required for human life. Furthermore, the fertilized egg cell, itself, constitutes an incredibly complex machine, possessing all of the metabolic systems necessary to function as a living thing. What Eldredge and his fellow evolutionists must explain is how life came into existence in the first place, in spite of the universal operation of the Second Law.

Eldredge brings up the favorite ploy of evolutionists when attempting to deal with evolution and the Second Law—open and closed systems. He makes the utterly false charge concerning creation scientists that ". . . at first they didn't realize that the law applies only to closed systems." Creation scientists defy Eldredge to document that statement. Discussions of evolution and the Second Law by creation scientists have always included the matter of open and closed systems. Eldredge's entire defense of evolution against the Second Law is based on the fact that the earth is an open system which receives energy from the sun. As pointed out in an earlier chapter, an open system and an outside energy supply are necessary, but not sufficient conditions for complex ordered systems to arise from disordered, simpler systems. Creation scientists deal with the problem of evolution and the Second Law in a rational, scientific, logical manner, but evolutionists reply only in a simplistic, irrational, and unscientific manner. They abandon reason for the god of evolution.

Eldredge's (and fellow evolutionists') simplistic answers to some of the most severe challenges to evolutionary theory may be seen in Eldredge's response to creationists' arguments based on the design and purpose so obviously seen in nature, expecially among living organisms. He says (p. 132) that:

> Anatomists were among the last holdouts against accepting
> the idea of evolution, so entranced were they with the
> intricate complexities of the organ systems they studied.

Imagining intermediate stages between, say, the front leg of a running reptile and the perfected wing of a bird seemed to them impossible, as it still does to today's creationists. That the problem perhaps reflects more the poverty of human imagination than any real constraint on nature is an answer not congenial to the creationist line of thought.

There's the answer to this challenge! Evolutionists just don't have big enough imaginations, or by jove, they surely would come up with the answers! That answer is about as simplistic as is possible, totally devoid of any intellectual content. Furthermore, evolutionary literature is littered with "Just So" stories. Evolutionists certainly don't suffer from a poverty of imagination! There are a multitude of examples, from nature, which are vastly too intricate and complex, exhibiting such a wealth of evidence of deliberate design and planning by a super-intelligent Creator, that evolutionists simply cannot explain how an evolutionary process, based as it is ultimately on blind, random chance mutations, could ever have produced them. No, neither great leaps of faith based on nothing more than the power of human imagination, nor, when this fails, an appeal to excuses based on the poverty of the human imagination is acceptable to the creationist line of thought.

In his book, *Evolution: A Theory in Crisis,*[5] Michael Denton devotes an entire chapter, "The Puzzle of Perfection," to this topic. He argues forcefully against the notion that an evolutionary process based ultimately on chance mutations could produce the intricate, incredibly complex machinery found in living organisms. In one of the closing remarks in this chapter, Denton says:

> Although the argument for design has been unfashionable in biology for the past century, the feeling that chance is an insufficient means of achieving complex adaptations has continually been expressed by a dissenting majority, and this dissent is undiminished today. As we have seen, the dissenters have not only been drawn from the ranks of fundamentalists, Lamarckists and vitalists such as Bergson

and Teilhard de Chardin, but also from very respectable members of the scientific establishment (p. 341).

Referring to the use, by creationists, of the analogy of organisms to complex machines built by intelligent human beings, Eldredge, after stating that it could be said simply that the Creator did it, says:

> The analogy is as meaningless as that: it 'proves' nothing. It could even be true—but it cannot be construed as science, it isn't biology, and in the end amounts to nothing more than a simple assertion that naturalistic processes automatically *cannot* be considered as candidates for an explanation of the order and complexity we all agree we do see in nature (p. 134).

What does Michael Denton have to say about this? He says:

> The almost irresistable force of the analogy has completely undermined the complacent assumption, prevalent in biological circles over most of the past century, that the design hypothesis can be excluded on the grounds that the notion is fundamentally a metaphysical *a priori* concept, and therefore scientifically unsound. On the contrary, the inference to design is a purely *a posteriori* induction based on a ruthlessly consistent application of the logic of analogy. The conclusion may have religious implications, but it does not depend on religious presuppositions (p. 341).

Eldredge says that the analogy is meaningless, that it proves nothing, and therefore is simply religion which must be excluded from science in general, and biology in particular. Denton soundly rejects this sort of faulty reasoning, pointing out that the concept is a purely *a posteriori* induction, moving from the undeniable evidence for design to the necessity of a Designer, not in the reverse direction. It is therefore not a metaphysical concept, devoid of any actual present-day physical evidence and dependent on religious presuppositions, but is based on a ruthlessly consistent application of the logic of analogy.

Eldredge concludes his book with a chapter on "Creationism, Religion and Politics," in which he maintains that the creation/evolution controversy is solely a religious and political exercise—the creationists using political means to wage war against the inroads of secular humanism, viewing evolution as the cutting edge of this man-centered, non-theistic religion. Citing a number of national polls that show a majority of the American people expressing a belief in creation and an even larger majority expressing an opinion that both creation and evolution should be taught in public schools, Eldredge expresses alarm, while stating, "Creationists have been making truly great inroads" (p. 148). He urges all those citizens interested in thwarting the efforts of scientific creationists to rally round the flag and enter the fray at both the state and local levels.

Creationist scientists say—"Welcome to the war. We are eager to join battle, for we have the truth on our side, and the consequences are as important as life (eternal life) and death." And, as Eldredge says, the gloves are off.

References

1. Niles Eldredge, *The Monkey Business. A Scientist Looks at Creationism,* Washington Square Press, New York, 1982.
2. S. J. Gould, *Paleobiology* 6:121 (1980).
3. Hannes Alfven, *American Scientist* 76(3):251 (1988).
4. D. T. Gish, *Evolution: The Fossils Say No!* Public School Edition, Creation-Life Publishers, 1978.
5. Michael Denton, *Evolution: A Theory in Crisis,* Burnett Books, London, 1985, pp. 326-343.

9

Science Confronts Evolutionists

Many books have been written during the last decade or so attacking creation and creation scientists (see the bibliography in the back of this book). These include a number of books by single authors and at least a half dozen or more by multiple authors. The book edited by Laurie Godfrey, *Scientists Confront Creationism*,[1] was one of the first of these latter books, and the authors of its 15 chapters include some of the most prominent American evolutionists, and all have been vigorous in their public opposition to the efforts of creation scientists. This chapter constitutes a critique of that book.

In her **Preface**, Godfrey states that "scientific creationism is not science; it is religion" (p. xiii). Later, she says, "They [scientific creationists] demand a response. Such is the task of *Scientists Confront Creationism*" (p. xiv). Godfrey says that the scientific creationists are uninformed by scientific developments of the past 150 years. Eldredge admitted, however, that in debates, the scientific creationists nearly always seem

252 Creation Scientists Answer Their Critics

better informed than their evolutionary opponents. If God-frey's statement is correct (it is pure propaganda, of course), then evolutionists are even more poorly informed than are creationists concerning scientific developments of the past 150 years.

In his **Introduction**, Richard Lewontin, a geneticist and professor at Harvard University, states, "The facts of evolution are clear and are not disputed by any serious scientific worker" (p. xxiii). That statement is as inaccurate as it is arrogant. There are literally thousands of serious scientific workers who reject the "facts" of evolution and who believe that creation is far more credible. Lewontin is simply another one of those evolutionists who believes that the incessant repetition of "Evolution is a fact" will, in itself, suffice to convince many people that, indeed, evolution theory is true. He asserts, on the same page, that:

> . . . the present complex living forms have evolved by an
> unbroken and continuous process from the simplest living
> forms of the pre-Cambrian era.

As we have documented in this book, as creation scientists have amply documented in many publications, and as non-creationist Michael Denton so conclusively and forcefully documents in his book[2] (and as other non-creationists have also demonstrated in their books), the record of both living organisms and the fossil record of the past prove beyond any reasonable doubt that these records are not records of an unbroken and continuous process, but are records of system-atic discontinuities, with many gaps that are both immense and indisputable.

Lewontin accuses creation scientists of honest confusion, of conscious attempts to confuse others, and of plunging deep-ly into dishonesty by taking statements of evolutionists out of context to make them say the opposite of what was intended. He claims that one of his statements was taken out of context to indicate that he rejects evolution. Anyone who would use any of Lewontin's statements for that purpose would certainly be either abysmally ignorant or outright dishonest. Lewontin, however, neither names the culprit nor provides any documentation whatsoever, so there is no possibility of the reader checking the accuracy of Lewontin's statement. Furthermore, to cite an isolated instance as being characteristic of creation scientists in general, is itself, at least bordering on dishonesty.

Lewontin casts the creation/evolution controversy in terms of class struggle, between poor, ignorant, rural Southerners and the rich, upper-class Easterners and Northerners. Lewontin declares that these rural Southerners perceived themselves, correctly, as being under control of the rich northern and eastern bankers and entrepreneurs. As a result, we are told, many flocked to populism and socialism, and there was an accent on revivalist, fundamentalist religion. Consequently, Lewontin says, evolution was hardly mentioned in textbooks. It, no doubt, greatly pleases Lewontin, a Marxist, to relive what he perceives to be the great and considerably successful class struggle of more than a half century ago. But to portray the creation/evolution controversy as a struggle between rural Southerners and the rich, well-educated, elite Northern and Eastern classes, is totally inaccurate. Creationists have always been just as numerous in the northern part of the U.S. as in the rural South, and their concentration in urban areas has been just as great as in rural areas. Furthermore, while there are numerous creation scientists today in southern states, a considerable majority of creation scientists are Northerners.

Lewontin describes what he believes to be the present-day success of the upper-class eastern and northern cultures in triumphing over the poor rural southern culture. He describes the success of the Biological Sciences Curriculum Study in securing a grant of several million dollars from the National Science Foundation, and using these funds to produce high school science texts which are dominated throughout by evolutionary theory. Then, he says:

> Suddenly the study of evolution was in all the schools. The
> culture of the dominant class had triumphed, and traditional

religious values, the only vestige of control that rural people had over their own lives and the lives of their families,
had been taken from them (p. xxv).

Here is a very frank admission, by a leading exponent of
evolution, a Harvard professor, concerning the powerful religious influence of evolution. According to Lewontin, *when
evolution got into the schools, traditional religious values
were put out,* and these rural Southerners lost control over their
own lives and the lives of their families. Lewontin, uninten-
tionally here, has made a powerfully convincing argument for
the balanced treatment of creation versus evolution in the free,
pluralistic, democratic society that we are supposed to have
in the United States. Academic and religious freedoms are two
of the most precious freedoms that Americans have enjoyed
for the first 200 years of the existence of our country, and the
desire for religious freedom is what brought the first settlers
to our shores and is that which inspired millions of other
immigrants to come to this country. But now, Lewontin tells
us, the traditional, religious values held by rural Southerners
was taken from them and replaced by the teaching of evolution. The god of evolution has replaced the God of creation
and the Bible. Creation and evolution are, as Lewontin states,
irreconcilable world views (p. xxvi). Humanists use evolution,
in the guise of science, in their determination to capture the
minds of young people throughout the world.

In his closing statement, Lewontin reveals total failure to
appreciate the difference between empirical science, the science of the here and now, the science of repeatably testable
and potentially falsifiable theories, and origins science, based
on inferences. He says:

Either the world of phenomena is a consequence of the
regular operation of repeatable causes and their repeatable
effects, operating roughly along the lines of known physical law, or else, at every instant, all physical regularities
may be ruptured and a totally unforeseeable set of events
may occur. One must take sides on the issue of whether the
sun is sure to rise tomorrow. We cannot live simultaneously

in a world of natural causation and of miracles, for if one miracle can occur, there is no limit. It is for that reason that creationism cannot survive, for fundamentalists, like the rest of us, live in a world dominated by regularity. Duane Gish, no less than I, crosses seas not on foot but in machines, finds the pitcher empty when he has poured out its contents and the cupboard bare when he has eaten the last of the loaf. Creationism, in the end, is defeated by human experience (p. xxvi).

First, let it be pointed out that creation scientists positively affirm that the world of phenomena is a consequence of the *regular operation of repeatable causes and their repeatable effects.* Yes, indeed, we all go hungry when the cupboard is bare and thirsty when the pitcher is empty. When interpreting the operation of the universe and the operation of living organisms, creation scientists perform their science in a purely scientific manner—in a more scientific manner than evolutionists, in fact, for their work is unencumbered with evolutionary myths. Furthermore, creation scientists ask, can Lewontin or any other evolutionist apply the regular operation of repeatable causes and their repeatable effects to the Big Bang theory, to theories on the origin of life, or, in fact, to theories on the origin of any living thing? Of course not. These all involve unrepeatable, unobservable events of the past. Creation scientists agree with Eldredge when he proclaims that it is the *consequences* of origins we must look for. Richard Lewontin, just like Duane Gish, can only infer how the universe and living organisms came into existence, although both may employ the regular operation of repeatable causes and their repeatable effects, operating roughly along the lines of known physical law, to explain the *operation* of the universe and of living organisms.

Finally, it is quite clear that Lewontin, *a priori,* could not accept the truth that God created the heavens and the earth, that a cloud by day and a pillar of fire by night led the people of Israel in the desert, or that Christ rose from the dead, for Lewontin has declared: " . . . if one miracle can occur there is no limit," not believing that there is a God who performs miracles while leaving His created universe to ordinarily function according to natural laws and processes.

In the opening chapter of this book, "**The Word of God**," by Alice Kehoe, a cultural anthropologist and professor of anthropology at Marquette University in Milwaukee, Kehoe (as do most evolutionists) casts the issue of creation versus evolution primarily as a struggle between fundamentalist Christians and what these fundamentalist Christians perceive to be the forces of evil, or, as she put it, "Scientific creationism is a modern version of the ageless myth of the battle between God and Evil." It is a battle, she believes, between fundamentalists who believe in an inerrant Bible, and those, including liberal theologians, who hold that the Bible is a mixture of myths, legends, and religious truth, and others who hold to no religious truths at all. She does admit, however, that:

> Some adherents of scientific creationism are not even particularly fervent Christians, but they have found the factual material provided by creationists quite convincing (p. 10).

This is a rather significant admission, since these converts obviously have been won over by the force of the scientific evidence, not religious convictions.

The classes of people involved in the struggle are, according to Kehoe, entirely different from those suggested by Lewontin. Lewontin viewed it as a class struggle based on economics, the rural, poor Southerners versus the upper-class, rich Easterners and Northerners. Kehoe, on the other hand, declares:

> The orthodox saw their hope of salvation threatened by theologians and scientists, by anarchists and socialists and nationalists who sought to deprive clergy of secular power, by freed slaves and illiterate immigrants and suffragette women who challenged the old order's ideas [p. 7].

There is a sharp contrast between the story spun by Lewontin and this tale contrived by Kehoe. Kehoe aligns the orthodox involved in the battle for creation against socialists, but

Lewontin says, of the rural Southern orthodox supporters of the Bible and creation, that:

> Large numbers became Populists and Socialists. Eugene Debs got more votes in 1912 from the rural, high tenancy counties of Arkansas, Texas, and Oklahoma than from the urban centers where industrial workers were concentrated [p. xxv].

Kehoe attempts to portray the fundamentalists of that day in the worst light possible, aligning them against freed slaves, "illiterate" immigrants and suffragette women. The freed slaves, however, for the most part, were deeply religious and held the Bible in highest respect. The claim that the immigrants of those years were illiterate is both a slur and largely inaccurate, for they came from many countries where education was just as strong as in the United States. Many of the immigrants came not only from Scandinavian and European countries where Protestant orthodoxy was just as strong there as in the United States, but many also were Roman Catholics, whose own orthodoxy had no more room for evolution than did Protestant orthodoxy. It is probable, furthermore, that suffrage for women was just as acceptable to fundamentalist Christians as it was to liberals.

As do most evolutionists, Kehoe portrays evolutionists as enlightened, objective scientists, free of the yoke of bias and preconceived notions, in contrast to creationists who begin with what they believe to be truth. She says:

> Both the Christian fundamentalist scientific creationists and their nonfundamentalist partners ignore the core principle of science, which is the observer's independence from any commitment to a preconceived idea.

Later she states:

> Science uses multiple working hypotheses, choosing the one that best explains the greatest number of observations. It is directly contrary to science, to declare in advance of observations, that they cannot possibly contradict a preferred hypothesis such as the Genesis account of the origin of life [p. 10].

First, why would nonfundamentalists hold dogmatically to the creationist view of origins? They are free to believe in either creation or evolution. Furthermore, didn't Kehoe, herself, proclaim that these nonfundamentalist believers in creation "found the factual material provided by creationists quite convincing" (p. 10)? Kehoe is so fervent in her desire to label all scientific creationists as misguided dogmatists that she publishes contradictory statements on the same page.

Of course, her claim, as we have thoroughly documented in this book, that evolutionists are free of bias, holding to the theory of evolution non-dogmatically as only one of several possible working hypotheses and one which they would quickly and willingly abandon were it shown to be questionable or false, is ridiculous. As we have already documented, Lewontin, in his Introduction, which just preceded Kehoe's chapter, declared evolution to be a fact. This is true of most leading evolutionists. Evolutionists begin with the assumption that evolution is a fact, and attempt to interpret all facts of nature in light of that assumption, without the slightest doubt as to the accuracy of this procedure.

In one of her concluding statements Kehoe completely twists what the creation/evolution controversy is all about. She says:

> For most of us, America's diversity and her tolerance of difference have been her greatest glory. For others, our plurality is a weakness exploited by Satan. The evangelicals believe that they know the single Truth and are called to battle Satan so that truth may prevail.
>
> Scientific creationists are making a mighty effort to impose their narrow doctrine upon all of us [p. 12].

This statement reveals either blindness or deliberate distortion. Evolutionists, including Kehoe and all authors of this book, are using every possible device to exclude the scientific evidence for creation from public schools and the popular media and to impose the theory of evolution exclusively, not only as the best explanation of origins but even as the final truth. Furthermore, the theory they teach is totally naturalistic and mechanistic, a metaphysical world view. They seek to impose their narrow doctrine on all of us. Creation scientists, on the other hand, do not seek to exclude the teachng about the theory of evolution from public schools. They are seeking to have *both* creation and evolution taught in a totally free and unbiased manner, devoid of any reference to religious literature. Now, who is for tolerance of differences? Who is for the pluralistic system our democracy supposedly guarantees? The answer is obvious.

John Cole, an archaeologist and cultural anthropologist, a professor in the Department of Sociology and Anthropology of the University of Northern Iowa, in his chapter, **"Scopes and Beyond: Antievolutionism and American Culture,"** views the creation/evolution controversy largely in terms of intellectualism versus anti-intellectualism and right wing religious groups. He asserts, "Antievolutionism is best understood as an aspect of the anti-intellectual tradition . . ." (p. 31). He links scientific creationists with those "right wing religious groups," declaring that:

> . . . activist right wing religious movements such as the 'Moral Majority' and the political sophistication of allegedly nonpartisan groups such as the Institute for Creation Research have proven to be potent lobbies for religious and social conservatism. Their success belies the liberals' myth that the Scopes trial settled the issues of evolution, education, and the value of intellectualism.

As sympathetic as it may be for religious and social conservatism, the Institute for Creation Research has never engaged in lobbying. It has never either sponsored or promoted legislation or court action relative to teaching creation.

One statement in his chapter is as ludicrous as it is false. He quotes Frances Fitzgerald as reporting[3] that:

> . . . the Reverend Jerry Falwell, leader of the Moral Majority organization, warned his followers not to read books other than the Bible [p. 30].

Falwell founded Liberty University, which now has in excess of 6,000 students and for which Falwell plans to institute a graduate school to issue advanced degrees in various subjects. The school has been fully accredited by the Southern Association of Colleges and Schools. These students, all 6,000 of them, must be a rare breed, indeed, to acquire accredited degrees in a variety of subjects, including primary and secondary education, without ever reading a book except the Bible!

George Abell, in his chapter, "**The Ages of the Earth and the Universe**," and Stephen G. Brush, in his chapter, "**Ghosts from the Nineteenth Century: Creationist Arguments for a Young Earth**," deal with the problem of the age of the earth and of the universe. These chapters will not be critiqued in this book, nor will the arguments on this subject found in other anticreationist books and literature be reviewed here. The subject of the age of the earth and the cosmos is certainly a very important subject and is frequently discussed in books and articles by creation scientists. There are two reasons why that subject will not be dealt with here. The first, and primary reason, is that the scope of this book is limited to the *how* of origins. This focuses attention on the core of the creation/evolution question. Secondly, significant numbers of both conservative theologians and creation scientists hold to an old age of the earth and long time intervals between the many acts of creation. Thus creationists take both sides of the controversy over the age of the earth and the universe while asserting that there is a mass of powerful, positive convincing evidence for special creation.

One statement of Abell's is worthy of note here. Referring to the creation with appearance of age theories held by a few creationists, Abell says:

> Perhaps the creationists' assertions are true (and many people accept them as such), but they are *not* part of science [p. 34].

Eldredge, in referring to the evidence for creation based on analogy that creationists use, remarked, "It could even be true—but it cannot be construed as science."[4] Other evolutionists have made similar statements. What they seem to be saying is that even though everybody knew that creation is true and evolution is false, we would still have to teach evolution because creation is religion and evolution is science. They have forgotten that science is defined as systematic *knowledge* of natural or physical phenomena; *truth* ascertained by observation, experiment, and induction.[5]

Chapter 5, "Probability and the Origin of Life," by Russell Doolittle, a biochemist and professor in the Department of Chemistry, University of California, San Diego, is one of the weakest in the entire book. Doolittle strings together a series of "Just So" stories based on imaginary scenarios, all of which are devoid of any intellectual content. It is amazing how Doolittle brushes aside insuperable difficulties to a naturalistic, evolutionary origin of life. In response to these difficulties, Doolittle extends this salve to his followers:

> Comfort yourself also with the fact that a mere thirty years ago (before the Watson and Crick era) no one had the slightest inkling how proteins were genetically coded. Given the rapid rate of progress in our understanding of molecular biology, I have no doubt that satisfactory explanations of the problems posed here soon will be forthcoming [p. 96].

The problem with Doolittle's assertion is that the more we learn about the living cell, the more incredibly complex it becomes and the further we are removed from any possible solution to its evolutionary origin. Thirty years ago we thought all that is involved in the synthesis of DNA were four nucleoside triphosphates and an enzyme, DNA polymerase. Now we know that there are at least twenty different enzymes involved in the synthesis of DNA, and there may be many more. Thirty years ago we knew that the ribosome, absolutely required for protein synthesis in the cell, consisted of ribonucleic acid and protein. Today we know that it consists of three different ribonucleic acid molecules and 55 different protein molecules.

In 1964, John Keosian published a book on the origin of life in which he optimistically looked forward to a solution of the many problems which seemed intractable at that time for the origin-of-life chemist.[6] Fourteen years later, drawing on much more knowledge and experience from his own research and that of many others in the field, Keosian was now much less optimistic, almost to the point of despair. He reports:

> The claims of chemical evolution are unreal. We are asked to believe that biochemical compounds, biochemical reactions and mechanisms, energy metabolism and storage, specific polymerizations, codes, transcription and translation apparatus, and more, appeared in probiotic waters with the functions they would have in a living thing before there were living things. Chemical evolution has become an end in itself. In many cases it represents contrived or ingenious laboratory syntheses which have no counterpart in abiotic organic chemical synthesis in an acceptable range of probiotic conditions. . . . There has been a good deal of uncritical acceptance of experiments, results, and conclusions which we are all too ready to acknowledge because they support preconceived convictions. . . . All present approaches to a solution of the problem of the origin of life are either irrelevant or lead into a blind alley. Therein lies the crisis. . . . The various approaches to a solution of the origin of life are examined and found wanting.[7]

This frank, honest, objective analysis of the true situation by this origin-of-life chemist is as different as night and day, when compared to Doolittle's fairy tale.

In his opening paragraph, Doolittle does admit that creationists' objections to evolutionary theories on the origin of life based on improbability are:

> . . . not easily parried by simply resorting to known facts. This is an area of active research where answers are not always obvious. But there are scenarios that satisfactorily explain how these events may have taken place [p. 85].

Doolittle certainly gets off to a bad start here. In this area of evolutionary speculation, Doolittle says, the evolutionist cannot resort to known *facts,* so he is forced to invent *scenarios* that can "explain" how these events *may* have taken place. What kind of science is this? Scenarios explain nothing—they are nothing more than the products of the human imagination.

Doolittle recounts several creationist arguments against an evolutionary origin of life based on the improbability of the chance formation of biologically active DNA or protein molecules. He then declares that the creationist claim that there could be no natural selection until there was reproduction is erroneous. Even though Doolittle is a biochemist and not a biologist, there is no excuse for such ignorance by one who pretends to be a well-informed evolutionist. He should know that, in modern terms, natural selection is defined as differential reproduction—thus, no reproduction, no natural selection. This fact has been amply supported by Doolittle's fellow evolutionists. Thus Harold Blum (also a biochemist) says:

> The present composition of living systems is the ultimate result of their past history, extending back to the moment of their origin from non-living material itself. Before that time mutation and natural selection could not exist, since they depend upon properties which are characteristic of living systems only, so the derivation of the basic materials must have involved other factors.[8]

Murray Eden, on the occasion of the Wistar Institute symposium on *Mathematical Challenges to the Neo-Darwinian Interpretation of Evolution,* remarked that:

> Dr. Wright [Sewell Wright] has objected that evolution should be reserved for biological phenomena and not for pre-biology, and I certainly agree with him.[9]

Peter Mora has shown, and as affirmed by Bernal, that the principles of experimental science do not apply to discussions on the origin of life, and, indeed, cannot apply to any problem of origin.[10] We see, then, that according to his fellow evolutionists, it is Doolittle who is erroneous on this point, not creation scientists.

Since creationists have cited published articles by non-creationist Hubert Yockey as support for their claims that a naturalistic evolutionary origin of the protein, DNA, and RNA molecules necessary for the origin of life is for all practical purposes impossible, Doolittle feels constrained to demolish Yockey, claiming that an article published by Yockey in the prestigious *Journal of Theoretical Biology*,[11] and most often cited by creationists (I cited this article in my debate with Doolittle at Lynchburg, Virginia, October 13, 1981), is "shot through with errors." Doolittle admits, as he must, that the *Journal of Theoretical Biology* is a refereed journal, but claims that "even well-refereed journals slip up" (p. 88). But how could a technical article, "shot through with errors," pass through several referees?

Yockey used information theory coupled with conventional probability calculations to estimate whether or not DNA, RNA, and protein sequences necessary for the origin of life could have arisen by random evolutionary processes. They could not have, Yockey concluded. Yockey's conclusions are that the probability of a functional cytochrome C evolving by random process is only 2×10^{-94}, far, far below the impossibility threshold, and that the best that could be accomplished in a billion years, as far as DNA is concerned, would be the origin of a small DNA molecule sufficient to code for a protein of only 49 amino acids, literally light-years short of what would be required to get life started.

Doolittle first proclaims that there must be an enormous number of amino acid sequences that could function as a cytochrome C. Such a molecule must have an amino acid sequence that would permit it to assume the necessary configuration to bind to a ring-shaped porphyrin molecule, and orient the porphyrin molecule in such a way that the approach of molecules that are electron donors, or acceptors, is facilitated. This would appear to require considerable specificity, but of the 3×10^{154} possible amino acid sequences of a protein with 100 amino acids (cytochrome C has 100 amino acids, consisting of 20 different kinds in present-day proteins, but these would total 39 if both the left-handed and right-handed forms are taken into account), Yockey very generously (for the benefit of evolution) estimated that perhaps 7×10^{60} (or more than a trillion multiplied times itself five times) of these randomly arranged amino acid sequences could function as a cytochrome C. That means that the probability of a functional cytochrome C arising by chance is no more than 2×10^{-94}, a probability so low that it wouldn't happen even once in the entire universe in 20 billion years, even if every star in the universe had a planet like the earth and one hundred amino acids could be assembled one trillion times a second on every planet (100 billon galaxies containing 100 billion stars each = 10^{22} stars; 20 billion years equal approximately 10^{17} seconds; one trillion = 10^{12}; $10^{22} \times 10^{17} \times 10^{12} = 10^{51}$; $2 \times 10^{-94} \times 10^{51}$ = 2×10^{-43}; one chance out of 2×10^{43} is, for all practical purposes, essentially a zero probability, and if by some miracle it did happen, we would have only one single molecule of one single protein).

Yockey's first error, according to Doolittle, is that his estimate of 7×10^{60} possible amino acid sequences that could function as a cytochrome C, is far too small. How Doolittle could possibly arrive at such a conclusion is a mystery, but just like the White Queen in Alice in Wonderland, Doolittle is able to imagine at least six impossible things before breakfast.

Doolittle then asserts:

> But Yockey's calculations still are completely without merit. He starts by assuming the existence of a three-letter code and, presumably, machinery for translating polynucleotide sequences into polypeptide sequences.

If Yockey starts out by assuming the existence of such machinery, Doolitle is right that this would invalidate Yockey's calculations, because this assumption eliminates one of the evolutionist's greatest problems—the origin of the genetic code and the transcription and translation apparatus. Yockey makes the task easier for the evolutionist, not harder. Why does Doolittle complain?

Doolittle then makes an absurd *ad hoc* assumption in order to get around one of the evolutionists' greatest origin-of-life problems—the fact that equal quantities of D- ("right-handed") and L- ("left-handed") amino acids would be produced by any origin of life scenario, and each is incorporated equally well into proteins by ordinary chemical means, but all proteins in living organisms today, without exception, consist 100% of L-amino acids. The presence of a single D-amino acid in a protein destroys all biological activity. Speaking of the transfer ribonucleic acid (tRNA) synthetases, the enzymes that link each amino acid to its specific tRNA, Doolittle says, "From the start of their existence, they probably bound only L-amino acids." Presto! There you have it! Give Doolittle a Nobel Prize—he has solved a mystery that has plagued evolutionists for decades. Transfer RNA's just did it, that's all. Of course, Doolittle does not venture a single word of explanation as to how they did it—they just did. Never mind that the hypothetical amino acids floating around in the hypothetical primordial ocean would consist of equal quantities of D- and L-amino acids; never mind that the hypothetical proteins floating in that ocean would consist of 50% each of D- and L-amino acids; never mind that the tRNA synthetases themselves would consist of 50% each of D- and L-amino acids; never mind that the transfer RNA's to which the amino acids must be bound by the tRNA synthetases must either magically contain the sugar ribose in 100% of the D-form, as is the case in all messenger RNA, transfer RNA and ribosomal RNA today, or the transfer RNA must contain equal quantities of D- and L-ribose. But then, Doolittle could easily get around this latter problem—he would just assume that 100% of the transfer RNA's had 100% D-ribose in them, just like he assumed that the tRNA synthetases consisted of 100% L-amino acids and bound only L-amino acids. After all, that is imagining only two impossible things before breakfast.

In his calculations, Yockey assumed that in the placement of each amino acid in a protein, the choice must be from 39 amino acids—glycine (which exists in only one simple form) and the D- and L-forms of the other 19 amino acids found in proteins today. Doolittle, however, says that is wrong. Since he has imagined that 20 (one for each amino acid) tRNA synthetases magically arose that consisted solely of L- amino acids and selected only L-amino acids from D- and L-mixtures, he has eliminated the 19 D-amino acids from the necessary probability calculations. Doolittle says he is right and Yockey is wrong. Nonsense!—unless you abandon all science in favor of black magic. Actually, the problem is much worse than Yockey makes it out to be. In all origin-of-life experiments (considerably contrived even to obtain trivial results), a large number of other amino acids are generated in addition to those found in proteins today—the so-called non-protein, or non-natural amino acids. Thus, in the random production of proteins before the hypothetical DNA-messenger RNA-transfer RNA system would have existed, these non-natural amino acids (both their D- and L-forms) would have been incorporated into proteins just as easily as the D- and L-forms of the amino acids that are found in natural proteins today. This would vastly reduce the probability of getting a biologically active protein similar to any found in living organisms. Thus, Yockey easily wins on this point against Doolittle, even though Yockey actually tilted the probability towards evolution.

Doolittle then complains (p. 89) about Yockey's estimate of the mutation rate. He claims that this would have been several orders of magnitudes greater than estimated by Yockey because Yockey bases his rate on the rate for modern proteins, and takes into account only those surviving natural selection. Moreover, Doolittle says, modern organisms have exquisite editing devices for repairing errors in base-pairing during the replication of DNA and thereby keeping the mutation rate low, and these could not have been operating in primitive systems. All of this may be so, but the pendulum swings back much too far in the opposite direction for origin of life theories to have any validity. DNA is not intrinsically stable, even inside the living cell. Its stability inside the cell is due largely to control and repair by specialized enzymes. Outside of the cell, floating around in the primitive ocean, DNA would be notoriously unstable. In living organisms, mutations are due to the placement of a wrong nucleotide in the sequence of DNA. These are often replaced with the correct nucleotide, by a repair mechanism found only in living cells. In the hypothetical primitive ocean, not only would wrong nucleotides be inserted frequently by the hypothetical synthesis system, but chemical bonds also would be easily ruptured at any point in the DNA molecule by ultraviolet light, hydrolysis, action of chemicals, etc. The DNA molecule (and, of course, the protein molecule as well) would have a very, very short life, far too short to permit the evolution of life. Doolittle completely ignores the rapid destruction of DNA, RNA, and protein molecules that would take place under the ordinary, natural conditions that would exist in the hypothetical primordial ocean.

Doolittle then discusses the assembly of nucleotides into the long chains which make up DNA molecules (genes in living organisms today usually consist of several thousand nucleotides to as many as the 186,000 nucleotides found in the gene that codes for blood-clotting factor VIII). He admits that it does present a formidable problem, but claims that there has been limited success, although no one regards the problem as completely solved. He refers to the work of Fakhrai, et al,[12] which produced a string of as many as twelve nucleotides, especially when metal catalysts were used. What he doesn't mention is that the chemical condensation did not involve simple nucleoside phosphates (which themselves could never be produced under primitive earth conditions) but involved the 5'- phosphorimidazolides. Now, how could these complex, unstable derivatives of nucelosides, such as those of guanosine and adenosine used in the experiments, have been generated on the hypothetical primitive earth? There would be no way to produce them naturally, and they are unstable to hydrolysis. The use of phosphorimidazolides in these experiments rendered them totally irrelevant to the origin of life.

The nucleotides in DNA and RNA in living organisms are linked together via 3'-5' linkages, but in the work of Fakhrai and co-workers, both 3'-5' and 2'-5' linkages were formed. Furthermore, they produced only short chains consisting exclusively of either the nucleotides of guanine or adenine. Mixed DNA molecules were not produced, nor did this system work to produce polynucleotides of the pyrimidines, cytosine and thymine.

Doolittle then goes on to mention that similarly, polypeptides can be formed from simple amino acids under certain conditions, but that "this is another area where there is much to learn" (p. 90). Actually, no protein-like polypeptide has been produced, as yet, under any plausible primitive earth conditions. What very limited success has been reported so far has involved nothing more than exercises in organic chemistry controlled by a chemist. Furthermore, the products consist of 50% each of the D- and L-forms of the amino acids, but even the presence of a single D-amino acid in a protein would obliterate all biological activity.

Doolittle then admits that the most puzzling problem remains—the invention of coding whereby the information in a polynucleotide sequence is transferred into a corresponding polypeptide. First, we must ask, why would there be "information" in a polynucleotide, before there was a living cell in existence with the required apparatus to "read" the information and utilize it as a set of instructions on how to proceed, say, to synthesize a protein? The primitive ocean couldn't care less what particular sequence was found in a DNA molecule. If tomorrow every human being on the face of the earth were to perish, all the "information" in every book in the entire world would be absolutely worthless. These books would no longer contain one iota of information. Why were languages invented in the first place? Only because there were human beings who had, first, the need for languages and, secondly, the ability to invent languages. The humans were there first.

Even if the means existed for DNA molecules and protein molecules to be produced in the hypothetical primitive ocean, their production would be totally useless. What would be the purpose of their existence? What would their presence accomplish? The whole exercise is pointless. Furthermore, the rates of destruction of these molecules in the primitive ocean would vastly exceed their rates of synthesis by many orders of magnitude. Speaking of double-stranded DNA, Doolittle says:

> These double-stranded forms, which tend to be stiff rods, are much more stable than the single-stranded oligonucleotides, so back reactions to the simpler monomeric units are discouraged [p. 90].

Such nonsense! Double-stranded DNA would be extremely unstable floating around in the primitive ocean—they would rapidly deteriorate. If Doolittle or some other biochemist isolates DNA from natural sources or synthesizes it in the laboratory, does he store it by dissolving it in water and placing the container on a laboratory bench at room temperature? Of course not. He would probably seal it in an ampule under nitrogen and store it in a deep freeze. Even under these conditions, chemical bonds in the molecule slowly rupture, and biological activity is gradually lost.

Doolittle goes on to say that once double-stranded oligonucleotides are produced, they could dissociate ("by warming them up to 80-90° centigrade!") and complementary copies of the separated strands could then be produced. "Self-replication is under way!" Doolittle doesn't tell us where the highly specific chemical energy required for such syntheses would come from; he doesn't tell us where the nucleoside phosphates required for the production of DNA would come from; he doesn't tell us where the highly specific enzymes required would come from (at least 20 enzymes are involved in the synthesis of DNA in living cells); he doesn't tell us what would stabilize the single-stranded DNA after the double-stranded DNA split apart; he doesn't tell us where the 80-90° temperature required to split apart the double-stranded DNA would be produced in the primitive ocean; he doesn't tell us how single-stranded DNA could survive long enough at 80-90° centigrade for a complementary strand to be produced.

"But," Doolittle tells us, "even more magic remains in these simple complementary oligonucleotides." Magic, indeed! But the magic exists in Doolittle's mind, not in these simple complementary oligonucleotides. These little strands, Doolittle claims, when not joined completely in a complementary manner but only partly overlapped, can use the exposed ends as templates to extend the other strand. Occasionally mistakes are made, the wrong nucleotide is put in, and diversity results. Thus, Doolittle asserts:

> Clearly, the complementary strands of nucleic acids are the Promethean sticks that were rubbed together to produce the spark of life.

What is clear is that Doolittle's complementary strands of nucleic acids producing the first spark of life are just as mythological as are the fire sticks of Prometheus in Greek mythology.

Concerning proteins, Doolittle envisions the production of a vast array of proteins which could be molded into an infinity of very precise forms. How all of this could happen Doolittle really can't tell us, but if proteins could be produced so that they could be shaped into an infinity of forms, that would not be the solution to the problem, that would be the problem. If an infinite number of sequences could potentially be produced, but only relatively few would have biological activity, the probability that the relatively few correct sequences would be produced rather than one of the infinite number of other useless sequences, is essentially infinitely low.

Doolittle declares that the complementary strands of nucleic acids were the Promethean sticks that were rubbed together to produce the spark of life. Later, however, he declares:

> But it wasn't until protein manufacture was coupled to the information in polynucleotide sequences that the roots were struck for genuine living systems [p. 93].

And it certainly is a giant leap from complementary strands of DNA to the utterly complex systems linking DNA to protein synthesis. First, utilizing the sequences of nucleotides in DNA to code for a protein with a specific amino acid sequence, a messenger RNA must be synthesized. This requires specific chemical energy, a supply of the pyrimidine and purine triphosphates, and several enzymes, among other things. The messenger RNA goes to the site of protein synthesis, where it attaches to ribosomes. Ribosomes, as we have mentioned earlier, consist of three different RNA molecules and 55 different protein molecules. A specific transfer RNA synthetase for each amino acid recognizes that specific amino acid and its specific transfer RNA and catalyzes the union of the amino acid with its transfer RNA. The transfer RNA, with its attached amino acid, moves to the site of protein synthesis. There, via three nucleotides which are part of its structure, the transfer RNA locates its proper place on the messenger RNA. Enzymes catalyze the union of the amino acid to the growing protein chain, break the bond between the amino acid and its transfer RNA, release the transfer RNA from the messenger RNA, and eventually release the completed protein chain.

This process is incredibly complex, involving DNA, three different RNA's, a variety of enzymes, and the structure of the cell. As someone has said, practically everything in the cell is involved in protein synthesis. Doolittle mentions the speculative idea of Francis Crick, that perhaps early in evolution polynucleotides directly "recognized" amino acids, rather than going through a transfer RNA and a transfer RNA synthetase.

The fact is that there is no recognition by polynucleotides for specific amino acids. This is simply another pipe dream.

Doolittle asks the question:

> How likely is it that a population of spontaneously replicating and mutating polynucleotides would generate an appropriate sequence for the formation of a polypeptide catalyst?

After warning us not to fall into Yockey's trap of dealing with absolute numbers for a process whose every mechanism and condition we don't know yet, Doolittle responds with an analogy—the probability of being dealt a perfect hand, say all 13 spades, in a game of bridge. The probability of that happening, we are told, is only one chance in 635,013,559,600. But it does happen! Even in the small country of England, it happens almost once each year. Doolittle thus is saying that since the probability of this happening is extremely low and yet it does happen, even the chance formation of a biologically active protein could take place. Next problem!

Not so fast! If 250,000 people played bridge every day in England, and each game consisted of ten deals, that would consist of 250,000 x 4 x 10 = 10 million hands each day, or 3,650,000,000 hands per year. Thus the probability of getting a perfect hand in bridge in England each year, making those assumptions, is 3,650,000,000 divided by 653,013,559,600, or one chance out of 179. Not something that anyone would want to bet on, but it could happen (obviously, we must have underestimated the number of bridge hands dealt each year, or the report of this happening on the average once each year is grossly exaggerated, or somebody is cheating at dealing the cards, because with those odds, on the average, a perfect deal would occur only once in 179 years!). Let us assume that all of this is true. A perfect deal results each year, in spite of the chance of that occurring is only one chance in, roughly, 179. The probability calculated by Yockey for the formation of a viable cytochrome C, however, was only one chance in 2×10^{94}! You have to multiply 179 times a trillion (10^{12}) roughly seven times to equal 2×10^{94}. In other words, the probability of getting a viable cytochrome C molecule by chance is a trillion times a trillion times a trillion times a trillion times a trillion times a trillion times a trillion times less probable than getting a perfect hand in bridge once each year in England, assuming there were 3 billion, 650 million bridge hands each year. The analogy is thus no analogy at all. Doolittle here has simply dealt a crooked hand. Furthermore, what if it did happen? What would we have? One single molecule of one single protein! But to get life started would require billions of tons each of hundreds of different protein molecules and billions of tons each of hundreds of different kinds of DNA and RNA molecules. We have 350 million cubic miles of water on this planet, and eventually everything produced on the earth would have been dissolved in and diluted by that enormous quantity of water. Thus, enormous quantities of each molecule is required.

Doolittle states that once a few polypeptide chains had formed which could catalyze a few critical reactions, things would be off and running. There are a few things critically wrong with this scenario. In the first place, almost all enzymes catalyze *degradative* processes—nucleases and proteases catalyze the rapid breakdown of nucleic acids and proteins, respectively. Deaminases and decarboxylases catalyze the deamination of amines and decarboxylation of carboxylic acids, respectively—and on and on. Supposing, for example, an enzyme approximating the catalytic properties of chymotrypsin should arise. It would happily set about hydrolyzing all the proteins in sight! End of origin of life! The activity of each enzyme in a living organism is carefully regulated by each cell in that organism so that its abilities are properly harnessed. Thus, life without enzymes is impossible, and enzymes without life is impossible.

Furthermore, if those nucleotides and proteins did exist, what held the system together? Where did membranes come from, the type of membranes specifically required by living organisms? Where did all the energy necessary to drive all the wide range of chemical reactions required for life come from? How did all that machinery just happen to get arranged in the precise manner required for life? Green and Goldberger have declared that:

> . . . the macromolecule-to-cell transition is a jump of fantastic dimensions, which lies beyond the range of testable hypothesis. In this area, all is conjecture. The available facts do not provide a basis for postulating that cells arose on this planet.[13]

G. Ledyard Stebbins, an evolutionist, as are Green and Goldberger, states:

> Organized structure, specific function, heredity, development and evolution are the distinctive properties of life *which are not even approached by those of the inanimate physico-chemical universe*[14] [emphasis added].

Doolittle airily dismisses all objections to a naturalistic, evolutionary origin of life. Sir Fred Hoyle has declared, on the other hand, that the probability of an evolutionary origin of life is equal to the probability that a tornado sweeping through a junkyard would assemble a Boeing 747. If Doolittle wants to believe that, that is his business, but he shouldn't call it science and teach it to his students.

Chapter 6, "Thermodynamics and Evolution," by John W. Patterson, has been critiqued in the chapter on thermodynamics, so need not be dealt with here, except to say its weakness is about on a par with the preceding chapter by Doolittle.

Chapter 7, "Molecular Evidence for Evolution," is by Thomas H. Jukes, a biochemist and professor in biophysics at the University of California, Berkeley. He is a virulent anticreationist. His chapter consists mainly of the standard textbook evolutionary explanation of the molecular similarities and differences found in plants and animals. Many evolutionists who have despaired of finding evidence for evolution in the fossil record have jumped on the molecular biology bandwagon, trumpeting that fossil transitional forms are no longer necessary or needed, for molecular biology will supply the evidence needed for evolution. In the case of the fossil record, we must attempt to infer how living organisms arose in the unobservable past, by the silent testimony of the fossils. We may feel comfortable with our conclusions based on that evidence, but we can never be certain. With molecular biology, we must also attempt to infer what has occurred in the unobservable past, but here we are worse off than with the fossil record. We have no fossil molecules, and thus we cannot go back into the past and actually analyze the hypothetical molecules that supposedly existed then. The only record we have, as far as these molecules are concerned, is what exists right now in living organisms. Based upon preconceived ideas, we can see how well the data from molecular biology fit these ideas, and where the data do not fit very well, we can modify our ideas to make a more comfortable fit. This can be done on the basis of either creation or evolution.

Let us first consider the similarities between what an evolutionist and a creationist would expect the data to show. An evolutionist would expect that all living organisms would reveal some similarities in their biochemical makeup, since he believes that life originated only once, or, at the most, a very few times. Primeval proteins, DNA, RNA, and other macromolecules would have existed in these first forms of life. As the first form or forms of life gradually evolved into higher and higher forms, finally culminating in man, these molecules would gradually change, or evolve. Thus, many, or most, of the macromolecules found in man would have been derived from distant ancestors, as would have been the case with similar molecules in all other living things. As living organisms evolved, these macromolecules would have changed, or evolved, through the accumulation of mutations. Differences in these molecules, the proteins, DNA, and RNA, would be small for closely related organisms, and greater, the more distant the relationship. Thus, the difference in the amino acid sequences of the cytochrome C's of man and chimpanzee would be less than those for the cytochrome C's of man and a reptile, or man and a fish, etc.

A creationist would also expect many biochemical similarities in all living organisms. We all drink the same water, breathe the same air, and eat the same food. Supposing, on the other hand, God had made plants with a certain type of amino acids, sugars, purines, pyrimidines, etc.; then made animals with a different type of amino acids, sugars, purines, pyrimidines, etc.; and, finally, made man with a third type of amino acids, sugars, etc. What could we eat? We couldn't eat plants; we couldn't eat animals; all we could eat would be each other! Obviously, that wouldn't work. All of the key molecules in plants, animals, and man had to be the same. The metabolism of plants, animals, and man, based on the same biochemical principles, had to be similar, and therefore key metabolic pathways would employ similar macromolecules, modified to fit the particular internal environment of the organism or cell in which it must function.

Furthermore, the creationist would expect these similarities, ordinarily, to be greater in creatures that are more similar to one another, and to be less, when dissimilar creatures are compared. We know, for instance, that man is more similar to a chimpanzee than he is to a bat; that he is more similar to either a chimpanzee or a bat than he is to a crocodile or a flea. Man, chimpanzee, and the bat are mammals. The creationist would expect, therefore, that his protein, DNA, and RNA molecules, those macromolecules that are among the most important molecules in metabolism, would be more similar to those of the chimpanzee and to those of the bat than to those of the crocodile or the flea. In the case of the evolutionist, he believes that these differences arose by mutations in the DNA molecules, or genes, and were the primary causes of the differences in all plants and animals. He believes that all the genes existing in all living organisms arose from preexisting genes by mutations or by gene duplication and mutations.

Creationists believe that all normal genes, the genes that account for the normal, healthy differences in plants and animals, were created. Each basic type of plant and animal was created with a sufficient genetic potential or variability (or gene pool, as geneticists say) to permit sufficient variability within the circumscribed boundaries of each kind, in order to adapt to various environments and conditions.

Using hemoglobin as a model, Jukes points out that the alpha and beta chains of human hemoglobin differ in each case from those of the chimpanzee by a single amino acid. The difference in the case of human and cattle alpha chains is 17 amino acids; the difference in the case of human and cattle beta chains is 24 amino acids, and so on. Eventually, we are told, as more information accumulated, it was possible to construct "family trees," utilizing the differences between the hemoglobins of various creatures. The divergences, Jukes says, showed the same relationships as those predicted from the classical taxonomic studies of various animals (p. 119).

Furthermore, it is explained, if it is assumed that mutations have accrued at a regular rate in all creatures, the amino acid differences of homologous proteins, or the nucleotide differences of genes, can be used as a "molecular clock" to assign dates to those times that various animals diverged in their evolutionary history. Of course, there is a great deal of circular reasoning involved here, for how do you "set" the clock to begin with? How do you "calibrate" the clock? This must be done, of course, by making assumptions concerning the times when certain organisms first evolved, or when two organisms diverged. For example, if it is assumed that two organisms diverged 600 million years ago, and the percent difference in their alpha hemoglobin chains is 60%, it is assumed that the mutation rate produced a one-percent difference every ten million years in the alpha hemoglobin chain. Thus, if the percent difference in the alpha hemoglobin chains of two other creatures is ten percent, it would be assumed that these creatures diverged 100 million years ago. Of course the accuracy of this procedure depends, first of all, on the assumption of evolution, and secondly, on the assumption that the time of divergence by which the clock was calibrated (600 million years) was correct. Maybe so. Maybe not.

A variety of problems soon began to crop up with this notion of using differences in proteins and DNA (which codes for the proteins, and therefore differences in proteins should parallel the differences in the respective genes) to establish evolutionary phylogenetic trees and to use as a molecular "clock." It was found that the differences that exist between different classes of proteins are enormous. Thus, the histones show very little differences, it being estimated that 600 million years is necessary to produce a one-percent difference in the histones of two different organisms. In the case of cytochrome C, the estimated time to produce a one-percent difference is 20 million years; for hemoglobin it is 5.8 million years; and in the case of the fibrinopeptides, it is only 1.1 million years, nearly 600 times faster than with the histones. Thus, we don't have all clocks running at the same rate—each clock chooses its own rate.

Furthermore, the phylogenetic tree that one obtains based on a particular class of proteins, say the cytochrome C's, may vary considerably from one drawn up on the basis of, say, the insulins, or the myoglobins, etc. Thus Vincent Demoulin has said:

> Who would seriously consider a phylogeny of vertebrates drawn from a comparison of myoglobin of some species and hemoglobin from others? The species for which myoglobin is used will cluster together far away from related species for which hemoglobin is selected. . . . The main problem here is the reliability of evolutionary reconstructions based on sequence data. . . . The composite evolutionary tree . . . encompasses all the weaknesses of the individual trees.[15]

When the cytochrome C's of purple nonsulphur photosynthetic bacteria were compared, the data was highly contradictory to evolutionary predictions. T. E. Meyer, *et al,* report that:

> Our results show that the deduction of phylogenetic information from the sequence of homologous bacterial proteins is not straightforward. . . . Sequence differences between similar species for these cytochromes C-551 are as large as those between mitochondrial cytochromes C of mammals and insects, although both classes of protein probably have similar redox functions.[16]

After examining some of the other cytochrome C's in these bacteria, R. P. Ambler, *et al,* state:

> . . . phylogenetic trees constructed from the results in Table 1 could never be interpreted as congruent, nor would they have any predictive value.[17]

This difficulty with the cytochrome C's of the above-mentioned bacteria is not unique among bacteria. Thus, when the cytochrome C's of two closely similar oganisms, *Desulfovibrio desulfuricans and Desulfovibrio vulgaris* are compared, it is found that although these proteins have similar molecular weights, partial specific volumes, chain lengths, and number of hemes, they differ markedly in amino acid composition.[18] We find many similar "anomalies" among the higher organisms. The insulins of the sperm whale and of the fin whale are identical to those of dog and pig, but differ from that of the sei whale.[19] The insulin of the guinea pig is unique, its structure being considerably different from all other insulins. For instance, there are 18 differences when the amino acid sequence of guinea pig insulin is compared to that of either human insulin or that of a fellow rodent, the rat.[20] What kind of a phylogenetic tree would one get, based on the insulins?

Among the cytochrome C's, the structure of that for the rattlesnake varies in 22 places when compared to that for the turtle, another reptile, but only in 14 places when compared to that for humans.[21] The amino acid sequence of the egg-white protein, lysozyme, of the Embden goose has no sequence homology (or very weak, if at all) with hen egg-white lysozyme.[22]

Based upon amino-acid-sequence data, most evolutionists declare that man's nearest kin among the apes is the chimpanzee, followed closely by the gorilla. The orangutan is more distantly removed, then the gibbon, and further yet, the monkeys. Thus, based on annealing experiments with nuclear DNA, it is said that the percent differences in the nuclear DNA of man with those of other primates are: chimpanzee, 1.6; gorilla, 2.2; orangutan, 3.7; gibbon, 5.2; baboon, 7.4; and spider monkey, 12.6. This is widely accepted, in evolutionary circles, as proof that man's nearest cousin is the chimpanzee. J. H. Schwartz, however, strongly disagrees with this. Relative to the molecular data, Schwartz says:

> . . . as has been a major point of this review, overall similarity is not necessarily, nor should it be assumed to be, reflective of closeness of relatedness.[23]

Creationists strongly agree that similarity does not necessarily indicate relatedness, in the sense of descent from a common ancestor. Based on morphological similarities and differences, Schwartz maintains that man is more closely related to the orangutan than he is to the African apes (chimpanzee and gorilla).

The data from radioimmunoassay and chromatography analyses of hypothalamic luteinizing hormone-releasing hormone (LHRH) reveal that LHRH of mammals is indistinguishable from LHRH of amphibians, but is chemically distinct from those of reptiles, birds and teleostean fishes. Of course, on all evolutionary phylogenetic trees, man and other mammals and birds are shown as direct descendants of reptiles, while reptiles are shown as the descendants of amphibians. This assigns the amphibians to a much more distant evolutionary place relative to mammals and birds than the reptiles, but the molecular data indicate just the opposite. This prompts J. A. King to state:

> The finding that amphibian LHRH is identical to the mammalian peptide and yet different from avian, reptilian, and teleostean LHRH's, which are in themselves

indistinguishable by the methods used, supports a contemporary phylogenetic scheme suggesting that mammals and amphibians may be more closely related than are mammals on the one hand and reptiles and birds on the other.[24]

Many more similar "anomalies" from the scientific literature are found. If amino acid sequence data, and the data based on DNA similarities and differences can truly be used to show evolutionary relationships and to construct an evolutionary phylogenetic tree, then many different phylogenetic trees should not emerge, but one single internally consistent phylogenetic tree should be derived that agrees with the phylogenetic tree based on morphological data. Instead, we see that it is not possible to derive a single internally consistent phylogenetic tree when the molecular data of different proteins are compared. Furthermore, even when data derived from a single protein are used to derive a phylogenetic tree, not only do many anomalies appear, but even to obtain the degree of similarity or homology seen, the data must be considerably "massaged." Thus, in order to align portions of proteins that show similarities in amino acid sequences, hypothetical insertions, deletions, frame shifts, hypothetical gene duplications and other genetic manipulations must be performed. In other words, even when working with a single protein, elements of the data must be ignored as reflecting "anomalies," and much of the rest must be molded to fit theory.

Evolutionists Christian Schwabe and Gregory Warr, and non-creationist Michael Denton have made some of the most concerted attacks on the notion that amino acid sequence data can be used to construct evolutionary phylogenetic trees. Schwabe and Warr, based on their data, reject the generally held dogma that assumes there was a single ancestral cell from which all other genes, cells, and organisms have arisen. They reject monophyletic evolution in favor of polyphyletic evolution, postulating that life arose many times, and that these distinctively basic forms of life have been separate from the beginning.[25,26] Thus, while Schwabe and Warr believe that the original forms of life evolved in the beginning, and each has undergone changes since then, these evolutionists, based on their data, agree with creationists that amino acid sequences of proteins and other molecular data cannot be used to construct an evolutionary phylogenetic tree. In fact, they insist that the data are actually incompatible with a monophyletic theory of evolution.

Schwabe and Warr point out that a single, well-documented inconsistency or contradiction is sufficient to invalidate a monophyletic interpretation as the sole explanation of evolution, for a monophyletic molecular clock theory to be correct requires that all individual phylogenetic trees, drawn from the structures of any orthologous family of proteins (insulins, cytochrome C's, myoglobins, etc.), should have superimposable branching sequences. Schwabe's special interest has been relaxin, a hormone that induces the widening of the symphysis pubis, and softening of the cervix and vagina, and is thus a hormone of viviparity (giving birth alive). The data of Schwabe and Warr show that pig and rat relaxins are as different from each other (55 percent) as shark relaxin is from either pig or rat relaxin. Based on these data, and the assumptions used in constructing phylogenetic trees from molecular data, the rat, pig, and shark all must have diverged at the same time, either at the assumed point of mammalian radiation (70 million years ago), or at the assumed time of divergence of the shark from the line that presumably later gave rise to mammals (700 million years ago). Neither interpretation is compatible with those based on paleontology and accepted by evolutionists. Similar problems arise when the relaxins of two sharks are compared, the sand tiger shark and the dogfish. The difference is about 20 percent, which places their divergence, based on assumptions used by molecular evolutionists, at 20 million years ago, in contrast to the 150 million years which is commonly accepted by evolutionists.

Schwabe and Warr then go on to discuss similar contradictions based on the data of other proteins. Schwabe and Warr feel forced into a position quite different from the popularly held theory of a branching evolutionary phylogenetic tree based on molecular data. They state:

> ... the major conclusion to which we wish to draw attention is that these findings strongly suggest that many of the genes purportedly produced by gene duplication have been present very early in the development of life. In fact, we can ask if they were not present so early that we must question whether any gene has come about by duplication or whether all have been there, from the beginning, as a potential for species development [p. 476 of their article].

These conclusions mesh amazingly well with those of creationists. The difference is, of course, that Schwabe and Warr believe that these living organisms bearing all those genes, somehow arose in the first place via some evolutionary process. Creationists would rephrase their statement to read:

> We maintain that the evidence indicates that no genes have come about by gene duplication but that all have been there, from the beginning, to maintain the integrity of each basic type of plant and animal and which provided the genetic material permitting variation within the limits of each kind.

Schwabe and Warr contrast the usual interpretation based on a branching phylogenetic evolutionary tree, using assumptions of molecular evolutionists, as shown in Figure 1, to their interpretation of these same data, as shown in Figure 2.

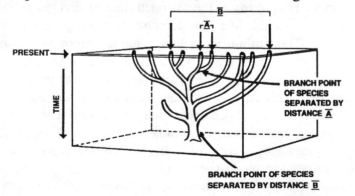

Figure 1. *The standard monophyletic evolutionary tree.*

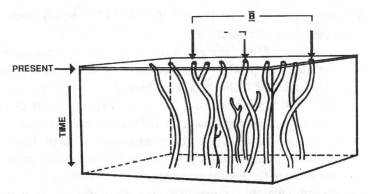

Figure 2. *The polyphyletic interpretation of molecular data according to Schwabe and Warr.*

Schwabe and Warr point out that if the notion of monophyletic evolution is abandoned, every single conclusion regarding relatedness of molecules or species becomes doubtful, because there would be no way of knowing whether branches of a single tree or similar branches of different trees are being compared. If the monophyletic notion is abandoned, then one is forced to abandon the interpretation that similarities automatically imply relatedness due to descent from a common ancestor. Creation scientists heartily agree with Schwabe and Warr on that point.

It must be emphasized that the only real data we have are found at the tips of the branches; all else is speculation based on preconceived ideas. Based on molecular differences derived from proteins and DNA of *living* organisms, evolutionists draw up a molecular evolutionary phylogenetic tree with hypothetical branching points. Numbers are supplied between the various hypothetical branching points that add up to the total molecular differences, usually expressed in percent, between present-day living organisms placed at the tips of the branches. Many of the unsuspecting public do not realize that the numbers between hypothetical ancestral proteins are not numbers that have actually been derived by analyzing real molecules, but are hypothetical numbers based on the assumption of monophyletic evolution. The *proof* of evolution thus is merely the *assumption* of evolution.

In several of the debates I have had with Vincent Sarich, a biochemist and professor in the Department of Anthropology, University of California, Berkeley, and one of the chief architects of the molecular clock hypothesis, Sarich has challenged his listeners to produce an alternative interpretation of the molecular data as offered by himself and other molecular evolutionists. Jukes, referring to the molecular evolutionist's interpretation of the amino acid sequences of the hemoglobins, also declared that there were no alternative explanations, when he said, "These data are important because they are *only* comprehensible within an evolutionary [branching tree] framework" (p. 119 of his chapter). Well, now, we have an alternative to that of molecular evolutionists (and very similar to that of creation scientists), and it comes from two of their fellow evolutionists! Sarich complains that Schwabe and Warr supply no numbers similar to his—that they have no data. Schwabe and Warr, as may be discovered by reading their paper, do have much data (and much more is available). They don't supply numbers similar to those supplied by molecular evolutionists, because they believe those numbers are fictitious, and since branching has not taken place, no such numbers are possible. Although they had no intention or desire to do so, Schwabe and Warr's research and conclusions offer powerful support to the interpretation of molecular data by creation scientists.

Michael Denton, in the chapter, "A Biochemical Echo of Typology," in his book, *Evolution: A Theory in Crisis,*[27] describes powerful evidence against the notion that molecular biology provides evidence for evolution. Denton, a molecular biologist and geneticist who earned his M.D. and Ph.D. degrees from British universities and who is now engaged in genetic research in Australia, says:

> Where fossils had failed and morphological considerations were at best only ambiguous, perhaps this new field of

comparative biochemistry might at last provide objective evidence of sequences and of the connecting links which had been so long sought by evolutionary biologists.

However, as more protein sequences began to accumulate during the 1960's, it became increasingly apparent that the molecules were not going to provide any evidence of sequential arrangements in nature, but were rather going to reaffirm the traditional view that the system of nature conforms fundamentally to a highly ordered hierarchic scheme from which all direct evidence for evolution is emphatically absent. Moreover, the division turned out to be more mathematically perfect than even most die-hard typologists would have predicted.[28]

Denton points out that when the molecular data of the cytochrome C's are examined, this reveals that each identifiable subclass of sequences is isolated and distinct. Every sequence can be unambiguously assigned to a particular subclass. That is, there is a group of similar amino acid sequences that is distinctive of reptiles, a group of similar amino acid sequences distinctive of mammals, of teleostean fishes, birds, insects, angiosperms (flowering plants), yeasts, etc. No sequence or group of sequences can be designated as intermediate with respect to other groups. Transitional or intermediate classes are completely absent. All sequences of each subclass are equally isolated from the members of another group.

Thus, as expressed in percent sequence differences, bacterial cytochrome C differs from that of the horse (a mammal) by 64%, from the pigeon (a bird) by 64%, from tuna (a teleostean fish) by 65%, from the silkmoth (an insect) by 65%, from wheat (a plant) by 66%, and from yeast (a fungus) by 69%. Thus, there are essentially no differences, whether mammal, bird, fish, insect, or plant. Silkmoth cytochrome C differs from horse cytochrome C by 27%, from pigeon by 25%, from turtle by 26%, from carp by 25%, and from lamprey by 30%, again no significant differences. Carp (fish) cytochrome C differs from horse and rabbit (mammals), turtle (reptile), and bullfrog (amphibian) cytochrome C's by 13% in each case, and from chicken (bird) by 14%. In the case of the hemoglobins, the hemoglobin of the lamprey (a cyclostome, or jawless fish, thus supposedly one of the most primitive fishes in existence today) differs from that of the carp (a jawed fish) by 75%, from that of the frog (amphibian) by 81%, from chicken (bird) by 78%, from kangaroo (marsupial) by 76%, and from human (placental mammal) by 73%. We see here, as in the other examples, that there is no indication of the traditional evolutionary series, which in the latter case would be cyclostome—jawed fish—amphibian—reptile—bird and mammal. Man is just as close to the lamprey as is the carp! The carp is not intermediate between lamprey and amphibian. The amphibian is not intermediate between fish and bird, marsupial or man. No group is intermediate between other groups. The same holds true when the hemoglobin of a snail (a gastropod mollusc) is compared to that of the lamprey, 85%; that of the carp, 87%; the frog, 87%; the chicken, 85%; and the kangaroo, 85%. These data, based on amino acid sequence data, so cherished by evolutionists today, do not allow us to classify the lamprey as primitive, with respect to other vertebrates, nor in any way intermediate between the snail (an invertebrate) and any of the vertebrates.

Denton looks at additional biochemical data and maintains that these data show systematic discontinuities, not the continuous grading of one form into another, beginning with "primitive" forms and moving on up into more and more "advanced" forms, even though thousands of different sequences of proteins and DNA have now been compared in hundreds of species. Since each class at a molecular level is unique, isolated, and unlinked by intermediates, Denton reminds us, then, that molecules, like fossils, have failed to provide the intermediates searched for so intensely by evolutionists ever since Darwin.

Before all of this was known, many evolutionists did predict that contemporary organisms that are supposed to be primitive in nature would have many protein sequences that would still be similar to those of their ancient ancestors, and thus intermediate between even more ancient types and the more modern types, such as mammals. Thus Denton[29] quotes Zuckerkandl as saying:

> Contemporary organisms that look much like ancient ancestral organisms probably contain a majority of polypeptide chains [proteins] that resemble quite closely those of ancient organisms. In other words, certain animals said to be 'living fossils', such as the cockroach, the horseshoe crab, the shark and, among mammals, the lemur, probably manufacture a great many polypeptide molecules that differ only slightly from those manufactured by their ancestors million of years ago.[30]

While mentioning that this view is controversial, Zuckerkandl says that this is the view he favors. Evolutionists are often heard to say that advances in scientific knowledge, particularly biology, are continually strengthening the evidence for evolution. Nothing could be further from the truth, and this evidence from comparative molecular biology, falsifying Zuckerkandl's prediction, is emphatic support for the fact that new knowledge, rather than strengthening evolutionary theory, widens the cracks in its facade.

If there is considerable variation in a family of proteins, say, the hemoglobins, within each class, such as the classes of mammals, birds, reptiles, amphibians, fish, etc., but the hemoglobins of none of these classes are intermediate between any others, as Zuckerkandl and many other evolutinists had expected, how do evolutionists explain this "anomaly"? Why is there about the same difference (approximately 85%) between the hemoglobins of lamprey, carp, frog, chicken, and kangaroo, and that of a snail? Why isn't the hemoglobin of a lamprey intermediate between snail and carp, or that of the frog intermediate between carp and chicken, etc.? Evolutionists attempt to get around this "anomaly" by pointing out that since the line leading to lamprey, carp, frog, and chicken split off from the invertebrates (the snail is an invertebrate, of course), say, about 500 million years ago, there has been 500 million years of molecular evolution in each one of these organisms, therefore it is not surprising that the hemoglobins, cytochrome C's, and other proteins of each one of these groups is equidistant from the snail, as expressed as percent differences. This is the "molecular clock" idea mentioned earlier. This is the notion that the mutation rate of the genes that code for each family of proteins in all animals, no matter how diverse, has been the same. This has produced, evolutionists believe, a one-percent change in histones of all creatures every 600 million years, a one-percent change in cytochrome C's every 20 million years in all creatures, a one-percent change every 5.8 million in the hemoglobins in all creatures, and a one-percent change in the fibrinopeptides in all creatures, whether insects, mammals, or fish, every 1.1 million years. Evolutionists must believe that the evolutionary molecular clock has ticked at a different rate for each family of proteins, and that means we must have hundreds of clocks all ticking at different rates.

There are some unknown factors, evolutionists must believe, that cause the same net mutation rate in the genes that govern each family of proteins, yet which produce tremendous differences in the mutation rates which code for different families of proteins.

Evolutionists have no empirical evidence to explain why the genes which code for one particular family of proteins would mutate much faster or slower than those that code for other families of proteins. Evolutionists did not expect or predict this. Furthermore, why would the genes that code for a family of proteins, say the cytochrome C's, mutate at the same rate in the lines leading to all organisms, no matter how "primitive" or "advanced," for hundreds of millions of years? Amphibians supposedly evolved about 400-450 million years ago. Since that time, variation of amphibians has been limited—amphibians are just as much amphibians today as when we first see them. The line that split off from amphibians, however, has supposedly evolved tremendously, giving rise successively to reptiles, birds, and mammals. Supposedly, animals change or evolve because genes mutate or evolve. If the genes that govern the cytochrome C's, the hemoglobins, and all other families of proteins, have evolved in amphibians during the past 500 million years just as much as the genes that code for all these proteins in all other creatures, why was evolution in amphibians essentially stopped dead in its tracks, while giving rise to a line that evolved all the way to man?

An insect is a very different creature than a mammal. If the genes in the insect that code for all the various families of genes have evolved or mutated at the same rate as those in the line leading to mammals for all the hundreds of millions of years since the insect became an insect, why is the insect still an insect, while the line that diverged from insects managed to evolve all the way to man? How could the same percentage of changes in the genes that code for proteins take place in the insect, yet leave dragonflies, cockroaches, spiders, mites, daddy longlegs, centipedes, etc., looking much like they did, supposedly, more than 350 million years ago?

Furthermore, the mutation rate is given as so many mutations per gene per generation, and the observed mutation rate is approximately the same for many genes. For higher organisms, a mutation rate of approximately 10^{-6}/gene/generation is estimated. In other words, for each gene, one could expect a mutation—good, neutral, or bad—to occur in one individual for each million individuals in each generation. In such species as man and the chimpanzee, where the generation rates do not differ widely, one might expect similar mutation rates. A mouse, however, produces four or five generations in one year. The time required for an elephant to reach reproductive age is about 14 years, and the period of gestation is 18-21 months. Thus, a mouse has a generation rate about 100 times greater that that of the elephant, but the proteins of the mouse have the same percentage differences from those of, say, the carp (or any other "lower" creature) as do those of the elephant.

Generation times differ much more drastically among insects. A fruit fly may produce offspring in two weeks, but the 17-year cicada requires 17 years to produce a single generation. Thus, the generation rate of the fruit fly is nearly a thousand times that of the cicada. If, as evolutionists believe, the modern orders of insects originated about 50 million years ago, then the fruit fly has undergone 50 billion more generations than the 17-year cicada, yet the proteins of all insect orders, including those of the fruit fly and the cicada, are equally divergent from those of vertebrates, and equally distant from bacteria, fungi, plants, etc. If one considers such divergent living things as trees and bacteria, the difference in generation times may differ by as much as 10,000.

What magic could have caused mutations to continue in the shark for hundreds of millions of years, but permitting the shark to remain a shark, while at the same time causing its fish relative to evolve successively into amphibian, then reptile, then mammal, and finally man? If the mutation rate is assumed to be the same in all classes of animals (thus a molecular clock is possible), and the mutation rate is measured as so many mutations per gene per generation, why are the proteins of organisms whose generation rates differ immensely, still equally divergent from their supposed common ancestors?

The mutation rate, as estimated by evolutionists, produces a one-percent change in the histones every 600 million years, and a one-percent change in the hemoglobins every 5.8 million years,—more than a 100-fold difference. What constraints could have caused *all* of the members of the hemoglobin family in *all* of the diverse phylogenetic lines, whether flea, snail, tuna, frog, crocodile, canary, cow, or man, to evolve precisely at 100 times the rates of *all* members of the histone family in *all* of the diverse phylogenetic lines? Even if one can come up with a scenario to "explain" that mystery, he must come up with other scenarios that would explain the systematic differences in mutation rates between cytochrome C's and hemoglobins, between hemoglobins and myoglobins, between hemoglobins and various proteases, *ad infinitum*. How could natural processes, involving random accidental genetic errors, supposedly eliminated or selected according to environmental conditions that vary tremendously around the world and having differential effects on a wide variety of organisms, produce the same mutation rate in all the hemoglobins of all creatures, but a different yet uniform mutation rate for all the cytochrome C's of all creatures, etc.?

In closing his chapter on this subject, Denton aptly states:

> Despite the fact that no convincing explanation of how random evolutionary processes could have resulted in such an ordered pattern of diversity, the idea of uniform rates of evolution is presented in the literature as if it were an empirical discovery. The hold of the evolutionary paradigm is so powerful, that an idea which is more like a principle of medieval astrology than a serious twentieth-century scientific theory has become a reality for evolutionary biologists.[31]

With this extensive critique of the notion of molecular evolution theory, and Denton's characterization of that idea as similar to medieval astrology, little further comment on Jukes' chapter on "Molecular Evidence for Evolution" need be given. One last comment may be worthwhile. Jukes says (p. 125) that it has been confirmed that procaryotes evolved into eucaryotes when some of these procaryotes were invaded by bacteria which shed most of their structure and activities to become mitochondria, and some were invaded by cyanobacteria, which, through a similar process, became chloroplasts. Contradicting this notion is the assertion by Jukes' fellow biochemist, Vincent Demoulin, who stated, "With regard to the origin of eucaryotic cells, the claim that the data support a symbiotic origin is also unfounded."[13] The notion that bacteria invaded other bacteria, or procaryotes, to enter into a symbiotic relationship and eventually become mitochondria or chloroplasts, is referred to as the theory of symbiotic origin of eucaryotes.

A link between procaryotes and eucaryotes is also denied by James Darnell. Based on his research, Darnell proclaims that:

> The differences in the biochemistry of messenger RNA formation in eucaryotes compared to procaryotes are so profound as to suggest that sequential procaryotic to eucaryotic cell evolution seems unlikely.[32]

So much for Jukes' "confirmation!"

Chapter 8, "Darwin's Untimely Burial—Again!" (pp. 139-146), is by Stephen Jay Gould and is a reprint of an essay published by Gould in *Natural History* in 1976.[33] This essay was an attack on an article by Tom Bethell in *Harper's Magazine*,[34] in which Bethell sets forth the thesis that the Darwinian theory of evolution, based on natural selection, was collapsing because it is finally being realized that the theory of natural selection is nothing more than a tautology. Since Bethell's claims and Gould's counterclaims advanced in these two articles have been critiqued in Chapter 3 of this book, it will not be necessary to discuss Gould's chapter further. It might be fitting at this point simply to restate that Gould's attempt to salvage the status of the theory of natural selection as a scientific theory failed miserably, according to philosopher Ronald Brady.[35]

Chapter 9, "The Geological and Paleontological Arguments of Creationism" (pp. 147-162), is by David M. Raup. Formerly Dean of Science at the Field Museum of Natural History, Raup is now Chairman of the Department of Geophysical Sciences at the University of Chicago. He is widely recognized for research in invertebrate paleontology and geology, having been elected to membership in the National Academy of Science. He is co-author with Steven M. Stanley of the textbook *Principles of Paleontology*.[36] It is greatly refreshing to read this chapter by Raup, for it is not an intemperate polemic against creation science and creation scientists

as are so many other chapters in this book. While Raup leaves
no doubt as to his belief in evolution, he approaches the
creation/evolution controversy calmly and objectively. In
sharp contrast to Gould's arrogant reference to creation scientists as "yahoos" and to claims of Raup's fellow evolutionists
that creation science has no vestige of science and is nothing
more than religion in disguise, Raup concedes that creation
scientists do use acceptable scientific methods (though sometimes poorly, in his opinion), and that the status and validity
of creation is independent of the ideology or of the religious
beliefs of creation scientists. Raup thus states:

> It is often argued that the creationists have allegiance
> to a single ideology (the Bible) and are thus not free enough
> intellectually to consider questions of origins in a scientifi-
> cally acceptable manner. There is no question that there is
> a strong correspondence between support of the creationist
> idea and commitment to a single religious view. Increas-
> ingly, however, people without strong religious commit-
> ment are being drawn into and are expressing some
> acceptance of the arguments made by the scientific crea-
> tionists. Therefore, control by an ideology may represent
> an argument in some quarters but certainly not in all. Fur-
> thermore, I think it can be argued that whether a body of
> reasoning is scientific or not should be decided indepen-
> dently of the question of whether the adherents are com-
> mitted to one ideology or another.

Creation scientists agree with this statement. Regardless
of the particular ideologies or religious beliefs held respectively by evolutionists and creationists, their scientific reasoning and conclusions concerning origins should be judged
independently of these beliefs and solely on the basis of the
scientific evidence each can marshal to support his views.
Certainly, concerning the matter of origins, very few people
approach this question free of preconceived ideas.

Raup confirms the fact that creation scientists do use
scientific methods in their procedures and do put the theory
of creation on the line in these tests. He says:

Several lists of "predictions" of the creation model
have been published (Gish 1978, pp. 50-51, for example).
Testing these predictions often involves rather elaborate,
and sometimes surprisingly conventional, research studies.
A recent example is a reappraisal of the well-known lime-
stone deposits of Silurian age at Thornton Quarry in Illinois
(D'Armond 1980). These deposits are conventionally understood to be buried reefs, and extensive work has been
done on them over many years. D'Armond attempts to
argue that the deposits are simply the result of catastrophic
flooding, and while I do not agree with his analysis or his
conclusions, the study is clearly an attempt to use geologic
data to support an aspect of the creation model.

Thus, while practitioners of scientific creationism
firmly believe in the authority of the Bible, they do not
attempt to rely on it as their sole authority. Rather, they
appear to be searching for corroborative data from a wide
range of sources. Theoretically, a creationist such as D'Armond could conclude that the creation model is not viable
because of a lack of corroboration from geologic data. This
is exceedingly unlikely for the committed creationist, but
the literature of scientific creation does provide the interested layman with the opportunity to conclude that the
biblical account is falsified by scientific data. In a real
sense, creationists are putting the biblical account of creation on the line by claiming that it *should* be subjected to
scientific testing.

Further, although Raup believes that errors of fact and of
understanding have crept into the work of creationists (this
could be said, of course, of *all* scientific work), he states:

In my view, a few of the arguments used by creationists are
'scientific' in the sense that they use the basic methods of
testing hypotheses normally considered to be scientific
[p. 159] . . . some scientific creationists have done a rather
remarkable job of absorbing a complex discipline . . .
[p. 160].

The main thesis of Raup's contribution to this book is, as
he says, a criticism of the geological and paleontological

arguments of creation scientists, a thesis he approaches confidently. He thus states:

> Gish (1978) has popularized the notion that the rocks and fossils say NO to evolution. As I will show here, the rocks and fossils say YES to evolution! [p. 147].

Creation scientists differ sharply with Raup on who is the winner on that point, and any reader of Raup's chapter should be able to discern that his arguments for evolution based on the fossil record are indeed exceedingly weak.

Raup begins his discussion of the fossil record with a rather frank admission that that record from the evolutionist's point of view is very poor. He says (p. 156):

> Darwin predicted that the fossil record should show a reasonably smooth continuum of ancestor-descendant pairs with a satisfactory number of intermediates between major groups. Darwin even went so far as to say that if this were not found in the fossil record, his general theory of evolution would be in serious jeopardy. Such smooth transitions were not found in Darwin's time, and he explained this in part on the basis of an incomplete geologic record and in part on the lack of study of that record. We are now more than a hundred years after Darwin and the situation is little changed. Since Darwin a tremendous expansion of paleontological knowledge has taken place, and we know much more about the fossil record than was known in his time, but the basic situation is not much different. We actually may have fewer examples of smooth transition than we had in Darwin's time because some of the old examples have turned out to be invalid when studied in more detail. To be sure, some new intermediate or transitional forms have been found, particularly among land vertebrates. But if Darwin were writing today, he would probably still have to cite a disturbing lack of missing links or transitional forms between the major groups of organisms.

Darwin admitted that one of the strongest arguments against his theory was the fossil record. He hoped and expected that future research would produce the transitional forms demanded by the theory and stated, as Raup reminds us, that if these transitional forms were not found, his general theory of evolution (the amoeba-to-man theory) would be placed in serious jeopardy. Here we are today, 133 years after the publication of Darwin's book, and the situation is even worse now than it was then. Not only have we failed to find the transitional forms that must exist if evolution is true, but even many of the fossils that contemporaries of Darwin claimed to represent transitional forms have since been shown not to be transitional forms at all. Raup, as do most evolutionists, does claim that there are at least some transitional forms, citing *Archaeopteryx* as an example. These examples are highly disputable, and, furthermore, if evolution is true, we should have many thousands of indisputable transitional forms.

In his chapter, Raup states he would show that the fossils say "YES" to evolution. How does he do this? First, as described above, he frankly admits the gravity of the problem that fossils pose for evolution theory. He then proceeds to tell us why transitional forms are not found, or in his words, "How does the evolutionist explain the lack of intermediates?" (p. 156). To start, Raup claims this in part results from an artifact in our system of taxonomic classification. For example, Raup says that although *Archaeopteryx* is a transitional form between Reptilia and Aves, taxonomists were forced by the rules of taxonomy to place it in one or the other class, and they arbitrarily classified it as a bird. With specific reference to his example of *Archaeopteryx,* creation scientists point out that research during the past few years on major anatomical features of *Archaeopteryx* has established, in every instance, that these features are bird-like rather than reptile-like, and thus its status as a transitional form is becoming more and more dubious with the passage of time. Furthermore, if a creature or a plant is transitional between two major categories, its intermediate status should be obvious to all, regardless in which category it is place by taxonomists. Thus, if

Archaeopteryx had elements that were half-way scales and half-way feathers rather than possessing feathers identical to those of modern birds, and if it had forelimbs part-way between feet and legs and wings rather than possessing the basic form and pattern of avian wings, it would easily be recognized as a true transitional form between reptiles and birds. As another example, if some invertebrates, such as trilobites, had evolved into fish, the transitional forms would be easily recognized as transitional whether taxonomists chose to place them in the Class Trilobita or in the Class Pisces.

Coming from such a well-informed geologist as Raup, his second argument is quite unexpected. In this argument, he pleads the poverty of the fossil record, an excuse used by Darwin but abandoned by many geologists today as untenable. We have a very rich fossil record in these modern times, with more than 250,000 different fossil species classified and resting on museum shelves. In this section (p. 158) Raup seems to have forgotten what he describes on p. 156. In the earlier section, he states:

> Since Darwin a tremendous expansion of paleontological
> knowledge has taken place, and we know much more about
> the fossil record than was known, in his time. . . .

Indeed we do! Paleontologists have searched intensely throughout the world for the "missing links." Rocks of every so-called geological period have been carefully searched. Many new discoveries have been made, but each new species is readily placed in an already established order, class, and phylum. No links between major categories have been discovered. If evolution were true, tens of thousands of the 250,000 known species should represent indisputable transitional forms. Raup's appeal to the poverty of the fossil record is totally without merit.

Raup encapsulates his third and final explanation for the lack of intermediate forms in these words:

> A third general explanation for the lack of intermedi-
> ates is that transitional forms constitute very short intervals

of geologic time if, as many theorists now believe, the change from one major type to another occurs rather rapidly (the punctuated equilibrium model of Eldredge and Gould [1972]. This simply lessens the probability of finding intermediates [p. 158]).

As creation scientists have pointed out,[37] the scenario of "punctuated equilibrium" was imagined for the purpose of explaining the absence of transitional forms between *species*, *not* the absence of transitional forms between *major* types of plants and animals, such as families, orders, classes, and phyla. The notion of "punctuated equilibrium" (the idea that a new species arises rapidly by a random process without the necessity of natural selection) does not even address the problem of the gaps between major categories, let alone solve the problem.

Raup, of course, avoids all discussion of the insuperable barriers the huge gap between single-celled organisms and the complex invertebrates and the equally huge gap between these invertebrates and fishes pose for evolutionary theory. These are by far the most serious problems the fossil record provides for evolution theory. Why then doesn't Raup address these problems? Simply because he, like all other evolutionists, has no solution to these problems. The explosive appearance, fully formed, of a great variety of complex invertebrates, and the abrupt appearance, fully formed, of each major type of fish without a trace of an ancestor provide as conclusive proof for creation as one could expect.

Raup concludes his discussion of the fossil record with the statement that:

> With these considerations in mind, one must argue that the fossil record is compatible with the predictions of evolutionary theory.

In an article Raup published a few years ago, he states that:

> Darwin's general solution to the incompatibility of fossil evidence and his theory was to say that the fossil

record is a very incomplete one—that it is full of gaps, and that we have much to learn. Well, we are now about 120 years after Darwin and the knowledge of the fossil record has been greatly expanded. We now have a quarter of a million fossil species but the situation hasn't changed much.[38]

If the fossil record was incompatible with Darwin's theory in Darwin's time, and the situation hasn't changed much, then how can it now be argued that it has become compatible with evolution theory? As mentioned above, the only really new development since Darwin's time has been the invention of the notion of punctuated equilibrium, and as noted, even if true, this notion would provide no solution whatsoever for the problem the gaps between the higher categories pose for evolution theory. Furthermore, if evolution is true, why would one have to go to great lengths to argue that the fossil record is compatible with the theory? Why is it necessary to provide explanations for the lack of intermediate forms? If evolution is true, the fossil record should provide undoubted *proof* of evolution. At the beginning of his chapter, Raup stated he would show that the rocks and fossils say "YES" to evolution. But even if one were to accept all of Raup's explanations for the lack of intermediate forms, the rocks cry out "NO" to evolution.

In his critique of the reasoning and conclusions of geologists who are creationists, Raup presents an accurate account of the position of these geologists. He then points out where he believes their conclusions to be faulty or out of date. Part of the blame, Raup maintains, is due to the dependence at times by creationists on the conclusions of evolutionary geologists who were advancing faulty or out-of-date ideas. For example, Raup points out that creationists strongly rely on the fact of catastrophism in geology, citing especially the possibility of a great worldwide flood to account for much of the great sedimentary rocks and vast fossil graveyards. At the same time, according to Raup, creationists attribute to evolutionary geologists the doctrine of uniformitarianism, the notion that present processes, acting essentially at present rates over vast stretches of time, can account for most geological features without resort to catastrophic events. Raup then points out, correctly, that the concept of uniformitarianism in geology is losing favor among present-day geologists. Raup says (p. 152):

> In the nineteenth Century, the combination of Lyellian geology and Darwinian biology did promote a conventional wisdom that the earth and life evolved by very gradual processes moving at uniform rates. Many of the examples of catastrophism now being cited by the scientific creationists were well known but were either ignored or given very secondary importance in nineteenth-century geology and paleontology. A great deal has changed, however, and contemporary geologists and paleontologists now generally accept catastrophe as a "way of life," although they may avoid the word catastrophe. In fact, many geologists now see rare, short-lived events as being the principal contributors to geologic sequences. In many instances, an exposure of rock records a series of special events (storms, hurricanes, landslides, slumps, or volcanic eruptions) that produced large volumes of sediment but that represent only a fraction of the elapsed time covered by the total sequence. The periods of relative quiet contribute only a small part of the record. The days are almost gone when a geologist looks at such a sequence, measures its thickness, estimates the total amount of elapsed time, and then divides one by the other to compute the rate of deposition in centimeters per thousand years.

Raup then acknowledges that part of the blame for misunderstanding falls on the evolutionary geologists. He states:

> The misunderstanding has been caused in part by the geologists themselves: the nineteenth-century idea of uniformitarianism and gradualism still exists in popular treatments of geology, in some museum exhibits, and in lower level textbooks. It is even still taught in secondary school classrooms, and one can hardly blame the creationists for

having the idea that the conventional wisdom in geology is still a noncatastrophic one.

The fact that, as Raup says, evolutionary geologists avoid the word "catastrophe," while generally accepting catastrophe as a "way of life," betrays their reluctance to embrace a concept long held by creationists but dogmatically rejected by the evolutionary establishment. Furthermore, Raup is a bit out of date with his own reading, as far as creationist literature is concerned. Not only are most creationists aware of this shift in thinking by evolutionary geologists, they delight in pointing out this shift to a position that is drawing ever nearer to their own. Evolutionary geologists, starting with James Hutton and Charles Lyell near the beginning of the Nineteenth Century, adamantly have excluded the possibility of worldwide catastrophes as contributing to geological features on the earth. More and more geologists now, however, are willing to concede the possibility of worldwide catastrophes. For example, while still refusing to accept the possibility of a worldwide flood (after all, that is described in the Bible!), many geologists are willing to believe that an asteroid struck the earth and hurled such a vast amount of dust into the air that the earth was blacked out for several years, causing the deaths of much of plant life and consequent extinction of all the dinosaurs, as well as wiping out many other forms of life. Now that is a worldwide catastrophe with a vengeance!

Raup challenges the claims of some creationists that the construction of the geologic column and the use of fossils in geologic dating is dependent upon biological theories of evolution. He points out that the geologic column, as we know it, was completed by 1815, nearly 50 years before Darwin published his book, and was developed largely by people who were creationists. Raup devotes a sizeable section of his chapter to denying that geologists date rocks by the stage of evolution of its fossils. Raup argues that while the oldest known fossils are of rather simple procaryotic organisms, and younger rocks contain more complex forms, there is no recognizable trend towards increasing complexity that is clear enough to use for dating purposes. He states that the process of evolution is not clearly directional. He does admit, however, that a surprising number of evolutionary geologists with specialties other than paleontology share the misconception, as pointed out by creationists, that the geological record reveals a series of organisms of gradually increasing complexity. Not only have creationists cited many statements in evolutionary geological literature to this effect, but creationists have been confronted frequently in their debates with the argument that fossils show gradually increasing complexity. Thus Raup is led to say:

> The creationists . . . come by their misunderstanding honestly, at least in part. Many teachers and textbook writers, especially in the late nineteenth and early twentieth centuries, have been so carried away by the elegance of the Darwinian model that they have ascribed powers to it that do not exist.

Raup goes on to say it is ironic that creationists accept, as fact, the mistaken notion that the geologic record shows a progression from simple to complex organisms, and go to great lengths to account for this in their Flood model. Now that he has made clear to creationists that this is a mistaken notion, he should work hard to root it out of evolutionary geology textbooks and the evolutionary geologic literature.

Perhaps I do not clearly understand what Raup is trying to say, but he does seem to contradict himself. He says (p. 154), "Geochronology depends upon the existence of a virtually exceptionless sequence of distinctive objects in rocks; that sequence just happens to exist in the fossils." But later (p. 160) he says, "Not uncommonly, however, demonstrably young rocks are found *beneath* older rocks." Of course, which are the younger rocks and which are the older rocks is determined by the fossils they contain, and if it is not uncommon for younger rocks to be found beneath older rocks, then it certainly cannot be claimed that geochronology is based upon a virtually exceptionless sequence. In fact, quite often subsidiary hypotheses must be invoked to explain why rocks containing supposedly older fossils rest on rocks containing allegedly younger fossils.

The final section in Raup's chapter is entitled, "Could the Evolutionists Be Wrong?" Here Raup states it would be wrong for evolutionists to claim they have a completely correct understanding of the history of life and the processes involved, reminding the reader of the many major paradigms in science that have proven to be wrong. He feels absolutely sure that evolutionists are correct that the age of the earth is in billions of years, but concedes that the mechanism of evolution may not yet be understood. He completely fails to grasp the creationist concept of teaching two models of origins. He asserts that since there are several biological models of evolution, that is, that there are several alternative mechanisms of evolution, it is wrong for creationists to insist that there are only two models of origins—a creation model and an evolution model. What Raup fails to understand is that while there are several possible sub-models within each model of origins, there are only two basic models of origins—a naturalistic, mechanistic non-theistic evolutionary model and a theistic, supernatural special-creation model. Lamarkism, neo-Darwinism, punctuated equilibrium, the hopeful monster mechanism, and theistic evolution are all sub-models within the evolutionary model or paradigm, while progressive creation, the gap theory, recent creation, etc., are sub-models within the special creation model. An evolutionist cannot claim he is teaching two models of origins if he is only offering his students alternative mechanisms of evolution.

Chapter 10, "Systematics, Comparative Biology, and the Case Against Creationism" (pp. 163-191), is by Joel Cracraft. At the time of publication of this book, Cracraft was an associate professor at the University of Illinois Medical Center. His special interests include functional morphology of birds, systematics theory (taxonomy), and vertebrate

biogeography. One of his burning interests today is defending
evolution and fighting creation science. His attitude sharply
contrasts with that of David Raup. Cracraft is extremely arrogant, heaping scorn and derision on creation scientists and
their science, accusing creation scientists of misquoting, of
quoting out of context, of employing distortions, of holding
childish myths, of being religious zealots, of lacking in com-
petence, of being extremists, of implying innuendos, and of
being guilty of outright deception. Not only has Cracraft taken
off his gloves to fight creation scientists, he has also donned
brass knuckles. No doubt many evolutionists applaud such
vicious and unprincipled attacks on creation scientists, but in
doing so, Cracraft is guilty of many of the charges he levels
against creationists. Furthermore, when evolutionists use such
tactics, it is a tacit admission that their own case is weak and
that creation scientists are hitting where it hurts.

Cracraft's first blast at creation scientists is their use of
the terms "created kinds" or "basic kinds." He charges that
creation scientists are guilty of using "superficial and illiterate
treatments" of the vast biological literature representing a
substantial body of knowledge on the subject of systematics.
Of course, few creationists, in fact, few evolutionists, have
had the time to make an extensive study of the science of
taxonomy or systematics, as has Cracraft. Most creationists,
however, certainly those among the biologists, have some
knowledge of what is involved in classification systems. One
of the largest categories of creation scientists, probably the
largest, are those who hold advanced degrees in botany, zoology, genetics, and biology, all of whom would have had
courses in taxonomy. There are, in fact, some creationists,
such as Dr. Wayne Frair of The King's College, who have had
a lifelong interest in systematics (Frair's specialty is the taxonomy of turtles). Furthermore, according to his own reasoning, Cracraft could have only a superficial and illiterate
knowledge of biochemistry, of the functional morphology of
primates and of most other creatures, of physics, of genetics,

of invertebrate anatomy, physiology, and paleontology; of hydrology, of geology, and numerous other fields of science, all important in the study of origins.

While Cracraft is throwing stones at creation scientists for using the term "kind" to refer to a created category or taxon, he and other evolutionists not infrequently use the term "kind."[39] Thus, Cracraft says (p. 164):

> So too is the realization that there exist groups of individual organisms that are defined in terms of their ability to interbreed with one another and thereby produce *like kinds*, but that at the same time lack the ability to interbreed freely with other such groups (although accidental interbreeding might be observed sometimes) [emphasis added].

Of course he is not using the term "like kinds" in a technical sense, but neither do creation scientists use the terms "basic types" or "created kinds" in a technical sense. Thus, if a creation scientist, through his study of genetics, natural breeding habits, and production of interspecific fertile offspring, became convinced that all creatures within the genus *Canis* (dogs, wolves, coyotes, jackals) were all one created kind, he might use the term "dog kind" in a general sense, or he might use the correct taxonomic term *Canis* in a technical sense.

Evolutionists, such as Cracraft, have repeatedly emphasized the difficulty that creationists have, at times, of precisely defining and indentifying what constitutes each basic type or created kind. At the same time, they fail to emphasize their own difficulty (and that of all taxonomists) in correctly identifying species, genera, etc. Most taxonomists, especially evolutionists, emphasize reproductive isolation in identifying species limits. Thus, Cracraft says (p. 164):

> The point to be made here is that the presence of reproductive isolation is not necessarily related to the degree of phenotypic difference, and at least in sympatric taxa

it is their reproductive discontinuity that is of significance when naming them as distinct species.

Just prior to that statement, however, Cracraft says:

> Accompanying the reproductive criterion has been the recognition that organisms show variability not only within species but among them as well. In fact, morphological discontinuity among clusters of like individual organisms has been the single most important basis for recognizing species limits, especially because information about interbreeding is known for only a very small percentage of the species currently recognized.

Thus, although evolutionists (as do creationists) attribute considerable significance to reproductive isolation (creationists do not use that as the sole criterion in identifying created kinds) as a criterion in identifying species limits, this is known for only a limited number of present-day species and for none of the species known only as fossils. Our common household pet, the dog (*Canis familiaris*) is not only very similar morphologically to wolves (*Canis lupus*) and to various species among coyotes (genus *Canis*), but on occasion they do interbreed with wolves and coyotes, and fertile offspring are produced. Why, then, do taxonomists place them in separate species rather than classifying them as varieties or subspecies?

A few examples from the literature will suffice to illustrate the difficulties that all taxonomists, including the arrogant Cracraft, have in identifying taxonomic limits. Roger Lewin, science writer for *Science,* in his article, "Recognizing Ancestors Is a Species Problem," writes:

> At the heart of the problem is the absence of any consistent relationship between speciation and morphological change. In other words, the origin of a new species might be accompanied by a very striking change in anatomy, which can be identified in fossils, or by little or no change at all, which cannot. Therefore, the absence of any marked anatomical difference between two individuals does not necessarily mean that they belong to the same species. The problem applies to all vertebrates.[40]

In an earlier article, Lewin discusses the same problem. Drawing on studies by Wake, Lewin says:

> There are many species of salamanders, some of which are physically very similar. "Two of them are virtually indistinct morphologically," says Wake. . . . For many years evolutionary biologists have equated morphological similarity with close genetic relationship. This is clearly not necessarily the case.[41]

George Gaylord Simpson has stated:

> Supposedly intergeneric hybridization, usually with sterile offspring, is possible in animals, for instance, in mammals, the artificial crosses *Bos x Bison, Equus x Asinus, and Ursus x Thalarctos.* In my opinion, however, this might better be taken as basis for uniting the nominal genera. I would not give generic rank to *Bison, Asinus, or Thalarctos.*[42]

The adult male and female snipe eels are so drastically different morphologically, that for over 50 years taxonomists mistakenly placed them in separate genera, and some even placed them in separate families and suborders![43] In another case, a group of organisms (snails) was classified into more than 200 species, but later and more careful research reduced them to no more than two species. These are just a few of a multitude of cases which illustrate that systematics is man-made, and, at least during most of its previous history, has significantly been determined by arbitrary and subjective analyses. That is not in any way intended to question the scientific value of systematics. Taxonomy as a science began with the work of Linnaeus in the 18th century, and it would be difficult for the modern sciences of zoology and botany to function without it. As stated earlier, creationists do have some difficulties in delimiting created kinds, especially when closely similar organisms are considered, but, as illustrated above, all taxonomists have difficulties in delimiting various taxa, from species on up through higher taxa—genera, families, orders, classes, and phyla.

Cracraft (pp. 165-167), as did Eldredge (see Chapter 7), quotes a portion of my comments concerning separate kinds in my book, *Evolution: The Fossils Say No!*[44] He claims, as did Eldredge, that my understanding of a created or basic kind is both contradictory and confusing. As I related in my discussion in Chapter 7 concerning similar charges by Eldredge, my discussion was thorough and clear enough that even a high school student should be able to understand what I meant by a separate or created kind. Evolutionists such as Eldredge and Cracraft are so determined to destroy the credibility of creation scientists that they skim through their writings in a hasty and superficial manner and then report inaccuracies and confusion on the part of the creation scientists, when it is their own thinking that is confused. Cracraft, as do others, accuses creationists of "selected quotations" (of course all quotations are selected!) and of quoting out of context. Here there is no question that Cracraft has lifted out of context a limited portion of my discussion of basic or created kinds. My discussion of this subject begins on p. 34 of the book cited above and closes on p. 37. If Cracraft had quoted this entire section, it would be clear to all, or at least to most readers who could read the passage with an open and inquiring mind rather than the closed mind-set of Eldredge and Cracraft, that my definition was clear and precise.

Cracraft further charges, (p. 165) in reference to creation scientists, that:

> The depth of their scientific acumen is illustrated by a particularly elementary example: they seldom even refer to taxa by their scientific names, preferring instead to adopt scientifically imprecise names such as dog, cat, bat, horse, and so on.

This charge against creation scientists is absurd, first, because creation scientists do refer to organisms by their scientific names when referring to specific organisms rather than general categories (see for example my book *Evolution: The Challenge of the Fossil Record*,[37] or my earlier book

Evolution: The Fossils Say No! which Cracraft quotes above). Having that book before him, Cracraft had to know his charge was false. Secondly, in referring to general types, evolutionists follow precisely the custom of creation scientists in referring to them as dogs, cats, bats, birds, fish, etc. For example, glance through Romer's book, *Vertebrate Paleontology*[45] (or any other similar book), and note his frequent references to dogs, bats, rats, fish, horses, birds, snakes, dinosaurs, etc. In fact, Romer, Cracraft, and other evolutionists very frequently refer to "horses"—from the tiny cony-like *Hyracotherium* (often referred to by evolutionists as *Eohippus,* in violation of the rules of taxonomy, since *Hyrocotherium* has priority) on up to our modern *Equus.* This is a very diverse group of creatures. *Hyracotherium* has little, if anything, in common with creatures commonly referred to as horses, but Cracraft and his fellow evolutionists have no qualms whatsoever in referring to all of these animals as "horses." Yet Cracraft condemns creation scientists for referring to "horses" and the use of similar general terms. When creation scientists refer to the individual creatures within this general group, of course they use the proper scientific names, such as *Merychippus, Hipparion, Pliohippus, Mesohippus, Equus,* etc. Cracraft's charge is false, and merely an attempt to belittle creation scientists for using a procedure commonly practiced by evolutionists themselves.

On p. 170, Cracraft begins a section entitled "Biological Comparison: A Natural Hierarchy or Analogical Similarity?" He states:

> The basis of any classification system is similarity. Long before the concept of evolution was accepted by the biological community, natural historians were making classifications of organisms and were attempting to identify those groups that could be called "natural." . . . In preevolutionary terms "natural" usually was interpreted to mean those groups assumed to be the product of a "creation event" and that evidenced a "divine plan." After the rise of an evolutionary viewpoint, natural groups were those

thought to have descended from a common ancestor. In both cases, some aspect of similarity was used to define the content of these natural groups.

Later on (p. 172) Cracraft says:

> To most comparative biologists, the concept of primitive and derived characters has evolutionary connotations, but it need not be interpreted in this way only.

Later, on the same page, Cracraft states:

> Thus embryological transformations can yield hypotheses about taxic hierarchies—without demanding an assumption of evolution (this is not to say, however, that an evolutionary interpretation cannot be applied).

It is quite apparent, even by Cracraft's own admissions, that the theory of evolution was not derived from the data mentioned above but was *imposed* upon the data, and then, using circular reasoning, it is commonly claimed by evolutionists that all of these data provide proof of evolution.

On p. 172, Cracraft states:

> The remainder of this section will discuss how creationists have viewed the problem of similarity and, most importantly, will argue that the *hierarchical pattern* produced by the shared similarities observed among organisms is predicted by a hypothesis of evolutionary descent with modification but *not* by an assumption of special creation.

Cracraft then describes two predictions which he claims are creationist predictions. His second prediction will be discussed first, since it is easily disposed of. It is, according to Cracraft (p. 173):

> All morphological similarities shared between separate 'created kinds' will exhibit strong correspondence in functions and biological roles that are tightly correlated with parallel ways of life.

This is substantially correct, if modified to read "most morphological similarities" (the substitution of "most" for "all" is not a major point, since, in contrast, evolutionary theory is shot through and through with exceptions and "anomalies"), and if by parallel ways of life Cracraft means sharing similar needs. Creation scientists believe it is obvious that teeth were designed for chewing, eyes for seeing, ears for hearing, grasping hands for grasping objects, noses for smelling, hair for protection and warmth, feet for walking, hearts for pumping blood, kidneys for filtration, lungs for breathing, hemoglobin for transporting oxygen and carbon dioxide, reproductive organs for reproduction, etc. Many creatures, including man, share these structures and organs in common because obviously they are required for their way of life. Here creation scientists plead guilty.

Cracraft's first "creationist prediction" is (p. 172): "The similarities observed among organisms cannot be shared so as to produce a hierarchical pattern of groups within groups." As noted earlier, Cracraft claims that:

> The *hierarchical pattern* produced by the shared similarities observed among organisms is predicted by a hypothesis of evolutionary descent with modification, but *not* by an assumption of special creation.

Here Cracraft makes his job easy. He creates a straw man by concocting a creationist prediction which no creation scientist would support, and then proceeds to destroy the straw man. As described in Chapter 7, Eldredge made similar claims. Thus he stated:

> This pattern of sharing similarities with an ever-widening array of biological forms must continue until all of life is linked up by sharing at least one similarity in common. *This* is evolution's grand prediction: that the patterns of similarities in the organic world are arranged like a complex set of nested Chinese boxes.

This pattern, "arranged like a complex set of nested Chinese boxes," is what is also described as the hierarchical pattern observed among organisms, and which both Cracraft and Eldredge claim is predicted by the hypothesis of evolution, but not by creation. This is false on both counts.

It was pointed out in Chapter 8 that the fact plants and animals can be arranged in hierarchical patterns or into sets of nested groups was recognized by Linnaeus and other taxonomists a hundred years before publication of Darwin's book, *Origin of Species,* and therefore could not have been a *prediction* based on evolutionary theory, nor was it in any way dependent on evolutionary theory, since Linnaeus and other pre-Darwinian taxonomists were creationists.

Colin Patterson, senior paleontologist at the British Museum of Natural History, and who, as discussed earlier in this book, is a systematist who has adopted a system of classification called pattern or transformed cladism, may be cited in support of the arguments given here and in Chapter 8. In his article, "Cladistics," Patterson says:

> 'Clade' is a term introduced by Julian Huxley in 1957 for 'delimitable monophyletic units,' and at its simplest cladistics is a technique for characterizing (delimiting) a *hierarchy* of groups. Of course, the same is true of *Linnean systematics* . . . [emphasis added].[46]

Patterson thus affirms what was stated earlier, namely, that arranging organisms in a hierarchy of groups is also true of the Linnaean system of taxonomy, invented a hundred years before Darwin, and thus is not a prediction based on evolutionary theory, nor does it provide evidence for the theory. Furthermore, the assertions by both Cracraft and Eldredge that this hierarchical pattern would not be a prediction based on creation theory is obviously false, since Linnaeus (as were other pre-Darwinian systematists) was a creationist, and what he discovered in nature tended to confirm rather than question his convictions as a creationist. In his chapter, Cracraft repeatedly asserts that the existence of a natural hierarchy refutes the creationist world view. This is obviously false.

On p. 177, Cracraft asserts that ". . . systematic biology is the very cornerstone of evolutionary analysis. . . ." If by this Cracraft means to say also that the converse is true, that is, that modern systematics is somehow dependent upon or inextricably intertwined with evolutionary theory, this is also false, or at the very least, not necessarily true. Thus, Patterson states:

> But as the theory of cladistics has developed, it has been realized that more and more of the evolutionary framework is inessential, and may be dropped. The chief symptom of this change is the significance attached to nodes in cladograms. In Hennig's book, as in all early work in cladistics, the nodes are taken to represent ancestral species. This assumption has been found to be unnecessary, even misleading, and may be dropped. Platnick refers to the new theory as 'transformed cladistics' and the transformation is away from dependence on evolutionary theory. Indeed, Gareth Nelson, who is chiefly responsible for the transformation, put it like this in a letter to me this summer: "In a way, I think we are merely rediscovering pre-evolutionary systematics; or, if not rediscovering it, fleshing it out."

> Mayr's and Simpson's criticisms (see quotes in Platnick for the latter) assume that cladistics is to do with evolution. But cladistics, as I have tried to show, is not necessarily about evolution—speciation, ancestry, and such things. It is about a simpler and more basic matter, the pattern in nature—groups, hierarchies, or nested sets of groups, and characters of groups.[47]

Please note that Gareth Nelson states that in the new theory of systematics called transformed or pattern cladistics, they are rediscovering, or fleshing out, *pre-evolutionary* systematics. Pre-evolutionary systematics was, of course, creationist, although this does not mean that transformed cladists are creationists. It does mean, however, that their systematics is completely divorced from evolutionary theory. In fact, according to Patterson, transformed cladistics has revealed some very unflattering facts about the modern neo-Darwinian theory of evolution, the current orthodoxy found in all textbooks. Patterson says:

> In my view, the most important outcome of cladistics is that a simple, even naive method of discovering the

groups of systematics—what used to be called the natural system—has led some of us to realize that much of today's explanation of nature, in terms of neo-Darwinism, or the synthetic theory, may be empty rhetoric.[48]

And just what is this pre-evolutionary (in pre-evolutionary times, certainly creationist) systematics all about? It is about a simpler and more basic matter, the pattern in nature— groups, hierarchies, or nested sets of groups, and characters of groups, Patterson tells us. Remember Eldredge's and Cracraft's claims that hierarchies and nested sets of groups are "predictions" based on evolutionary theory but not creation. Patterson, Platnick, Nelson, and their fellow transformed cladists obviously don't agree. Cracraft's "Creationist Prediction #1" thus is not a creationist prediction whatsoever. Furthermore, the existence of these hierarchies and sets of nested groups could be a genuine prediction based on creation, since creation was widely accepted long before these hierarchies and sets of nested groups were recognized and placed in a formal system of classification by Linnaeus in the 18th century, but Darwinism did not appear on the scene until 100 years after the Linnaean system was devised.

In case some may feel that I have somehow misinterpreted what transformed or pattern cladistics is all about, or, as Cracraft might claim, I have quoted out of context or misquoted the transformed cladists, I will quote further from an article by John Beatty, "Classes and Cladists." Beatty, from the general tone of his article, does not appear to be sympathetic to the transformed cladist point of view. He says,

> The new cladists, on the other extreme, have explicitly argued against incorporating any particular models of the evolutionary process into cladistics (a seminal paper in this regard is Platnick, 1979). Moreover, and more importantly with regard to the purpose of this essay, the new cladists have even given up the goal of representing genealogy (e.g., Nelson and Platnick 1981; Patterson, 1981). Descent with modification is too much of an assumption. Even descent is too much. Genealogy smacks too much of

evolution, and evolutionary hypothesizing is under too much fire. Put more positively, the new cladists believe that cladistics per se has no "necessary connection" with evolutionism (e.g., Nelson and Platnick, 1981; Patterson, 1981). What they mean by that is that no evolutionary suppositions are necessary to discover the sort of "pattern" that they hypothesize/assume is characteristic of the living world. Hence the name "pattern" cladists. What sort of pattern is this? It is a strict hierarchy of groups, where the groups at one level are nonoverlapping, or mutually exclusive, and where the groups at one level is completely included in the group at the next highest level.[49]

Later, Beatty asserts that:

But the neutrality of pattern cladism with respect to evolutionary theory is, I believe, a myth. I will not argue that it reflects or reinforces any particular evolutionary theory— i.e., that it is positively theory laden. I will argue instead that it is theory antagonistic with respect to evolutionary theory. It is at odds with current evolutionary theorizing. And it undermines, and is undermined by, evolutionary theory for the same reasons that the traditional class concept of species is.[50]

Later, on the same page, Beatty states:

For the pattern cladists, groups are *just* collections of organisms, distinguished by the sorts of characters that allow the collections to be so hierarchically ordered.

In summary, the new transformed or pattern cladism is actually antagonistic to evolutionary theory, and to transformed cladists, groups are just collections of organisms, distinguished by the sorts of characters that allow the collections to be hierarchically ordered. No wonder evolutionary biologists despise transformed cladism! No wonder creation scientists welcome transformed cladism as a breath of fresh air, a true science unencumbered by story-telling, the "problem solving strategies" of Philip Kitcher, and other mindless pap. Transformed cladism (if not the transformed cladists) is antagonistic to evolutionary theory and ascribes no evolutionary significance or theorizing to the hierarchies and sets of nested groups that result from the true science of systematics or taxonomy. Thus, the shallow thinking and bogus charges against creation science derived from systematics by Cracraft stands exposed as a fraud. Cracraft descends into the depths of what Colin Patterson calls empty rhetoric, or what might less sympathetically be called mindless pap, in his evolutionary theorizing. Cracraft says (p. 176):

> The concept of change being due to "chance" is philosophically and psychologically offensive to a creationist—it conjures up a world lacking purpose, direction, or design. But evolutionary change occurs not by "chance," if that word is taken to mean "at random," because the probability of evolutionary change in phenotype is not equal in all directions. The adult phenotype is the result of a highly regulated developmental (ontogenetic) history in which the phenotype is influenced not only by direct genetic controls over elaboration of biochemical products and their expression in developmental pathways, but also by epigenetic (environmental) factors modifying those pathways (Løvtrup 1974; Alberch 1980).

> The development of organisms is thus canalized, or constrained; consequently, changes in the underlying genetic control or in environmental factors having an influence on ontogeny do not produce a random ("chance") array of phenotypic responses, but rather a very narrow spectrum of possible alterations. In this way, then, much of evolutionary change can be viewed as being "directed" by developmental canalization, the exact direction being determined by a host of genetic and epigenetic factors.

Then, a bit later, Cracraft goes on to say:

> Thus, unlike the simplistic characterization of evolution proposed by creationists (and unfortunately by some evolutionists) in which natural selection is envisioned as the primary, if not only, mechanism of directional change, modern evolutionary biologists are realizing that

the magnitude and directionality of phenotypic change is primarily a problem of developmental genetics.

What Cracraft is saying here is highly significant. Ever since Darwin, evolutionists have maintained that evolution has no purpose, no goals, no direction, or directing force. Furthermore, the primary, if not the sole source, of new variations required for evolutionary change is largely, if not totally, a random process. Ernst Mayr and George Gaylord Simpson were two of the leaders in establishing the neo-Darwinian theory of evolution, which, as already mentioned, is the present orthodoxy found in textbooks and is still accepted by most evolutionists, although the notion of punctuated equilibrium (even more based on chance than Neo-Darwinism) is making significant inroads. Mayr has declared that:

> The basic framework of the theory [the modern synthetic or neo-Darwinian theory] is that evolution is a two-stage phenomenon: the production of variation and the sorting out of the variants by natural selection.[51]

The first stage of the evolutionary process, according to the neo-Darwinians, is the production of variations. What is the source of these variations? Mayr declares:

> . . . it must not be forgotten that mutation is the ultimate source of all genetic variation found in natural populations and the only raw material available for natural selection to work on.[52]

On that same page, while stating that the probability of mutation is much higher at some loci than at others, and that the number of possible mutations at any given locus is severely limited by other mutational sites and by the total epigenotype, Mayr says, with reference to the randomness of mutations, (a) that the locus of the next mutation cannot be predicted, and (b) that there is no known correlation between a particular set of environmental conditions and a given mutation. What comes out of his statement is that mutations are indeed random—no prediction can be made where the next mutation will occur, and none occurs because it is required or would be useful in any way.

Simpson states:

> The random nature of changes in heredity must be particularly emphasized. The shuffling of existing stocks of genes in sexual reproduction is, in the main, random. The appearance of chromosome and gene mutations is also largely, although not completely, random and the nature of their effects seems to be altogether random with respect to the needs or adaptation of the organisms and with respect to the direction in which evolution has, in fact, been progressing in the given group.[53]

Thus, the first stage in the evolutionary process according to neo-Darwinians, the production of variations through mutation and the shuffling of existing stocks of genes during sexual reproduction, is largely a random process. The second stage of the evolutionary process according to this view of the evolutionary mechanism is adaptation via natural selection. Simpson states:

> With no pretense at having plumbed the whole mystery or excluded all other possibilities, it is concluded that the major (if not the only) nonrandom, orienting factor in the process of evolution is reasonably identified as adaptation.[54]

Now, of course, the second stage of evolution, the "nonrandom orienting factor" of adaptation via natural selection, is totally dependent upon the first stage—the random production of mutations and the random reshuffling of genes during sexual reproduction. Everything in the evolutionary process must await the production of new variations produced by these random processes. Thus, ultimately, the rate-determining step in evolution, the production of new variations, is a random process. Thus, evolution is a random process, just as is the deal of the cards from a shuffled deck.

Creation scientists, ever since Darwin, have pointed out that such a random process could never have produced the millions of incredibly complex species now living or extinct in a few billion years (or in 500 billion years, for that matter). Many evolutionists have been troubled by these same considerations, although most evolutionary biologists, including Cracraft, have, in the past, simply glossed over the difficulties. These considerations served as the basis for a challenge by a group of mathematicians to neo-Darwinian theory at a Wistar Institute symposium. On that occasion, one of these mathematicians, Murray Eden, went so far as to say that:

> It is our contention that if "random" is given a serious and crucial interpretation from a probabilistic point of view, the randomness postulate is highly implausible and that an adequate scientific theory of evolution must await the discovery and elucidation of new natural laws—physical, physico-chemical and biological.[55]

Because of these and many other challenges to the neo-Darwinian mechanism of evolution, evolutionists have cast about for other mechanisms of evolution that reduce the chance or random factors in evolution. Some, as has Cracraft in his chapter here, and as has Stephen Jay Gould, who is postulating that a directive force may somehow be found in DNA,[56] are suggesting that there exists certain evolutionary processes which "canalize" or "constrain" the development of organisms into a "narrow spectrum of possible alterations" so that "much of evolutionary change can be viewed as being 'directed' by developmental canalization," as Cracraft has put it. This is pure fiction, or empty rhetoric, more of the same kind of story-telling that fills so many volumes of evolutionary fiction published throughout the world. Cracraft does not have one shred of empirical evidence to support his scenario.

The scenario that Cracraft is seeking to adopt here is decidedly non-Darwinian. Proof of that is one of the authorities he cites in support of his scenario: Søren Løvtrup. Remember, it was Løvtrup who has declared, "I believe that one day the Darwinian myth will be ranked the greatest deceit in the history of science."[57] But earlier in his chapter, Cracraft

322   Creation Scientists Answer Their Critics

had warmly adopted the neo-Darwinian interpretation of evolution. Thus, on p. 169, Cracraft states:

> It should be apparent that small changes accumulated
> during speciation, as in Darwin's finches, when extrapo-
> lated through geological time provide a plausible basis for
> apparent large scale differences among groups of organ-
> isms.

Cracraft is saying here exactly what neo-Darwinians have
always claimed: Small-scale changes, or microevolution, ac-
cumulating during vast stretches of time, are sufficient to
account for the origin of all higher taxa—genera, orders,
classes, and phyla. In other words, macroevolution is nothing
more than microevolution writ large.

Have I somehow misunderstood what Cracraft is trying
to explain? Am I wrong in supposing that the evolutionary
scenario he proposes on p. 176 is contradictory to the neo-
Darwinian scenario he cites on p. 169? But then, if his scenario suggested on p. 176 is not non-Darwinian and
non-neo-Darwinian, why does he cite Løvtrup as a supporter,
an evolutionist who condemns all of the Darwinian mechanisms, including neo-Darwinism, as a myth, the greatest deceit
in the history of science? But then, evolutionary theory is like
a bowl of Jello—it is too slippery to get a hold on. Evolutionary theory has been made so plastic that one way or another,
no matter what the data are, they can be made to fit.

In one breath, Cracraft can extol the neo-Darwinian
mechanism as adequate to account for all evolutionary progress, and then later, he feels free to advance non-Darwinian
notions to avoid fatal flaws in the neo-Darwinian mechanism.

Speaking of the feathers of birds and the hair of mammals
(p. 171), Cracraft says, "Both these characters are interpreted
by biologists to be derivatives of scales." This is a statement
very commonly found in evolutionary literature. After all, if
birds and mammals evolved from reptiles, as evolutionists
believe, where else did feathers and hair develop from, if not
from scales? Feathers supposedly began as frayed-out scales.

This is pure myth, empty rhetoric, no matter how imaginative such stories may be. What are scales? They are thin, flat, overlapping horny plates. This horny epidermal covering in reptiles is shed periodically. Feathers, on the other hand, are incredibly complex structures, an engineering marvel, the flight feathers being precisely designed for aerodynamic function.

As Raymond has pointed out, feathers are fundamentally different structures than scales, arising from different layers of skin.[58] Scales are merely folds in the epidermis, while feathers and hairs develop from follicles. The development of a feather is in itself an engineering marvel. Furthermore, if hairs in mammals developed from scales, no one could claim they began as frayed-out scales. How did a hair develop from thin horny plates? Why is the mode of development of feathers and hair so fundamentally different from that of scales, if feathers and hairs evolved from scales? Here evolutionists like Cracraft are clutching at straws—or should we say feathers?

Beginning on p. 177, Cracraft has a section on the fossil record. Rather than making a calm and reasoned attempt to explain the fossil record versus evolutionary theory as Raup did, Cracraft, as is his custom, immediately descends into muckraking. He arrogantly asserts that creation scientists have used misrepresentation and outright distortion in making the "blatantly false claim that the fossil record supports the creationist world view." Enough evidence has already been presented in this book to make crystal clear that the fossil record not only provides powerful positive support for creation, but that it also provides irrefutable evidence that evolution has not occurred.

Cracraft twists and distorts statements by creation scientists and then accuses them of misquoting evolutionists. An example is found on p. 180. He accuses me of both distortion and misquoting. He cites a quotation I used in my book *Evolution: The Fossils Say No!*,[44] taken from an article by Leigh

Van Valen, which consists of a review of the 6th volume of *Evolutionary Biology.*[59] In that quotation, Van Valen says:

> Three paleontologists (no less) conclude that stratigraphic position is totally irrelevant to determination of phylogeny and almost say that no known taxa is derived from any other.

A statement like this, from within evolutionary circles, certainly does lend support to the position of creation scientists, and it is perfectly legitimate for creation scientists to quote such statements taken from the evolutionary literature, which purportedly state facts derivable from the fossil record. Cracraft resents this and attempts to twist things around.

First, he claims that Van Valen is overstating the position of the paleontologists, and Cracraft then accuses me of using Van Valen's statement in a highly biased fashion. Let us suppose that Cracraft is correct, and that Van Valen did overstate their position. Who then is guilty of distortion—Van Valen or Gish? Furthermore, even if Van Valen did overstate their position, their position would still lend support to creation scientists. Later, on that same page, Cracraft accuses me of misquoting Van Valen. This is an outright falsehood. I quoted Van Valen's statement precisely correctly—not one word was misplaced; not one word was left out; not one word was added. Cracraft could not help but know that—he had both my book and Van Valen's article before him, and if he did not, he is guilty of inexcusable carelessness. Cracraft has thus proven himself guilty of the very charges he makes against creationists—distortion and misquoting.

He accuses me of further distortion (pp. 180, 181). He cites a statement in which I say:

> It cannot be emphasized too strongly that even evolutionists are arguing among themselves whether these major categories appeared *instantaneously* or not! It is precisely the argument of creationists that these forms *did arise instantaneously* and that the transitional forms are not recorded because they never existed![60]

First, Cracraft takes exception with my use of the term "categories" rather than the term "taxa." But as we will see shortly, that is the term that has been similarly used by David Raup, one of Cracraft's esteemed evolutionary colleagues. Cracraft then accuses me of distortion. He claims that I was attempting to equate "instantaneous creation" with the term "geologically instantaneous," used by evolutionary geologists to indicate events that appear to be instantaneous geologically, but may have transpired during tens of thousands of years, or possibly longer. If Cracraft had not lifted my statement out of context, but had quoted, in full, the preceding statement from Simpson, which was cited in my book, it would be obvious to the reader that I had accurately quoted Simpson, and that I was not attempting to make Simpson's statement say more than Simpson himself had said. The statement from Simpson, which I quoted in my book immediately before my statement quoted by Cracraft, and critical to that statement, but which Cracraft deliberately chose to omit, reads as follows:

> The process by which such radical events occur in evolution is the subject of one of the most serious remaining disputes among qualified professional students of evolution. The question is whether such major events take place instantaneously, by some process essentially unlike those involved in lesser or more gradual evolutionary change, or whether all of evolution, including these major changes, is explained by the same principles and processes throughout, their results being greater or less according to the time involved, the relative intensity of selection, and other material variables in any given situation.

> Possibility for such dispute exists because transitions between major grades of organization are seldom well recorded by fossils. There is in this respect a tendency toward systematic deficiency in the record of the history of life. It is thus possible to claim that such transitions are not recorded because they did not exist, that the changes were not by transition, but by sudden leaps in evolution.[61]

Now, did Simpson say "instantaneously" or did he say "geologically instantaneously?" Obviously, he said "instantaneously." But by this did he mean geologically instantaneously, as Cracraft claimed, or did he actually mean instantaneously? It is equally obvious that he meant instantaneously, as the term ordinarily means. Note what Simpson says:

> It is thus possible to claim that such transitions are not recorded because *they did not exist*, that the changes were *not by transition*, but by *sudden leaps* in evolution [emphasis added].

If no transitional forms ever existed, but the changes were by sudden leaps from one major type to a basically different basic type, then the changes were indeed truly instantaneous. And if Cracraft, or any other evolutionist should claim that Simpson was not referring to macroevolution or the origin of basically different types in the sentences immediately preceding the section from Simpson's book that I quoted, Simpson says:

> Nonadaptive and random changes have another possible role in evolution which is important and which has so far been suggested only in passing. They have a bearing on changes in broad types of organization, the appearance of new phyla, classes, or other major groups in the course of the history of life.

Thus, as I pointed out in my book, just as creation scientists maintain that the higher categories—families, orders, classes, phyla—have appeared instantaneously, even some evolutionists are arguing the same (by as yet some unknown mechanism, of course). As clearly proven, these evolutionists certainly meant instantaneously in the true sense of the word, instead of, as Cracraft falsely claims, geologically instantaneously, involving tens to hundreds of thousands of years.

Now who is the guilty party in this affair? Who distorted the facts and lifted things out of context, Gish or Cracraft? Cracraft, beyond a shadow of doubt, was guilty of precisely what he accused me, and I am innocent. After these obvious distortions and false charges, what confidence can be placed in any of Cracraft's polemics against creation scientists? Cracraft also indicated, on p. 180, that I was wrong in referring to higher taxa as higher "categories." It is more technically correct, of course, to use the term taxa rather than categories, but the latter term conveys the true meaning just as well. As mentioned earlier, this term has been used in that sense by David Raup (and Steven Stanley). Thus, in their book on the principles of paleontology, Raup and Stanley say:

> Unfortunately, the origins of most higher categories are shrouded in mystery: commonly new higher categories appear abruptly in the fossil record without evidence of transitional forms.[62]

Of course, if such eminent paleontologists as Raup and Stanley can use that term in a standard text on paleontology, Cracraft has no business criticizing creation scientists for using the same term. (Perhaps he would like to scold his seniors in evolutionary biology and paleontology for doing so.)

Cracraft's section on paleontology is hardly worth further comment except to point out that he, like almost all other evolutionists, makes no references whatsoever to the most positive evidence for creation, the evidence that, on the other hand, demonstrates conclusively that evolution has not taken place. That evidence is, of course, the abrupt appearance, fully formed, of each major invertebrate type—snails, clams, trilobites, sponges, jellyfish, etc.—and the abrupt appearance, fully formed, of each major group of fishes—the so-called first vertebrates.

Beginning on p. 182, Cracraft has a section on biogeography, that is, the distribution of organisms, both living and fossil, throughout the world. He states that the predominant explanation which was accepted by many pre-evolutionary (evolutionists cannot bring themselves to frankly call pre-evolutionary biologists and other scientists "creationists," which almost all were) and post-evolutionary biologists as well was that of dispersalism. He says that dispersalism has been, until quite recently, the primary explanation used by evolutionists. He claims that biogeography has been ignored by creation scientists, since it offers such strong evidence for evolution. As a matter of fact, one of the earliest books marking the resurgence of the modern creation science movement, the book by Whitcomb and Morris, *The Genesis Flood*, has a section on animal distribution, or biogeography,[63] as Cracraft acknowledges. Furthermore, this subject should be an embarrassment to evolutionists because, until about 20 years ago, biogeography was explained by evolutionists via dispersalism, assuming that all the continents have always been right where they are now. Cracraft informs us that dispersal from one area to another, followed by differentiation, is now apparently not as important as once thought. What do they believe today? Cracraft tells us that:

> . . . it is becoming apparent that these patterns of biotic separation are correlated with changes in earth history, continental drift being the most obvious example [p. 185].

How plastic, how fluid is this theory of evolution! No matter what the data may be, they can be accommodated in vastly different evolutionary mechanisms and earth history. The concept of static continents versus the notion of continents drifting all over the world are *drastically* different versions of earth history. Previously, evolutionists took the data of biogeography, the data of plant and animal distributions, and fit them into a theory of earth history that assumed the continents have always been where they are today. They felt smug in their explanations, while ridiculing the attempts of creation scientists to fit the data into their views of earth history. Now geologists have adopted a totally different view of earth history, assuming that sometime in the past all land masses consisted of one massive continent, Pangea, which then somehow, by some as yet unknown mechanism, began to split apart, and continents have been drifting apart ever since. Evolutionists take the same old data (certainly fossils didn't hop from one continent to another) and claim they can fit these data into this new and drastically different view of earth history! It is obvious that either their present view of earth history, incorporating the notion of continental drift, is incorrect or what they were teaching previous to this was nonsense.

Cracraft claims (p. 183) that creationists have to explain how all the different kinds of organisms were able to find their way to Noah in order to avoid the Flood. If Cracraft is going to criticize ideas based on Biblical data, he should at least read it first. The Bible does not indicate that the animals had to find their way to Noah on their own, but rather, the suggestion is clear that God would direct them to Noah.[64] Furthermore, creationists believe that the nature and distribution of land masses, and thus biogeographical distributions, were drastically different before the Flood than now.

Beginning on p. 186, Cracraft has a section entitled "Classification," but the matter of classification, that is, taxonomy or systematics, has already been extensively discussed, so no further comments are necessary. Cracraft closes his chapter with a section entitled "Discussion." Here he merely reiterates some of his outrageous characterizations of creation scientists. What really enrages evolutionists like Cracraft is the astounding success that creation scientists have had in the last quarter century in challenging the dogma of evolution and winning so many hundreds of thousands, if not millions of scientists, students, and the lay public to their view of the origin and history of the universe and its living inhabitants.

Chapter 11, Creationism and Gaps in the Fossil Record (pp. 194-218), is by Laurie Godfrey. Since an extensive discussion concerning the fossil record has already been included in this book, comments here need be only brief. It is obvious that no evidence could shake Godfrey's religious faith in evolution. On p. 200, she says, "The 'sudden appearances' of various extant mammalian orders in no way disconfirms their evolution." On p. 207, she informs us that speciation is often "hidden" in the fossil record. Thus, Godfrey is willing to believe that transitional forms between species can somehow be "hidden" in the fossil record, but even the transitional forms leading up to major groups of organisms, such as the 32 orders of mammals, can somehow be hidden (in other words, be simply invisible, in spite of intense searching by paleontologists for 150 years).

On p. 199, Godfrey states that the origin of bats is enigmatic, admitting that the world's oldest known bat, *Icaronycteris index,*[65] is a perfectly good flying bat. But then Godfrey tells us that:

> . . . the inference drawn from neontological data that bats evolved from some primitive eutherian (or placental) mammal is well supported by fossil bat teeth.

In the first place, if all that can be found are teeth, how could it be known with any degree of certainty that the teeth were bat teeth? Secondly, as noted in Cracraft's case that he was grasping for straws in seeking to explain the origin of feathers from reptilian scales, Godfrey, in resorting to nothing but teeth in claiming that bats had evolved from some non-flying mammals, is also grasping for straws. The fact remains that the oldest known bat, believed to be 50 million years old, was 100% bat, essentially identical to modern bats, and even possessed the incredibly complex sonar or echolocation organs found in some modern bats.[66]

On p. 201, Godfrey says:

> Transitions exist at two levels in the fossil record. First, there are species-level transitions. These are the transitions the young Darwin expected to see in the fossil record. They are rare, but are known. Second, there are intermediates between groups at higher levels of the taxonomic hierarchy: families, orders, classes, phyla. These exist in abundance in the fossil record. . . .

This claim has already been refuted in Chapter 5, but it would be good to once again compare this claim against statements of Godfrey's fellow evolutionists. George Gaylord Simpson says:

> Gaps among known species are sporadic and often small. Gaps among known orders, classes, and phyla are systematic and almost always large.[67]

Eldredge has declared that:

> . . . there are all sorts of gaps: absence of gradationally intermediate 'transitional forms' between species, but also between larger groups—between, say, families of carnivores, or the orders of mammals. In fact, the higher up the Linnaean hierarchy you look, the fewer transitional forms there seem to be.[68]

Goldschmidt states:

> When a new phylum, class, or order appears, there follows a quick, explosive (in terms of geological time) diversification so that practically all orders or families known appear suddenly and without any apparent transitions.[69]

Godfrey claims there is an abundance of transitional forms at higher levels—families, orders, classes, phyla. Goldschmidt says that it is at the level of phyla, classes, orders, and down to and including almost every family, that these groups appear suddenly and without transitions. Simpson declares it is at these higher levels—orders, classes, and phyla—where the gaps are systematic and almost always large. Eldredge says the higher we go up the Linnaean hierarchy, the fewer the transitions there seem to be. Either Godfrey doesn't read the literature of her fellow evolutionists or she deliberately ignores it to create her own story.

On p. 203, Godfrey asserts that the claims of creation scientists that there are no intermediate forms between basic kinds, such as sharks and whales is nonsense. Then she says:

> There are multitudes of intermediates between such 'kinds' as Morris cites, both in the paleontological and contemporary worlds. Between sharks and whales, for example, we find bony fishes, amphibians, reptiles, mammal-like reptiles, and some mammals.

On the next page she declares, "In the case of the shark and whale, the common ancestor was a primitive fish!" With those kinds of arguments, one could prove anything. The transformed cladists arrange these creatures in the same way Godfrey is doing, but assert that there is no connection between this procedure and evolution, with Beatty declaring that their system of taxonomy is actually antagonistic to evolutionary theory. We must not allow ourselves to be confused by Godfrey's use of the terms "intermediates" and "transitional forms." An evolutionist may believe that an ape is intermediate between monkey and man, but it certainly does not constitute a transitional form between them, anymore than the earth is a transitional form between Mars and Venus, though it occupies a position intermediate between these two planets.

On pp. 201 and 202, Godfrey discusses the origin of angiosperms (flowering plants). She refers (p. 202) to the 1978 edition of my book, *Evolution: The Fossils Say No!*,[70] in which she claims that the treatment in that book of angiosperm origins was misleading, incomplete, full of half-truths, and outright falsehoods. As I pointed out in Chapter 4, that would have been quite an accomplishment, since in that book I nowhere even discussed the origin of angiosperms! Neither the words "angiosperm" nor "flowering plants" can be found anywhere in the book. As pointed out, it was Godfrey's charges that were misleading and an outright falsehood.

Godfrey's only attempt, if that is what it can be called, to deal with the tremendous problem of the origin of complex invertebrates is merely to claim that:

> We *have* found sources in Pre-Cambrian rocks for the famous Cambrian explosion of multicellular life forms (see Cloud, 1977; Valentine 1977; and Valentine, in press).

The article by Cloud, which Godfrey cites, was published in *The Humanist*,[71] the publication of The American Humanist Society, and not a technical publication. In that article, Cloud provides no evidence for evolutionary ancestors for the Cambrian invertebrates, other than mentioning evidence for the discovery of fossil bacteria and algae (microscopic single-celled organisms) in pre-Cambrian rocks. As described in Chapter 5, her choice of Valentine to support such a statement was a poor one, for, in reference to the origin of the complex invertebrates found in Cambrian rocks, it was Valentine who said, in a book edited by Godfrey, that:

> The fossil record is of little use in providing direct evidence of the pathways of descent of the phyla or of invertebrate classes. Each phylum with a fossil record had already evolved its characteristic body plan when it first appeared, so far as we can tell from the fossil remains, and no phylum is connected to any other via intermediate fossil types. Indeed, none of the invertebrate classes can be connected with another class by series of intermediates.[72]

This statement by Valentine exposes, as pure bluff, Godfrey's statement concerning the origin of the Cambrian invertebrates, and it is in a book she had edited! Furthermore, it exposes the spurious nature of Godfrey's claim, mentioned earlier, that there is an abundance of transitional forms at higher levels (orders, classes, phyla). Note that Valentine asserts that there are *no* transitional forms between *any* of the invertebrate classes and phyla—not one! And since, as Valentine points out, about 300 different invertebrate types, with basically different body plans appear in the Cambrian, there is a multitude of opportunities to find transitional forms at this level, if such ever existed, *but not one has ever been found!* Just as is the case with Cracraft, it is Godfrey, not the creation scientists whom she accuses, who is guilty of distortions and falsehoods.

In the latter part of her chapter, Godfrey discusses the notion of "punctuated equilibrium" and Goldschmidt and his "hopeful monster" mechanism. Since a thorough treatment of Goldschmidt's "hopeful monster" notion of evolution is included in Chapter 5, and the idea of punctuated equilibrium is described and discussed in my book, *Evolution: The Challenge of the Fossil Record,*[73] no discussion of that portion of

Godfrey's chapter is necessary. As described in this chapter and elsewhere in this book, Godfrey viciously attacks creation scientists, accusing them of various forms of perfidy, but she is the one who is guilty of careless, superficial treatment of both creationist and evolutionist literature, resulting in distortions and outright falsehoods.

Steven D. Schafersman is the author of **Chapter 12, "Fossils, Stratigraphy, and Evolution: Consideration of a Creationist Argument"** (pp. 219-244). Schafersman received a Ph.D. in geology from Rice University and at the time of publication of this book was employed as a research geologist in the oil industry. He is a virulent anti-creationist and is very active in the campaign to silence creation scientists and other critics of evolutionary theory. In order to know just where Schafersman is coming from, and why he is so vicious in his attacks on creation scientists, one has only to read the conclusion to his chapter (p. 243). He says that he has descended from an ape-like creature, in fear and wonder at an uncaring universe, both at oneness with nature and alienation from nature, and is a participant in man's evolutionary journey, which has prepared him to face life and the universe with acceptance in the face of meaninglessness, and hope in the face of ignorance. As an atheist, Schafersman has no choice but to believe in blind, chance evolution. On the other hand, he accuses the creationists—the "true believers"—of arrogance and self-righteousness, and as those who regard themselves as being created in the image of God, and acting like it.

One has only to read Schafersman's chapter, however, to recognize the supreme arrogance of this man as he levels all sorts of reckless charges against creation scientists, particularly Dr. Henry Morris, president of the Institute for Creation Research, whom Schafersman singles out because of Morris's comments on the way evolutionists handle the data on biostratigraphy. Schafersman immediately loses all pretense at any ability to consider the evidence related to origins in an

objective manner. In perfect accord with his stated philosophy
and religious beliefs, he refers, in the second sentence of his
chapter, to evolution as a fact of science. On p. 228, he states
that biologists accept evolution

> . . . because spontaneous generation of complex organisms
> has been shown not to occur and because evolution is the
> only *materialistic* alternative [emphasis added].

Of course, he then asserts that another reason they accept it is
because the evidence for it is strong, but the strongest and
primary reason they accept it, at least according to Schafersman, and certainly in his own view, is because it is the only
materialistic theory available today.

Schafersman here, also, reveals a most significant fact
concerning evolutionary theory and how it is viewed by evolutionists—a fact that provides a powerful tool for creationists
in their attempt to obtain recognition of creation as an alternative to evolution. David Kitts, professor of geology at the
University of Oklahoma, in a statement quoted by Henry
Morris (which will be discussed in more detail later), says,
"For most biologists the strongest reason for accepting the
evolutionary hypothesis is their acceptance of some theory
that entails it."[74] Schafersman, in his reply to this statement
by Kitts, states:

> In that quotation Kitts betrays an ignorance of certain
> aspects of both philosophy and science. First, biologists do
> not accept evolution because of their acceptance of some
> theory that entails it, but because spontaneous generation
> of complex organisms has been shown not to occur and
> because evolution is the only materialistic alternative. They
> also accept evolution because the evidence for it is very
> strong; recognition of this fact does not require acceptance
> of any specific theory or process (see Gould 1981).

Note what Schafersman has said—that the acceptance of
evolution does not require acceptance of any specific theory
or process, citing a publication of Stephen Jay Gould[75] in
support. One of the reasons most often cited by evolutionists

for including evolutionary theory in science and excluding creation is because it is obvious that it is impossible for us to ever know the process by which God created. Yet here we have Schafersman and Gould, the latter one of the chief spokesman for evolutionary theory in the U.S., claiming it is not necessary to understand the process of evolution or to accept any particular theory about that process, in order to accept evolution. Thus, what these evolutionists are saying is that creation must be excluded from consideration as an explanation for origins because creationists don't know the mechanism, but evolution must be included in science even though they don't know the mechanism of evolution either. Evolutionists may immediately reply that at least the mechanism of evolution is knowable, even if they do not as yet know it. But how do they know it's knowable? Only by faith.

On p. 233, Schafersman says, with reference to the book, *Scientific Creationism,* by Henry Morris:[76]

> For example, it claims that the "creation model" predicts the first and second laws of thermodynamics, the constancy of natural law, the existence of intelligence in man, gaps in the fossil record, and so forth. Clearly, these "predictions" are for phenomena that are either self-evident or readily acceptable to the average layman. But they are not predictions of creationism at all because their relationship to a "Creator" (or any supernatural phenomenon) cannot be tested.

First, it should be pointed out that certainly, beyond a shadow of doubt, gaps in the fossil record are a prediction based on creation. The concept of special creation was formulated well before Darwin, with vast numbers of adherents, both in and out of the scientific community, and before armies of geologists and paleontologists went out to search for the "missing links." Certainly the systematic gaps were not self-evident at that time to either scientists or laymen.

Furthermore, as described earlier in the discussion of Raup's chapter, Raup acknowledged that creation scientists, based on their creation model, have made legitimate predictions and have sought to confirm them. Thus, as will be recalled, Raup says (p. 150):

> . . . the creationist could be content simply to present, and perhaps interpret the biblical account and leave it at that, with no reference to observational data from natural history. But this is not the approach. Rather, they claim, the biblical account is used as a model or hypothesis, and its predictions are tested with data from geology, paleontology, and other fields.
>
> Several lists of "predictions" of the creation model have been published (Gish 1978, pp. 50-51, for example). Testing these predictions often involves rather elaborate, and sometimes surprisingly conventional research studies.

Later (p. 159), Raup states:

> In my view, a few of the arguments used by the creationists are 'scientific' in the sense that they use the basic methods of testing hypotheses normally considered to be scientific.

We see, then, that Schafersman and Raup are in substantial disagreement on this point. Schafersman is guided by his preconceived notions and anger at creation scientists, while Raup's views are far more calm and reasoned.

On p. 234, Schafersman declares that:

> Fossils do not provide the main evidence for evolution. This is a myth, not popularized, I hope, by paleontologists.

Some other evolutionists have made similar claims. They, as does Schafersman, realize that in some of its most important aspects, the fossil record is an embarrassment to evolutionary theory, and thus they attempt to downgrade its importance. As noted earlier in this book, however, Pierre-Paul Grassé, France's most distinguished zoologist, sharply disagrees with the notion that the fossil record is not important as evidence for evolution. He says:

> Naturalists must remember that the process of evolution is revealed only through fossil forms. A knowledge of paleontology is, therefore, a prerequisite; only paleontology can

provide them with the evidence of evolution and reveal its course or mechanisms. Neither the examination of present beings, nor imagination, nor theories can serve as a substitute for paleontological documents. If they ignore them, biologists, the philosophers of nature, indulge in numerous commentaries and can only come up with hypotheses.[77]

Carl Dunbar, an eminent geologist, declares, "Fossils provide the only historical, documentary evidence that life has evolved from simpler to more and more complex forms."[78]

Schafersman doesn't like the fact that such a prominent geologist could be cited to contradict Schafersman's claim that fossils constitute only a minor part of the evidence, and he especially didn't like the fact that Morris had used Dunbar's statement in his book, *Scientific Creationism*.[78] Schafersman thus accuses Morris of misrepresenting Dunbar and of misquoting him. This latter charge is obviously false, because Morris quoted Dunbar's statement with precise accuracy. No words were left out, none were added, and no words were transposed in the statement quoted. At most, Schafersman could only accuse Morris of softening Dunbar's statement by omitting the qualifying words preceding the statement quoted, in which Dunbar says, "Although the comparative study of living plants and animals may give convincing circumstantial evidence. . . ." However, the fact that Morris used Dunbar's statement accurately and in context remains, because what Morris wished to establish is that Dunbar agrees with Morris that (if evolution is true) fossils could provide the *only historical, documentary* evidence that evolution has occurred. All the rest is merely hypothetical reconstructions, heavily salted with imagination.

Morris also quotes a statement by G. A. Kerkut, an evolutionist who published a book in 1960 which challenged the dogmatism of his fellow evolutionists. In that statement, Kerkut says that ". . . fossils . . . provided the main factual evidence for evolution."[79] Of course, Schafersman doesn't like that statement, so he just simply declares that Kerkut is wrong.

Schafersman cites many of the quotations used by Morris in *Scientific Creationism,* statements which powerfully support Morris's contention that biostratigraphy, as constructed by evolutionists today, is significantly dependent on the assumption of evolution and involves an important element of circular reasoning. The approach that Schafersman uses in his attempts to refute Morris's use of these supporting statements is to accuse Morris of quoting out of context, misquoting, distortion, deception, and of using illogical and invalid claims. Another common tactic he uses is attempting to destroy the credibility of the authorities Morris quotes, even though they may be fellow evolutionists.

On p. 225, Schafersman cites a statement by Gareth Nelson, which Morris quotes in one of the Impact articles published by the Institute for Creation Research.[80] In that statement, Nelson says:

> That a known fossil or recent species, or higher taxonomic group, however primitive it might appear, is an actual ancestor of some other species or group, is an assumption scientifically unjustifiable, for science never can simply assume that which it has the responsibility to demonstrate. It is the burden of each of us to demonstrate the reasonableness of any hypothesis we might care to erect about ancestral conditions, keeping in mind that we have no ancestors alive today, that in all probability such ancestors have been dead for tens or hundreds of millions of years, and that even in the fossil record they are not accessible to us.[81]

Schafersman then quotes the statement by Morris which followed the quotation above. In that statement, Morris says, "There is, therefore, really no way of proving scientifically any assumed evolutionary phylogeny, as far as the fossil record is concerned." Schafersman attacks Morris's statement, asserting that it is a gross distortion; that Morris was putting words into Nelson's mouth. In the first place, it is quite clear, from Morris's article, that the words of Morris just quoted above were coming from Morris's mouth, and not from that of Nelson's. Furthermore, as extensively documented earlier in this chapter when discussing Cracraft's contribution, it is abundantly clear that Morris is precisely correct in his interpretation of what Nelson is saying. Nelson is one of the transformed cladists whom Beatty declared is undermining evolutionary theory, and whose approach to cladistics is actually antagonistic to evolutionary theory.

On p. 222, Schafersman quotes a statement by J. E. O' Rourke[82] which was used by Morris to support Morris's contention that biostratigraphy is heavily dependent on the use of and accuracy of index fossils. Although Schafersman acknowledges that O'Rourke's paper was published in a respectable geological journal, and that no geologist had ever published a reply critical of O'Rourke's paper, he condemned it as being full of errors of fact and loaded with grossly mistaken notions. On pp. 226-227, Schafersman repeats another statement of O'Rourke's[83] which had been quoted by Morris[84] to document Morris's claim that geologists are guilty of circular reasoning when they use rocks to date fossils, and then use fossils to date rocks. Again, Schafersman accuses O'Rourke of error in judgment.

As noted earlier, Schafersman took exception to the views of David Kitts, a fellow evolutionist, whose remarks offered support to Morris's contention that the temporal ordering of biological events (biostratigraphy) as used by evolutionists entails the assumption of evolution and involves circular reasoning. In that statement, Kitts says:

> But the danger of circularity is still present. For most biologists the strongest reason for accepting the evolutionary hypothesis is their acceptance of some theory that entails it. There is another difficulty. The temporal ordering of biological events beyond the local section may critically involve paleontological correlation, which necessarily presupposed the non-repeatability of organic

events in geologic history. There are various justifications for this assumption but for almost all contemporary paleontologists it rests upon the acceptance of the evolutionary hypothesis.[74]

First, in order to downgrade Kitts' scientific credibility, Schafersman refers to him as "philosopher Kitts" (p. 227). Although Kitts may have had considerable interest in the philosophy of science during the latter stage of his career, he is a professor of geology at the University of Oklahoma who received his Ph.D. in vertebrate paleontology under George Gaylord Simpson, one of the premier evolutionary paleontologists in the nation. Kitts' qualifications as a bona fide scientist, sufficiently experienced and informed to speak on this subject, needs no defense, and far exceed those of Schafersman. Later (p. 228), Schafersman accuses Kitts of betraying ignorance of certain aspects of both philosophy and science; he accuses Kitts of accepting "the creationists' myth that acceptance of some aspect of evolution is necessary to perform stratigraphy"; that Kitts is erroneous in implying that acceptance of evolution justifies the assumption of nonrepeatability of organic events; and finally, that Kitts' assertion that biostratigraphy "necessarily" presupposes the nonrepeatability of organic events is false.

On p. 229, Schafersman accuses Morris of hiding or distorting the true meaning of a series of authors whom Morris quotes. One author refers to the possibility of landing in an impossible circular argument (Ager); another of being guilty of circular reasoning in using the Darwinian theory of evolution to interpret the fossil record, and then saying the fossil record supports this theory (West); and others assert that the prime difficulty with the use of presumed ancestral-descendant sequences to express phylogeny is that biostratigraphic data are often used in conjunction with morphology in the initial evaluation of relationships, which leads to circular reasoning (Schaeffer, Hecht, and Eldredge).

On p. 234, Schafersman notes that Morris cites Berry,[85] "a well-known biostratigrapher, who apparently does believe that biostratigraphy is 'based on the evolutionary development of organisms.'" In fact, just as Schafersman notes, the subtitle of the book by Berry is *Growth of a Prehistoric Time Scale, Based on Organic Evolution.* In each of these cases, Schafersman attempts to establish that Morris has simply misunderstood, distorted, and deliberately and deceptively twisted what these people are trying to say. Schafersman's arguments are, themselves, artful in distortion and obfuscation. It is he who puts words in the mouths of his fellow evolutionists in attempts to make them appear to say something other than what the plain reading of the text yields. Schafersman uses this approach throughout the entire chapter; it is his *modus operandi.*

Two other assertions of Schafersman may warrant comment. On p.241 he says, ". . . cladistic analysis today provides evidence that is superior to fossil evidence for documenting evolutionary relationships." This is truly an astounding statement, for how can one provide a cladistic analysis without using fossil evidence? If fossil evidence is not used, then the analysis would be strictly limited solely to present-day living organisms. What a foolish statement! Furthermore, the transformed cladists strongly disagree that cladistic analysis should be used in attempts to establish evolutionary relationships. They wish to keep cladistics free of evolutionary theory.

On p. 227, Schafersman recalls a talk by Morris that he heard in Houston, in which Schafersman claimed that Morris "belittled" the biostratigraphers working in the oil industry because their discipline was "extremely inefficient in locating oil" (the success rate is about 10%, that is, 90% of the wells drilled are dry holes). This enraged Schafersman, claiming Morris is ignorant of the many real reasons that the great majority of wells are failures. Then Schafersman states that the acceptance of evolution by these biostratigraphers is irrelevant, since they never use evolution in their work. But how many times have we creation scientists been confronted by statements from scientists, professors, and laymen that if evolution is false, how can we account for the fact that oil companies employ thousands of geologists who are guided by evolution in their search for oil? At least now, when confronted with that statement, creation scientists can quote Schafersman in their response.

Schafersman might have made a useful contribution to the creation/evolution controversy if he had limited himself to a thorough and objective analysis of the creationist and evolutionist interpretations of biostratigraphy and had advanced a reasoned defense of his views on these subjects, rather than merely attacking the creation scientists (mainly Henry Morris) in a vicious and distorted manner. Attacks of this nature may sound good when "preaching to the choir," but by the nature of their personal invective directed at the integrity of creation scientists, these tirades lose credibility in the eyes of those honestly searching for the true explanation for origins.

Chapter 13, Humans in Time and Space (pp. 245-282), is by C. Loring Brace. Brace is professor of anthropology and Curator of Physical Anthropology at the Museum of Anthropology, University of Michigan, and is the author of several books on human evolutionary theory. He is a bitter opponent of creation science. He apparently accepts the neo-Darwinian view of evolution, for he says (p. 271), speaking of minor variations within the human population:

> Biologists refer to changes of such a nature as "micro-evolution." Although the time through which microevolutionary changes are observed is not sufficient to produce the transformation in "kind," or "macroevolution," that creationists refuse to credit to the evolutionary process, all one needs is more time. As has been written, "macroevolution is nothing more but microevolution over longer time spans" (Alexander 1978, p. 101).

He asserts that no creationist has ever bothered to study the fossil material available. Whether this is true or not, creation scientists are scientifically trained; they can read, and they can understand what physical anthropologists have published about the available fossil evidence. They have trained themselves to be skeptical and to investigate thoroughly the various claims and counterclaims that are made about the fossil evidence by anthropologists, rather than skimming through standard textbooks and accepting, uncritically, all the claims that are made about alleged evidence for human evolution. Creation scientists are apt to give greater credibility to physical anthropologists, such as Charles Oxnard, who has tirelessly applied the best methods of anatomy to his analysis of fossil material, than to Donald Johanson and Tim White, who laid their fossil material out on a table for eye-ball examination, a process decried by Lord Zuckerman as the "myth of anatomy." Furthermore, it is often the outsiders, the non-believers who are the better judges, rather than the insiders, who have fame, fortune, prestige, and power to gain from extravagant and unwarranted claims, as did the patrons of Piltdown Man.

Brace's choice of creationist publications as his source of the latest thinking of creationists is indeed at times strange and highly questionable. For example, in reference to his claims concerning analyses of australopithecines by evolutionists, he says (pp. 251-252):

> Contrast this with the cavalier treatment accorded by creationists, based only on hearsay evidence, secondary sources, and without any firsthand familiarity with the original specimens—"these creatures were nothing but apes" (Gish 1974, p. 16).

A check of his references reveals that he is quoting from a little booklet I had published, entitled, "Have You Been Brainwashed?", and based on a lecture I gave at the University of California, Davis, in 1972. Why would Brace choose to quote this little, unreferenced booklet, based on a lecture given eleven years before the chapter he was writing, rather than my fully referenced book, *Evolution: The Fossils Say*

No!,[44] published in 1979, and which Brace had available, since he quotes from it (p. 268). As Brace could have learned by consulting that book, and as one may now learn by consulting my 1985 book, *Evolution: The Challenge of the Fossil Record*,[37] the work of such authorities as Charles Oxnard has greatly strengthened the view, noted by Brace in the little booklet, that the australopithecines were neither intermediate between ape and man nor ancestral to man. Furthermore, all anthropologists, including Brace, who write books on anthropology, are almost totally dependent upon secondary sources, since they do not have the time or opportunity to travel all over the world for firsthand familiarity with the original specimens. Nor is there any need for this, since they can consult articles (secondary sources) published by their colleagues who do have firsthand familiarity.

On p. 246, Brace says:

> Human beings, anthropoid apes, monkeys, tarsiers, lemurs, and lorises are grouped in the Linnaean order Primates (Clark 1950; Simons 1972). Initially this classification was based solely on the recognition of shared anatomical similarities. Linnaeus, as a good creationist, interpreted the similarities as evidence of God's plan. Over a century later, after Darwin taught scientists to look at the world in the perspective of time and adaptive change, it was realized that the similarities among members of a classificatory unit reflected community of descent (Simpson 1953, 1961).

Here, again, is an admission that the theory of evolution was *not* derived *from* the data, but the theory was *imposed on* the data, and then these data are submitted as proof of the theory—circularity, if there ever is such a thing.

On p. 246, Brace states:

> The spectrum of living primates runs from that most modified and aberrant species, Homo sapiens, to prosimian forms that are so little modified from non-primate insectivores that scientists have been arguing for a century about their correct classification (Luckett 1980). The important

thing, in reality, is not the "correct" pigeonhole but the fact
that they represent a condition intermediate between the
two orders and suggest to us the kind of evolutionary
changes by which primates could have diverged from the
generalized mammalian stem.

This statement by Brace reveals that he is guilty of precisely the charge he makes against creation scientists—a
cavalier treatment of the subject based on secondary sources
and without any firsthand familiarity with the original specimens. Furthermore, the secondary sources he is depending on
are sadly out-of-date and rejected by many of his fellow
evolutionists today. It is textbook orthodoxy, and repeated by
many evolutionists with wearisome regularity, that primates
evolved from insectivores, more particularly, the tree shrew.

This idea was based on the work of Wilfred LeGros Clark,
a famous British anthropologist, in the 1920's. LeGros Clark
studied the Asian tree shrew, *Tupaia,* and believed that he had
identified characteristics in these tree shrews that revealed a
close relationship to living primates. A. J. Kelso, a physical
anthropologist, states:

> The transition from insectivore to primate is not documented by fossils. The basis of knowledge about the transition is by inference from living forms.[86]

Kelso, as did Brace and almost all other anthropologists,
bowed to the authority of LeGros Clark and assumed LeGros
Clark had indeed established that the order Primates was
closely related to tree shrews, and thus that primates must
have evolved from tree shrews. Please note that Kelso must
admit there is no evidence whatsoever for this in the fossil
record. The alleged evolution of primates from tree shrews
was merely inferred from the study of present-day tree shrews
and primates. Brace accepts this without question—cavalierly, and based on hearsay evidence and secondary sources
which were sadly out-of-date when he wrote his chapter.

As far back as 1966, C. B. G. Campbell published an article in *Science,* challenging the notion that primates are related to tree shrews. He states:

> I have attempted to indicate the large number of recent studies whose results indicate that a close relationship between tupaiids and primates is unlikely. . . . There is no doubt that the inclusion of the tree shrew as the most primitive primate in the morphological sequence: tree shrew-lemur-tarsier-ape-man is an attractive picture. Its innate attractiveness may have been in large measure responsible for its acceptance.[87]

Acceptance of a notion in science largely because of its innate attractiveness would certainly qualify for what Brace calls cavalier. Furthermore, even more recent research has confirmed Campbell's conclusions. In an article published in 1982 (prior to the writing of Brace's chapter), R. D. Martin reports on his studies of the maternal behavior of tree shrews compared to that of primates. He found that maternal behavior in tree shrews is totally different from that of primates. Primate mothers devote great care to their babies. Tree shrew mothers, on the other hand, visit the nest only once every 48 hours, spending ten minutes nursing the young, and not returning for another 48 hours. Furthermore, the fat content of tree shrew milk is 25%, while that of primates is typically 1-3%. Martin says:

> Contrary to reports, the tree shrew is not on the roster of human ancestors. Its maternal instincts are decidedly unlike those of a primate. . . . After researchers widened their comparisons to include other placental mammals and even marsupials, they found many of the features that supposedly link tree shrews to primates in other mammals as well. . . . The consensus now is that tree shrews are not relatives of the Primates.[88]

Martin reports that many authorities now place the tree shrews in their own order, Scandentia. Now this discussion demonstrates, first of all, that it is not only permissible, but most often necessary for scientists to use secondary sources and to defer to those who have actually done the original research. Secondly, this discussion shows that scientists, especially in the field of origins, are often wrong, reaching conclusions because of the innate attractiveness of those conclusions as related to their preconceived ideas. What is inexcusable is for Brace to parrot old discredited notions, ideas which give credence to his evolutionary prejudices, while at the same time condemning creation scientists for cavalier treatment of data and reliance on secondary sources. Finally, this recent research establishes the fact that there is no evidence in the present world to link primates to any other creature, and, as Kelso has admitted, there is no fossil evidence, or evidence from the world of the past, to link primates to other creatures. Here we find another of the multitude of huge gaps which shows that organisms consist of groups that are separate and distinct—a record of discontinuity, rather than the continuum demanded by the theory of evolution.

On p. 247, Brace reproduces a diagram taken from a publication by Gingerich,[89] purportedly showing the gradual evolution of *Notharctus* from *Pelycodus*. All of the data in the diagram are based solely on the cross-sectional area of the lower first molar of these creatures. This is obviously extremely limited data, restricted to a single dimension of a single tooth. Even at that, the data reveal a reversal at the 1,200-foot level of the 1,600-foot-thick sequence, the cross-sectional area decreasing rather than continuing to increase. Because of the paucity of evidence, evolutionists are forced to ascribe great significance to such data, which is far less significant than the natural variation within a single species.

On p. 247, Brace mentions the appearance of the monkey grade of organization. He makes absolutely no reference whatsoever to any material that bridges the considerable gap between prosimians (lemurs, lorises, and tarsiers are present-day prosimians) and monkeys. This is, of course, because there is none.[90] He refers to *Aegyptopithecus zeuxis* as being the best documented of these first monkeys. He describes certain characteristics of this creature as completely monkey-like, stating that *A. xeuxis* had the body plan of a monkey. Brace says it had the patterns of cusp arrangement on the molar teeth that are unlike modern monkeys but that are indistinguishable from those of modern anthropoid apes and man, and, as such, can thus be regarded as a "dental ape." He goes on to say, "All told, it provides a splendid representation of the ancestral condition from which modern apes—and humans—descended."

Something seems strange about this scenario. What is supposed to be one of the oldest fossil monkeys found is unquestionably a monkey with no fossil evidence to link it to its alleged prosimian ancestors, and yet what is supposed to be the most ancient monkey yet known already has traits that are supposed to indicate it was on its way to becoming an ape—and man.

On p. 249, Brace mentions that debate is still continuing today whether *Ramapithecus* and *Sivapithecus* should be placed in separate genera, or whether they constitute a single genus. Then he says:

> Whatever designation finally achieves accepted recognition, most anthropologists feel comfortable with the idea that the specimens that constitute that group make good representatives of the form that was ancestral to both more recent apes and to human beings.

This notion that *Ramipithecus* and *Sivapithecus* (or both lumped together) could be the ancestors of both modern apes and man was quite popular among leading paleoanthropologists until about ten years ago. Again, Brace is sadly out-of-date with his use of secondary sources. These earlier conclusions were based on a study of scanty material, a few teeth and jaw fragments, and advanced the idea that, as Brace declares, these creatures were on the direct line that led to man. Recent discoveries by David Pilbeam[91-93] and by Alan Walker and Richard Leakey[94] have definitely established that *Ramapithecus-Sivapithecus* was a pongid. Pilbeam, who previously had been one of the strongest supporters of the idea

that these creatures were ancestral to man, has declared that
they must be stripped of their status as a hominid (in the line
leading to man).[93] Walker and Leakey report that their fossils
of *Sivapithecus,* supposedly 17 million years old, reveal an
uncanny resemblance to the modern-day orangutan. In fact,
Walker was quoted as saying that "it's heretical to say so, but
it may be that orangs are 'living fossils.'"[94]

The track record of evolutionists in this area is sad indeed.
Two others, whose demise as ancestors to man preceded that
of *Ramapithecus-Sivapithecus,* were *Dryopithecus* and *Oreopithecus.* In fact, *Oreopithecus* had been declared by various
investigators, at one time or another, to be a monkey, an ape,
a hominid, and even a pig![95] Thus, it is Brace and his fellow
evolutionists who warrant criticism for evolutionary scenarios
that are outdated and obviously contradictory to known evidence.

On pp. 249-256, Brace gives the standard textbook explanation of the australopithecines, including Johanson's "Lucy"
and her fellow creatures. This does reflect the consensus of
evolutionary paleoanthropologists—that at least one branch of
Australopithecus was in the line leading to man. It is claimed
that these creatures, barely four feet tall and essentially ape
from the neck up, nevertheless walked in a totally human
manner and were therefore on their way to becoming people.
This, however, has been challenged by some of the best experts in the field. These include Lord Zuckerman (Professor
Solly Zuckerman was raised to the peerage in recognition of
his distinguished scientific career) and Dr. Charles Oxnard,
now professor of Anatomy and Human Biology at the University of Western Australia, Perth. These scientists did not use
the eyeball type of examination, but they used the most sophisticated methods of anatomical analysis available.[96-98]
Lord Zuckerman spent fifteen years studying fossils of the
australopithecines with a scientific team that rarely numbered
less than four. After these many years of research, Lord Zuckerman declared, concerning the claims that *Australopithecus*

should be placed in the family of man, Hominidae, rather than in a genus of the anthropoid apes:

> But I, myself, remain totally unpersuaded. Almost always when I have tried to check the anatomical claims on which the status of *Australopithecus* is based, I have ended in failure.[99]

Oxnard describes a multitude of morphological characteristics in which the australopithecines are more ape-like than man-like, which indicate they had many characteristics designed for an arboreal way of life, although they may have had some indications of bipedality (of course, modern apes and some monkeys display limited bipedality, the gibbon walking habitually upright during its brief excursions on the ground). Oxnard is convinced that the australopithecines were unique, neither intermediate between apes and man nor ancestral to any modern ape or man. He says:

> The information presented above for the different fragments of australopithecines from Olduvai and Sterkfontein that are here in contention shows that, *compared with humans and African apes,* each fragment is far more different from the equivalent part of humans and apes than are these latter from each other; the fossils are indeed uniquely different from these extant hominoids. It is in this sense that I use the term 'unique' (Oxnard, 1979c). This uniqueness leads inexorably to the possibility that these fossils are not ancestral to either humans or apes.[100]

Later, he says:

> The foregoing results of multivariate morphometric studies of australopithecines are the following: in terms of morphology, the various australopithecines are generally more similar to one another than any individual specimen is to any living primate. They are different from any living form to a degree greater than the differences between bipedal humans and terrestrial apes. Some of their similarities to living forms are especially reminiscent of the arboreal habitat.[101]

Some evolutionists maintain that Zuckerman's and Oxnard's conclusions cannot apply to Johanson's "Lucy" and fellow creatures (given the designation of *Australopithecus afarensis* by Johanson), because they have never studied Johanson's material. However, the fossils studied by Zuckerman and Oxnard are supposedly one to two million years younger than "Lucy," so if anything, they should be more advanced, more modern, than "Lucy." Furthermore, in an addendum to Oxnard's book, entitled "Grounds for Doubt? New Confirmations!", he describes much recent work on the *Australopithecus afarensis* fossils of Johanson by various workers which confirms Oxnard's conclusions based on the australopithecine fossils Oxnard had studied earlier.

Brace mentions not one word about the work of Zuckerman, Oxnard, or anyone else who may have published views on the australopithecines contrary to those he prefers to believe. Creation scientists are predicting that Zuckerman, Oxnard, and others who hold similar views will turn out to be right, and as a human ancestor, *Australopithecus* will suffer the same fate as Piltdown Man (a hoax), Nebraska Man (a pig's tooth), Neanderthal Man (*Homo sapiens*), *Dryopithecus, Oreopithecus,* and *Sivapithecus-Ramapithecus* (all just apes with no relationship to man).

One other interesting point in Brace's discussion of the australopithecines is an apparent contradiction in his discussion of australopithecine dentition. Speaking of "Lucy," the creature that Donald Johanson claims is directly in the line leading to man, Brace says (p. 253-254):

> The dentition also shows enough pongid features so that if one simply had a better part of the skull, face, and teeth, an expert could quite reasonably conclude that the creature could not be distinguished from a fossil ape.

On p. 253, however, Brace displays a drawing of "An early Australopithecine palate, AL 200, from Hadar in the Afar depression of Ethiopia." This is one of the fossils of *Australopithecus afarensis,* that is, one of "Lucy's" fellow creatures. Brace declares: "This is perfectly intermediate between the apelike and the human condition." How can the dentition of these creatures (and the skull and face) be so apelike that an expert could not distinguish the creature from a fossil ape, and yet, as Brace declares, be "perfectly intermediate between the apelike and human condition?"

Brace faults Morris (p. 266) for suggesting that civilization is contemporaneous with modern man. Brace says that:

> The gradual development of agriculture after the end of the Pleistocene ten thousand years ago has also repeatedly been tested and confirmed.

As Morris points out, however, it is significant that domestication of both plants and animals is believed to have occurred at about the same time and place.[102] He quotes Halbaek, who says:

> In rough outline, the available evidence now suggests that both the level of incipient civilization and animal domestication and the level of intensive food-collecting were reached in the Near East about 9000 B.C.[103]

Cambel and Braidwood state that:

> The sheep, on the basis of statistics found at Shanidar Cave and at the nearby site of Zawi Chemi Shanedar, now appears to have been domesticated by around 9000 B.C., well before the earliest evidence for either the dog or the goat.[104]

Dyson reports that:

> The oldest known artificially shaped metal objects are some copper beads found in northern Iraq and dating from the beginning of the 9th millennium B.C.[105]

On pp. 264-266, Brace tells us that:

> The evidence from archaeology shows that a basic and successful hunting and gathering mode of subsistence had been established before the beginning of the Middle Pleistocene three-quarters of a million years ago. This remained relatively unchanged until just before the onset of the last glacial episode about 100,000 years ago.

Thus, for about 650,000 years, we are told, there was essentially no progress in human technology and civilization. Then, so it is said, Neanderthal people, with a fully *Homo sapiens* status (Brace, p. 254) abruptly appeared in Europe and other places, possessing an average cranial capacity of about 1600 cc, even greater than that of present-day man (averaging about 1450 cc). If the Neanderthal people were fully developed when first noted in Europe, they would have had a large cranial capacity for perhaps tens of thousands of years prior to 100,000 years ago, if evolutionary theory is accepted. The questions then are, what in the world were our advanced hominid ancestors doing for almost a million years? Why was evolution, both physical and cultural, so quiescent for such a vast stretch of time? If *Homo sapiens* had evolved perhaps as much as 150,000 years ago or even longer, why was it that he invented agriculture and domestication of animals so recently and so abruptly? (Certainly "abruptly" is an appropriate term, if we use the evolutionary time scale.)

On pp. 261-263, Brace tells us that:

> The changes in cranio-facial anatomy that occur as *Australopithecus* becomes *Homo* can be comfortably accounted for in the perspective of the changes in the forces of natural selection that accompany such a transition in subsistence strategy (Brace 1979a, 1979c).

> It is just such circumstances that would lead to a marked increase in brain size. Certainly the other aspects of hominid anatomy by themselves are pretty unpromising for a would-be predator. As modes of locomotion go, bipedalism is not notably rapid, and a bipedal primate could hardly expect to capture much of anything by outrunning it. Nor could a creature whose canines did not project beyond the level of its incisors pose much of a threat by trying to bite its would-be prey if it did succeed in catching up with it. Its only hope would be in learning so much of the seasonal, species, and individual peculiarities of the various members of the animal world that it could plan their capture from ambush with the aid of hand-held tools and

weapons. Such are the circumstances under which we would predict a relatively rapid increase in the size of the organ by which such planning is accomplished, namely the brain, and it is surely no accident that the available skeletal finds show that hominid brain size effectively doubled during just that period when big game hunting became an important hominid subsistence activity.

Thus we are told that bipedalism, in itself, does not bring with it the advantages needed to survive. Thus, natural selection comes to the rescue, and brain size practically doubled just when needed, since it is brain power that a bipedal creature needs to give him the cunning to fashion tools and weapons and to ambush his prey. This is another "just-so" story, or what Kitcher calls "a problem-solving strategy." Brace's own account shows, indeed, that it is nothing more than a "just-so" story, and obviously false. He tells us (p. 252) that the australopithecines go back 3.5 million years ago, and that there is no doubt that they were erect bipeds (p. 253). On p. 261, Brace says:

> Given a terrestrial biped lacking enlarged canine teeth, the existence of some kind of hand-held defensive weapon would hardly be a surprise. However, the fossil record shows that our biped has an antiquity of at least 3.5 million years, and, given the locomotor development already achieved by that date, there is reason to suspect that its bipedal adaptation must predate that by at least another half million years. Yet stone tools do not appear until 2 million years ago.

Thus Brace tells us earlier that without an enlarged brain and the mental capacity to fashion weapons and to use cunning in ambushing prey, bipedalism would carry with it no survival benefits (and, by inference perhaps, even loss of benefits). But yet we are told *bipedalism existed for up to two million years before tools and weapons were invented,* and certainly there was no substantial, if any, increase in brain size during that alleged vast stretch of time. How, then, could these poor ignorant creatures survive for two million years until they

finally figured out how to make tools and weapons? Why
would natural selection have converted them to slow, disad-
vantageous, bipedal locomotion, without the mental capacity
to cope by fashioning tools and weapons? The only suggestion
Brace can offer is that perhaps during those two million years,
these supposed bipeds were using tools of perishable materials, such as pointed wooden sticks! And Brace accuses creationists of a cavalier treatment of the evidence!

Brace, as do all evolutionists, attaches great evolutionary
significance to variations in dental characteristics and dimensions. It will be remembered that he traced the supposed
evolution of *Notharctus* from *Pelycodus* through increases in
the cross-sectional area of the lower first molar, even though
this trend actually reversed itself. But later (p. 273), he says:

> When one then looks at the differences in dento-facial
> robustness in the various populations in modern *Homo
> sapiens,* one can observe a range of variation that is more
> than just the expression of chance individual differences.
> In aboriginal Australia, for example, fully Middle Pleisto-
> cene levels of tooth size continue right up to the pre-
> sent. . . .

Thus, living today, we have aborigines in Australia with
levels of tooth sizes possessed, according to Brace, by homi-
nids of the Middle Pleistocene, which places them about one
million years in the past, as far as tooth sizes are concerned.
It thus seems that one should be quite skeptical, or at the least
cautious, in accepting conclusions based solely on dentition
(and practically all of supposed early primate evolution, and,
in fact, practically all of early mammalian evolution is based
on dentition).

It is evident that much of what Brace so confidently states
is open to serious doubt, and, in fact, has been challenged by
those within the evolutionary camp. His arrogant disdain of
creation scientists and their interpretation of the data related
to human origins is certainly not warranted. He ought to clean
up his own house, and at least base his conclusions on an

updated search of the literature. In closing this discussion, we should first remind ourselves that all of this fuss over what may or may not be considered as intermediates between ape and man is irrelevant, because it has already been established that neither the complex invertebrates nor the vertebrates (fishes) have a trace of an ancestor, and thus, obviously, ultimately, man has no ancestors. Furthermore, one of the great experts in anatomy and paleoanthropology, and certainly not a professing creationist, Lord Zuckerman, after a lifetime of research in the field, declared:

> ... no scientist could logically dispute the proposition that man, without having been involved in any act of divine creation, evolved from some ape-like creature in a very short space of time—speaking in geological terms—without leaving any fossil traces of the steps of the transformation.[106]

Thus, Brace describes what he maintains is a wealth of evidence that documents man's evolution from some apelike creature, ". . . a burgeoning mass of data, all of which fit comfortably within an evolutionary framework, and are hard to account for in any other way" (p. 246). Lord Zuckerman, on the other hand, says that there are no fossil traces of the transformation—not even a single trace. Creation scientists agree with Lord Zuckerman, whom Brace would not dare to accuse of treating the evidence cavalierly and of having no acquaintance with the original material.

Chapter 14, The Evolution of Bible-Science (pp. 283-299), is by Robert J. Schadewald, a freelance science writer. One of his special interests has been the flat-earth movement, which has a miniscule number of followers and certainly no scientific supporters, so his special area of expertise is in a moribund society, of little interest to anyone except its few members and Schadewald. Schadewald is a bitter anti-creationist, fully in keeping with his atheistic or agnostic philosophy. He begins by stating that "Bible-scientists have waged war on conventional science, sometimes defending their beliefs with such potent arguments as the rack, rope, or stake." He doesn't describe what took place, or when and who these "Bible-scientists" were. One must just accept his word for all of this. He does admit, later (p. 298), that the rack, rope, and stake are fortunately obsolete, but claims the Bible scientists have once again given their doctrines the force of law. This latter statement is sheer nonsense, for it is evolutionary theory that is now being backed by the force of law, every attempt being made to establish evolutionary theory as the sole explanation for origins, with complete exclusion of the scientific evidence for creation. It is the creationists who would be tortured with rope, rack, and stake if evolutionists had their way.

In order to prejudice the reader against creation science, Schadewald links creation scientists to flat-earthers, geocentrists, and other categories that he says fall under pseudoscience. He says that modern creationists march under the banner of science and make a great "pother" about science, but they offer a complex pseudoscience, which they call scientific creationism (p. 284). Of course, Schadewald himself has no scientific credentials whatsoever. In fact, in this book's description of the contributors to the book, in the section devoted to Schadewald, no mention is made of any degree held by Schadewald, although it may be assumed that he may have earned some sort of a degree in philosophy, or writing, or some related field. His discussion is a mere hodgepodge of jibes at creation scientists and those who hold to a Bible-centered faith. Most of his chapter is devoted to a discussion of the Flat Earth Society, his obvious tactic being aimed at linking creation scientists to flat-earthers.

He maintains that the Bible does teach a flat earth (pp. 270, 293). This is manifestly false. The Bible refers to the *circle* of the earth (Isaiah 40:22). From every point in space, the earth appears as a circle, which it must, of course, if it is a sphere. The Bible is thus scientifically accurate on that point, and Schadewald simply reveals his ignorance of the Bible.

On p. 297, Schadewald declares that present-day creation scientists are just like the British flat-earthers a century ago— "A corps of skilled lecturers crisscrosses the country speaking in churches, before religious organizations, or wherever they can get a hall and a crowd." Schadewald's statement is deliberately deceptive. He has followed the creation science movement practically since its beginning. He doubtlessly, regularly receives the monthly periodical, *Acts & Facts,* published by the Institute for Creation Research, that lists the speaking schedule of its scientific staff members (now numbering nine, all but one of whom hold a doctorate in their fields of science), and carries reports of the lectures and debates of these staff members. He must know, then, that these staff members (and many other creation scientists as well) have lectured in major colleges, universities, and science institutes in practically every state of the U.S., in practically every province of Canada, and in at least 25 other countries, as well. Schadewald deliberately omits any references to these lectures, seminars, and debates, and attempts to convey the notion that the activities of creation scientists are restricted to churches and religious organizations. Nothing could be further from the truth.

On p. 297, Schadewald mentions the debates participated in by members of the Institute for Creation Research (many other creation scientists have also debated, with exemplary results). He claims that these debaters take their text from John Hampden, a flat-earther of a century ago. Of course, none of the creation scientists has ever heard of John Hampden, let alone being aware of his admonition against his opponents. Schadewald, in effect, admits that creationists have won most of the debates, when he says, "The poor evolutionist, up against an experienced creationist debater, often looks like an unarmed man assaulting a fortress." Exactly! Unarmed, because he cannot present a credible scientific case for evolution, and up against the fortress of powerful positive evidence for creation! Here Schadewald and creation scientists are in agreement.

The final chapter of the book, Chapter 15, "Is It Really Fair to Give Creationism Equal Time?" (pp. 301-316), is by Frederick Edwords. Philosophy is one of his main interests. He is administrator for the American Humanist Association, the main atheist organization in the U.S. He enjoys debating creationists and lectures against creation science wherever he can get a hearing.

Edwords presents a fairly thorough and substantially correct description of the various creationist sub-models—recent creation, the day-age theory, the gap theory, and progressive creation. He states that Christianity isn't the only religion that claims an active role for a divine power in creating organisms. This is obviously true, because Christians accept all of the Hebrew Scriptures. Furthermore, not only do orthodox Jews accept the Genesis record of creation, but so do Moslems. And, as creation scientists have often pointed out, the scientific evidence for creation supports all concepts of an all-knowing, all-powerful Creator bringing the universe and its inhabitants into being by direct fiat, and is thus not limited to the Judeo-Christian record derived from Genesis. Edwords proceeds to document the fact that the Hare Krishnas reject evolution and embrace creation, although they do accept the notion of a cyclical universe. Thus the claim of evolutionists that creation science represents the views only of Christian fundamentalists is obviously untrue.

In rejecting the claim of creationists that academic and religious freedoms, supposedly guaranteed in our pluralistic democratic society, demand that the scientific evidence for both creation and evolution be taught in our tax-supported public schools, Edwords employs Schadewald's tactics of linking creation science with astrology, flat-earthers, pyramid power, and Mary Baker Eddy's Christian Science theory of disease (p. 308). Therefore, he tells us, if we present the evidence for creation along with evolution, we must also permit the teaching of astrology, a flat earth, pyramid power, and Eddy's theory of disease! Later on (p. 311), for good measure, he throws in the Theosophists, the Rosecrucianists, and Erich Von Däniken!

On p. 313, Edwords asserts that just because humanists accept evolution doesn't make evolution Humanism. The creationist can quickly retort that just because fundamentalists accept creation doesn't make creation science Fundamentalism. But practically every author in this book, certainly including Edwords, asserts that scientific creation is nothing more than Christian Fundamentalism parading as science. He says (p. 314) that:

. . . Special Creationists aren't really fighting for fairness but rather are fighting to have their religion taught in public schools at taxpayer expense.

This is absolutely untrue, and Edwords knows it. Creation scientists have repeatedly pointed out, and Edwords has heard them state this, that they want only scientific evidence that supports creation (along with evolution, of course) taught in public schools, devoid of any references to Genesis or any other portion of the Bible. In fact, the legislation enacted by the states of Arkansas and Louisiana was explicit in excluding all religious literature and permitting only scientific evidence. What we have today, on the other hand, is a *de facto* state-sanctioned humanistic religion, with evolution as its basic dogma, being taught in our public schools while concealed under a pseudo-scientific mantle.

On p. 313, Edwords tells us, "The simple solution in cases where students are offended at evolution would seem to be discreet removal of the student from the class." This is no solution at all, because this still denies the right of all students to hear the scientific evidence for creation. Furthermore, it is a solution against which the American Humanist Association, the American Civil Liberties Union, and all their humanist colleagues argued so strenuously against in the case of prayer and Bible reading in public schools.

According to Edwords, most humanists and evolutionists would have no objection to the teaching of creation science in public schools if restricted to classes in comparative religions. Creation scientists maintain that, following a similar line of thinking, it could be argued even more effectively that evolution should be restricted to courses in comparative religions.

References

1. L. R. Godfrey, Ed., *Scientists Confront Creationism,* W. W. Norton, New York, 1983.
2. Michael Denton, *Evolution: A Theory in Crisis,* Burnett Books, London, 1985 (available from Woodbine House, 5615 Fishers Lane, Rockville, MD 20852, and the Institute for Creation Research, P.O. Box 2667, El Cajon, CA 92021).
3. Frances Fitzgerald, *New Yorker,* 18 May 1981, p. 99.
4. Niles Eldredge, *The Monkey Business,* Washington Square Books, 1982, p. 134.
5. *Websters Dictionary,* compiled by J. G. Allee, Literary Press, Baltimore, 1981.
6. John Keosian, *The Origin of Life,* Reinhold Publishing Co., New York, 1964.
7. John Keosian, *Origin of Life,* 1978, pp. 569-574.
8. Harold Blum, *Times Arrow and Evolution,* Princeton University Press, 3rd. Ed., 1968, p. 194.
9. Murray Eden, in *Mathematical Challenges to the Neo-Darwinian Interpretation of Evolution,* P. S. Moorhead and M. K. Kaplan, Eds., Wistar Institute Press, Philadelphia, 1967, p. 9.
10. P. T. Mora, in *The Origins of Prebiological Systems and of Their Molecular Matrixes,* S. W. Fox, Ed., Academic Press, New York, 1965, p. 52.
11. H. P. Yockey, *Journal of Theoretical Biology* 67:337-343 (1977).
12. H. Fakhrai, J. H. G. van Roode, and L. E. Orgel, *Journal of Molecular Evolution* 17:295-302 (1981).
13. D. E. Green and R. F. Goldberger, *Molecular Insights into the Living Process,* Academic Press, New York, 1967, p. 407.
14. G. L. Stebbins, *Bioscience* 17:83 (1967).

15. Vincent Demoulin, *Science* 205:1036-1038 (1979).

16. T. E. Meyer, R. G. Bartsch, M. D. Kamen, R. P. Ambler, Margaret Daniel, and J. Hermoso, *Nature* 278:659-660 (1979).

17. R. P. Ambler, T. E. Meyer, and M. D. Kamen, *Nature* 278:661-662 (1979).

18. H. Drucker, E. B. Toysil, L. L. Campbell, G. H. Barlow, and E. Margoliash, *Biochemistry* 9:1515 (1970).

19. R. V. Eck and M. O. Dayhoff, *Atlas of Protein Sequence and Structure 1966*, National Biomedical Research Foundation, Silver Springs, MD, 1966, p. 110.

20. *Ibid.*, p. 191.

21. *Ibid.*, p. 170.

22. M. G. Grutter, L. H. Weaver, and B. W. Matthews, *Nature* 303:828-831 (1983).

23. J. H. Schwartz, *Nature* 308:501-505 (1984).

24. J. A. King, *Science* 206:67-69 (1979).

25. Christian Schwabe and Gregory Warr, *Perspectives in Biology and Medicine* 27(3), Spring 1984, pp. 465-485.

26. Christian Schwabe, *Trends in Biochemical Sciences* (July 1986).

27. Reference 2, pp. 274-307.

28. *Ibid.*, p. 278.

29. *Ibid.*, p. 291.

30. Emile Zuckerkandl, *Scientific American* 212(5):111 (1965).

31. Reference 2, p. 306.

32. James T. Darnell, *Science* 202:1257-1260 (1978).

33. S. J. Gould, *Natural History* October 1976, pp. 24-30.

34. Tom Bethell, *Harper's Magazine* 252(1509):70-75 (Feb. 1976).

35. R. H. Brady, *Systematic Zoology* 28:600-621 (1979).

36. D. M. Raup and S. M. Stanley, *Principles of Paleontology*, W. H. Freeman, New York, 1978.

37. See for example D. T. Gish, *Evolution: The Challenge of the Fossil Record*, Master Books, El Cajon, CA, 1985, pp. 247-250.

38. D. M. Raup, *Field Museum of Natural History Bulletin* 50:22 (1979).

39. For example, see E. Mayr, *The Growth of Biological Thought*, Harvard University Press, Cambridge, MA, 1982, p. 282.

40. Roger Lewin, *Science* 234:1500 (1986).

41. Roper Lewin, *Science* 214:42 (1981).

42. G. G. Simpson, *Principles of Animal Taxonomy,* Oxford University Press, London, 1961, p. 90.

43. Anonymous, *Nature* 278:307 (1979).

44. D. T. Gish, *Evolution: The Fossils Say No!* 3rd Edition, Creation-Life Publishers, San Diego, 1979, pp. 36-37.

45. A. S. Romer, *Vertebrate Paleontology,* 3rd Ed., Chicago University Press, Chicago, 1966.

46. Colin Patterson, "Cladistics," in *The Pattern of Nature,* pp. 110-120. This article first appeared in *Biologist* 27:234-240 (1980).

47. Colin Patterson, *ibid.,* p. 118.

48. Colin Patterson, *ibid.,* p. 119.

49. John Beatty, *Systematic Zoology* 31(1):29 (1982).

50. John Beatty, *ibid.,* p. 30.

51. Ernst Mayr, *Animal Species and Evolution,* The Belknap Press of Harvard University Press, Cambridge, MA, 1966, p. 8.

52. E. Mayr, *ibid.,* p. 176.

53. G. G. Simpson, *The Meaning of Evolution,* Yale University Press, New Haven, 1949, pp. 218-219.

54. G. G. Simpson, *ibid.,* p. 159.

55. Murray Eden, in *Mathematical Challenges to the Neo-Darwinian Interpretation of Evolution,* Wistar Institute Press, Philadelphia, 1967, p. 109.

56. S. J. Gould, *Natural History* 95:27 (October 1986).

57. Søren Løvtrup, *Darwinism: The Refutation of a Myth,* Croom Helm, New York, 1987, p. 422.

58. P. E. Raymond, *Prehistoric Life,* 5th Ed., Harvard University Press, Cambridge, MA, 1967, p. 184.

59. Leigh Van Valen, "Review of *Evolutionary Biology* Vol. 6," *Science* 180:488 (1973).

60. D. T. Gish, Ref. 44, pp. 165-166.

61. G. G. Simpson, *The Meaning of Evolution,* Yale University Press, New Haven, 1949, p. 231.

62. D. M. Raup and S. M. Stanley, *Principles of Paleontology,* W. H. Freeman and Co., San Francisco, 1971, p. 306.

63. J. C. Whitcomb and H. M. Morris, *The Genesis Flood,* The Presbyterian and Reformed Publishing Co., Philadelphia, 1961, pp. 79- 86.

64. Genesis 6:20.

65. G. L. Jepsen, *Science* 154:1333-1338 (1966).

66. M. J. Novacek, *Nature* 315:140-141 (1985).

67. G. G. Simpson, in *Evolution of Life,* Sol Tax, Ed., University of Chicago Press, Chicago, 1960, p. 149.

68. Niles Eldredge, *The Monkey Business,* Washington Square Press, New York, 1982, p. 65.

69. R. B. Goldschmidt, *American Scientist* 40:97 (1952).

70. D. T. Gish, *Evolution: The Fossils Say No!* Public School Edition, Creation-Life Publishers, San Diego, 1978.

71. Preston Cloud, *The Humanist,* Jan./Feb. 1977.

72. J. W. Valentine, "The Evolution of Complex Animals," in *What Darwin Began,* L. R. Godfrey, Ed., Allyn and Bacon, Inc., Boston, 1985, p. 263.

73. D. T. Gish, Ref. 37, pp. 247-250.

74. D. G. Kitts, *Evolution* 28:466 (1974).

75. S. J. Gould, *Discover,* May 1981, pp. 34-37.

76. H. M. Morris, *Scientific Creationism,* Creation-Life Publishers, San Diego, 1974.

77. P.-P. Grassé, *Evolution of Living Organisms,* Academic Press, New York, 1977, p. 4.

78. H. M. Morris, Ref. 76, p. 135.

79. G. A. Kerkut, *Implications of Evolution,* Pergamon Press, Oxford, 1960, p. 134.

80. H. M. Morris, *Impact,* Series No. 48, Institute for Creation Research, El Cajon, CA, 1977, pp. i-ii.

81. G. J. Nelson, *Annals of the New York Academy of Sciences* 167:27 (1969).

82. J. E. O'Rourke, *American Journal of Science* 276:51-52 (1976).

83. J. E. O'Rourke, *ibid.,* p. 47.

84. H. M. Morris, Ref. 80, p. ii.

85. W. B. N. Berry, *Growth of a Prehistoric Time Scale, Based on Organic Evolution,* W. H. Freeman, San Francisco, 1968.

86. A. J. Kelso, *Physical Anthropology,* 2nd Ed., J. B. Lippincott, New York, 1974, p. 142.

87. C. B. G. Campbell, *Science* 153:436 (1966).

88. R. D. Martin, *NaturalHistory* 91:26-32 (1982).

89. P. D. Gingerich, *American Journal of Science* 276:1-28 (1976).

90. See A. J. Kelso, Ref. 86, pp. 150-151.

91. D. R. Pilbeam, *Nature* 295:232 (1982).

92. W. Herbert, *Science News* 121:84 (1982).

93. D. R. Pilbeam, *Natural History* 93:2 (1984).

94. See B. Rensberger, *Science 84* 5(1):16 (1984).

95. D. R. Pilbeam, *The Evolution of Man*, Funk and Wagnalls, New York, 1970, p. 99.

96. S. Zuckerman, *Beyond the Ivory Tower*, Taplinger Pub. Co., New York, 1970, pp. 75-94.

97. C. E. Oxnard, *Nature* 258:389-395 (1975).

98. C. E. Oxnard, *The Order of Man*, Yale University Press, New Haven, 1984.

99. S. Zuckerman, Ref. 96, p. 77.

100. C. E. Oxnard, Ref. 98, p. 320.

101. C. E. Oxnard, Ref. 98, p. 328.

102. H. M. Morris, *Scientific Creationism*, 2nd Ed., Creation-Life Publishers, El Cajon, CA, 1985, p. 190.

103. Hans Halbaek, *Science* 130:365 (1959).

104. Halet Cambel and Robert J. Briadwood, *Scientific American*, 222 (March 1970), p. 52.

105. R. H. Dyson, Jr., *Science* 144:674 (1964).

106. Solly Zuckerman, Ref. 96, p. 64.

10

Out of Their Own Mouths*

I believe that one day the Darwinian myth will be ranked the greatest deceit in the history of science.[1]

Søren Løvtrup

. . . but if Mayr's characterization of the synthetic theory is accurate, then that theory, as a general proposition, is effectively dead, despite its persistence as textbook orthodoxy.[2]

Stephen Jay Gould

So heated is the debate that one Darwinian says there are times when he thinks about going into a field with more intellectual honesty: the used-car business.[3]

Sharon Begley

Most of us might opt for rejection in most circumstances. Yet in the case of the synthetic theory, we hold it, not with a light hand as advocated by T. H. Huxley, but with an

---

*All quotes in this chapter are from evolutionists except for non-evolutionists Denton, Hoyle, and Van Wylen, and creationists Chesterton and Job. The position of Huston Smith is not known.

ironclad grasp, unwilling to let go, unwilling to explore
alternatives.[4]
                                            E. O. Wiley

. . . contrary to what is widely assumed by evolutionary
biologists today, it has always been the anti-evolutionists,
not the evolutionists, in the scientific community who have
stuck rigidly to the facts and adhered to a more strictly
empirical approach.[5]
                                          Michael Denton

Just as pre-Darwinian biology was carried out by people whose faith was in the Creator and His plan, post-
Darwinian biology is being carried out by people whose
faith is in, almost, the deity of Darwin.[6]
                                          Colin Patterson

It is as a religion of science that Darwinism held, and holds
men's minds. . . . The modified, but still characteristically
Darwinian theory has itself become an orthodoxy, preached
by its adherents with religious fervor, and doubted, they
feel, only by a few muddlers imperfect in scientific faith.[7]
                                          Marjorie Grene

. . . there is no escape from the fundamental contradiction
between evolution and creationism. They are irreconcilable
world views.[8]
                                          Richard Lewontin

Humanism is the belief that man shapes his own destiny. It
is a constructive philosophy, a non-theistic religion, a way
of life.[9]
                                          Anonymous

I use the word "Humanist" to mean someone who believes
that man is just as much a natural phenomenon as an animal
or plant; that his body, mind, and soul were not supernaturally created but are products of evolution, and that he is
not under the control or guidance of any supernatural being
or beings, but has to rely on himself and his own powers.[10]
                                          Julian Huxley

Our theory of evolution has become . . . one which cannot
be refuted by any possible observations. Every conceivable
observation can be fitted into it. It is thus "outside of

empirical science" but not necessarily false. No one can think of ways to test it. Ideas, either without basis or based on a few laboratory experiments carried out in extremely simplified systems have attained currency far beyond their validity. They have become part of an evolutionary dogma accepted by most of us as part of our training.[11]

                                        Paul Ehrlich and L. C. Birch

I have suggested that the neo-Darwinian theory of evolution rests on the axioms that all heritable variations in fitness result from chance mutations and that there is natural selection for fitness. There are several consequences for evolution and for biology in general.

First, the axiomatic nature of the neo-Darwinian theory places the debate between evolutionists and creationists in a new perspective. Evolutionists have often challenged creationists to provide experimental proof that species have been fashioned de novo. Creationists have often demanded that evolutionists show how chance mutations can lead to adaptability, or to explain why natural selection has favored some species but not others with special adaptations, or why natural selection allows apparently detrimental organs to persist. We may now recognize that neither challenge is fair. If the neo-Darwinian theory is axiomatic, it is not valid for creationists to demand proof of the axioms, and it is not valid for evolutionists to dismiss special creation as unproved as long as it is stated as an axiom.[12]

                                                 C. Leon Harris

The fact of evolution is the backbone of biology, and biology is thus in the peculiar position of being a science founded on an unproved theory—is it then a science or a faith? Belief in the theory of evolution is thus exactly parallel to belief in special creation—both are concepts which believers know to be true but neither, up to the present, has been capable of proof.[13]

                                         L. Harrison Matthews

. . . Gillespie recasts the debate as a contrast between two 'epistemes' or world views—creationism and positivism . . . Creationism and positivism do not represent religion

versus science, but two styles of doing science. . . . The
positivist, Gillespie claims, "limited scientific knowledge,
which he saw as the only valid form of knowledge, to the
laws of nature and to processes involving 'secondary', or
natural causes exclusively" . . . Creationists believed that
an understanding of nature would reveal the working of
God's mind. "The creationist", Gillespie argues, "saw the
world and everything in it as being the result of direct or
indirect divine activity. His science was inseparable from
his theology."

To be sure, they found God manifest in his works (nature),
but their tool was science, their commitment to regularity
of law and 'knowability'.[14]

Stephen Jay Gould

(Here Gould is speaking of the pre-Darwinian creationists—in
his mind, the true "scientific creationists.")

The theory of dialectic materialism postulates matter as the
ultimate reality, not to be questioned. Evolution is more
than a useful biologic concept: it is a natural law controlling
the history of all phenomena.[15]

J. E. O'Rourke

Dobzhansky believed and propounded that the implications
of biological evolution reach much beyond biology into
philosophy, sociology, and even socio-political issues. The
place of biological evolution in human thought was according to Dobzhansky, best expressed in a passage that he
often quoted from Pierre Teilhard de Chardin. "(Evolution)
is a general postulate to which all theories, all hypotheses,
all systems must hence forward bow and which they must
satisfy in order to be thinkable and true. Evolution is a light
which illuminates all facts, a trajectory which all lines of
thought must follow—this is what evolution is."[16]

Francisco Ayala

Darwinism removed the whole idea of God as the creator
of organisms from the sphere of rational discussion . . . we
can dismiss entirely all idea of a supernatural overriding
mind being responsible for the evolutionary process.[17]

Julian Huxley

A religion is essentially an attitude to the world as a whole. Thus evolution, for example, may prove as powerful a principle to coordinate man's beliefs and hopes as God was in the past.[18]

Julian Huxley and Jacob Bronowski

Suddenly the study of evolution was in all the schools. The culture of the dominant class had triumphed, and traditional religious values, the only vestige of control that rural people had over their own lives and the lives of their families, had been taken from them.[19]

Richard Lewontin

Meantime, let me say that the conclusion I have come to is this: the law of Christ is incompatible with the law of evolution—as far as the law of evolution has worked hitherto. Nay, the two laws are at war with each other; the law of Christ can never prevail until the law of evolution is destroyed.[20]

Sir Arthur Keith

Christianity has fought, still fights, and will fight science to the desperate end over evolution, because evolution destroys utterly and finally the very reason Jesus' earthly life was supposedly made necessary. Destroy Adam and Eve and the original sin, and in the rubble you will find the sorry remains of the son of God. If Jesus was not the redeemer who died for our sins, and this is what evolution means, then Christianity is nothing.[21]

G. Richard Bozarth

[Natural] selection is the blindest, and most cruel way of evolving new species, and more and more complex and refined organisms. . . . The struggle for life and elimination of the weakest is a horrible process, against which our whole modern ethics revolts. An ideal society is a non-selective society, one where the weak is protected; which is exactly the reverse of the so-called natural law. I am surprised that a Christian would defend the idea that this is the process which God more or less set up in order to have evolution.[22]

Jacque Monod

I am convinced that the battle for humankind's future must be waged and won in the public school classroom by teachers who correctly perceive their role as the proselytizers of a new faith: a religion of humanity that recognizes and respects what theologians call divinity in every human being. These teachers must embody the same selfless dedication as the most rabid fundamentalist preachers, for they will be ministers of another sort, utilizing a classroom instead of a pulpit to convey humanist values in whatever subject they teach, regardless of the educational level— preschool day care center or large state university. The classroom must and will become an arena of conflict between the old and the new—the rotting corpse of Christianity, together with all its adjacent evils and misery, and the new faith of humanism. . . . It will undoubtedly be a long, arduous, painful struggle replete with much sorrow and many tears, but humanism will emerge triumphant. It must if the family of humankind is to survive.[23]

John Dunphy

One reason education undoes belief is its teaching of evolution; Darwin's own drift from orthodoxy to agnosticism was symptomatic. Martin Lings is probably right in saying that "more cases of loss of religious faith are to be traced to the theory of evolution . . . than to anything else." (*Studies in Comparative Religion*, Winter 1970.)[24]

Huston Smith

How could evolution be true? Did we all really come from a single cell? Did an organ like the eye evolve by mere chance? These questions are still being asked.

Once again, in classrooms and laboratories across the land, Darwin's theory of evolution is being challenged.

This is nothing new. Charles Darwin has been under almost constant attack since 1859.

Darwin's most spirited critics include the "creationists." They are religious Fundamentalists who insist that evolutionary theory is no more than "an animal fairy tale," in the words of one believer. The creationists are not alone; the journal *Nature* reports that almost half the adults in the

United States believe we are directly descended from Adam and Eve.

Darwin's model has faced scientific challenges as well. Critics point to the many evolutionary puzzles they say the theory has failed to explain:

How can unrelated animals who evolve in different areas end up looking alike by chance?

How could a turtle shell have evolved gradually from a rib cage when nothing in between would have been a viable structure for the reptile?

How could the panda evolve a stronger skull, specialized genitalia, and a thumb different from that of other bears?[25]

John Gliedman

Another way of stating the second law then is: "The universe is constantly getting more disorderly!" Viewed that way, we can see the second law all about us. We have to work hard to straighten a room, but left to itself it becomes a mess again very quickly and very easily. Even if we never enter it, it becomes dusty and musty. How difficult to maintain houses, and machinery, and our own bodies in perfect working order: how easy to let them deteriorate. In fact, all we have to do is nothing, and everything deteriorates, collapses, breaks down, wears out, all by itself—and that is what the second law is all about.[26]

Isaac Asimov

The author has found that the second law tends to increase his conviction that there is a Creator who has the answer for the future destiny of man and the universe.[27]

Gordon J. Van Wylen

The claims of chemical evolution are unreal. We are asked to believe that biochemical compounds, biochemical reactions and mechanisms, energy metabolism and storage, specific polymerizations, codes, transcription and translation apparatus, and more, appeared in probiotic waters with the functions they would have in a living thing before there were living things. Chemical evolution has become an end in itself. In many cases it represents contrived or ingenious laboratory syntheses which have no counterpart in abiotic organic chemical synthesis in an acceptable range of probiotic conditions. There is no point in further pursuing this line of investigation to add more biochemicals to the list. Let it be assumed that the probiotic waters contained all of the material that "chemical evolution" is supposed to have brought about. Then how, and in what form, could life have arisen from such a scattered melange? That question must be answered, if there is an answer, to give meaning and direction to the pursuit of chemical evolution, otherwise that pursuit will continue to be an endless series of laboratory experiments unrelated to the central problem. There has been a good deal of uncritical acceptance of experiments, results, and conclusions which we are all too ready to acknowledge because they support preconceived convictions. . . .

All present approaches to a solution of the problem of the origin of life are either irrelevant or lead into a blind alley. Therein lies the crisis. . . . The various approaches to a solution of the origin of life are examined and found wanting.[28]

John Keosian

More than 30 years of experimentation on the origin of life in the fields of chemical and molecular evolution have led to a better perception of the immensity of the problem of the origin of life on Earth rather than to its solution. At present all discussions on principal theories and experiments in the field either end in a stalemate or in a confession of ignorance.[29]

Klaus Dose

. . . the longest genome which could be expected with 95% confidence in 10^9 years corresponds to only 49 amino acid residues. This is much too short to code a living system so evolution to higher forms could not get started. Geological evidence for the "warm little pond" is missing. It is concluded that belief in currently accepted scenarios of spontaneous biogenesis is based on faith, contrary to conventional wisdom.[30]

Hubert P. Yockey

I don't know how long it is going to be before astronomers generally recognize that the combinatorial arrangement of not even one among the many thousands of biopolymers on which life depends could have been arrived at by natural processes here on the Earth. Astronomers will have a little difficulty at understanding this because they will be assured by biologists that it is not so, the biologists having been assured in their turn by others that it is not so. The "others" are a group of persons who believe, quite openly, in mathematical miracles. They advocate the belief that tucked away in nature, outside of normal physics, there is a law which performs miracles (provided the miracles are in the aid of biology). This curious situation sits oddly on a profession that for long has been dedicated to coming up with logical explanations of biblical miracles.

Now imagine 10^{50} blind persons each with a scrambled Rubik cube, and try to conceive of the chance of them all *simultaneously* arriving at the solved form. You then have the chance of arriving by random shuffling of just one of the many biopolymers on which life depends. The notion that not only the biopolymers but the operating programme of a living cell could be arrived at by chance in a primordial organic soup here on the Earth is evidently nonsense of a high order. Life must plainly be a cosmic phenomenon.[31]

Sir Fred Hoyle

An honest man, armed with all the knowledge available to us now, could only state that in some sense, the origin of life appears at the moment to be almost a miracle, so many are the conditions which had to have been satisfied to get it going.[32]

Francis Crick

It is clear that if not one but two or more cells had started life, every single conclusion regarding relatedness of molecules or species is doubtful simply because one cannot know whether branches of a tree or similar branches of different trees are being compared. If we admit the possibility that life started from more "individuals" than the solitary *Urzelle*, we are forced to abandon our interpretation of similarities as automatically implying relatedness . . . the major conclusion to which we wish to draw attention is that these findings strongly suggest that many of the genes purportedly produced by gene duplication have been present very early in the development of life. In fact, we can ask if they were not present so early that we must question whether any gene has come about by duplication or whether all have been there, from the beginning, as a potential for species development.[33]

Christian Schwabe and Gregory Warr

To a large extent, the mutual affinities of the mammalian orders continue to puzzle systematists, even though comparative anatomy and amino acid sequencing offer a massive data base from which these relationships could potentially be adduced. . . . Qualitative comparisons between the morphologically based and molecularly based trees were also made; only moderate congruence between the two was observed. Moreover, there was a general lack of congruence between the cladograms specified by each of the four proteins. . . . Because the cladograms specified by the four proteins herein considered were widely incongruent, we question how much confidence can be placed in the results of tandem-alignment analyses.[34]

A. R. Wyss, J. M. Novacek, and M. C. McKenna

Despite the fact that no convincing explanation of how random evolutionary processes could have resulted in such an ordered pattern of diversity, the idea of uniform rates of evolution is presented in the literature as if it were an empirical discovery. The hold of the evolutionary paradigm is so powerful, that an idea which is more like a principle of medieval astrology than a serious twentieth-century theory has become a reality for evolutionary biologists.[35]

Michael Denton

In any case, no real evolutionist, whether gradualist or punctuationist, uses the fossil record as evidence in favor of the theory of evolution as opposed to special creation.[36]

Mark Ridley

The last word on the credibility and course of evolution lies with the paleontologist.[37]

Gavin de Beer

Naturalists must remember that the process of evolution is revealed only through fossil forms. A knowledge of paleontology is, therefore, a prerequisite; only paleontology can provide them with the evidence of evolution and reveal its cause and mechanisms. . . . That is why we constantly have recourse to paleontology, the only true science of evolution.[38]

Pierre-Paul Grassé

The fossil record affords an opportunity to choose between evolutionary and creationist models for the origin of the earth and its life forms.[39]

B. F. Glenister and B. J. Witzke

. . . The facts of greatest general importance are the following. When a new phylum, class, or order appears, there follows a quick, explosive (in terms of geological time) diversification so that practically all orders or families known appear suddenly and without any apparent transitions.

. . . Moreover, within the slowly evolving series, like the famous horse series, the decisive steps are abrupt, without transition: . . .[40]

R. B. Goldschmidt

The almost universal absence of fully documented transitions between species (a key creationist argument) has recently been underlined by scientists like Eldredge and Gould. Unfortunately, the biological processes involved in their own punctuated equilibria model are not yet all that clear, and anti-evolutionists can and have made effective use of these problems to undermine their opponents' arguments.[41]

M. R. Johnson

Missing links in the sequence of fossil evidence were a worry to Darwin. He felt sure they would eventually turn up, but they are still missing and seem likely to remain so.[42]

E. R. Leach

Unfortunately, the intermediate stages hardly ever seemed to exist in the fossil record (Huxley's later trumpeting about *Archaeopteryx* notwithstanding).

Anderson and Evensen's data does not support Eldredge and Gould's claim that speciating populations are very small. It can also be asked whether evolution is rapid in small populations. Smaller populations have lower total rates of mutation which can cause lower rates of evolution (e.g., Maynard Smith, *Am. Nat.* 110,331: 1976).[43]

Mark Ridley

Despite the bright promise that paleontology provides a means of "seeing" evolution, it has presented some nasty difficulties for evolutionists the most notorious of which is the presence of "gaps" in the fossil record. Evolution requires intermediate forms between species and paleontology does not provide them.[44]

David B. Kitts

Much evidence can be adduced in favour of the theory of evolution—from biology, bio-geography and paleontology, but I still think that, to the unprejudiced, the fossil record of plants is in favour of special creation.[45]

E. J. H. Corner

The fossil record is of little use in providing direct evidence of the pathways of descent of the phyla or of invertebrate classes. Each phylum with a fossil record had already evolved its characteristic body plan when it first appeared, so far as we can tell from the fossil remains, and no phylum is connected to any other via intermediate fossil types. Indeed, none of the invertebrate classes can be connected with another class by series of intermediates.[46]

J. W. Valentine

All three subdivisions of the bony fishes first appear in the fossil record at approximately the same time. They are already widely divergent morphologically, and they are heavily armored. How did they originate? What allowed them to diverge so widely? How did they all come to have heavy armor? And why is there no trace of earlier, intermediate forms?[47]

Gerald T. Todd

... But whatever ideas authorities may have on the subject, the lungfishes, like every other major group of fishes that I know, have their origins firmly based in *nothing*. ...

... I have often thought how little I should like to have to prove organic evolution in a court of law.[48]

Errol White

Where information regarding transitional forms is most eagerly sought, it is least likely to be available. We have no intermediate fossils between rhipidistian fish and early amphibians or between primitive insectivores and bats; only a single species, *Archaeopteryx lithographica* represents the transition between dinosaurs and birds. On the other hand, certain genera of fish, amphibians, and reptiles are known from thousands upon thousands of fossils from every continent.

Perhaps we should not be surprised that vertebrate paleontologists did not support the prevailing view of slow, progressive evolution but tended to elaborate theories involving saltation, orthogenesis, or other vitalistic hypothesis. Most of the evidence provided by the fossil record does *not* support a strictly gradualistic interpretation, as pointed out by Eldredge and Gould (1972), Gould and Eldredge (1977), Gould (1985), and Stanley (1979, 1982).[49]

R. L. Carroll

The theory that birds evolved from dinosaurs, which has gone in and out of fashion since the 19th century and is now back in vogue, leads the scientists who subscribe to it to imagine that dinosaurs were highly mobile and very active, like birds today, and that they even had feathers. ... Unfortunately the bird theory requires "fixing" too often to inspire confidence. . . . The theory linking dinosaurs to birds is a pleasant fantasy that some scientists like because it provides a direct entry into a past that we otherwise can only guess about. But unless more convincing evidence is uncovered, we must reject it and move forward to the next best idea.[50]

Larry D. Martin

At the higher level of evolutionary transition between basic morphological designs, gradualism has always been in trouble, though it remains the "official" position of most Western evolutionists. Smooth intermediates between *Baupläne* are almost impossible to construct, even in thought experiments; there is certainly no evidence for them in the fossil record (curious mosaics like *Archaeopteryx* do not count).[51]

S. J. Gould and Niles Eldredge

The extreme rarity of transitional forms is the trade secret of paleontology. . . . The history of most fossil species includes two features particularly inconsistent with gradualism:

1. Stasis. Most species exhibit no directional change during their tenure on earth. They appear in the fossil record looking much the same as when they disappear; morphological change is usually limited and directionless.

2. Sudden appearance. In any local area, a species does not arise gradually by the steady transformation of its ancestors; it appears all at once and "fully formed."[52]

S. J. Gould

Of course there are many gaps in the synapsid fossil record, with intermediate forms between the various known groups almost invariably unknown. . . .

Gaps at a lower taxonomic level, species and genera, are practically universal in the fossil record of the mammal-like reptiles. In no single adequately documented case is it possible to trace a transition, species by species, from one genus to another. . . .

The apparent rate of morphological change in the main lineages of the mammal-like reptiles varies. The sudden appearance of new higher taxa, families and even orders, immediately after a mass extinction, with all the features more or less developed, implies a very rapid evolution.[53]

T. S. Kemp

Well, we are now about 120 years after Darwin and the knowledge of the fossil record has been greatly expanded. We now have a quarter of a million fossil species but the situation hasn't changed much. The record of evolution is still surprisingly jerky and, ironically, we have even fewer examples of evolutionary transition than we had in Darwin's time. By this I mean that some of the classic cases of Darwinian change in the fossil record, such as the evolution of the horse in North America, have had to be discarded or modified as a result of more detailed information—what appeared to be a nice simple progression when relatively few data were available now appears to be much more complex and much less gradualistic. So Darwin's problem has not been alleviated. . . .[54]

David Raup

It must be significant that nearly all the evolutionary stories I learned as a student, from Trueman's *Ostrea/Gryphea* to Carruther's *Zaphrentis delanouei,* have now been "debunked." Similiary, my own experience of more than twenty years looking for evolutionary lineages among the Mesozoic Brachiopoda has proved them equally elusive.[55]

Derek V. Ager

Some paleontologists, like Johanson's colleague Owen Lovejoy, believe that the so-called valgus angle of the knee, the extent to which the leg bends 'outward' at the knee, is an important indication of bipedality, because such a bend enables the foot to be placed more directly under the centre of gravity of the body, giving better balance and more time for the free leg to swing forward during walking.

Jack Prost, of the University of Illinois at Chicago Circle, maintains the opposite view; he says that the angle reflects the ability to climb, and circumstantial evidence in favor of this alternative theory is that among monkeys and apes the greatest angle of valgus is found in the orangutan and the spider monkey, extremely able arborealists who have the same knee angle as humans . . . Lucy's more human knee could be an adaptation to tree-climbing.[56]

Jeremy Cherfas

. . . the australopithecines known over the last several decades from Olduvai and Sterkfontein, Kromdraai and Makapansgat, are now irrevocably removed from a place in the evolution of human bipedalism, possibly from a place in a group any closer to humans than to African apes and certainly from any place in the direct human lineage.[57]

Charles Oxnard

Though the standard idea is that some of the australopithecines are implicated in a lineage of humanlike forms, the new possibility suggested in this book, a radiation separate from either humans or African apes, has received powerful corroboration. It is now being recognized widely that the australopithecines are not structurally closely similar to humans, that they must have been living at least in part in arboreal environments, and that many of the later specimens were contemporaneous or almost so with the earliest members of the genus *Homo*.[58]

Charles Oxnard

(Here Oxnard is speaking relative to recent studies on *Australopithecus afarensis*—Donald Johanson's "Lucy.")

. . . for example, no scientist could logically dispute the proposition that man, without having been involved in any act of divine creation, evolved from some ape-like creature in a very short space of time—speaking in geological terms—without leaving any fossil traces of the steps of the transformation.[59]

Lord Zuckerman

Creationists claim that their law broadened the freedom of teachers by permitting the introduction of controversial material. But no statute exists in any state to bar instruction in 'creation science.' It could be taught before, and it can be taught now.[60]

S. J. Gould

Unless we are vigilant, the recent Supreme Court victory for evolutionists could also turn sour. The actual decision in the Louisiana case was weaker than Judge William Overton's earlier ruling overturning a similar law in Arkansas. The Supreme Court ruling did not, in any way, outlaw the teaching of "creation science" in public school classrooms. Quite simply it ruled that, in the form taken by the Louisiana law, it is unconstitutional to demand equal time for this particular subject. "Creation science" can still be brought into science classrooms if and when teachers and administrators feel that it is appropriate. Numerous surveys have shown that teachers and administrators favor just this route. And, in fact, "creation science" is currently being taught in science courses throughout the country.[61]

Michael Zimmerman

No teacher should be dismayed at efforts to present creation as an alternative to evolution in biology courses: indeed, at this moment creation is the only alternative to evolution. Not only is this worth mentioning, but a comparison of the two alternatives can be an excellent exercise in logic and reason. Our primary goal as educators should be to teach students to think and such a comparison, particularly because it concerns an issue in which many have special interests or are even emotionally involved, may accomplish that purpose better than most others. . . .

Creation and evolution in some respects imply backgrounds about as different as one can imagine. In the sense that creation is an alternative to evolution for any specific question, a case against creation is a case for evolution and *vice versa.*[62]

R. D. Alexander

. . . that the search for knowledge and understanding of the physical universe and of the living things that inhabit it should be conducted under conditions of intellectual freedom, without religious, political or ideological restrictions. . . . That freedom of inquiry and dissemination of ideas require that those so engaged be free to search where their inquiry leads . . . without political censorship and without fear of retribution in consequence of unpopularity of their conclusions. Those who challenge existing theories must be protected from rataliatory reactions.[63]

National Academy of Sciences

The world does not explain itself . . . it is absurd for the
Evolutionist to complain that it is unthinkable for an
admittedly unthinkable God to make everything out of
nothing, and then pretend that it is *more* thinkable that
nothing should turn itself into everything.[64]

G. Chesterton

But ask now the beasts, and they shall teach thee; and the fowl
of the air, and they shall tell thee: Or speak to the earth, and
it shall teach thee: and the fishes of the sea shall declare unto
thee. Who knoweth not in all these that the hand of the LORD
hath wrought this? (Job 12:7-9 KJV).

References

1. Søren Løtrup, *Darwinism: The Refutation of a Myth,* Croom Helm,
    New York, 1987, p. 422.
2. S. J. Gould, *Paleobiology* 6(1):120 (1980).
3. Sharon Begley, "Science Contra Darwin," *Newsweek,* April 8,
    1985, p. 80.
4. E. O. Wiley, *Systematic Zoology* 24(2):270 (1975).
5. Michael Denton, *Evolution: A Theory in Crisis,* Burnett Books,
    London, 1985, pp. 353, 354.
6. Colin Patterson, as quoted by Brian Leith, *The Listener,* 8 October
    1981, p. 392.
7. Marjorie Grene, *Encounter,* November 1959, p. 48.
8. Richard Lewontin, in *Scientists Confront Creationism,* L. R. God-
    frey, Ed., W. W. Norton and Co., New York, 1983, p. XXVI.
9. "What Is Humanism?" Humanist Community of San Jose,
    San Jose, California, 95106.
10. Julian Huxley, as quoted in Ref. 9.
11. Paul Ehrlich and L. C. Birch, *Nature* 214:352 (1967).
12. C. L. Harris, *Perspectives in Biology and Medicine,* Winter 1975,
    pp. 179-184.
13. L. H. Matthews, in his Introduction to *The Origin of Species,* Char-
    les Darwin, J. M. Dent & Sons, Ltd., London, 1971, p. X.
14. S. J. Gould, *Nature* 285:343 (1980).
15. J. E. O'Rourke, *Journal of Science* 276:51 (1976).

16. Francisco Ayala, *Journal of Heredity* 68:3-10 (1977).

17. Julian Huxley, in *Issues in Evolution*, Sol Tax, Ed., University of Chicago Press, Chicago, 1960, p. 45.

18. Julian Huxley and Jacob Bronowski, *Growth of Ideas*, Prentice-Hall, Inc., Englewood Cliffs, 1986, p. 99.

19. Richard Lewontin, in *Scientists Confront Creationism*, Laurie Godfrey, Ed., W. W. Norton & Co., New York, 1983, p. XXV.

20. Arthur Keith, *Evolution and Ethics*, Putnam, New York, 1947, p. 15.

21. G. R. Bozarth, *The American Atheist*, September 1978, p. 30.

22. Jacque Monod, "Secret of Life," Transcript of a television interview with Laurie John on the Australian Broadcasting Co., June 10, 1976.

23. John Dunphy, *The Humanist*, Jan./Feb. 1983, p. 26.

24. Huston Smith, *Christian Century*, July 7-14, 1982, p. 755.

25. John Gliedman, *Science Digest Special*, Sept./Oct. 1980, pp. 55-57.

26. Isaac Asimov, *Smithsonian Institute Journal*, June 1970, p. 6.

27. G. J. Van Wylen, *Thermodynamics*, John Wiley and Sons, New York, 1959, p. 169.

28. John Keosian, *Origin of Life* 1978:569-574.

29. Klaus Dose, *Interdisciplinary Science Reviews* 13(4):348 (1988).

30. H. P. Yockey, *Journal of Theoretical Biology* 67:377 (1977).

31. Sir Fred Hoyle, *New Scientist*, 19 November 1981, pp. 526-527.

32. Francis Crick, *Life Itself*, Simon and Schuster, New York, 1981, p. 88.

33. Christian Schwabe and Gregory Warr, *Perspectives in Biology and Medicine* 27(3):468,474 (1984).

34. A. R. Wyss, M. J. Novacek, and M. C. McKenna, *Molecular Biological Evolution* 4(2):99 (1987).

35. Michael Denton, Ref. 5, p. 306.

36. Mark Ridley, *New Scientist* 90:830 (1981).

37. Gavin de Beer, *Science* 143:1311 (1964).

38. Pierre-Paul Grassé, *Evolution of Living Organisms*, Academic Press, New York, 1977, p. 4.

39. B. F. Glenister and B. J. Witzke, in *Did the Devil Make Darwin Do It?*, D. B. Wilson, Ed., Iowa State University Press, Ames, 1983, p. 58.

40. R. B. Goldschmidt, *American Scientist*, 40:97 (1952).

41. M. R. Johnson, *South African Journal of Science* 78:267 (1982).

42. E. R. Leach, *Nature* 293:19 (1981).

43. Mark Ridley, *Nature* 286:444 (1980).

44. D. B. Kitts, *Evolution* 28:467 (1974).

45. E. J. H. Corner, in *Contemporary Botanical Thought,* A. M. MacLeod and L. S. Cobley, Eds., Quadrangle Books, Chicago, 1961, p. 97.

46. J. W. Valentine, in *What Darwin Began,* L. R. Godfrey, Ed., Allyn and Bacon, Inc., Boston, 1985, p. 263.

47. G. T. Todd, *American Zoologist* 20(4):757 (1980).

48. Errol White, *Proceedings of the Linnaean Society of London* 177:8 (1966).

49. R. L. Carroll, *Vertebrate Paleontology and Evolution,* W. H. Freeman and Co., New York, 1988, p. 4.

50. Larry D. Martin, *Sunday World-Herald,* Omaha, Nebraska, January 19, 1992, p. 17b. (Dr. Martin is professor of systematics and ecology at the University of Kansas and head of the vertebrate paleontology division in the university's museum of natural history.)

51. S. J. Gould and Niles Eldredge, *Paleobiology* 3:147 (1977).

52. S. J. Gould, *Natural History* 86:14 (1977).

53. T. S. Kemp, *Mammal-Like Reptiles and the Origin of Mammals,* Academic Press, New York, 1982, pp. 3, 319, 327.

54. David Raup, *Field Museum of Natural History Bulletin* 50(1):25 (1979).

55. D.V. Ager, *Proceedings Geological Association* 87:132 (1976).

56. Jeremy Cherfas, *New Scientist,* January 20, 1983, p. 173.

57. Charles Oxnard, *The Order of Man,* Yale University Press, New Haven, 1984, p. 332.

58. Charles Oxnard, *ibid.,* pp. iii and iv of Nota Bene.

59. Solly Zuckerman, *Beyond the Ivory Tower,* Taplinger Publishing Co., New York, 1970, p. 64.

60. S. J. Gould, *New York Times Magazine,* July 19, 1987, p. 34.

61. Michael Zimmerman, *Bioscience* 17(9):635 (1987).

62. R. D. Alexander, in *Evolution Versus Creationism: The Public Education Controversy,* J. Peter Zetterberg, Ed., Oryx Press, Phoenix, 1983, p. 91.

63. National Academy of Sciences Resolution, "An Affirmation of Freedom of Inquiry and Expression," April 1976.

64. G. Chesterton, as quoted by P. E. Hodgson in his review of *Chesterton: A Seer of Science,* by Stanley L. Jaki, National Review, June 5, 1987.

Appendix I

The following articles appeared as Impact Articles No.'s 57 and 58 in March and April 1978, respectively, in the ICR Impact Series, published monthly by the Institute for Creation Research, P.O. Box 2667, El Cajon, California, 92021. They were written in response to the often mistaken notion that Ilya Prigogine, Nobel Prize winner in physics in 1977, had solved the problem of evolution and the Second Law of Thermodynamics, or at least had made significant headway.

THERMODYNAMICS AND THE ORIGIN OF LIFE - PART I

Number 57
March 1978
by Henry M. Morris

Evolutionists are embarrassed by the Second Law of Thermodynamics. Dr. V. F. Weisskoff, President of the American Academy of Arts and Sciences, has recently pointed up the problem in the following words:

> The evolutionary history of the world from the 'big bang' to the present universe is a series of gradual steps from the simple to the complicated, from the unordered to the organized, from the formless gas of elementary particles to the morphic atoms and molecules and further to the still more structured liquids and solids, and finally to the sophisticated living organisms. There is an obvious tendency of nature from disorder to order and organization. Is this tendency in contradiction to the famous second law of thermodynamics, which says that disorder must increase in nature? The law says that entropy, the measure of disorder, must grow in any natural system.[1]

The "obvious tendency of nature from disorder to order and organization" is, of course, only an assumption of evolutionists. The real tendency in the natural world, as expressed by the Second Law of Thermodynamics, is from order and organization to disorder. This very obvious problem is commonly bypassed by evolutionists with the naive statement that the earth is a system open to the energy of the sun and that this fact resolves the problem! Creationists in turn have reminded them that while an open system and available energy constitute *necessary* conditions before a growth in order (or information) can take place, they are not *sufficient* conditions. In addition, there must be a pre-coded program containing the necessary information to direct the growth of the system and one or more conversion mechanisms to convert the external energy into the highly specific work of internal growth. Since the vast system of the hypothetically evolving biosphere as a space-time continuum seems to lack both a program and mechanism, it is clearly precluded by the Second Law.[2]

It has been especially difficult to imagine ways to get life started in the first place. How can unordered non-living chemical elements be combined naturalistically into the extremely sophisticated ordered information in a replicating system? The common belief that this problem has been practically solved by modern biochemists is premature, to say the least. Freeman Dyson says:

We are still at the very beginning of the quest for understanding of the origin of life. We do not yet have even a rough picture of the nature of the obstacles that prebiotic evolution has had to overcome. We do not have a well-defined set of criteria by which to judge whether any given theory of the origin of life is adequate.[3]

The nature of the problem in trying to account for the origin of a replicating system has been well expressed by Angrist and Hepler:

Life, the temporary reversal of a universal trend toward maximum disorder, was brought about by the production of information mechanisms. In order for such mechanisms to first arise it was necessary to have matter capable of forming itself into a self-reproducing structure that could extract energy from the environment for its first self-assembly. Directions for the reproduction of plans, for the extraction of energy and chemicals from the environment, for the growth of sequence and the mechanism for translating instructions into growth all had to be simultaneously present at that moment. This combination of events has seemed an incredibly unlikely happenstance and often divine intervention is prescribed as the only way it could have come about.[4]

Small wonder! In the real world, every effect must have an adequate cause, but the usual laws of science do not seem to intimidate evolutionists. In the strange land of evolutionary credulity, wonderful things may happen—plans draw themselves, mechanisms design themselves, order generates itself from chaos, and life creates itself! Yet evolutionists call creationists unscientific because they postulate an adequate Cause (divine intervention) to account for the marvelous Effect called life.

In creation/evolution debates, creationists commonly place great emphasis on the Second Law of Thermodynamics as an overwhelming evidence against evolution. Although there have been approximately a hundred such debates held within the past four years, with leading evolutionist professors on major college and university campuses, the latter have never yet been able to come up with an answer of any consequence to this problem. Even more amazingly, most of them do not even seem to understand the problem, either dismissing it as irrelevant or else making some vacuous reference to ice crystals or open systems!

There are apparently only a few evolutionists who realize the magnitude of the problem and have been trying to find a solution. Some of these attempts have been discussed in previous Impact articles.[5,6]

By far the most important of these efforts, however, has been the suggestion of a Belgian scientist named Ilya Prigogine. Dr. Prigogine is a widely known chemist and thermodynamicist, with faculty appointments both at the University Libre de Bruxelles and at the University of Texas at Austin. An indication of the strategic significance of Prigogine's ideas is that they have recently won for him the Nobel Prize in Chemistry. Judging from the popular announcements, the main reason for this award was the ray of hope Prigogine has given evolutionists in their battle with entropy!

According to *Newsweek,* for example, the significance of Prigogine's work is as follows:

> Scientists who have sought to explain the origin of life as the result of chemical interactions have been confounded by the second law of thermodynamics: energy tends to dissipate and organized systems drift inevitably toward entropy, or chaos. . . . Prigogine's insights will give biologists new grounds for learning how the first random molecules organized themselves into life forms. . . . Prigogine thinks the Nobel committee recognized that his work is building a bridge between the physical and human sciences.[7]

According to an interview in a professional chemical journal, Prigogine himself was "really surprised" at the decision of the Nobel committee. He also said: "The fact that the Nobel committee has chosen this one subject is a great encouragement."[8]

If, indeed, Prigogine had shown that the tremendous amount of information necessary for molecular self-replication can be produced naturalistically despite the entropy law, his achievement would be well worth the Nobel Prize. It would be all the more remarkable in view of the fact that Prigogine himself has "not actually worked in a chemistry lab for decades."[9] At best, however, he has only offered a theoretical speculation, not an experimental demonstration. It is hard to avoid the suspicion that the Nobel award in this case was due less to the scientific value of Prigogine's achievement than to the urgent need of the evolutionary establishment for some kind of answer, no matter how superficial, to the entropy problem.

Just how has Dr. Prigogine proposed to harmonize molecular evolution with the Second Law? Here it is, in his own words:

> In all these phenomena, a new ordering mechanism . . . appears. For reasons to be explained later, we shall refer to this principle as *order through fluctuations*. The structures are created by the continuous flow of energy and matter from the outside world; their maintenance requires a critical distance from equilibrium, that is, a minimum level of dissipation. For all these reasons we have called them dissipative structures.[10]

These "dissipative structures" are supposed to exhibit a higher degree of structure, or order, than they possessed before being subjected to a large influx of outside energy, while at the same time their generation is accompanied by a large dissipation of energy in the form of heat. The main example cited by Prigogine is the formation of convection currents and vortices in a fluid subjected to a temperature gradient.

Under such conditions, vortices (or other fluctuations or instabilities) may be generated and maintained. These, supposedly, manifest higher "order" than the system possessed previously, even though such order has been produced at the cost of excessive over-all energy dissipation. This phenomenon has long been familiar to hydrodynamicists, but Prigogine suggested that it may also apply in certain chemical and biological reactions which are proceeding under non-equilibrium conditions.

That such vortices or any other analagous "dissipative structures" could actually be called a device for naturalistic generation of higher order, and then that such a description could be awarded a Nobel Prize is almost unbelievable! This writer's own Ph.D. dissertation over a quarter of a century ago described in quantitative and analytical form the generation of turbulent vortices in fluid flow over rough surfaces.[11] These, indeed, are dissipative structures, requiring the dissipation of much flow energy in the form of heat for their generation. Their own rotational energies in turn are soon dissipated by breaking up into smaller vortices, so that no permanent increase in order is produced, even if such vortices are assumed (very questionably) to possess a higher degree of order than the energy gradient which generated them. "Big whirls make little whirls that feed on their velocity; little whirls make tiny whirls, and so on to viscosity!"

In any case dissipative structures could hardly serve as a substrate for still *higher* order, since they themselves require an abnormally large input of energy just to maintain their own structures. Prigogine himself says that, as far as chemical or biological reactions are concerned, the generation of dissipative structures is apparently limited to "auto-catalytic" processes. But catalytic processes, like fluid vortices, do not generate higher order—they merely speed up reactions which themselves are already going downhill thermodynamically in the first place. And any imaginary "auto-catalytic" processes would certainly require already-living systems for their own generation, so they can hardly explain the generation of living systems!

Although Prigogine wistfully expresses the hope that his speculations may someday lead to an understanding of how life may have evolved from non-life, he is at least more cautious than those of his fellow evolutionists who are currently exuberating over it. He warns:

> It would be too simple to say that the concepts of life and dissipative structures are intermingled. . . . But it is not just one instability that makes it possible to cross the threshold between life and non-life; it is, rather, a succession of instabilities of which we are only now beginning to identify certain stages.[12]

In a later section, he again suggests caution:

> But let us have no illusions. If today we look into the situation where the analogy with the life sciences is the most striking—even if we discovered within biological systems some operations distant from the state of equilibrium—our research would still leave us quite unable to grasp the extreme complexity of the simplest of organisms.[13]

One thing is clear. Whatever of scientific value may be deduced from Prigogine's analysis, he has *not* solved the problem of harmonizing entropy with evolution and he has certainly *not* shown that life can evolve from non-living chemicals. His dissipative structures do not constitute either the required program or the required mechanism to enable any kind of permanently increased order to be produced in an open system. However, he should perhaps be commended for trying. Maybe next he can work on a perpetual motion machine!

The problem of the origin of life can really only be resolved by recognition of the omnipotent Creator. The only alternative to belief in special creation is credulous faith in impotent Chance.

> We are faced with the idea that genesis was a statistically unlikely event. We are also faced with the certainty that it occurred. Was there a temporary repeal of the second law that permitted a "fortuitous concourse of atoms"? If so, study of the Repealer and Genesis is a subject properly left

to theologians. Or we may hold with the more traditional scientific attitude that the origin of life is beclouded merely because we don't know enough about the composition of the atmosphere and other conditions on the earth many eons ago.[14]

Yes, not knowing how life could be formed would indeed becloud the understanding of the origin of life! The problem is why this should be called the scientific attitude when all the scientific evidence continues to support special creation.

References

1. Victor F. Weisskopf, "The Frontiers and Limits of Science," *American Scientist*, Vol. 65, July-August 1977, p. 409.

2. Henry M. Morris, *The Scientific Case for Creation* (San Diego: Creation-Life Publishers, 1977) pp. 11-26.

3. Freeman Dyson, "Honoring Dirac," *Science*, Vol. 185, September 27, 1974, p. 1161. Dyson is at Princeton's Institute for Advanced Study.

4. Stanley W. Angrist and Loren G. Hepler, *Order and Chaos* (New York: Basic Books, Inc., 1967), pp. 203-204.

5. Henry M. Morris, "Entropy and Open Systems" (ICR Impact Series No. 40) *Acts & Facts*, October 1976.

6. Jerry R. Bergman, "Albert Szent-Gyorgyi's Theory of Syntropy and Creationism" (ICR Impact Series No. 54), *Acts & Facts*, December 1977.

7. "Chemistry: The Flow of Life" *Newsweek*, October 17, 1977, p. 87.

8. *Chemical and Engineering News*, October 17, 1977, p. 4.

9. *Newsweek, op. cit.*

10. Ilya Prigogine, Gregoire Nicolis and Agnes Babloyants, "Thermodynamics of Evolution," *Physics Today*, Vol. 25, November 1972, p. 25.

11. Henry M. Morris, *A New Concept of Flow in Rough Conduits* (Minneapolis, University of Minnesota, 1951, 157 pp.).

12. Ilya Prigogine, "Can Thermodynamics Explain Biological Order? *Impact of Science on Society,* Vol. XXIII, No. 3, 1973, p. 169.
13. *Ibid.,* p. 178.
14. Angrist and Hepler, *op. cit.,* p. 205.

THERMODYNAMICS AND THE ORIGIN OF LIFE - PART II

Number 58
April 1978
by Duane T. Gish

Prigogine's speculative model is enshrouded with a considerable amount of complex mathematics that is difficult if not impossible to understand by non-mathematicians. This immediately renders it incomprehensible to most scientists, certainly to most biologists. Nevertheless, Prigogine's model sounds deliciously scientific and it has been eagerly welcomed by evolutionists who are looking for a way to overcome the insuperable barrier the Second Law of Thermodynamics poses against an evolutionary origin of life. When Prigogine moves his mathematical model off of paper and out into the real world, however, it then becomes possible for a non-mathematician to examine the chemical and biological assumptions which serve as the basis of his model. An examination of these assumptions reveals that they are totally devoid of any foundation. His model offers no solution whatsoever.

In Prigogine's "evolution model,"[1] a system open to the flow of two monomer species a and b (which may correspond to two kinds of nucleotides, for example, adenylic acid and thymidylic acid) is assumed. Although he doesn't say much about it, a steady in-flow of energy in the form of energy-rich organic chemical molecules must also somehow be provided, and a way must exist to link this in-flow of energy to the synthetic process assumed in the model. Right at this preliminary stage, even before the more serious difficulties of his model are encountered, the model loses all plausibility.

In the absence of living organisms, it would be impossible to supply a sufficient quantity of either the nucleotides or the energy-rich organic molecules to provide the required concentration of these molecules. Under any plausible primitive earth conditions, the rate of destruction of these compounds would so far exceed their rate of formation that no detectable quantities of either could ever accumulate.[2,3]

Even if the ocean were swarming with these molecules, however, Prigogine's model could not explain how life could have evolved. From monomer a, which for the purpose of illustration Prigogine takes to be the nucleotide, adenylic acid (A), Prigogine assumes that the homopolymer, poly-adenylic acid (poly-A) is formed. Poly-A codes for (provides the template for) poly-thymidylic acid (poly-T), so in the presence of poly-A and a supply of thymidylic acid, Prigogine assumes that poly-T will form. Since poly-A not only codes for poly-T, but poly-T codes for poly-A, Prigogine asserts that when this stage is reached, an autocatalytic cycle is switched on. Let us pause here to examine assumptions made at this stage of the model.

First of all, Prigogine assumes that the monomers (the nucleotides) will combine to form polymers in huge quantities (many billions of tons of each polymer must form in order to produce a significant concentration in an ocean containing 350 million cubic miles of water). Actually, for all practical purposes, no polymer at all could form. To form the bonds linking the monomers to form the polymer requires an input of energy. As a consequence this process is energetically highly unfavorable. Rupture of the bonds linking the nucleotides in the polymer, or rupture of the bonds within each nucleotide subunit (such as the sugar-purine bond), on the other hand, releases energy and is thus energetically favorable. Furthermore, to form a polymer of, say, 100 nucleotides requires the formation of 100 inter-nucleotide bonds, the formation of each bond being energetically highly unfavorable. *The destruction of the polymer, however, requires the rupture of only a single bond,* the rupture of which releases energy and is thus energetically favorable. As a consequence, formation of a polymer of even just a few nucleotides would be incredibly slow, but if any polymer did exist, it would break down at a relatively rapid rate. The rate of destruction would enormously exceed the rate of formation, and thus no significant concentration of polymer, even of a dinucleotide, could form under any plausible primitive earth conditions.

Secondly, even if formation of polymer occurred at a significant rate to produce a significant overall amount of polymer, with two monomers present, such as adenylic acid (A) and thymidylic acid (T), it would still be impossible for a significant amount of a particular polymer to form. How in the world would formation of polymers be restricted to poly-A (A-A-A-A-A-A-A-A——A) and poly-T (T-T-T-T-T-T-T-T——-T)? Every possible sequence of A and T would form. For example, the polymer T-A-A-T-A-T-T-T-A-T-A-A-A-T-T, or any other sequence of A and T, would be just as likely to form as a polymer containing 15 A's or 15 T's exclusively. If polymers of 100 nucleotides were formed under assumed primitive earth conditions from only two monomers, 2^{100} (10^{30}, or a million billion billion) different combinations would be produced. This would completely eliminate the possibility of producing a significant quantity of any one particular polymer.

Thirdly, to claim that the presence of two polymers, such as poly-A and poly-T, would establish an autocatalytic cycle is sheer nonsense. Such a system could not be autocatalytic, since neither poly-A nor poly-T (or any other polynucleotide) is catalytic. Neither has the ability to speed up any chemical reaction, in this case the rate at which the bonds linking the nucleotides are formed. Thus neither can be called a catalyst. Prigogine nevertheless calls the assumed cycle autocatalytic, since poly-A codes (provides a template) for poly-T, which in turn codes for poly-A. Thus, he asserts, the rate of production of poly-A would at least be proportional to its concentration. But what Prigogine neglects to mention is *that the rate of destruction of poly-A (or poly-T) would also be proportional to its concentration.* Since both the rate of production and the rate of destruction would tend to increase as the concentration tended to increase, no net effect on the overall concentration would result.

But now, going on with further assumptions in Prigogine's model (in spite of the impossibilities encountered so far), Prigogine assumes that in the formation of poly-A under the coding action of poly-T, errors occur, and as a result a new polymer is formed (let us call it polymer-X). Polymer-X, Prigogine assumes, may now direct the synthesis of a new substance E. He further assumes that E might possibly be a "primitive" protein enzyme which catalyzes the production of polymer-X, as well as its own production. The appearance of this catalyst, it is assumed, produces polymer-X at a much more rapid rate than either poly-A or poly-T is being produced, so the system rapidly shifts far from equilibrium until a new equilibrium is established. Now let us pause once again to see what is wrong with Prigogine's assumptions.

Firstly, no polynucleotide can direct the synthesis of a protein. All enzymes are proteins and consist of long chains of amino acids. In living organisms the gene (a polynucleotide consisting of deoxyribonucleic acid or DNA) for each protein provides only the code for the sequence in which the amino acids occur in the protein, *and that is all it does.* The translation of this information, and the actual synthesis of the protein, requires much, much more.

DNA is only one of many different kinds of molecules required for the synthesis of a protein. To assert that a DNA molecule could direct the synthesis of a protein in the absence of the entire complex apparatus required for this task is simply absurd.

Furthermore, to say that the process was much simpler in the first step toward a living thing is totally contradicted by the evidence. For example, amino acids cannot align themselves along either a DNA or an RNA molecule. There is no "lock-and-key" fit, or any other kind of fit, between any amino acid and any nucleotide. It is chemically and physically impossible, for this reason alone, then, for a DNA or RNA molecule to "direct" the synthesis of a protein. In fact, the chemistry that would naturally occur would wreak havoc on any evolving life.

Secondly, no enzyme is capable of catalyzing both the synthesis of a polynucleotide, such as DNA or RNA, and itself. Thus, there is no enzyme known that catalyzes the formation of chemical bonds between nucleotides to form polynucleotides, and which also catalyzes the formation of chemical bonds between amino acids to form proteins. The chemistry involved in the formation of inter-nucleotide bonds is just too different from the chemistry involved in the formation of chemical bonds between amino acids for that to be possible.

Thirdly, as mentioned above, Prigogine assumes that the "primitive enzyme" catalyzes the production of polymer-X, which codes for his "primitive enzyme." The action of an enzyme cannot be restricted to the formation of any particular polynucleotide, however. There is a single DNA-polymerase in a cell which catalyzes the formation of all DNA molecules. Thus, if Prigogine's hypothetical primitive enzyme did arise, it would not only catalyze the formation of polymer-X, but it would also catalyze the formation of every other polynucleotide that could possibly exist. Thus it would catalyze the formation of the original polymers, poly-A and poly-T, just as readily as it would catalzye the formation of polymer-X. Polymer-X, since it arose originally in a very small amount by error, would remain in very small quantity, relative to the original polymers.

Fourthly, the possibility that just by chance an error in the synthesis of poly-A would produce a new polymer (polymer-X) that is capable of directing the synthesis of a primitive enzyme defies the laws of probability, even if a polynucleotide could indeed direct the synthesis of a protein. No one knows just how an enzyme is capable of catalyzing a particular chemical reaction, but we do know that for the catalysis of a particular chemical reaction only one, or a very few, of the almost infinite possible arrangements of the amino acids in the protein enzyme will work. Each particular chemical task establishes rigid limits on what particular molecules can act as catalysts.

Most present-day enzymes consist of protein molecules containing several hundred amino acids (there are 20 different kinds of amino acids in these proteins). Thus, even a "primitive" enzyme would probably require at least a hundred amino acids. No one really knows, of course, for we have no "primitive" enzymes to study today. Usually the removal of just a few amino acids from either end of present-day enzymes completely destroys their activity, leaving nothing that possesses "primitive" enzyme activity. If we assume, however, that the "primitive" enzyme consists of 100 of the 20 different amino acids that now exist in proteins and that a hundred billion (10^{11}) different possible arrangements of these 100 amino acids, rather than only one or a very few, precise arrangements (as is true in present-day living things) might be able to function as the primitive enzyme, the possibility by chance of getting even a single molecule, let alone billions of tons, of any one of these hundred billion primitive enzymes would essentially be nil.

One hundred amino acids of 20 different kinds can be arranged in 20^{100} (10^{130}) different ways. If 10^{11} of these could function as the primitive enzyme, and if a billion trillion (10^{21}) of the various protein molecules of 100 amino acids formed each second for five billion years (approximately 10^{17} seconds) the chance of getting a single molecule of one of the required sequences is $10^{130}/10^{21}$ x 10^{17} x 10^{11}, or only one chance out of 10^{81}. This is, for all practical purposes, equal to zero probability, since the value of negligible probabilities may be set at $1/10^{50}$ on a cosmic scale.[4]

Summarizing, in Prigogine's model he assumes:

   1. A steady net production of enormous quantities of nucleotides and amino acids on the hypothetical primitive earth by the simple interaction of raw energy and simple gases.

2. A steady net production of enormous quantities of energy-rich organic molecules to supply the required energy.

3. The combination, in enormous quantities, of the nucleotides to form polymers (DNA).

4. The selective formation of homopolymers (such as poly-A and poly-T) rather than the formation of mixed polymers of random sequences.

5. The establishment of an autocatalytic cycle.

6. Errors in the formation of the polymers producing a new polymer which directs the synthesis of a primitive protein enzyme.

7. The primitive protein enzyme catalyzes the formation of both itself and the nucleotide polymer (DNA).

8. The above molecules somehow manage to spontaneously separate themselves from the rest of the world and concentrate into condensed systems coordinated in time and in space.

Not a single one of the above assumptions has any shred of probability under any plausible primitive earth conditions. Improbability piled on improbability equals impossibility.

A mathematical model of almost any imagined process can be made to work on paper as certain assumptions are made. When the model is moved off the paper and out into the real world of chemistry and physics and the assumptions of the model are translated into processes which can actually be tested, it then becomes possible to determine whether the model has any validity. As can be seen from the above discussion, Prigogine's model has no validity whatsoever.

References

1. Ilya Prigogine, G. Nicolis, and A. Babloyantz, *Physics Today,* December 1972, p. 42.
2. D. T. Gish, *Speculations and Laboratory Experiments Related to Theories on the Origin of Life: A Critique,* Creation-Life Publishers, San Diego, 1972.
3. D. T. Gish, "Origin of Life: Critique of Early Stage Chemical Evolution Theories" (ICR Impact Series No. 31) *Acts & Facts,* January 1976.
4. Emil Borel, *Probabilities and Life,* Dover Publishing Company, New York, 1962, p. 28.

Appendix II

The following is all of the correspondence in the possession of the author that pertains to the allegations concerning alleged gross errors in a paper published by David R. Boylan in the *Creation Research Society Quarterly,* Volume 15(3), pp. 133-138 (1978), and the supposed incompetence of creation scientists relative to evolution and the Second Law of Thermodynamics.

Alleged Major Errors in Boylan's *CRSQ* Paper[*]

Major Error I

Consider Boylan's equation (3) which reads as follows:

$$Q_t - W_t^{**} = E_2 - E_1 + \Delta U + \Delta PV + \Delta v^2/2g_c + \Delta Xg/g_c \quad \text{(B3)}$$

---

[*] Personal communication from J. W. Patterson to D. T. Gish in a letter dated May 27, 1980.

[**] As the reader will note in examining Equation (3) of Boylan's paper, W_i actually reads W_s, so Patterson's version of Boylan's Equation (3) contains this error (typo?).

By changing the first "plus sign" on the right side (a "typo"?) to an "equal sign," one could eliminate the obvious mistake. That is, the term $E_1 - E_1$ is really supposed to be the total energy difference ΔE, which in common engineering usage is often written as the sum $\Delta U + \Delta PV + \Delta v^2/2g_c + \Delta X g/g_c$. Hence, as written, Boylan's eq. (3) actually reads: $Q_i - W_i = 2 \Delta E$ which is nonsensical. That the error is a real one, however, and *not* just a "typo," is suggested by Boylan's very next sentence which asserts in effect that under steady flow conditions only one (and not both!) of these ΔE's vanishes! Thus as I see it, the situation with Boylan's equation (3) is hopeless. Beyond that, of course, it is difficult to justify the steady flow condition, $E_2 - E_1 = 0$, which is then conveniently carried on throughout the rest of the analysis.

Major Error II

In order to appreciate the gravity of Boylan's second major error, which is introduced in connection with eq. (10) we must review a fundamental point about entropy, and especially the way in which entropy changes are to be evaluated. In short one can*not* use the differential heat exchanges δQ_i for a real process; i.e., over the actual path when evaluating entropy changes with the formula

$$\Delta S = \int dQ_r/T$$

It is of paramount importance that some sort of reversible path or process be concocted between the two states of interest if one is going to evaluate ΔS with this formula. The subscript r is used precisely to emphasize this extremely important point. To replace δQ_r as Boylan did with a δQ_i quantity such as dQ_i obtained from the First Law in a "typical" process is to totally destroy the equality required for evaluation purposes. In other words, Boylan's eq. (10) is not an equation at all but rather is an inequality based on the famous Clausius inequality for the Second Law and entropy.*

Letter from D. R. Boylan to D. T. Gish, July 9, 1980

David R. Boylan
1516 Stafford
Ames, Iowa 50010
Professional Engineer
Telephone: 515-232-5739

July 9, 1980

Dr. Duane T. Gish
Associate Director
Institute for Creation Research
2716 Madison Avenue
San Diego, CA 92116

Dear Duane:

Thank you for your letter of June 30 and the attached material from Patterson. I am amazed that you can keep up correspondence and be gone so much. I have to admit failure in that department.

---

*   From Mark Zomansky, *Heat and Thermodynamics*, McGraw Hill (1951) QC 311 Z4h3 c.1

10.7 Entropy and Irreversibility. When a system undergoes an irreversible process between an initial equilibrium state and a final equilibrium state, the entropy change of the system is equal to

$$s_f - s_i = R\int_i^f \frac{dQ}{T}$$

where R indicates any reversible process arbitrarily chosen by which the system may be brought from the given initial state to the given final state. No integration is performed over the original irreversible path. The irreversible process is replaced by a reversible one. This can easily be done when the initial and the final state of the system are equilibrium states. When either the initial or the final state is a nonequilibrium state, special methods must be used. At first, we shall limit ourselves to irreversible processes all of which involve initial and final states of equilibrium.

First, let me comment about Patterson's criticisms of my paper. I am surprised that there are only two alleged "errors," after he characterized it as "so bad." His citations are, in fact, not errors at all. They show either a misunderstanding of my paper or a lack of understanding about the subject. Major Error I relates to Equation 3 in my paper. Patterson apparently doesn't recognize this equation as the First Law expression for "open" systems. I purposely chose to use an equation for open systems, since evolutionists generally argue that life processes are "open." In an open system, there is transfer of matter in or out of the system. As a result, the energy balance must be made on the system before and after, as well as on the matter that either enters or leaves the system. Equation 3 does just that. I introduced Equation 3 as "For open systems . . ." In this equation, E, as I have indicated, is the energy of the system. However, the system in this case is not a constant mass system, and E_1 is the energy associated with the initial state. E_2 is for the final state of the system. All of the other terms refer to the mass which is entering or leaving the system. For steady flow, $E_2 = E_1$, i.e. the system parameters are constant. The result is, of course, Equation 4 which is the well-known steady state flow equation. Regardless of the interpretation of Equation 3, it should have been obvious what was intended by Equation 4. It's the one most used in engineering work.

To be more specific, when an initial system, E_1, loses mass, the energy of the final state will be E_2, the energy of the final system, plus energy imparted to the mass lost, which is all the other terms on the right side of Equation 3. E_1 is the initial system state and E_2 is the final system state. Neither of those terms takes into account the energy imparted to the mass leaving.

For steady flow processes, the rate of mass flow into the system equals the rate of mass flow out of the system, and the quantity of material within the system remains constant. All conditions (temperature, pressure, composition) are assumed constant, as well as the rate of heat flow across the boundaries and the rate of work done on the boundaries. For such cases, the system is at any time the same as for any other time and $E_2 = E_1$, giving Equation 4. It applies whether the operation in question is reversible or not. Patterson's analysis is totally wrong. Equation 4 can be viewed as a constant mass equation. Equation 3 cannot. It's as simple as that.

To further establish the validity of Equation 3, I attach developments from two thermodynamics books of the "open" system First Law Equation. The first is from Thermodynamics for Chemical Engineers, by Harold C. Weber and Herman P. Meissner, both Professors at M.I.T. It has been a "standard" for many years. Equation (5.5) on page 69 is the same as my Equation 3, except that I have replaced

$$\Sigma \int \left(h + \frac{Xg}{g_c} + \frac{U_2}{2g_c} \right) dm \quad \text{with the integrated expression.}$$

The second is from Fundamentals of Classical Thermodynamics, by Gordon I. Van Wylen and Richard E. Sonntag, Professors at the University of Michigan. (5.43) on page 124 is the equivalent of Equation 3, with different notations.

Major Error II relates to evaluation of ΔS in Equation 10. It is well known that the expression $\int \dfrac{dQ_i}{T}$ is to be evaluated over a reversible path. If dQ_i includes irreversible heat efforts, a reversible path must be conceived for the integration. Nothing in Equation 10 suggests otherwise. Since ΔS can be determined if a reversible path is conceived, Equation 10 is indeed valid. If a reversible path is not conceivable, corrections for irreversibility can be used. This is the domain of irreversible thermodynamics. The intent of Equation 10, however, is to show the effect of introducing the required $-W_o$ term in an energy balance around any process and not to demonstrate how to integrate $\int \dfrac{dQ_i}{T}$ (by reversible paths) or how to quantitatively determine the other terms.

The fact that reversible paths may be difficult to conceive for life processes is immaterial. I mention at the upper left of page 132 that "It is not always possible quantitatively to evaluate the various states of thermodynamic systems, but it is possible to predict the probable state of a system from thermodynamic principles." I made no attempt to evaluate

$$\int \frac{dQ_i}{T} .$$

It seems Sophomoric to point out that it must be evaluated over reversible processes. In concept, the equation is true and holds for any process.

Now, most processes with which engineers deal, and I suspect with which most scientists deal, are in some measure irreversible. Nevertheless, we go about calculating entropy changes and, in fact, make great use of Equation 10. Engineers, particularly recognize irreversibility. Many scientists calculate properties as if all systems were either ideal, frictionless or reversible. Engineers have long learned that there is irreversibility in most processes and that most things are not "ideal." In dealing with gasses, we use fugacity coefficients which correct for non-ideality, or compressibility factors to simplify calculations. In some cases, we use the reversible integration of Equation 10 to show the limits on the process and then demonstrate that irreversibility prevents us from reaching those limits. If any reversible process can be conceived between the two states in Equation 1, then the calculation is straightforward. If a reversible process cannot be conceived, irreversibility factors must be added or the equation must be used as the limiting case. Actually, Equations 2 through 10 are not directly related to Equation 1. Just above Equation 2, I stated that "In general . . ." these equations apply. The only reason for the development was to demonstrate that open systems and steady flow systems can be readily handled thermodynamically and that a general approach drawn from thermodynamics can be used for life systems. I have not advocated, necessarily, that thermodynamics principles apply to living systems. I have used Stull's pronouncement that they are applicable (see p. 133) and Calvin's assertion that "life is a logical consequence of known chemical principles operating on the composition of matter." The evolutionist position apparently is that life processes are <u>ordinary</u> and <u>simple</u> processes, easily understood by the laws of chemistry and physics. I have then asserted that what we know about ordinary and simple processes should be valid for life processes. My main theme is for emergence of order, a work term, $-W_o$, must be added to the First Law expression.

If these citations of Patterson's are the "Major Errors," the paper in no way is ". . . so gross as to make a laughing-stock of him, of the Editorial Board, of the <u>Quarterly</u>, and of all the <u>C.R.S.Q.</u> readers who have read the paper and failed to even comment on its colossal blunders." Patterson himself has failed to find even one "colossal" blunder! His critique shows the extent to which he will go to discredit the views of those with whom he disagrees.

Sincerely,
Dave Boylan
DRB/srl

Letter from Emmett L. Williams to D. T. Gish, July 9, 1980

5093 Williamsport Drive
Norcross, GA 30071

July 9, 1980

Dr. Duane T. Gish
Institute for Creation Research
2716 Madison Avenue
San Diego, California 92116

---

* G. J. Van Wylen and R. E. Sonntag, *Fundamentals of Classical Thermo-dynamics*, John Wiley and Sons, New York, 1973, pp. 116-121.

Dear Duane:

Thank you for your letter of June 30. I read Boylan's paper over a year ago and thought that it was excellent. I saw no problems with it then and I see none now. May I address Dr. Patterson's allegations. He questions equation 3 in the paper. Enclosed are some pages from an engineering thermodynamics text.[*] You can follow the derivations up to equation 5.44 pg 120 which is very close to Boylan's equation 3

$$Q_{cv} + \Sigma \, \dot{m}_i \left(h_i + \frac{V_i^2}{2} + gZ_i \right) = \frac{dE_{c.v.}}{dt} + \Sigma \, \dot{m}_e \left(h_e + \frac{V_e^2}{2} + gZ_e \right) + W_{c.v.}$$

Consider the process per unit time (integrate the equation over a unit of time).

$$Q_{cv} + \Sigma \, m_i \left(h_i + \frac{V_i^2}{2} + gZ_i \right) = dE_{cv} + \Sigma \, m_e \left(h_e + \frac{V_e^2}{2} + gZ_e \right) + W_{cv}$$

$$Q_{cv} - W_{cv} = dE_{cv} + \Sigma \, m_i \left[h_e - h_i + \frac{V_e^2 - V_i^2}{2} + g \, (Z_e + \, Z_i) \right]$$

$\Sigma \, m_i = \Sigma \, m_e$ steady state, steady flow (SSSF) process equation of continuity

$$Q_{cv} - W_{cv} = E_e - E_i + h_e - h_i + \frac{V_i^2 - V_i^2}{2} + g(Z_e - Z_i)$$

$dE_{cv} = E_e - E_i,$ and express changes per unit mass $\Sigma \, m_i = 1$

$$h = U + PV$$

$$dh = h_e - h_i = dU + d \, (PV)$$

$$Q_{cv} - W_{cv} = E_e - E_i + dU + d(PV) + \, d \left(\frac{V_{cv}^2}{2} \right) + dgZ_{cv} \quad \text{(a)}$$

$$\text{since} \quad \frac{V_e^2 - V_i^2}{2} = d \left(\frac{V_{cv}^2}{2} \right)$$

$$\text{and} \quad g(Z_e - Z_i) = dgZ_{cv}$$

Equation a is essentially Boylan's equation 3. Boylan further reduces the equation for the SSSF process, $E_e - E_i = 0$. Patter-son's second objection about $dS = \int \dfrac{dQ}{T}$ is meaningless.

Anyone working with $dS = \int \dfrac{dQ}{T}$ understands the limitations he mentions.

However, entropy is a state function and $dS = S_2 - S_1$ is the same for reversible and irreversible processes between states 1 and 2. Let me use an example to illustrate the problem solving method.

A system at -5°C contains 1 mole of supercooled water at this temperature at a pressure of 1 atm. By seeding with an ice crystal the water turns into ice at -5°C. What is the entropy change?

This is an <u>irreversible</u> transition. To solve, find a reversible path. The water is first warmed reversibly from -5°C to 0°C, then allowed to turn into ice at 0°C (removal of latent heat of fusion) and the ice is cooled reversibly from 0°C to -5°C.

$$ds = \int_{268}^{273} \frac{C_w dT}{T} - \frac{H}{273} + \int_{273}^{268} \frac{C_i dT}{T}$$

C_w = specific heat of water/mole

C_i = specific heat of ice/mole

H = latent heat of fusion

The entropy change for the irreversible process is the same as that for the imagined reversible process and no inequality is needed as stated by Patterson. Boylan explains how to solve equation 10 in subsequent paragraphs and explains the limitations of a solution.

I repeat, there are no major errors in Boylan's paper. Let me know if I can help you again.

Sincerely,

Emmett L. Williams
Enclosure
ELW/mmw

Memo from D. R. Boylan to J. W. Patterson, July 16, 1980

July 16, 1980
To: Dr. John Patterson
Materials Science & Engineering
102 Engineering Annex

From: D. R. Boylan, Dean
College of Engineering
104 Marston

In regard to my paper on "Constraints,"

1. Equation 3 is the common First Law expression for an open system model where the development of the steady flow Equation 4 is contemplated. It is found in similar form, or with possible different notation, in most comprehensive thermodynamics textbooks. Or, it can be easily developed from an open system flow model. Because of the nature of the readership, I deliberately chose to use the Δ notation rather than the more correct $\Sigma\int$ notation. This was probably a poor choice.

2. As I have indicated, Equations 2 through 10 are for the "general" case. As such, both reversible and irreversible heat effects must be considered. Since the intent of the paper was to examine a view of origins and not to develop techniques for the evaluation of any of the energy terms, the evaluation of $\int \dfrac{dQ_i}{T}$ where irreversible effects are present was omitted. It is well known that for irreversible heat effects, the integral must be strictly evaluated over a reversible path, or special techniques from irreversible thermodynamics used.

3. The typo in Equation 10 was so obvious, I did not bother the Editor to make a correction.

DRB/srl

Memo from J. W. Patterson to D. R. Boylan, July 18, 1980

July 18, 1980
To: Dean Boylan
College of Engineering
104 Marston
From: John W. Patterson
Materials Science and Engineering
102 Engineering Annex

I greatly appreciate receiving your memo re "constraints" which clears up part of the confusion. Ordinarily I would deliberate longer before replying but under the circumstances I think I should respond as promptly as possible—by return mail.

First of all, I can certainly be understanding of typographical errors such as the error of omission which apparently crept into the work integral $\int \frac{W_o}{T}$ (*sic*).

Secondly, I think your memo also clears up the misunderstanding regarding your first law expression. Realizing that the $\Sigma \int$ notation had been suppressed enables me to see how your term $\Delta E = E_2 - E$ could correspond to an energy "accumulation rate" which I tend to visualize at the volume integral $\frac{\partial}{\partial t} \int_v e\rho dV$ taken over the entire open system, or control volume, as we say, (see Joachim E. Lay, Thermodynamics, p. 112-118, Merrill (1963)). This integral would, of course, vanish after the onset of steady flow conditions. I still have serious reservations about assuming typical life processes to be of the steady flow variety. But if that is your assumption, I retract my allegation about the "1 = 2" first law mistake in your *CRSQ* paper. Moreover, I am relieved that this got settled before any of my allegations were commmitted to print.

But your second law (entropy change) derivation is quite another matter. The explanation offered in your memo simply does not seem tenable to me. However, I would certainly welcome further clarification or perhaps one or more pages of relevant reference material which I could scrutinize. Pending receipt of that from you or someone else, I hold that your attempt to embrace both the typical process *and* the corresponding reversible process with one derivation or one expression is out of order. Such a practice totally obscures the most important rule that must be followed when deriving entropy change expressions or when calculating entropy changes numerically. As it is, students have enough trouble getting this straight even when the necessity for employing reversible paths—which are actually fictional in nature—is emphasized repeatedly. As it is, they simply can't resist the tempting mistake of using the δQ of the actual process under consideration when trying to calculate entropy changes from the formula $\int dQ/T$. But from all appearances this is exactly what you did in the "constraints" paper. I can now imagine being challenged on this important point by creationist students, especially those who study *CRSQ* and other creationist literature to supplement the subject matter we teach in our science and engineering classes here.

As you know, I also hold that the anti-evolution second law arguments so widely publicized by ICR, CRS, and other creationist groups are badly mistaken. Moreover, the mistake has been explained to creationists many times and yet they continue to insist on perpetuating their mistaken version. Consequently, speaking as a teacher, an engineer, and as a strong proponent of improved science education for our young people, I feel I can make an important contribution by exposing the mistaken thermodynamic arguments promoted by the likes of Duane Gish and Henry Morris, among others. I also feel that if I am successful, it may restore some of the respect for engineers which many scientists and intellectuals have lost because of the relative visibility of engineers in the creationist camp and the fallacious positions which they have advanced.
cc: Duane Gish

Memo from D. R. Boylan to J. W. Patterson, July 21, 1980

July 21, 1980

To: Dr. John W. Patterson
Materials Science & Engineering
102 Engineering Annex

From: D. R. Boylan, Dean
College of Engineering
104 Marston

Thank you for your note of July 18. I must also respond "off the top," as I will be leaving tomorrow for a two-week vacation.

The constraints on Equation 9 are such that entropy changes could be calculated directly if it were not for the term W_o . Because of the introduction of this term, Equation 10 must, as you point out, be strictly limited to evaluation over a reversible path. To emphasize that point, it might have been better to have used special notations, such as Q_{rev} or "greater than or equal to."

A proper balance between extended development of detail and focus on content or ideas is difficult to achieve. Most editors prefer the latter. Most writers, the first.

DRB/srl

Memo from J. W. Patterson to D. R. Boylan, August 29, 1980

August 20, 1980

To: Dean Boylan
College of Engineering
104 Marston

From: John W. Patterson
MSE
102 Engineering Annex

I am replying to the enclosed Gish-Williams letters but I need some clarifications from you to be sure they haven't misrepresented you in the analysis they have put forward.

First of all, do you feel that the Williams analysis is a faithful representation of what you had in mind in your "process Constraints . . ." paper?

Second, does the ΔS_{TOT} expression* of your eq. (10) apply to the same control volume (taken as the system) as does your quantity $E_2 - E_1 (= \Delta E_{TOT})$? In other words isn't $\Delta S_{TOT} = S(t_2) - S(t_1)$? Where $S(t_i)$ is the total entropy inventory inside the CV at time $t_i = t_2$ and t_1 . Or did you change systems without saying so in going from eq. (4) to eq. (10)? Williams entropy comments would, in my view, be applicable to a unit mass of throughput taken as the system but not to the control volume system.

Finally do you agree with Williams that your system is of the steady state, steady flow (SSSF) variety? In my view, that is the only kind of system to which William's analysis applies (a la the Van Wylen and Sonntag enclosure)?

For now, I will answer Duane the best I can and then provide a more definitive reply later, after receiving your answers to these specific questions.

JWP:mjm

Letter from Emmett L. Williams to Duane T. Gish, September 11, 1980

5093 Williamsport Drive
Norcross, GA 30071

September 11, 1980

---

* Could you supply a reference which uses your integration approach to arrive at an integrated expression like (eq. 10) for ΔS_{TOT} ? I can't find anything on that in my library of thermo books. That would help a lot in clearing this up, I think.

Dr. Duane T. Gish
Institute for Creation Research
2716 Madison Avenue
San Diego, California 92116

Dear Duane:

Thank you for sending me a copy of Patterson's letter of August 20 to you. I am enclosing a copy of his original allegations. As you will note from these and the allegations of August 20 he has completely side-stepped his original objections and moved to new areas. We are dealing with intellectual "sliding sand." No where in his original letter did he deal with reactants and products; he objected to equations and maintained a totally theoretical argument. I assume by his movement away from this issue he has conceded the original arguments.

Let me discuss his "new" first objection keeping in mind his "old" first objection. He claimed that Boylan's equation 3 is suspect. I started with the first law of thermodynamics for open systems and derived Boylan's equation 3. Now considering $aA + bB \leftrightarrow cC + dD$ one simply can move back through the derivation where the entering and existing masses are taken in account. You then solve the equation plugging in the entering and existing masses in the proper places accounting for any unreacted material. The term Q_{cv} would account for any heat of reaction. Any scientist would be aware of this procedure I have just described. In Van Wylen and Sonntag's book several solutions to the first law for open systems are presented. Various forms of the equation are used. You can look in other thermo books and find slightly different forms of the first law for open systems. There isn't an engineer or scientist living who doesn't realize that different forms of an equation must be used to solve different problems. Again I repeat, there is absolutely nothing wrong with Boylan's equation 3.

Also he accuses me of not understanding the life process mentioned by Boylan, and also states that Boylan's equation 3 applies only to steady flow processes (a bad omen to use his words). A rather brief perusal of thermo books will reveal that generally living systems are treated as steady states! This concept is very useful when trying to represent living systems (particularly an adult form).

Patterson's "old" second objection dealt with entropy and irreversibility. This was answered in my letter of July 9 to you. He again sidesteps and discusses another issue. To briefly answer, entropy changes per unit or per unit mass are discussed in thermodynamics textbooks quite often, particularly in irreversible open system processes. Therefore his last objection is meaningless. The entropy change could be expressed per unit mass of reactants.

Sincerely,
Emmett L. Williams
ELW:mmw

Letter from D. R. Boylan to D. T. Gish, December 26, 1989

David R. Boylan
1516 Stafford
Ames, IA 50010

December 26, 1989

Dr. Duane Gish
Institute for Creation Research
10946 N Woodside Ave.
Santee, CA 92071

Dear Duane:
I have just finished reading your Chapter 6 on thermodynamics, the Attack and Counterattack. It is excellent and well written. The references should give anyone who wishes, the opportunity to get informed on this issue and to see that

evolutionists' attacks on creationists are a diversion to suppress serious consideration of the true nature of 'origins'. I am sorry for the delay in responding, but the end of semester activities prevented me from doing so.

I believe your treatment of the issue is fair and accurate. One can't help wonder why evolutionists persist in believing a scenario that is scientifically barren. The answer, of course, is that they do not and will not acknowledge God as the Creator. As others have pointed out, it is not the 'facts' that are in conflict but the 'interpretation' of those facts. Your review of this conflict will help to put this issue in proper perspective.

As to my interaction with Patterson, I can only add a few thoughts. At the beginning, I thought that he might have found some mistakes. I told him that anyone could make a mistake and that I would be willing to address any errors he might have found. He declined to point out any errors, saying it was a 'professional' matter, and instead tried to vilify me in the media. The "Major Error I and Major Error II" never materialized. He called my Equation 3 (in the CRS article) "nonsense" until I pointed out that it was the generally accepted expression of the First Law for open systems and referred him to Van Wylen and Sonntag's "Fundamentals of Classical Thermodynamics".

As you point out, Patterson kept changing his mind on just what were the errors. He tried to make a point of my use of "systems" and "processes" by some strange analogy of ". . gas combustion (a process) being like a tire or an engine . .". He apparently hasn't worked any thermodynamic problems related to gas combustion. In thermodynamic analysis one is at liberty to choose the "system", as Van Wylen puts it (p.17), as "a quantity of matter of fixed mass and identity upon which attention is focused for study . ."

And, on page 220, Van Wylen states ". . the principle of the increase of entropy can be considered as a quantitative general statement of the second law from the macroscopic point of view, AND APPLIES TO COMBUSTION OF FUEL in our automobile engines, the cooling of our coffee, and the processes that take place in our body . ." Note these examples. They are all 'processes'. Obviously, he either doesn't understand the terms himself, or he is just making up criticisms to justify his own personal vendetta of creationists.

Patterson's paper in the American Atheist showed clearly that he doesn't understand the nature of the issue. As you have shown, the ram-jet pump is not an example of ". . how natural evolution works . ." as he claims. The ram-jet pump was 'designed'. It is not a 'natural' occurring development. And it only works where a significant hydraulic head is available. It also requires frequent maintenance (by the same intelligence that designed it) which is one of the reasons you don't see many of them anymore. For someone who claims to be an expert, this is unbelievable!

The article in the Proceedings of the Iowa Academy of Science, which I had not seen until reprinted by the Spirit of the Lord Charitable Fund (whatever that is), is by far the most telling "blunder" that Patterson has made. In his article "An Engineer Looks at the Creationist Movement" he states ". . by definition of steady state there can be no change in the entropy inventory (nor of any other extensive property) for steady state systems . . All these properties including entropy must remain steady or fixed in value . ." He references Van Wylen, page 235. Unfortunately, he is not well read in the book he references. On page 127 of that book, the authors state under the heading Steady-State, Steady Flow Process, ". . consider a centrifugal air compressor that operates with constant mass rate of flow into and out of the compressor, constant properties AT EACH POINT across the inlet and exit ducts, a constant rate of heat transfer to the surroundings, and constant power input. At each point in the compressor the properties are constant with time, even though the properties of a given elemental mass of air VARY AS IT FLOWS THROUGH THE COMPRESSOR." What Patterson didn't read in his reference on page 235 were the words ". . at any point within the control volume . .". Even so, only the first term of the second law control volume equation equals zero. On the very next page, 236, the authors give the resulting equation which has a change in entropy term for the mass crossing the control volume boundary. Again, the claimed "blunder" is his own not mine.

As I told Patterson, I am willing to correct any error which might have been made. The letters to the editor of most scientific journals show that errors do creep in the best of manuscripts. Most of these letters are gracious attempts to help the scientific community. This is not the case with Patterson. His purpose, unfortunately, is to discredit anyone who holds the creationist position.

I enclose a copy of page 249, Van Wylen. I believe you will find it interesting.

Duane, I hope these comments are helpful. Actually, your manuscript doesn't need help. It will, on the other hand, help others who have not been in the midst of the controversy.

Sincerely,
D. R. Boylan

On the following pages is an article by D. R. Boylan as it appeared in the Creaion Research Society Quarterly, Volume 15, December, 1978.

PROCESS CONSTRAINTS IN LIVING SYSTEMS
D. R. Boylan*

Received 21 April 1978

During the past ten years major advances have been made in understanding living systems. Of particular importance is the unfolding of the chemical nature of these systems. It is instructive, therefore, to examine living systems as ordinary chemical processes. Constraints known to be applicable to such processes should then be applicable to living systems. It is the purpose of this presentation to suggest a few such constraints.

Recently, the Office of Student Life sponsored a Religion and Life Seminar on campus. One of the topics was "Finding Our Roots: Created or Evolved." The subject is of timely interest, and much debate in regard to "roots" is current. Some of this debate centers on the age-old argument of creation vs. evolution. The issue will not be settled in this discussion, or in any other for that matter, since origins cannot be subjected to scientific scrutiny. Some will argue that evolution has been proved and, therefore, any other view is either not scientific or not worthy of serious consideration. Such an attitude is naive since *any* construction of origins must remain speculative. Neither creation or evolution can be proved, except possibly by inductive reasoning, as no life existed at the "beginning," and no extra-Biblical record is available of the event or the occurrence. We can examine only a small spectrum of the system and that only over a small segment of time.

Some Terms Defined

Since the subject of origins is highly controversial and often misunderstood, a few definitions are necessary. The words "creation" and "evolution" have different meaning for different people. In this presentation the

*D. R. Boylan, Ph.D., is Dean of the College of Engineering, Iowa State University of Science and Technology, Ames, Iowa 50011.

words are intended to mean the following:

Evolution—the belief that the world in which we live, including the complexities of life, came about by natural causes.[1]

Creation—the belief that natural causes or processes are impotent in themselves to effect either the origin or development of the complexities of life.

These definitions have been elaborated in a position paper on the teaching of creation/evolution in public schools by the Iowa Department of Public Instruction as:

Evolution

"The theory of evolution . . . states that modern biologic organisms descended,with modification, from pre-existing forms which in turn had ancestors. Those organisms best adapted, through anatomical and physiological modifications to their environment, left more offspring than did nonadapted organisms. The increased diversity of organisms enhanced their ability to survive in various environments and enabled them to leave more progeny . . . ."[2]

Creation

". . . all permanent, basic life forms originated thousands of years ago through directive acts of a Creator independent of the natural universe. Plants and animals were created separately with their full genetic potentiality provided by the Creator. Any variation, or speciation, which has occurred since creation has been within the original prescribed boundaries. Since each species contains its full potentiality, nature is viewed as static, reliable and predictable . . . "[3]

It needs to be emphasized that these fundamental postulates are not "religious" in themselves. They do not involve worship. They are legitimate areas of investigation and constitute appropriate classroom inquiry. The fact that people who hold either belief may also be "religious" is only a testimony that people have a religious nature. Fortunate is the man or woman whose religious perspectives do not conflict with his or her scientific perspectives. Indeed, they need not conflict. The tendency to discredit creation views as only religious perspectives is obviously an attempt to minimize a growing mistrust in the evolutionary explanation of origins.

Development

Observations of the world about us show the development of increasing order in matter and cases of the apparent operation of abiogenesis, ontogenesis, and phylogenesis. These processes are sometimes referred to as the "facts of evolution". They are, in the same manner, the "facts of creation". Being observations of the present, they offer little to an understanding of origins, except by inductive reasoning. And it is just such reasoning that form the bases of any theory of origins. By examination of the processes of life on the basis of equilibrium, free energy and entropy, rather significant inference can be made however, in regard to the competing theories.

Application of Thermodynamics

To do this requires information gained from the application of thermodynamics to the life systems. That thermodynamics is applicable is asserted by Stull.

"The laws of thermodynamics and thermochemistry are linked and govern the behavior of all the matter in the Universe."[4]

"Combination of the energy and entropy with the absolute temperature yields quantitative information on the thermodynamic behavior and stability of chemical substances."[5]

Dr. Melvin Calvin has proposed a sequence of chemical reactions from hydrogen to present life in an article on chemical evolution. He states that

"Life is a logical consequence of known chemical principles operating on the atomic composition of matter."[6]

A particularly important thermodynamic principle applicable to life systems seems to be the Second Law. Dr. L. Brillouin introduces his interesting and informative article on Life, Thermodynamics and Cybernetics by:

> "How is it possible to understand life, when the whole world is ruled by such a law as the second principle of thermodynamics, which points toward death and annihilation?"[1]

Later in the same article he states:

> "Let us simply state at this point that there is a problem about "Life and the second principle" . . . "Nobody can doubt the validity of the second principle, no more than he can the validity of the fundamental laws of mechanics . . . We do not know of any experiment telling against the second principle . . . ."

Such a universal acceptance of thermodynamic principles is testimony to the soundness of those principles. Thermodynamic laws have been shown to apply to open as well as closed systems, unstable as well as stable systems, and irreversible as well as reversible systems. It is not always possible quantitatively to evaluate the various states of thermodynamic systems, but is possible to predict the probable state of a system from thermodynamic principles.

Therefore, let us consider life systems as processes. A typical process can be represented as

$$aA + bB \rightarrow cC + dD \tag{1}$$

This general expression relates reactants A and B to products C and D. The small letters represent amounts. (Any number of reactants or products could be considered). The energies associated with the reactants and products are: internal energy, U, potential energy, X, kinetic energy, $v^2/2g_c$ and pressure-volume energy, PV. The "system" can absorb heat, Q_i, from the surroundings and do work, W_s, on the surroundings. In addition, the system may be subject to other work efforts, such as electrical, W_e, gravitational, W_g, magnetic, W_m, etc. If other than random work effects are present, appropriate additional terms must be included. Examples of non-random work are the separation of products, stacking a deck of cards, and the increase in system order in complex processes of life. Such processes require a work term, $-W_o$, to account for the work done on the system in directing the process outcome.

All of these energy terms can be included in a First Law expression for the process represented by Eq. 1. In general

$$dQ_i - dW_s = dE \qquad (2)$$

where: Q_i = heat added to the system, W_s = work done by the system in expansion or shaft work, and E = total energy of the system. For open systems, the integral expression is

$$Q_i - W_s = E_2 - E_1 + \Delta U + \Delta PV$$
$$+ \Delta v^2/2g_c + \Delta X \, g/g_c \qquad (3)$$

For steady flow $E_2 = E_1$ and only expansion or shaft work considered,

$$Q_i - W_s = \Delta U + \Delta PV + \Delta v^2/2g_c + \Delta X \, g/g_c \qquad (4)$$

Where the other work effects are important, Equation 4 must be written as

$$Q_i - W_s = \Delta U + \Delta PV + \Delta v^2/2g_c + \Delta X \, g/g_c + W_e$$
$$+ W_g + W_m - W_o \qquad (5)$$

since $U + PV = H$ (the enthalphy of the system)

$$Q_i - W_s = \Delta H + \Delta v^2/2g_c + \Delta X \, g/g_c + W_e + W_g$$
$$+ W_m - W_o \qquad (6)$$

For systems where potential, kinetic, electromagnetic and gravity effects are negligible:

$$Q_i - W_s = \Delta H - W_o \qquad (7)$$
$$\text{and} \quad Q_i = \Delta H + W_s - W_o \qquad (8)$$

If the system or process is not doing expansion or shaft work on the surroundings, the term W_s is zero, and

$$Q_i = \Delta H - W_o \qquad (9)$$

For such a system the Second Law expression for the entropy (S) change is

$$\Delta S_{TOT} = \int \frac{dQ_i}{T} = \int \frac{d(\Delta H - W_o)}{T} = \int \frac{dH}{T} - \int \frac{W_o}{T}$$

$$= \Delta S_R - \Delta S_o \qquad (10)$$

where: ΔS_{TOT} = total entropy change, ΔS_R = entropy change due to random effects, and ΔS_o = entropy change due to increasing order. The expression for the change in entropy is, therefore, the sum of the change in entropy due to the chemical reaction, i.e., the integral of dH/T, and the entropy change due to the increase in order or information in the system, ΔS_o.

Equation 10 in its later forms is useful in explaining complex processes having both random and non-random character. As an example, crystallization takes place partially by well defined change of state heat effects which are reversible and purely random. The crystal formation, however, is not random, and the atoms deposit themselves in a specific order. This order is so precise that many very sophisticated analytical techniques depend on crystalline structures being *exactly* ordered. The entropy of the random cooling process is quantitatively measured by the term $\int dH/T$. The non-random part of the process, or the ordering of the crystal, is represented by the term $\int -W_o/T$. It cannot be quantitatively measured for it represents the information contained in the atomic structure of the atom species. The second term effect is, however, clearly evident in the regularity of the crystal!

The final form is helpful in analyzing processes in which chemical effects are negligible and probability effects prominent. As an example, the process of "stacking" a deck of cards as opposed to a random "shuffle" involves $-W_o$ only and

$$\Delta S_{TOT} = O - \Delta S_o \qquad (11)$$

In this case the $-\Delta S_o$ can be calculated from probability theory since $S = k \ln p$ where p = the probability of the "stacked" order, and k = Boltzman constant. It should be emphasized that the two entropy terms in the different forms of Equation 10 result from different "types" of energy transfer, and the interchange of energy between the system and its surroundings in terms of entropy exchange must be of the same "kind". The argument that an "open" system will provide the necessary entropy sink for life systems is erroneous. The decrease in entropy due to increasing order cannot be financed by an increase in entropy in the sun or in any other random process in the surroundings. It can only be financed by energy from an equivalent "quality" source.

This can be illustrated by considering a process of putting a watch together. If the parts of a watch were arrayed on a table, "opening" the system to the sun, or to the universe for that matter, would not be effective in making a watch. Only the application of a certain "kind" of energy—intelligence or ordered energy—could do it. And, of course, we know that is just what happens. The watchmaker provides the $-W_o$ energy work on the system in accord with Equation 9.

The introduction of the $-W_o$ term into Equation 5 does not *a priori* imply a Creator. It does imply a certain kind of operation that must take place. The term, having been introduced, could be omitted once the proper understanding of energy interchange is achieved. Evolutionary theory claims that the term $-W_o$ is a result of natural selection, random chance, and long time spans. Creation theory claims that $-W_o$ comes from supernatural causes.

Development of Matter and Abiogenesis

Let us now examine the process of abiogenesis. The proposal (or allegation) is:

$$\text{non-living matter} \rightarrow \text{living matter} \qquad (12)$$

Dr. Calvin proposes possible processes (for abiogenesis) from what we know about present-day chemistry. (Figure 1).

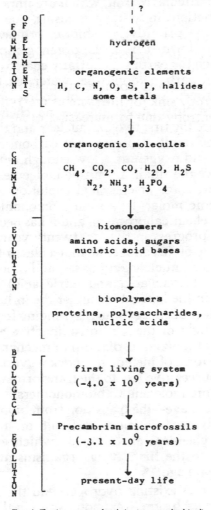

Figure 1. The time sequence of evolution (as commonly claimed), from the formation of the elements up to the present. After Calvin, reference 6, page 171.

"In the beginning most of the elements of the universe were in the form of hydrogen, which eventually had to undergo fusion reactions, giving rise to higher elements in the periodic table, particulary those important to living things: carbon, nitrogen, oxygen, sulfur, phosphorous, halides and certain

metals, particularly iron, which are important catalytic functions in living organisms.

Then, the primitive (prebiotic, primeval) molecules were formed from the organogenic elements
with which the earth was initially coated: methane,
ammonia, carbon monoxide, water, carbon dioxide, hydrogen sulfide, and of course, hydrogen.
These first three stages present no chemical problem, since the first two are nuclear and the third is
simply the result of presence of carbon, hydrogen,
nitrogen and oxygen at a low enough temperature
to produce the small, primitive molecules.

The next stage of chemical evolution—from the
organogenic molecules to the biomonomers—does
present a chemical problem, and it has been an area
of major progress in the last twenty years . . . The
conversion of organogenic molecules into amino
acids, sugars, nucleic acid bases, and other carboxylic acids (acetic acid and citric acid) has been
achieved in the laboratory under the influence of a
wide variety of energy sources, ranging from the ultraviolet light of the sun to radioactive energy (in
the form of ionizing radiation) to mechanical energy (in the form of meteoritic shock waves). All these
energy sources give rise to the transformation of the
organogenic molecule to biomonomers.

The next stage—the transition from biomonomers
to biopolymers—is more difficult to achieve in
terms of chemical evolution . . . which eventually
gave rise to the first living organisms about four
billion years ago."[8]

Calvin *assumes* existing hydrogen and the necessary
conditions for a "fusion" reaction. Now, in the state in
which there were no suns or stars for such reactions and
certainly no fusion furnaces, could this fusion take
place? Modern fusion work is testimony to the difficulty
in "arranging" such reactions, even with sophisticated
laboratories. The proposition that . . . "hydrogen had
to undergo fusion reactions, giving rise to the higher
elements in the periodic table . . ." is contrary to the
Second Law. And, of course, the hydrogen had to come

from somewhere. It was "created". The formation of higher elements in the periodic table from hydrogen is not a "natural" process. As Stull points out, the free energy difference is prohibitive.

The equilibrium for any reaction or process is derivable from heat quantities alone. These heat quantities are related as follows:

The Gibbs free energy, G, is defined as

$$G = U + PV - TS \qquad (13)$$

where: $U =$ is internal energy, $P =$ pressure, $T =$ temperature, and $S =$ entropy.

Since $H = U + PV$ and $G = H - TS$, at constant temperature and standard states

$$\Delta G° = \Delta H° - T\Delta S° \qquad (14)$$

This free energy change is related to equilibrium by

$$\Delta G = -RT \ln K \qquad (15)$$

where K is the equilibrium constant, given in terms of the things in Equation 1 by $K = C^c D^d / A^a B^b$. Combining Equations 14 and 15

$$-RT \ln K = \Delta H° - T\Delta S° \qquad (16)$$

which can be written

$$\ln K = -\frac{\Delta H°}{RT} + \frac{\Delta S°}{R} \qquad (17)$$

According to Stull, these

". . . relationships clearly indicate that the atoms present in a reaction will prefer the molecular configurations in which the entropy is maximized and in which the energy is minimized (algebraically). The maximum entropy is associated generally with the molecular configurations having the largest number of states available to the system, thus providing more "freedom" for the system. The minimum energy is associated generally with the molecular structure in which its atoms are most strongly bound to each other (or the structures in which the atom will have the maximum stability)" . . . "At low temperatures the equilibrium is determined largely by the value of ΔH°, the "stability" term, while at high temperatures the equilibrium is determined largely by the value of the ΔS°, the 'freedom' term."[9]

Calvin suggests that, higher elements in the periodic table eventually "evolve" into organogenic molecules by stages . . ."the first". . . nuclear and the third simply the result of carbon, hydrogen, nitrogen, and oxygen at a low enough temperature. This process demands that simpler molecules evolve into more complex molecules. It is a classic case of increasing order. The The Second Law expression, Equation 10, tells how this takes place, viz.:

$$\Delta S = \int \frac{dH}{T} - \Delta S_0 = \Delta S_e - \Delta S_0 \qquad (18)$$

Since increasing order is the goal of the reaction, the process must have, in addition to the chemical heat effects, an energy source which can establish order. The molecules themselves must either be credited with intelligence (molecular predestination) or some other intelligent or order direction tapped. The limited success achieved in laboratory experiments is directly attributable to the order-directing force—the scientist. Calvin admits to this . . . "I designed an experiment . . ." This is just what the Second Law demands—a "creative" force. It is not evolution that Calvin describes. It is creation (in the limited sense).

Ontogenesis

The development of the embryo is many times taken as evidence of evolution. Here, the Second Law clearly requires a $-\Delta S_0$ term apart from the chemical process. A "direction" of energy is clearly evident. Brillouin recognizes this.

"There are many strange features in the behavior of living organisms, as compared with dead structures. The evolution of species, as well as the evolution of individuals, is an irreversible process. The fact that evolution has been progressing from the simplest to the most complex structures is very difficult to understand, and appears almost as a contradiction to the law of degradation represented by the second principle. The answer is, of course, that degradation applies only to the whole of an isolated system, and not to one isolated constituent of the system. Nevertheless, it is hard to reconcile these two opposite directions of evolution. Many other facts remain very mysterious: reproduction, maintenance of the living individual and of the species, free will, etc."[10]

". . . we must be prepared to accept a 'life principle' that would allow for some exceptions to the second principle" . . . "What about life and the second principle? Is there not, in living organisms, some power that prevents the action of the second principle?"[11]

". . . a living organism is a chemical system in unstable equilibrium maintained by some strange "power of life" which manifests itself as a sort of *negative* catalyst."[12]

This "negative catalyst" is the $-\Delta S_o$ term of Equation 10 and which is the needed "power of life."

Phylogenesis

The development of species is generally considered to have occurred through random chance and long time spans. Random chance is supposed to provide the negative entropy necessary for the "upward mobility" in speciation. However, the only energy identified is random energy from the sun. As stated before, such energy cannot provide the energy of order ($-\Delta S_o$ of the last form of Equation 10). There must be an energy which can direct the speciation process. Much of this "direction" is found in the DNA coding. The coding in these molecules has been shown not to be randomly derived. Dr. L. Quinn[13] has demonstrated by molecular modeling that the codon structure of proteins is not redundant and represents unique molecular instructions.

Prigogine proposes that "fluctions" or "instabilities" in what he calls "dissipative" structures" can generate higher order in an open system. He acknowledges, however, that there is no evidence that life originated by any such means.

"The probability that at ordinary temperatures a macroscopic number of molecules is assembled to give rise to the highly ordered structures and to the coordinated functions characterizing living organisms is vanishingly small . . . ."[14]

That random chance cannot be effective in DNA coding can be seen in an example of chance formation of a simple protein. Assume a hypothetical molecule consisting of 100 amino acids using 20 distinct amino groups. The number of possible arrangements of these amino acids is $20^{100} = 10^{130}$, and the probability that one essential arrangement would occur by random chance is 10^{-130}, which is a fantastically small number. It is fantasticaly small because 10^{130} is fantastically large. For comparison, consider that the total number of electrons in the universe (5 billion light-years radius) has been estimated to be 10^{80}. And the total number of seconds elapsed since the beginning of time (according to the evolutionary theories) is 10^{18}.

Thus, the number of possible arrangements which could occur by chance is so very great in relation to any number with meaning that the probability of any such molecule occurring by chance is for all practical purposes zero.

With such small probabilities it is necessary to propose long time spans for the "improbable to become probable." George Wald[15] says:

". . . the important point is that since the origin of life belongs in the category of at-least-once phenomena, time is on our side. However improbable we regard this event . . . given enough time it will almost certainly happen at least once . . . Time is in fact the hero of the plot . . . given so much time, the impossible becomes possible, the possible probable, and the probable virtually certain. One has only to wait; time itself performs miracles."

This statement is repeated frequently in defense of evolution. The idea of time being a "hero" was recently repeated by Dr. K. E. Boulding.

"That which has probability of one percent in a year, such as a 100-year flood, has a 66 percent chance of occurring in 100 years and 99.9 percent chance of occurring in 1000 years."[16]

Such statements have some basis in fact for repeated and independent trials of an experiment with two outcomes—success and failure.

If p = probability of success and q = probability of failure, $q = 1 - p$. The probability of a number of successes, k, in a number of repeated trials, n, is[1] $b = p^k q^{n-k}$. So, the probability of no successes, or $k = 0$, is $b = q^n$ and therefore the probability of at least one success is $1 - q^n$.

Now, with numbers of the order of magnitude used by Dr. Boulding, the quoted statement is valid. For example, if the probability of an event is 1% ($p = .01$) and there are 100 trials ($n = 100$), the following probability of at least one success ($1 - q^n$) or occurrence in 100 years is $1 - q^n = 1 - (0.99)^{100} = 0.634$ or 63.4%. For 1000 trials (or 1000 years in Dr. Boulding's example) $1 - q^n = 1 - (0.99)^{1000} = 0.99996$ or 99.99%. But, for very small probabilities such as for random chance of protein formation, the inference of "time as a hero" is simply erroneous. Even at relatively large probabilities, as 1/10%, the statement is erroneous. If $p = .001$ and $q = 0.999$, for 100 trials $1 - q^n = 1 - (0.999)^{100} = 0.0952$, or 9.52%.

For $n = 1000$, $1 - q^n = 1 - (0.999)^{1000} = 0.6323$ or 63.23%.

With this ten-fold decrease in probability, repeated trials do not produce the certainty which Dr. Boulding's statement might lead one to believe. However, as for protein production by random chance, for even a very simple molecule of only 100 amino acids, the probability is not only small, it is *infinitesimally* small. As developed above, it is of the order of magnitude of $1/10^{130}$. For this case, then, $p = 1/10^{130}$, and $q = 1 - p = 1 - 10^{-130}$, which would be written: $q = 0.9999 \ldots 999$, there being 130 nines altogether.

The probability equation for at least one success would be $1 - q^n = 1 - (1 - 10^{-130})^n$.

An expansion according to the binomial theorem, in which only two terms are retained, is legitimate here; and that gives for the result $n/10^{130}$.

Even if $q = 1 - 10^{-9}$ and $n = 1000$, $1 - q^n$ comes to only 0.0001%. And if $q = 1 - 10^{-130}$, as discussed above, the resulting $1 - q^n$ is small beyond all imagining.

Thus, the evolutionary theory demands long spans of time, which is another way of saying that many more repetitions than 100 or 1000 would be necessary. But even if repetitions occurred a billion times a second since the beginning of evolutionary time (30 billion years) the probability is still infinitesimally small.

In this case, $n = 10^{27}$, so if $q = 1 - 10^{-130}$, then $1 - q^n = 1 - [(1 - 10^{-130})$ raised to the power $10^{27}]$. Even a large computer could not readily work this out as a direct problem in arithmetic. However, the binomial theorem may be used again, to give for the result $10^{27}/10^{130} = 10^{-103}$. This number is still inconceivably small. So time is not a hero; it is simply impotent to make an impossible event (evolution) possible.

In conclusion, living systems seem to be negative entropy processes. It is evident that abiogenesis, ontogenesis and phylogenesis proceed from lower order to higher order. Application of the First Law to such systems shows that the entropy change must include a random and a non-random contribution. The random contribution explains the general demise of the system through aging. The non-random contribution explains growth and development. The non-random contribution, or the $-\Delta S_o$ term in Equation 10, is necessary to account for the increasing order of living systems.

Equation 12: *non-living matter* → *living matter* is therefore not correct. It has a missing term. This missing term is the $-W_o$ contribution to Equation 10. It is the required intelligence (coding, design, direction, etc.) that the scientist (or creator) provides to the process. Intellectual activity is the highest form of energy. By this

people do things. They build. They make. They
CREATE. Intelligence is seen in the DNA coding, in the
assembly of a watch, in the design of a pump to get water to go uphill, and in any higher order energy requirement to finance the processes of life. Equation 12 therefore needs to be modified. The equation is then[17]

$$\text{matter} + \text{intelligence} \rightarrow \text{life} \qquad (19)$$

This equation fits the universe in which we live. The key
component in the transformation of non-living matter
into living matter is intelligence. This intelligence must
come from a source outside of "matter" itself. It must
reside in the scientist, the designer or, in the case of life,
in the Creator.

References

[1]By natural causes will be understood here those which can be
studied by the methods of natural sciences. As for what constitutes
natural sciences, there is fairly general agreement on that question.
[2]Creation, Evolution and Public Instruction, pp. 2-3. The Position
Paper of the Iowa Department of Public Instruction, Curriculum
Division, Grimes State Office Building, Des Moines, Iowa.
[3]*Ibid.*, pp. 1-2.
[4]Stull, Daniel L., 1971. The thermodynamic transformation of
organic chemistry. *American Scientist* 59(6):734-743.
[5]*Ibid.*, p. 736.
[6]Calvin, Melvin, 1975. Chemical evolution. *American Scientist*
63(2):169-177.
[7]Brillouin, L., 1949. Life, thermodynamics, and cybernetics.
American Scientist 37(4):554-568.
[8]Calvin, *op. cit.*, p. 171.
[9]Stull, *op. cit.*, p. 736.
[10]Brillouin, *op. cit.*, p. 465.
[11]*Ibid.*, pp. 554-555.
[12]*Ibid.*, p. 563.
[13]Quinn, Loyd Y., 1975. Evidence for the existence of an intelligible
genetic code. *Creation Research Society Quarterly* 11(4):188-198.
[14]Prigogine, Ilya, Gregoire Nicolis, and Agnes Babloyants, 1972.
Thermodynamics of evolution. *Physics Today* 25(11):23-28.
[15]Wald, George, 1955. The origin of life (in) The Physics and
Chemistry of Life. Simon and Schuster, New York. P. 12.
[16]Boulding, K. E., 1976. The importance of improbable events. *Technology Review.* (February) P. 5.
[17]Wilder, Smith, A. E., 1970. The creation of life. Harold Shaw Pub.
p. 26.

Bibliography

Creation Science Literature

1. Sunderland, L. D., *Darwin's Enigma,* Master Books Publishers, San Diego, CA 92115, 1984.
2. Thaxton, C. B., Bradley, W. L., Olsen, R. L., *The Mystery of Life's Origin: Reassessing Current Theories,* Philosophical Library, New York, 1984. (Available from Foundation for Thought and Ethics, P.O. Box 830721, Richardson, TX 75083-0721.)
3. Morris, H. M., *Scientific Creationism,* 2nd Ed., Creation-Life Publishers, El Cajon, CA 92022, 1985.
4. Morris, H. M., and Parker, G. E., *What Is Creation Science?,* 2nd Ed., Master Books, El Cajon, CA 92022, 1987.
5. Morris, H. M., *History of Modern Creationism,* Master Book Publishers, San Diego, CA 92115, 1984.
6. Whitcomb, J. C., and Morris, H. M., *The Genesis Flood,* The Presbyterian and Reformed Publishing Company, Philadelphia, 1961.
7. Taylor, I. T., *In the Minds of Men,* TFE Publishing, Toronto, 1984.
8. Andrews, E. H., Gitt, W., and Ouweneel, W. J., *Concepts in Creationism,* Evangelical Press, Welwyn, Herts, England, 1986.
9. Gentry, R. V., *Creation's Tiny Mystery,* Earth Science Associates, Knoxville, TN, 1986.
10. Rusch, W. H., Sr., *The Argument: Creationism Versus Evolutionism,* Creation Research Society Books, Norcross, GA 30092, 1984.

11. Mulfinger, George, Jr., Ed., *Design and Origins in Astronomy*, Creation Research Society Books, P.O. Box 28473, Kansas City, MO 64118, 1983.

12. Williams, E. L., Ed., *Thermodynamics and the Development of Order*, Creation Research Society Books, P.O. Box 28473, Kansas City, MO 64118, 1981.

13. Gish, D. T., *Evolution: The Challenge of the Fossil Record*, Creation-Life Publishers, El Cajon, CA 92022, 1985.

14. Huse, S. M., *The Collapse of Evolution*, Baker Book House, Grand Rapids, MI, 1983.

15. White, A. J. Monty, *What About Origins?*, Dunestone Printer, Ltd., Kingsteignton, Newton Abbot, Devon, England, 1978.

16. Wilder-Smith, A. E., *The Scientific Alternative to Neo-Darwinian Evolutionary Theory: Information Sources and Structures*, TWFT Publishers, Costa Mesa, CA 92683, 1987.

17. Pitman, M., *Adam and Evolution*, Rider and Company, London, 1984.

18. Chittick, D. E., *The Controversy. Roots of the Creation-Evolution Conflict*, Multnomah Press, Portland, OR 1984.

19. Lester, L. P., and Bohlin, R. G., *The Natural Limits to Biological Change*, Zondervan Publishing House, Grand Rapids, MI, 1984.

20. Geisler, N. L., and Anderson, J. K., *Origin Science. A Proposal for the Creation-Evolution Controversy*, Baker Book House, Grand Rapids, MI, 1987.

21. Lubenow, M., *From Fish to Gish*, Creation-Life Publishers, San Diego, CA, 1983.

22. Morris, H. M., *Evolution in Turmoil*, Creation-Life Publishers, San Diego, CA, 1982.

23. Bowden, M., *Ape-Men: Fact or Fallacy?*, Sovereign Publications, Bromley, Kent, 1977.

24. Bowden, M., *Rise of the Evolution Fraud*, Creation-Life Publishers, San Diego, CA, 1982.

25. Thompson, B., *The History of Evolutionary Thought*, Apologetics Press, Montgomery, AL, 36117, 1981.

26. Davidheiser, B., *Evolution and the Christian Faith*, Presbyterian and Reformed Publishing Company, Nutley, NJ, 1969.

27. Wiester, J., *The Genesis Connection*, Thomas Nelson Publishers, New York, 1983.

28. Frair, W., and Davis, P., *A Case for Creation,* Moody Press, Chicago, 1983.
29. Bird, W. R., *The Origin of Species Revisited Volume I: Science; Volume II; Phylosophy of Science, Philosophy of Religion, History, Education, and Constitutional Issues,* Philosophical Library, New York, 1989.

Anti-Evolution and Anti-Darwinian Books

1. Denton, M., *Evolution: A Theory in Crisis,* Burnett Books, London, 1985. (Available from Woodbine House, 5615 Fishers Lane, Rockville, MD 20852, and the Institute for Creation Research, P.O. Box 2667, El Cajon, CA, 92021.)
2. Hoyle, F., and Wickramasinghe, C., *Evolution from Space,* Simon and Schuster, New York, 1981.
3. Fix, W. R., *The Bone Peddlers. Selling Evolution,* Macmillan Publishing Company, New York, 1984.
4. Macbeth, N., *Darwin Retried,* Gambit, Boston, 1971.
5. Cohen, I. L., *Darwin Was Wrong - A Study in Probabilities,* New Research Publications, Greenvale, NY, 1984.
6. Rifkin, J., *Algeny,* The Viking Press, New York, 1983.
7. Hitching, F., *The Neck of the Giraffe,* Ticknor and Fields, New Haven, NY, 1982.

Anti-Creationist Books

1. Hanson, R. W., Ed., *Science and Creation,* Macmillan Publishing Company, New York, 1986.
2. Young, W., *Fallacies of Creationism,* Detselig Enterprises, Calgary, Alberta, 1985.
3. Kitcher, P., *Abusing Science,* The MIT Press, Cambridge, MA, 1982.
4. Futuyma, D. J., *Science on Trial,* Pantheon Books, New York, 1983.
5. Ruse, M., *Darwinism Defended,* Addison-Wesley Publishing Company, London, 1982.

6. Selkirk, D. R., and Burrows, F. J., *Confronting Creationism: Defending Darwin,* The New South Wales University Press, Kensington, NSW, 1987.

7. Wilson, D. B., Ed., *Did the Devil Make Darwin Do It?,* The Iowa State University Press, Ames, 1983.

8. Godfrey, L. R., Ed., *Scientists Confront Creationism,* W. W. Norton and Company, New York, 1983.

9. Montagu, A., *Science and Creationism,* Oxford University Press, Oxford, 1984.

10. Conway, F., and Siegelman, J., *Holy Terror,* Doubleday and Company, Garden City, NY, 1982.

11. Nelkin, D., *Science Textbook Controversies and the Politics of Equal Time,* The MIT Press, Cambridge, MA, 1977.

12. McGowan, C., *In the Beginning - A Scientist Shows Why the Creationists Are Wrong,* Macmillan of Canada, Toronto, 1983.

13. Zetterberg, J. P., Ed., *Evolution Versus Creationism: The Public Education Controversy,* Oryx Press, 1983.

14. Eldredge, N., *The Monkey Business,* Washington Square Press, New York, 1982.

Name Index

Subject Index